SING,
MEMORY

SING,
MEMORY

∾

The Remarkable Story of
the Man Who Saved the Music
of the Nazi Camps

Makana Eyre

W. W. NORTON & COMPANY
Celebrating a Century of Independent Publishing

For information about permission to reproduce selections from this book,
write to Permissions, W. W. Norton & Company, Inc.,
500 Fifth Avenue, New York, NY 10110

For information about special discounts for bulk purchases, please contact
W. W. Norton Special Sales at specialsales@wwnorton.com or 800-233-4830

Manufacturing by Lake Book Manufacturing
Book design by Chris Welch
Production manager: Lauren Abbate

ISBN 978-0-393-53186-2

W. W. Norton & Company, Inc., 500 Fifth Avenue, New York, N.Y. 10110
www.wwnorton.com

W. W. Norton & Company Ltd., 15 Carlisle Street, London W1D 3BS

1 2 3 4 5 6 7 8 9 0

For Ewelina

For Gavan

In the dark times
Will there be singing?
There will be singing
Of the dark times.

—BERTOLT BRECHT

Contents

Author's Note

In 1989, the newly established but not yet open United States Holocaust Memorial Museum (USHMM) received a tip that an archive, unique in topic and scope, was gathering soot in a former prisoner barracks at the Auschwitz-Birkenau Memorial and Museum. The archive, museum representatives learned, had been built by the late Sachsenhausen camp singer Aleksander Kulisiewicz and contained thousands upon thousands of documents and recordings about music and poetry in the Nazi camps.

Whether or not the USHMM knew it at the time, the archive was in a precarious position. Over the last decade of his life, Aleksander Kulisiewicz had desperately tried to convince a Polish institution to acquire it, yet each museum and university he contacted rebuffed him. After his death in 1982, his family continued the task of searching for a permanent home. Through contacts in Milwaukee and New York City, they even approached American institutions, only to receive refusals, if they heard back at all. As a temporary solution and because of its large size, the Auschwitz Museum agreed to store it, but only in the short term.

In the fall of the same year, Jacek Nowakowski, the director of Collections and Acquisitions at the USHMM, flew to Poland to investigate. After Auschwitz Museum archival staff showed him the files, he quickly understood that this collection was important and that the USHMM must acquire it. Before the end of the year, the crates were in transit to Washington, D.C. When they arrived some weeks later, the original inventory was: Approximately eight hundred folders that contained some seventy thousand pages of documentation about music in the Nazi camps; over 620 Polish camp songs from thirty-four camps and two hundred songs written by prisoners of other nationalities; several thousand microfilmed and original prisoner notebooks, diaries, prints, sketches, photographs, maps, leaflets, letters, postcards, memoirs, manuscripts, and paintings related to the musical life in the camps; tens of thousands of feet of open reel and cassette tape with recordings of camp songs, poetry, and commentary; and the original unpublished story of Kulisiewicz's life, entitled "How My Voice Was Dying."

I offer this anecdote because it serves as an origin story of this book. Had the USHMM not chosen to acquire the archive, the songs and documents that Aleksander Kulisiewicz spent his life collecting might very well have been lost—and with it, any chance of telling the complete stories of Kulisiewicz, Rosebery d'Arguto, and the Jewish choir of Sachsenhausen.

This anecdote also helps me answer an important question: How did I approach the sourcing, research, and verification of this book? I wrote *Sing, Memory* thanks to several important categories of sources, including the memoirs of camp survivors, oral history and testimony, scholarly books and articles, and information from the descendants of the characters. Yet above all, this was an archival project in which I relied on thousands of pages of documents to piece together the complex and powerful narrative of Kulisiewicz and d'Arguto, their lives, and the time they spent in the Sachsenhausen concentration camp.

Though I consulted various archives around Europe, the United States, and Israel, two collections were most important. The first was what is now known as the Aleksander Kulisiewicz Collection at the United States

Holocaust Memorial Museum. This archive contains the voices of hundreds of camp survivors and the music and poetry they created. At the core, Aleksander Kulisiewicz was a gatherer, an accumulator of anything related to music making in the Nazi camps. Over more than three decades, he collected microfilms, correspondence, personal narratives, newspaper clippings, artwork, poetry, research notes, manuscripts, and photographs. He made copies of camp diaries, musical scores, drawings, and maps. It is these documents that make up the foundation of this book.

The other archive I relied on heavily was the Sammlung Rosebery d'Arguto at the Akademie der Künste, Berlin (the Rosebery d'Arguto Collection, Academy of Arts, Berlin), assembled in large part by the pioneering German musicologist Inge Lammel. Over many years, Lammel tracked down friends, colleagues, and choir members of Rosebery d'Arguto and interviewed them in great detail. The result is hundreds of pages of information, photographs, scores, and programs that paint a rich picture of d'Arguto and his accomplishments, particularly during his years in Berlin and his imprisonment in Sachsenhausen.

I am far from the first person to study these archives. Over the last three decades, scholars and archivists such as Barbara Milewski, Bret Werb, Peter Konopatsch, Guido Fackler, and Juliane Brauer, among many others, have examined these collections and meticulously scrutinized the stories they tell for accuracy. The result is a trove of scholarly material about music in the Nazi camps broadly and Kulisiewicz and d'Arguto in particular that was crucial for me during my research.

Thanks to these archives, the descendants of the characters in the book, and scholarship, I have been able to write *Sing, Memory* as a work of nonfiction. Each detail, anecdote, and scene comes from primary sources. The same applies to any instances of dialogue in the book or places where I include the thoughts of a character.

Based on guidance and recommendations from scholars of the Nazi camps, I approached survivor memoirs and testimony from a perspective of trust and respect. Yet no camp survivor, Kulisiewicz included, can offer a perfect account of incarceration and trauma at the hands of the Nazis. I have thus buttressed these accounts with fact-checking and corroboration and have done my best to correct the record where necessary, fill in any blanks, and offer historical context where it proved useful.

It is also essential to note that the experiences of prisoners at Sachsenhausen or any Nazi camp varied considerably, depending on a person's nationality, ethnicity, religion, sexual orientation, status, and so-called camp privilege. The story in *Sing, Memory* is only that of Aleksander Kulisiewicz, Rosebery d'Arguto, and the other men in their orbit. It should not be seen as an account of Sachsenhausen as a whole. The same proviso applies to music in the Nazi camps. Kulisiewicz, d'Arguto, and many of their camp friends found joy, satisfaction, and strength in their music-making activities. Yet for some prisoners, especially in the context of forced singing or SS-sanctioned musical groups, music was a source of suffering and despair, which sometimes persisted long after the war had ended.

If you study the Kulisiewicz Collection at the USHMM, you will repeatedly see words, sentences, and even pages in the various files where Kulisiewicz struck through the text. He did this when he tried but failed to verify a fact. His aim was always to make the archive as accurate as possible. I have taken inspiration from his approach. As Kulisiewicz maintained, to embellish is to tarnish the memories of those who did not survive.

PART I

Chapter 1

~⁓~

Cieszyn, Poland. August 1939

I n the heat of late summer, at the close of the 1930s, Aleksander
Kulisiewicz was strolling in his hometown, a swagger in his step, a
tune running through his head.

The three years since he earned his high school diploma had exhila-
rated the twenty-one-year-old. Poland was again sovereign. Culture was
blossoming. Poets, writers, philosophers, and painters filled the cafés
of the country's great cities, drinking and chattering as cars and horse-
drawn carriages clattered by on the paving stones outside. The generation to which Aleks belonged experimented; they argued, founded literary
magazines, discussed new ideas, slept with one another. At night in dim
clubs, women in elegant dresses and men in dark suits swayed to tango
rhythms imported from South America in this nation in the midst of a
revival. It was a time when Aleks could sing, act, pursue love. For this
slim law student of medium height with dark eyes and straight black hair,
which he slicked back over his forehead, the future glimmered. So much

was there for the taking, and Aleks, who had talent, burning ambition, and just enough privilege, wanted in on all of it.

Until those final summer days, 1939 had been a good year for Aleks. During the university term, he lived in the cosmopolitan city of Kraków in a student dorm just west of the old town, near the vast green meadow of Błonia Park. Cabarets and clubs in the city, filled with young people and tobacco smoke, booked him to sing onstage or to whistle, which he did with the finesse of an accomplished instrumentalist. When classes drew to a close at the end of the spring term, he returned to his hometown of Cieszyn for his summer break. At Cieszyn he passed his time as he pleased. He wrote articles on politics and current affairs and sold them to local newspapers or magazines. He reposed on the sunny riverbanks of the Olza, which cut through the edge of town. He unwound with friends and sometimes knocked back glasses of vodka late into the night with the editors who published his writing.

Aleks's generation was coming of age in a country free after decades of foreign domination. From Lwów in the east to Poznań in the west, Poles once again received their education in their mother tongue. They read and celebrated their great poets and writers. Independence returned to Poland's artists an ardent sense of freedom. Creating art for the national cause no longer constrained them. That obligation vanished when the Prussians, Austrians, and Russians—the three countries that had divided up and ruled Poland since the third partition in 1795—withdrew in the year of Aleks's birth, liberating young creatives to experiment, refute, and innovate. Aleks's peers made art for its own sake; they explored sex, humor, futurism, and radical politics. They could flout the rules. Even homosexuality occasionally appeared in art and society. The old class structures, which had always vexed Aleks, were shifting, too. Though serious economic and social troubles seethed under the surface, and poverty still ravaged big tracts of the country, Poland radiated a certain confidence, a bravado not seen in generations. By and large, Aleks could say what he wanted. No grand state ideology silenced him. Freedom and opportunity permeated the air. He often said to himself: the whole world belongs to me.

During those heady years, Aleks took advantage of the freedoms Poland afforded a young man in his position, though it intensely irritated his father, Franciszek. Franciszek believed his son should be a lawyer, or at least someone with a career of the mind, not the pensive artist Aleks wished to become. Thanks to Franciszek, the fate of the Kulisiewicz family had been on an upward swing, toward a solid, prosperous life. It was he who had shed the rural, peasant struggle for middle-class contentment in Cieszyn, a good-sized town with colorful buildings and an ornate church. Franciszek was the son of a poor, vodka-drinking carpenter. He grew up in a hamlet outside the village of Nowy Wiśnicz, 100 miles east of Cieszyn. Franciszek's mother, her hands in fists and her teeth clenched shut, birthed him and eleven other children in a wood and mud hut where the black soil could be seen through gaps in the floorboards.

It took a great deal of determination and luck for Franciszek to peel himself away from that shack and a life where in summer he toiled under the heat of the sun; in winter, the wind cut through cracks in the window frames no matter how much straw his mother stuffed around them. Every day, he walked 4 miles there and back to a town called Bochnia for the education that would give him a decent life. He had overcome immense obstacles to become a teacher of classics at a prestigious private school. His only son had to keep the family on the right trajectory. Art was out of the question.

But like many young men, Aleks cared little about what his father thought. The artistic world was too tantalizing for him to focus his attention on his studies at the Jagiellonian University, and he failed the end-of-year exam for an important class on ancient Roman law. As he saw it, too much time with his nose in a tome meant missing out on all the dancing and singing and romance.

Yet Aleks's carefree life would soon come to an end. By the middle of August, rumors of war were circulating. People in Poland were growing anxious, afraid that life was about to change in a drastic, frightening way. Together with his family in their modest apartment, Aleks awaited news of an invasion.

Though confined in his childhood home, memories of performing in Kraków sustained Aleks. He mused about how he moved before the crowd, how he held them in his hands. He reflected on the joy he felt strumming his guitar for university friends at private parties. He yearned for a life of music and performance. For all he cared, he could flunk out of law school and leave the elaborate halls of Jagiellonian University forever. Yet now, as the summer of 1939 came to a close, the future was uncertain. Life seemed on the edge of collapse. Perhaps he'd have to endure a war before making for himself a life of music.

FOR A YOUNG man who heard magic in music, for whom a tune could touch the heart, the borderland town of Polish Cieszyn had been an ideal place to be raised. Throughout Aleks's childhood, many Poles as well as Germans, Czechs, and Jews called his town and region home. Each group prayed at its own house of worship, celebrated its own holidays, spoke its own languages—and, importantly for Aleks, played its own music. Groups of Romani also traveled through the region and sometimes stopped at Cieszyn to perform music of great energy in the rynek, the town square, for coins tossed into a hat or the case of a violin. The musical richness of Aleks's hometown meant a childhood surrounded by a range of melodies. He could stroll through town and hear the cantor chanting in the synagogue or hear traditional Polish and Czech songs, German folk music, and Romani singing. He absorbed it all.

At six years of age, Aleks had begged his father for violin lessons. Music didn't mean much in the Kulisiewicz household, so no one could sit the boy down and teach him even the simplest of melodies. Yet for a reason Aleks never understood, Franciszek agreed. One day he returned home with a violin under his arm, a small one meant for a child. The instrument thrilled Aleks, and he hugged it preciously to his body. With a teacher Franciszek hired, Aleks learned to play German folk songs. Sometimes he also picked up songs from the household servants or friends of his stepmother, who often dropped by and took an interest in the proud little boy with his violin. When friends and family praised his talent, he beamed with happiness, delighted to perform the tunes he had learned, hungry for the attention. Even at that young age, music and performance were knotted tightly together. He loved the music, but performing what he learned was half the draw. He felt compelled to show what he could do and impress those around him.

The melodies that first caught Aleks's ear were carefree and flowing. Sometimes he sang to them, too, although he didn't yet think of himself as much of a singer. He loved the music he was learning on the violin, but he was lazy with his practice. Music moved him greatly, but the discipline of learning scales and doing exercises bored him. Instead, he wished to wander off into the forest, his little cat at his heels, to listen to the twitter of birds and the rhythm of their songs. In the birdsong, he perceived a call and response, as though the birds were singing as an ensemble. The language of the chirping also fascinated him. Nothing of it resembled the waltzes or mazurkas he was learning in his private lessons.

Aleks absorbed the full richness of music around him in Cieszyn. German melodies caught his ear. The church songs he heard on Sundays with booming organ tracks impressed him. In Czechoslovakia, on holiday, he wandered from village to village with his father and stepmother, listening to the shepherds' songs, to wedding couplets, or the way highlanders sang in beautiful harmony. Yet of all the music he encountered, it was the Romani troupes that thrilled him most. When he first heard a band of them playing, he thought it was the most beautiful sound he'd ever heard. That day, he and his father and stepmother were traveling along Poland's southern border. Early in the morning, the family took a boat on the Dunajec River, which made up part of the frontier with Czechoslovakia. They floated down the waterway watching the Pieniny Mountains, tall and lush and green, that stood on each side. Near a town called Spišská Stará Ves on the Czech side, they disembarked and walked to the market square where a group of Romani sat, tuning their instruments. Aleks looked at the violin one Roma man held. It was different from his own— bigger, black, strung with bristly cord. The man who held it towered above him. A deep scar stretched above his eyebrows. When he began drawing out notes on his instrument, the others in the band joined in. The music was unlike anything Aleks had heard before, departing completely from what he'd been taught on his violin, that he heard in church, or that cantors sang in Cieszyn's synagogue. Even the Polish Highlanders's melodies seemed like nothing special compared with the music this band was playing. It seemed truer, purer. The timbre the instruments produced and the pulsating melodies felt eternal. Aleks perceived an affirmation of life that he hadn't felt in the music he'd heard before. At times, the Romani musicians played such sorrowful melodies, lamenting a bad turn of fate, the death of a loved one. Other times the music glistened with joy. In between, they improvised with virtuosity, and it seemed to Aleks that they always understood one another, always knew the musical direction the others would take, as if they could communicate telepathically.

One soloist caught Aleks's eye. He would begin to play, and Aleks thought the man had entered a trance. His eyes closed; he seemed deep in a maze of sounds. Turn one way and his tune went off down a melancholy path. Turn another, and jubilation filled the air. Aleks thought of his mother; he pictured her face, although he wasn't sure if he had a true memory of her or rather had come to know her from the portrait photographs from Lwów, taken over twenty years earlier, where she stood beside a bouquet of flowers in a long white dress, her dark hair flowing down to her waist. Or perhaps it was from the other photo he had of her in which she wore braids.

The Romani music so moved Aleks that he begged his father to take him back to the Polish side of the river where they were staying so he could fetch his little violin. In Aleks's mind, there was no option but to retrieve his instrument from their lodgings in Poland and return to Spišská Stará Ves to play alongside the Romani band. Though music stirred little sentiment in Aleks's father or stepmother, they both understood the boy's need and acquiesced, taking the short trip by boat across the river to their lodgings on the Polish side. Once back at the town square with the Romani band, Aleks stood, ever so pleased, his violin under his chin, bow in hand.

During a break in their performance, Franciszek approached the Romani to ask if Aleks could play with them. They looked at him askance. "He's still a tiny boy, a child," one said. Aleks, listening in on the conversation, jumped in. "Sir, I can play. I am not afraid. I can't do much yet, but I'll try. Let me!" The Romani relented and said Aleks could join them for a song, though on the condition that Franciszek add a bit extra to their tip.

Aleks stood on the little stage, a skinny boy with a beginner's violin. Where other children his age might have felt intimidated by the audience before him, Aleks seemed not to care. For him, the stares of a crowd evoked no fear; no anxiety welled up within him. Later, he remembered the moment like this: when the music started, he closed his eyes, thought about the woods he wandered in and their birdsong, and in that state of mind, he started to draw out notes on his little violin. He tried to impart his hope, pain, and love, as trivial as these emotions may have been for a boy still so young. And the melodies flowed out of him, seemingly all on their own. He tried to imitate the beautiful music he'd heard just an hour or so before. Behind him stood the tall Roma with the black violin and the scar. When Aleks played a melody, the man echoed it note for note. It was just like the call and response of birds in the forest.

THAT CULTURE AND art flourished during the time of Aleks's youth was thanks to the end of the First World War. The year 1918, the year of his birth, brought an end to three empires—the Russians in the east, the Austro-Hungarians in the southwest, and the Prussians in the northwest—the countries that had cut up and ruled Poland for 123 years. Not in four generations had a Kulisiewicz child been born in a Poland governed by Poles, on land that occupying powers hadn't stripped for resources and profit.

Before the Great War, Poland did not exist on the map of Europe. Its lands had been swallowed up by its neighbors, hungry for territory, power, and people to place under their dominion. Like their parents and grandparents before them, the twenty to thirty million men and women who considered themselves Polish at the start of the twentieth century were subjects of either the tsar in Saint Petersburg, the kaiser in Berlin, or the emperor-king in Vienna. In November 1918, just three months after Aleks came into the world and with the end of the Great War, Józef Piłsudski and his legions took control of a Poland without borderlines, a government, a constitution, or recognition of national sovereignty from its neighbors. Vyacheslav Molotov, the Russian statesman and diplomat, called the new country "the monstrous bastard of the Peace of Versailles." The British economist John Maynard Keynes described it as "an economic impossibility whose only industry is Jew-baiting." Thus began the Poland of Aleks's youth.

During the first years of Aleks's life, Poland struggled to regain the lands it called home before the partitions. It took six border wars for the country to win back its heartland, bringing cities like Warsaw, Lublin, and Kraków into the Polish realm once again. From the far east to the far west, young Poles killed and died to reclaim the frontiers. Even in Cieszyn, border disputes turned violent when Czech soldiers crossed the river to take control of the city in 1919. A year later, in July, the town was split in two, the Olza River defined as the frontier.

Though Poles once again could determine their present and future, the country lacked integration, unity. While Aleks was playing his violin with the Romani band or strolling in the forest to reflect on birdsong and the rhythm of the melodies he was learning, policymakers were trying desperately to bring cohesion to the country. At the start of the 1920s, six currencies circulated in Polish hands. Military commands were given in four languages. Five regions of the country kept separate administrations, of which Cieszyn was one. Three legal codes governed Polish citizens. Two incompatible railway gauges caused headaches and delays. Aleks's boyhood was a time when the leaders of the new Polish state had to build national institutions from scratch. The most basic parts of a state system—administrative buildings, courts, and schools—had to be constructed. The culture and habits people followed were also deeply different. Until that moment, citizens of Poland had spent their lives in Russia, Prussia, or Austria.

By the time Aleks reached his teens, Poland had achieved a stability of sorts. In this new environment, his ambition to perform intensified. He had by now abandoned any wish to become a violinist and instead picked up the guitar. For his father, it was high time for the boy to focus, to pass the finishing exams that would allow him entry to university. But the stage tugged at Aleks with such force that, at sixteen, he dropped a rope out his window one night, rappelled down the facade of the several-story building, and disappeared into the darkness. With some pocket money from selling postage stamps to friends of his father, Aleks made his way to the nearby town of Wisła, where he knew of a nightclub called the Oaza.

At sixteen, Aleks projected that same convincing, precocious confidence he had displayed as a skinny six-year-old performing with the Romani band while on holiday with his parents. He knew how to build relationships, to get what he wanted. After an impromptu audition on the doorstep of the club, in which Aleks impressed the manager with the purity and range of his whistling, he was booked as the "Lithuanian Nightingale" and put onstage that very night. Wearing a pair of leather breeches that revealed the thin legs of a boy, he whistled waltzes by Strauss and other Austrian or German composers for an eager crowd.

The bookings kept Aleks away from home for three days. So drawn was he to perform that everything else fell away—the tyranny of his father, his coursework, the approaching exams. He could focus only on one goal: to get onstage every night to whistle for the crowd. There was a rush about it, a unique feeling of power that he couldn't resist. Back in Cieszyn, Franciszek brooded, wondering what had become of his son. He knew Aleks hadn't fallen into trouble. To his irritation, the boy had run off before. It was a matter of finding him and dragging him home. A tip about his whereabouts came one evening from a waitress at a Cieszyn café who had heard through friends about Aleks performing in Wisła. When Franciszek gave her a look of anger, she said, "Professor, why are you worried? You have such an independent son!" Franciszek hired a taxi and set out toward Wisła. There he lingered until night fell and Aleks's act, scheduled to begin around eleven o'clock, drew near. When Aleks took the stage,

Franciszek waited for the perfect moment to cut in. Partway through a waltz, he had heard enough. From the back rows of the theater, in the darkness, he yelled, "You! You fool, are you getting off the stage yet?" Aleks ignored the heckle. He recognized his father's voice but couldn't believe he had come all this way to intervene. "Get off, I'm telling you! Or else I will rip your legs off your ass!" Franciszek shouted. Then, in what felt like a fraction of a second, Franciszek strode across the stage, grabbed Aleks by the arm, and pulled him away, shattering a mirror in the process. The trip home was long and quiet.

Despite his best efforts, Franciszek never managed to quell his spirited child. Once Aleks passed his exams, earned his high school diploma, and, in 1936, enrolled at the Jagiellonian University's Faculty of Law, he could pretty much do as he pleased, so long as he remained in school. The freedom Aleks had in those brief years of Poland's independence meant he could travel the European continent and experience life in a way no Kulisiewicz before him could have dreamed of. With friends that same year, he embarked on a tour of the Balkans and Central Europe. He explored Vienna, Budapest, Belgrade, Sofia, and Bucharest. He heard captivating music in villages and towns in Yugoslavia, where the tunes reminded him of the imitations of Arab music he heard in films. The singing seemed stretched out, mournful, with so much soul. It enchanted him, and sometimes, when a particularly wonderful song was played, he and his friends joined the townsfolk in dance, his hands grasping his neighbor's arms, theirs grasping his, as they spun in circles to the music, sometimes with frenzied speed, sometimes slowly and tenderly. All along the way, he absorbed the culture around him, picking up songs like the gorgeous waltz in Zagreb, which charmed him so much that he memorized it.

Of all the places Aleks visited, Tarnovo, in Bulgaria, burned itself most strongly in his memory. When he and his friends arrived, they marveled at the town, which was built up against several steep hills with the Yantra River flowing below it. Aleks never forgot the first morning in Tarnovo when, after tossing all night on mattresses infested with bedbugs, he and his friends awoke to a foggy dawn and the scent of roses. When the sun emerged red over the horizon, they could see the fields of flowers stretching out before them.

THOUGH SO MUCH opportunity lay before Aleks in the Poland of the 1930s, there was also a dark side of the era that blemished the country he loved. In the early days of its independence, a series of crises had unfolded. The country's first president, Gabriel Narutowicz, was assassinated just two days after his inauguration. Disastrous hyperinflation took hold, during which the Polish mark soared from a conversion of one to nine against the US dollar in 1918 to, at one point, one to twenty million in 1923. In 1926, Józef Piłsudski, the man who presided over Poland's rebirth eight years earlier, arrived in Warsaw, overthrew the legal government, and installed what became known as the Sanacja regime. By the latter half of the 1930s, a deep anxiety had taken hold in most corners of the country. Hitler turned his spite toward Poland's neighbors, one after another. In 1936, he took the Rhineland. In 1938, he took Austria. Many feared it was only a matter of time before he would focus his sights on Poland.

In this tenuous situation, Poland's minorities began to fret. Ethnic Germans were allying themselves with Nazism at a rapid and worrying pace. Disaffection among Ukrainians was taking hold. Anti-Semitism in the political arena was on the rise, making Jews fear harassment and abuse. Dread set in among ethnic Poles as well.

As he began his law studies in 1936, Aleks sought a worldview of his own. He toggled between sympathies for the leftists, many of whom felt the allure of communism, and Poland's newly regalvanized and energetic right. Though he chiefly saw himself as a musician, trepidation about politics and what he stood for grew within him. In the political arena, a great debate about Poland and its future was taking place. Politicians argued over the "Jewish Question," with some, especially on the right, demonizing Poland's Jews. The right's calls for limiting what they saw as outsized Jewish influence caught Aleks's eye.

Being targeted because of their ethnoreligious identity was not new for Jews living on Polish soil or indeed in Europe broadly. Despite the fact that by 1939 they had lived in Poland for the good part of a millennium, their coexistence with ethnic Poles being sometimes harmonious, anti-Semitism had taken hold in tone and occasionally in action in the decade or so before the Germans invaded. Some politicians on the right believed the delusion of a great Jewish conspiracy and advocated for anti-Jewish boycotts or forced emigration. Sometimes, anti-Semitism led to violence, although this was relatively rare.

The "Jewish Question" also permeated institutions of higher learning, including the Jagiellonian University, where Aleks was studying law. Though forbidden on paper, from the early 1920s, nationalist and far-right student groups began to form at most of Poland's elite universities. These groups openly preached anti-Semitism and schemed about ways to exclude Jews and other minorities and make Poland a pure ethnic state. By the early 1930s, they had become more venomous and violent, calling for the complete removal of Jewish students, sometimes dragging them from lecture halls or carrying out brutal attacks. All around the country at this time, the far right was growing in strength. Their members were intoxicated by fascism and its ideology as a modern response to social problems, a new system that could rein in chaos and propose a coherent vision for all of ethnic Polish society.

During his first year at university in 1936, Aleks got caught up in the right-wing fervor. In little time, he transformed into a hyperpatriotic, chauvinistic version of himself. At the Jagiellonian University, one nationalist student group that echoed the anti-Semitic calls for limiting or restricting the admission of Jews caught Aleks's attention. Soon, he joined the group, and his newly minted nationalist views began to appear in the newspaper articles he wrote, such as one headlined "Land, You've Returned!" in which he voiced his support of Poland absorbing certain Czech borderlands, including land in his home region. Aleks still regarded himself primarily as an artist, concerned with performing, with honing his musical abilities and impressing those around him—especially the young women. Yet alongside some of his peers, he began to regard Jews as a problem, as competition, both political and economic. Though he and his classmates lacked any evidence, they believed that Jews held too much power, succeeded too easily in business. Many of them believed that Poles, especially those of modest means, ought to have more access to universities—for social reasons, but also to make up for the consequences of occupation by the partitioning powers that had always kept the Polish working class from education. The group that Aleks joined was composed of students from more modest backgrounds. They weren't the sons of workers, but they also hadn't been raised in the aristocratic palaces of Kraków or nearby country estates. The majority of them felt great jealousy toward their Jewish peers and cheered when, in 1937, the rectors of Poland's universities voted to allow bench ghettos, which banished Jewish students to one side of lecture halls. Emboldened by the ruling, the group Aleks belonged to became stridently vocal, making anti-Semitic remarks in the classroom and in marches on surrounding streets. Far-right students regularly attacked their Jewish classmates; violence turned into a near daily occurrence on Polish university campuses. At its most virulent, these nationalist student groups echoed some politicians in advocating for the deportation of Jews through forced emigration to Mandatory Palestine or Madagascar.

Though Aleks belonged to this group and shared some of its views, he rarely participated in marches and never joined acts of violence. His ideas about the world were facile, malleable. He was in search of a worldview and felt drawn to whatever was current, contemptible as it may have been. As the threat of Hitler grew ever more menacing for Poland, and as news of pogroms against Jews in Berlin hit the newspapers, he left the group and swore off any sympathies for nationalism or a more authoritarian state. Yet to some degree, he retained his suspicions about Jews and their role in Polish society. Perhaps these views went deeper than he understood. Perhaps, like many Poles in his milieu, a current of anti-Semitism ran within him, whether he realized it or not.

BY THE THIRD week of August 1939, Aleks's life—and the lives of almost every other Pole—began to disintegrate. His breezy summer of social calls, music, and writing for the local press faded into the past. Now the approach of war animated everything; it hung as a great weight over Cieszyn. Schoolchildren and workers carried out antiaircraft drills. Civilians learned to operate radios and treat wounds. People in the town square going about their daily shopping seemed jittery, breathless.

To Aleks and the people of the town, war seemed certain as early as August 23, when a group of local Nazi sympathizers, likely drawn from the many ethnic Germans who had turned to Nazism, set off explosives and damaged several local monuments around Cieszyn. In the days that followed, the government in Warsaw mobilized Polish troops, and because Cieszyn lay on the border, Polish soldiers there began to organize a defense. When German troops massed along the frontier in the final days of August, Aleks knew he would not return to university in the fall. The rector had not canceled the term, but many of Aleks's classmates dispersed, anxiously awaiting what was rumored to come.

The first news of invasion on that Friday, September 1, came in the form of radio broadcasts. Before dawn that morning, German aircraft had showered bombs over the Polish city of Wieluń, a place of no military significance. They dropped 70 tons of munitions, flattening the city and killing hundreds of civilians. At the port of Danzig, a free city, a German battle cruiser on a so-called friendship mission unmoored and sailed a short distance to a bend in the Vistula. Once in position, the ship aimed its guns on land and fired on a Polish military depot. In the city of Danzig proper, paramilitary units attacked the Polish Post Office, and fierce fighting ensued. At home in Cieszyn, Aleks heard the thunder of warplanes, high in Polish skies, streaking toward Kraków and nearby Katowice.

Though the residents of Cieszyn knew about the invasion, their morning carried on almost as usual. Local shops opened, workers arrived at factories. But artillery blasts rumbled in the distance. Just before noon, shops closed and factory managers evacuated workers. Polish soldiers had set up points of defense on the perimeter of the town, but any sense of safety was short-lived. As the German army poured across the border slightly north of town, residents realized that Cieszyn and its surroundings were essentially undefended. By noon, the last of the local officials, clerks, and their families had fled. So had the local military command. Some Polish soldiers tried to delay the invading armies, but their commanding officers called for an eastward retreat. By three that afternoon, with Cieszyn's three bridges in ruins, any Polish attempt to slow the invading army had failed. The Germans arrived, met no resistance, and took the town.

When the Wehrmacht paraded victorious through town, ethnic Germans welcomed them, distributing sandwiches and smiling as the soldiers marched over the cobblestones. Local militants—mostly fifth columnists of German origin—appeared too, wearing SA or even SS uniforms that German officials across the border had issued them. These men occupied themselves by tearing down Polish monuments.

In many places in western Poland, more intense fighting unfolded. Air raids shook the foundations of Warsaw, Łódź, Kraków, Poznań, and other cities. The invading Germans destroyed bridges and derailed trains, and as crowds of new refugees made their way out of razed towns, heading for what they hoped would be safety in the cities, Luftwaffe aircraft strafed them.

With Cieszyn now in German hands, Aleks and his family retreated to their home. They could hear commotion outside. Sometimes German soldiers passed by the house. Sometimes a blast would ring out from a distant battlefield.

When night fell on that first day of September, Aleks wondered whether Poland as a whole would fall as Cieszyn had done. Like many Poles around the region, he believed that surely, in the north of the country, the defense lines would hold. The national government had assured them that the military was capable and that the British and French would honor their pact and come to the aid of Poland. Perhaps, Aleks thought, Cieszyn under German rule would be temporary. Perhaps the interruption of his quest for a life of music would be short. All he could do was wait.

Chapter 2

⁓

In the morning light of September 2, the Germans set Cieszyn's main synagogue ablaze. Within hours, what remained of the ornate, L-shaped structure was a pile of scorched white bricks and heaps of ash.

A short time later, the new German town government announced that Jews could no longer own a business. Their shops, factories, and grocery stores would be commandeered without compensation. Wehrmacht soldiers commenced a series of arrests, harassing residents of all backgrounds and loading people onto trucks. The dragnet of detentions had begun. Just hours after the invasion, German intentions were absolutely clear. It didn't matter if a person was a professor or businessman or farmer, the Germans had one goal for most of Poland's people—to make them slaves of the Reich.

Over the next few days, Aleks, holed up in the family apartment, frightened by the German forces swarming around town, likely found a bit of solace in listening to the radio at hushed volumes. In the modest Kulisiewicz family apartment on Solna Street, south and slightly east of the town square and just a 15-minute walk from the river border with Czechoslovakia, Aleks and his family huddled around the most direct source of information they had. The newscasts, in Polish and likely emitted from the capital, swung between accounts of Wehrmacht advances and upbeat assurances of the resilience of the Polish army. The truth lay somewhere in between, and few Poles had the full picture. During the first days of the invasion, a million and a half German troops stormed across the border from three frontiers—East Prussia, Germany, and Czechoslovakia, the country from which the troops now marauding in Cieszyn had originated. The Germans possessed a sizable advantage, having faster and more sophisticated hardware and weapons than the Poles, especially when it came to armored vehicles. The Polish tank force, for instance, was dwarfed by the Wehrmacht's. Though Germany possessed the edge, the Polish army was not by any means frail. With a million men in arms, Poland boasted the fifth largest military on earth. It also had some advanced weaponry, including Polish-made and highly effective anti-tank rifles, machine guns, and pistols. Most important, regardless of how disadvantaged the Polish army was, their goal was never to defeat the Germans. Rather, they were meant to hold off the invaders for two weeks while France and Britain mobilized for their own attack on Germany.

In Kraków, the closest major city to Cieszyn and Aleks's home during the university term, bombs from Luftwaffe jets damaged an airfield, a train station, and a major church. Not long after, the mayor of the city and other government and military officials fled eastward, leaving the city undefended, ungoverned, and its residents abandoned. Knowing that Kraków could mount no defense, the remaining leaders declared the city open on September 5, hoping that surrender might reduce destruction and bloodshed. The next day, when the city's deputy mayor drove to the suburbs to observe the placing of two white sheets that would signify Kraków's yielding, a gunshot halted him. The Germans had already arrived. By the following morning, Wehrmacht troops marched through Kraków, and the city's residents watched tanks, motorized units, and huge guns pulled by horses drive by. They heard the thud of boots on their cobbled streets.

In Warsaw, German bombs rained down. Though the air raids first targeted aviation and industrial sites in the suburbs, the terror soon struck residential neighborhoods. On September 10, seventeen air raids took place, destroying buildings and killing civilians. The destruction by air of a major European city by an enemy force was unprecedented. On the ground, transport workers fitted trams with dim blue lights so they wouldn't be seen from above at night. Residents taped their windows to prevent shattering from the impact of falling bombs. When the Wehrmacht encircled the capital by the end of the second week of September, they began launching artillery fire. By some estimates, the Germans fired twenty-five thousand shells into Warsaw in one day during the siege. Shortages of food became a crisis.

Though lacking the promised assistance from their French and British allies, the Poles fought well. They stunned the German invaders in several battles, including at the fort of Westerplatte, where Polish forces repelled repeated German assaults, and during the nineteen-day siege of Warsaw, when the capital fought off an initial invasion and then resisted the Germans for several weeks. As the third week of September began, the Poles had inflicted some fifty thousand casualties on the Wehrmacht and were still fighting.

WITH EACH DAY, the Gestapo plucked people off the streets of Cieszyn, loaded them at gunpoint into trucks, and deported them to unknown destinations. Few returned. For the Germans, anyone vaguely tied to the Polish intelligentsia presented a threat. Teachers, journalists, academics, priests, doctors, and members of the gentry would leave their homes to do errands or to see relatives and never return. Sometimes their family found out that their loved one lay beaten in the local Gestapo-run jail. Just as often, they disappeared, presumably sent west to the Nazi camps that Polish journalists had written about in the years before the war. Then more sinister rumors began to spread. As the days passed, people around Cieszyn whispered to one another that the Gestapo had begun to take prisoners to the forests north of town and shoot them into trenches.

For the Germans, eliminating the upper stratum of society was an essential part of their plan to destroy Poland as a functioning state. From those first days of September, they dismantled the country's bureaucracy and administration with speed. The aim: to render the citizens of Poland a pliable mass of faceless, nameless people, unable to determine their present or future, incapable of resisting foreign rule.

In the Kulisiewicz household, Aleks's father, Franciszek, seemed most at risk. None of the Kulisiewiczs were activists, politicians, or university professors. The family didn't belong to the local gentry or the military. They didn't hold government posts. But teaching, as Franciszek did, made one a target. Over some fifteen years, Franciszek had taught in several of the elite private schools that dotted the region. Until 1937, he even held the headmaster's job at a school in the nearby town of Pszczyna, 40 minutes away, where some of Poland's noblest families sent their sons to read the classics. For the Germans, simply instructing young Poles about culture and history was cause enough for arrest. To make matters worse for Franciszek, he had also published several newspaper articles before the invasion and at its start, writing sharp pieces condemning Hitler's desire to annex Danzig, then a free city.

Aleks also fretted about arrest. In local newspapers, he, too, had condemned Hitler and the Nazi state. He feared that the secret police, now a dark presence in Cieszyn, were bound to find old copies of his articles. And even if they didn't, denouncing him as anti-German would be easy. The Gestapo had begun their sweep of the town, interrogating their captives for information. Perhaps an old friend, even a newspaper editor, would succumb to the torture and betray him.

While Aleks and Franciszek were keeping a low profile during those first weeks of September, trying their best not to bring attention to themselves or their household, the Germans replaced every bit of Polishness in Cieszyn they could. A quickly established German occupying administration lowered flags and wrenched Polish government signs off of buildings, leaving red and white eagle plaques lying on the sidewalks. They Germanized Polish street names. They renamed the town market, where so much of local life took place, to Adolf Hitler Platz.

Though the invasion itself had not surprised Aleks, what did shock him was how fast the Germans had swept across Poland and that the French and British had sat on their hands, not intervening as they had promised. Like many others in his country, he had believed the Polish government and newspapers, which made it seem as though the country's armed forces could withstand a German attack—perhaps not indefinitely, but for longer than actually happened. Once the French and British mobilized, the three countries would together defeat Hitler, attacking Germany on two fronts. Aleks thought the war would only last a few months, that soon he'd be back in Kraków, singing in cabarets and clubs, procrastinating with his law studies, sending his father into fits of dread about the destiny of the Kulisiewicz family.

Though the radio reported increasingly grave news during those first two weeks of September, detailing stories of German victories and Polish defeats, Aleks didn't believe what he was hearing. As some hoped, he may have interpreted Polish retreats as an attempt by the army to straighten its line or regroup. It was likely hard, however, for him to maintain that hopeful thinking when news reached Cieszyn that in Kraków the Germans had torn down the statue of Poland's great poet, Adam Mickiewicz, in the market square, which they also renamed Adolf-Hitler-Platz.

Across the region, the Germans shut down schools, theaters, newspapers, and any other sector that could not be absorbed to serve the German war machine. It became clear to Aleks that the Germans were settling in, preparing to subsume his country and incorporate it as a colony of the Reich. Any hope for continued Polish resistance to its totalitarian neighbor melted away on September 17, when half a million Red Army troops crossed into Poland from two regions, the Byelorussian Front and the Ukrainian Front. To support these forces, over forty-eight hundred tanks and fifty-five hundred armored vehicles drove alongside the infantry, and two thousand aircraft flew overhead. Poles received the Soviet troops with a mix of hope and fear, some wanting to believe that this new invading force had come to fight the Germans. It didn't take long, though, for the intentions of the Red Army to become clear. Though Soviet propaganda claimed that their forces arrived to protect Poland's large Byelorussian and Ukrainian populations, this was no more than a cover for Stalin's hunger for Polish land. Though Polish troops again mounted solid resistance, the defense line was shattered; they simply could not hold out against two massive armies invading from opposite ends of the country. Not long after the invasion in the east, Polish leaders issued evacuation orders.

The Polish government and its military leaders first fled to Romania. The civil and military officials who managed to escape then formed a government in exile, first in France, then in England. The Germans and Soviets divided their spoils, establishing a demarcation line along the rivers Bug and San on September 28. After twenty short years of renewed political sovereignty and cultural revival, Poland again vanished from the map of Europe. Soldiers who didn't flee or were not captured went underground, forming a resistance network. Germany absorbed several northern and western Polish districts directly into the Reich, including the one in which the Kulisiewicz family lived in Cieszyn. In the vast central and southern areas on the German side of the new Nazi-Soviet line, Hitler created the "General Government" and installed his former lawyer Hans Frank as its governor-general. From the Wawel Castle in Kraków, once the residence of Polish kings, Frank ruled the region. In the east, the Soviets staged elections that purported to signal Poland's wish to be annexed. In reality, they simply swallowed up huge swaths of land, incorporating them into the USSR.

AS THE GERMANS erased as much Polishness as they could, something changed in Aleks. At the beginning of the occupation, he feared the Germans, worried about being picked up by the Gestapo. But that nervousness lifted as autumn began. The days darkened; the nighttime temperature plummeted.

Aleks's first small rebellion took the form of teaching as part of an underground network of tutors. Starting from the early days of occupation, the Germans forbade education in the Polish language. As occupiers had done for centuries before, Hitler, stamping out the languages of those he conquered, followed the old playbook of subjugation, stripping away what it meant to be Polish. During Aleks's first years at the Jagiellonian University, he had tutored young students to earn pocket money. Though this was now illegal, he continued taking students, teaching them in Polish about the culture and history of their lost country. This small act of defiance meant a great deal to him, as though he was playing a part in keeping Polishness alive in the face of the Germans.

Life under occupation quickly became strenuous and cruel for most citizens throughout the country, regardless of ethnicity or religion. There was one exception to this rule. Ethnic Germans residing in Poland suddenly found themselves a privileged class. In Cieszyn, Nazi rules and regulations had begun to govern all aspects of daily life. The Germans quickly imposed a racial hierarchy, which they enforced brutally. As in most of German-controlled Poland, trams, certain park benches, and the best shops around Cieszyn bore a sign that read "For Germans Only." What was more, every citizen had to register with the authorities. Under orders from Heinrich Himmler, every person in Poland had to be assigned a group: Reichsdeutsche, the category for Germans born within the old borders of Imperial Germany; Volksdeutsche, for those who claimed German lineage within three generations; Nichtdeutsch, for those who were neither German nor Jewish; and finally, Juden, for Jews.

When the Germans imposed this hierarchy in Cieszyn, Aleks found himself in an ambiguous position. While his father's roots were firmly Polish, Aleks's mother, Isabella Ludmila Czorba-Bromowicz, came from a prosperous Austro-Hungarian family that settled in Kraków during the partitions of Poland. Isabella died of intestinal tuberculosis when he was a boy, but her father, an engineer known to Aleks as grandfather Czorba-Bromowicz, took an interest in him.

For much of Aleks's childhood, he felt a strong, if confusing, connection to a certain Germanic identity—thanks in large part to his grandfather. Czorba-Bromowicz, a proud, sometimes arrogant man who built railroads and bridges and wore long whiskers, lived among Kraków's elite class, speaking German and moving in circles with ties to Vienna, Budapest, and Berlin. He flaunted, in German, his disdain for much of Polish society—Aleks's father included. Ever since Aleks was a boy, Czorba-Bromowicz drilled into him that he was not Polish but Germanic like his mother and grandfather, part of a superior stock of people.

From early on, German culture had made a great impact on Aleks, partly because of his grandfather but also because of the proximity of his world to Germanic lands. As a child, he read the Brothers Grimm tales of "Hansel and Gretel" and "Little Red Riding Hood." Among the first songs he remembered learning was one called "Sneaky Fox, You Stole a Goose," a German melody. With a pair of scissors and sheets of paper, he cut out little houses, whose architecture always mirrored the Tyrolean tradition he saw in picture books. At school, Germanized nuns taught him to write in the gothic alphabet, using a fountain pen with a flat nib to compose sentences with thick and thin lines. All around him in Cieszyn there lived Germans. They held some of the top posts in the region—mine managers, engineers, supervisors—all positions of the higher class. When Aleks's mother eloped with his father and fled to Czechoslovakia, grandfather Czorba-Bromowicz sent the Austrian police to wrench his daughter from the arms of a lousy Pole. So opposed was he to his daughter marrying Franciszek that, according to family lore, he tried to conceal Aleks's birth from him and raise the boy without a father. Surely that was better than bringing a Pole into the family.

Throughout Aleks's upbringing, old Czorba-Bromowicz, with his thick Franz Joseph–like whiskers extending past his upper lip and up his cheeks, never stopped reminding Aleks of his Austro-Hungarian roots. He would take young Aleks to cafés around Kraków and assert with the strongest conviction in his voice, "Only Austro-Hungarian blood plays music in your veins. Remember that."

Being connected to German culture signified privilege to Aleks—wealth, status, family. It meant the grand townhouses of Kraków, like the red brick one with the medusa on its facade that his grandfather owned in Salwator, the leafy, coveted quarter of the city. Now, with the Germans looting

Poland, Aleks had to reckon with this part of his identity. Just as his grand-father had, the occupying Germans saw the Poles and anyone to the east of the Reich as an inferior race—men, women, and children cut from the stone of a primitive culture whose adherents were at best fit for slave labor.

As the grandson of a man with citizenship in the old Austro-Hungarian Empire, Aleks could have claimed to be Volksdeutsche, which, though a Faustian bargain, would likely have made his life significantly better in the short term. A man with the Volksdeutsche designation received coupons for more and better food than his Polish or Jewish compatriots. Declar-ing loyalty to the German state might also have meant that Aleks could avoid imprisonment, although that was not certain, given how strongly he had decried Hitler in the press. He identified as a patriotic Pole through and through, and he viewed the Germans with nothing but contempt. Yet another reason may have dissuaded him from declaring himself as Volks-deutsche. Strong and young as he was, the Germans might enlist him in the Wehrmacht and send him to the front, something he wished to avoid at all costs.

Regardless of the privilege the Volksdeutsche status might have meant for Aleks, he had no interest in joining the ranks of the Nazis. An earlier version of him may have felt pulled in two opposing directions, toward his Germanic roots and toward his staunch love for Poland, its people, and its culture. But by the time he reached early manhood, and certainly when the invasion took place, he aligned himself firmly with Poland, forsaking all that his grandfather had once tried to make him believe. He felt no con-nection to the ever-expanding Germandom that now ruled Europe with terror. In fact, he felt more allegiance to his homeland than ever. When his time came to register, he marked the box that read Nichtdeutsch, not German. Perhaps he could lie low and ride out the turmoil.

EVEN BEFORE WARSAW capitulated on September 27, the national press struggled to print and distribute newspapers, and information about the war slowed to a trickle. The best source of news for Aleks, the radio, rarely picked up anything not broadcast from German sources. Either way, own-ing a radio was now illegal, so Aleks and his family stopped huddling around it as they had done during the first few weeks of the invasion.

In the absence of news, Aleks could only make deductions about the German occupation based on what he saw and heard in Cieszyn. What he did suspect from observing events in town was that something horri-ble seemed to be happening to the Jews. Over a month had passed since the Nazis destroyed Cieszyn's synagogue. Now the Germans harassed and assaulted Jews in Cieszyn. Over time, Jews began to disappear. Whole families vanished, and their shops and businesses, already stolen from them, were to be handed over to Nazi-controlled trusts.

What Aleks was witnessing had begun to take place all over occupied Poland. Before invading, Nazi officials instructed their soldiers that the Jews they would encounter were savages who spoke a corrupted version of German and lived in filthy, subhuman conditions. When the Wehrmacht passed through villages and towns on their march east, often razing them as they went, they saw communities of Jews that resembled nothing like the assimilated, often secular Jews of Germany. The Polish Jews they con-fronted living in shtetls and rural settlements followed religion and tradi-tion. Men wore sidelocks and long beards. Women wore sheitels. It took no time for the Germans to abuse Poland's Jews. Soldiers repeatedly shaved the beards and sidelocks of the Jewish men they encountered during the invasion. They raped Jewish women. Once hostilities had ceased in early October, the Nazis began rounding up Jews in villages and small towns. Often, the soldiers herded them into ghettos. Some they summarily shot.

In Cieszyn, a local underground formed, and Aleks felt drawn again to resisting the Germans. But joining the organized resistance didn't interest him. Instead, he returned to writing, his second small rebellion against the Germans. One day in mid-October, Aleks sat at the family typewriter and composed an article he titled "Homegrown Hitlerism." Over the last couple of years, he had gotten to know the editor of a local Cieszyn news-paper, *Głos Stanu Średniego*. On some nights before the invasion, Aleks and the newspaperman had binge-drunk together at local bars late into the darkness, and the man had already published some of Aleks's work. He now operated the presses underground at immense personal risk and despite the German interdiction on Polish media. On October 25, "Homegrown Hitlerism" appeared under Aleks's middle name, Tytus. "With a fist," a part of Aleks's article read, "we will squeeze every insult against the Polish nation down your throat, and we will use the broken teeth to make an inscription in front of the theater in Cieszyn: 'People who are passing by! Tell Adolf that this is the way we broke the teeth and hit the face of the Hitlerite system.'" The publication of this article made Aleks a Gestapo target. For the next several days he rarely left the house. As risky as it was before, doing so now posed an even greater threat.

As Aleks expected, the Gestapo had indeed taken notice of him. Little did he know that an old friend of his from high school had been drawing up a list of young men for the police to arrest. The friend had added Aleks's name. A few days after his article was published, Aleks heard a loud pounding on the door of the family apartment. He was home alone, not expecting anyone.

In the hours leading up to that moment, with little to do, Aleks had been reflecting on the loss of his country, mourning for the Poland he had known and loved. He thought in particular of Biłgoraj, a town in the far east of Poland, which he heard the Nazis had bombed and then burned a few weeks earlier. Because it was an old, poor place, where most houses were built of wood, the town disappeared in a matter of hours. Only piles of ash and a forest of orphaned chimneys remained. He thought about the little six-year-old Ewunia, his final student to whom he had taught the work of Poland's great literary heroes, such as Adam Mickiewicz and Henryk Sienkiewicz, and the rich history and beauty of their mother tongue. He thought about Ewunia again later that night after several German policemen dragged him from his apartment and threw him into a Gestapo interrogation cell in the local jail. As the secret police beat Aleks, breaking his teeth with each blow, he thought of Ewunia once more. For each bloody tooth that fell to the floor, the Germans shouted, "Count, you dog!" and Aleks had to bow and count, saying *Danke schön!* each time.

He thought of Ewunia growing, changing, but holding onto the literature and language he had taught her, keeping it alive in her mind. And somehow, thinking of that child made the blows less painful.

During the first days of his imprisonment in Cieszyn, Aleks wondered why the Nazis didn't just shoot him. They jumped at the opportunity to execute other prisoners. On most nights, as the communal cell darkened and the stone walls chilled, a selection took place. The peephole in the iron door would slide open, the sound of which would quell any chatter and render the men frozen in fear. The guard would call a prisoner by name. The chosen man would have to approach the peephole and give his personal details. Who might be called each night and why was always a mystery. What was certain, though, was that once the guards summoned a prisoner, he had little time left to live. After the first week or so in jail, Aleks and the other prisoners got word from Polish jail guards, who treated them better than the Germans who oversaw the facility, as to what happened after the Gestapo summoned a prisoner. First, guards would lead him to the forest just beyond the jail walls and order him to dig graves for a pile of corpses lying there. Once he'd finished the digging, the man would be led to a holding cell for a final night. When morning came, the Gestapo would take him back to the forest and shoot him, often with several others. Later in the day, the next round of condemned men arrived to dig the graves of those before them. And so it went, one man digging the grave of his comrade. Again and again and again.

The beating from the Gestapo had an important effect on Aleks. It woke him up to the reality he faced and the urgent task ahead if he wished to survive. It also made him acutely aware of the risk of death. The fragility of life was suddenly in stark relief. The fearlessness of a young man left him, and a keen awareness of human weakness replaced it. Most important was Aleks's determination to live. The burning ambition he felt in the years before the invasion had not evaporated, though no longer was it directed to performance. As he sat within the walls of the jail, Aleks began to obsess on how he could survive. Imprisonment, it seemed, would not be a short affair. It was plausible that he would be locked up perhaps for the duration of the war, perhaps longer still. To pass the time, he hummed songs to himself, such as "Morning Song," which his childhood friend, Stanisław Hadyna, had written when his sister Wanda died in 1936. Imagining the shining sunlight the song depicted gave him strength.

Aleks also began to tell the fortunes of his fellow prisoners, analyzing the creases on their palms, pretending to be clairvoyant. For years he had dabbled in the supernatural. Since his boyhood, he and Stanisław had read everything they could about metaphysics, parapsychology, clairvoyance, and mysticism. They even sought out local soothsayers and begged for lessons in the supernatural. Together, they honed their seeing powers and also the skills required to make the recipient of their predictions believe them. The two boys adopted the parlance of the soothsayers they met, greeting each other in Hindi, putting their right hands on their hearts and saying: "*Efendi!*" These paranormal topics at once fascinated Aleks and stoked a deep skepticism in him. He loved the performance of soothsaying, the attention it brought him. But did he believe any of it was true? That was another matter.

In December, when a new group of prisoners arrived in his Cieszyn cell, they spoke of a miraculous sight they claimed to have witnessed. They recounted a story about the final Polish-language church service the Germans permitted in town, on December 12, a Tuesday. They claimed that during mass, an image of Mother Mary decorated with rubies and pearls began to sag from the heat of an unknown source. When the priest raised the monstrance, a great crack was heard inside the vaulted hall of the church. The churchgoers looked up from their moment of prayer and saw that many of the decorations had fallen, and those that remained seemed to show the number twelve. To the new prisoners, this number held significance; it meant something, though they didn't exactly know what.

When Aleks heard the tale, he didn't think much of it. He could be an incredulous man, keen on reading about and performing such mysticism but not one to believe in miracles or signs from a higher power. Yet when one of the guards, a man the prisoners called Little Bee who treated them humanely, approached Aleks to ask him what he made of the story, Aleks saw an opportunity. Evidently, his cellmates and now even a guard saw him as a sage, a young man with prophetic powers. This, Aleks thought, could be a way to protect himself, to make himself useful, indispensable even, and thus harder to kill. In the moment that Little Bee approached him, Aleks decided he'd run with the clairvoyant act, and speaking loud enough for everyone in the cellblock to hear him, said, "Mr. Little Bee, please tell the city of Cieszyn and its residents that just as today's last service in the Polish language happened on the twelfth day of the twelfth month and on a Tuesday, the last service in German will also take place in this same church, in a year when the twelfth day of the twelfth month is also a Tuesday." Something impulsive inside Aleks drew the prophecy out of him. It was a split-second decision where an opportunity appeared and he had to decide what to do with it immediately. When he uttered those words, the men around him stood silent. At first, they tried to calculate the next time December 12 fell on a Tuesday. But without a calendar, none of them could.

In the days that followed, Aleks's cellmates came to him frequently for predictions. They regarded him as a haunted young man, one who could contact the spiritual world and call forth information about the future. Aleks saw that his scheme was working. For the men around him, his predictions were a respite, a moment of relief, something to help divert the mind from the wickedness they endured. Playing this role made Aleks important to his cellmates; it raised his standing from a skinny young man with little experience in the world to someone of some significance. He was building goodwill, a sort of currency he might draw on if he needed a bit of food or an extra blanket. In these circumstances Aleks figured out how to use his skills to survive. He loved the performance of giving predictions, the feeling of the men fixing their gaze on him with deep trust and interest as he doled out a piece of information about their wives or children or the future of the war. Ever since he was a boy playing his little violin for his family, Aleks had sought the spotlight. It was fuel for him, a pathway to a feeling he loved. Aleks also excelled at building relationships of mutual interest. He could be transactional, not in a cynical way, but in a way that would benefit himself and the person with whom he was exchanging something. He had a shrewd eye for spotting resources or opportunities, and he built relationships with this in mind.

One evening, a few days after Aleks made his grand prediction about the end of the war, the hour came when the prisoners felt the nightly fear in their guts, when the next man would be selected. That night, the guard slid open the peephole and yelled, "Aleksander Kulisiewicz." Aleks was seated beside another prisoner and halfway through telling his fortune. At the sound of his name, heat blanketed Aleks's body. He stood up and walked to the door. The men around him—who'd come to him for predictions and trusted him—suddenly saw him as a charlatan. Aleks heard one prisoner whisper, "The idiot talked so much, tried to bewitch us, and he didn't even know what he had coming." Aleks turned around, and in a state of rage cursed at his cellmates. The room fell quiet, and none of the men shook Aleks's hand to express their sympathy, to say goodbye, as they had done with others before him. All he received were a few cubes of sugar one prisoner slipped into his pocket before he reached the door.

When Aleks walked into the corridor, Little Bee led him to a cell on the second floor that was empty of prisoners. No Gestapo agents in their pressed uniforms sat waiting for him. Aleks instead saw a girl who, Little Bee explained, was his own daughter. Seated at a table, she held a round calendar with sliding numbers. Little Bee explained that she had been thinking about Aleks's prediction. But Little Bee was incredulous. "The next Tuesday, December 12, will happen in 1944! In five years! You're crazy." Aleks watched the girl sliding the numbers around the calendar. He heaved a quiet sigh of relief that on this day he would not be harmed. He repeated his prediction.

Back in the cellblock, the other prisoners were shocked to see Aleks return unharmed. When the surprise wore off, some viewed him with suspicion. Had Aleks become a Gestapo informant who would rat out his fellow prisoners? How else could he have survived?

What the others thought didn't matter to Aleks. Most important was that he was still alive. Almost as essential was the realization that being a prisoner of high standing—being known or useful in some way—could grant him great power. So long as he struck a good balance with it, he could use clairvoyance as a way to get favors from other prisoners, put himself above the others, and thus achieve a sort of protection. Just as his first beating toughened him for what was to come, understanding the power of relationships in prison proved to be one of the most important lessons of the early months of the war.

ON THE DAY of Aleks's arrest, his life as he had envisioned it ended. As with just about all the middle-class young men and women of the Second Republic of Poland, war obliterated the freedom and opportunities the 1930s had afforded those with enough privilege. With the fall of Poland came the end of Aleks's youth and the destruction of the life he thought he would live—that of a half-interested but jolly lawyer by day, a man-about-town by night, someone who attended the performances of Poland's great singers and from time to time got onstage to sing himself. Aleks and his entire generation watched as the dream of Polish liberty their parents had fought for disintegrated in the course of a few short weeks. Unlike their mothers and fathers before them, they had had a fleeting taste of a free Poland during their youth. They had come of age in a version of the country where they could celebrate their history and culture. It was a bitter loss to everyone, but Aleks's generation felt a unique sense of sorrow. With the Germans in the west and the Russians in the east, Polish identity again risked fading away.

By then, Kraków's cafés were no longer filled with Polish intellectuals talking about revolution and music and art. Wehrmacht soldiers, Nazi officials, even Gestapo agents lit cigarettes, leaning against local bars. School halls were locked up. Government buildings, in Polish hands for just two decades, again housed the administration of an occupying power. At least on paper, the cabarets and nightclubs Aleks had frequented or performed at were now for German use. Far off in his mind lived the memories of the scent of roses in the Balkans, of nights out with friends in Brussels, of singing onstage.

In December, winter came with full force, and with it, an aching, painful cold. In fact, a deep freeze had begun to spread through Central Europe in the last weeks of 1939. In the Cieszyn jail, Aleks and the others suffered within the stone walls. Shivering in his cell, he sought comfort in one particular set of memories—of a Czech girl he loved in 1938 called Bożena. Though Aleks had courted many young women since his late teens, Bożena was special. He had been infatuated with her, intent on impressing her by any means. Early on most mornings, Bożena would cross from the Czech side of the Olza River into Polish Cieszyn, poor and sometimes barefoot, to sell vegetables. To impress her, Aleks often rose before dawn and snuck out of the house to help her pull her cart of produce through the quiet streets to where she'd stand and sell. Then he stood beside her, barefoot too, in solidarity, with her baskets of potatoes and onions, parsnips, carrots, and turnips.

Bożena knew about Aleks's music, how he whistled or performed onstage. She often warned him about standing shoeless, saying in Czech, "You will go hoarse and won't impress the world with your singing anymore." Aleks knew she was trying to get rid of him. During the times of terror in the Cieszyn jail, between fear and boredom and all the emotions in between, Bożena came alive in Aleks's mind. He yearned for the simplest moments with her, waiting silently together at her stand for a customer, watching the carriages pass by. He recalled the day when he had some money after playing a two-bit role in a Belgian film the summer before. When a carousel was installed in the Cieszyn town square, Aleks paid extra for the manager to announce over the loudspeaker, "And now one round for the most beautiful girl in the city." Bożena went pale. She fled, wanting nothing of the attention.

Though Aleks never managed to spark feelings in Bożena for him, he savored the memories of her. When Poland invaded the Zaolzie region of Czechoslovakia in 1938, she and her family moved deep into the Czech interior. From then on, all Aleks knew about her was the name of the town she supposedly lived in.

FOR THE ENTIRETY of the winter of 1939–40, Aleks sat in the Cieszyn jail. Throughout those cold months, he watched as men came and went. Sometimes, men he got to know disappeared. Others, like Aleks, remained in the jail, though no one knew exactly why.

In early April, the guards assembled Aleks and a group of other prisoners, marched them out of the jail, and led them through town to a railway station, where a train stood, closely guarded. There, under the watchful eyes of German soldiers, Aleks and the others were prodded onto empty box cars. Once everyone was inside, the guards slammed the doors shut. The men waited in the darkness. Then came the tug of the locomotive, and the train slowly pulled out of town. No one knew where it was headed.

Chapter 3

The train rumbled out of the Cieszyn station, slowly picked up speed, and chugged along at a steady pace. Aleks sat against the walls of the dark box car, one among many detainees. Little fresh air seeped through the cracks in the paneled walls. There was a pervasive stink of urine.

Aleks recognized several of the men from his weeks in the local jail. Some he knew well after telling their fortunes or analyzing their handwriting, which they scrawled in the dust of the jail floor. As the train headed northwest, leaving behind the more mountainous terrain of southern Silesia, it seemed certain to Aleks that a quick end to his detention would be unlikely. He knew that the Nazis rarely released the men they arrested, and now that he was departing from his hometown, perhaps his homeland altogether, it seemed near certain that he would not return anytime soon. He wondered where he'd end up and what he might be forced to endure there.

The train eventually slowed and screeched to a stop. The car doors slid open and light streamed onto the sullen faces of the men around Aleks.

Though he wasn't yet sure where his captors had taken him, the fact that German was bellowed as guards offloaded the prisoners from the train to buses made him assume they'd crossed the border and were now in German Breslau.

From the station, the Germans marched the prisoners to a jail. By then, Aleks had spent months in Nazi custody. What struck him was the size of this new facility and the fact that he was now among prisoners from other countries—Czechoslovakia, Germany, Poland.

Aleks's time in Breslau was short but treacherous. Though the cold had lifted somewhat, he and the other men shivered in the stone cells of the prison, waiting for whatever was to come. Shortly after arriving, guards marched him and many of the men around him into another train. They resumed their journey northwest, sitting in the darkness of the box car for hours.

When the train doors opened, it didn't take long for Aleks to see where he was—Berlin, the heart of the Nazi state. From the station, the guards took him and the others to a Gestapo prison facility. Aleks's cell block, a large, damp room that held many other men, stood in the basement of the building, near what looked like interrogation cells. Everything was piercingly white, the space burning with the light of enormous bulbs that shone day and night. To Aleks, it felt as if the light went straight through his eyes, traveling into his brain. Some prisoners seemed to have gone mad. They chewed at blankets, smiled dumbly at nothing, bashed their heads against the walls. Others were silent. Passing guards taunted them. Then the guards began to say that the inmates would soon be sent to the "end station," the end of the line, their final destination.

For three weeks, Aleks cowered in the Gestapo jail. Without a glimpse of the darkness of night or the light of day, he began to lose track of time. Dawn or dusk, the lights always shone. Sleep was impossible, and he grew ever more exhausted. The lights emitted such intense heat that it seemed he lived under the radiance of four big suns that never fell below the horizon. To cope, he pretended he was sitting at the riverbank in Cieszyn, tanning under the warmth of summer light, far away from the terrifying scene before his eyes. He began to hum his childhood friend Stanisław's "Morning Song." The music helped him believe he was there, grass underneath his back, watching the water slide over the stones on the riverbed.

Aleks began to change the song's lyrics. The vision of the water comforted him, yet he wanted the song somehow to reflect the situation he now faced, to process the loss of his freedom and country. He wrote: *You are a great thing—I am small, / you wretched Poland. / Ach, from beneath Berlin I'm calling for you, / I shed tears in longing.*

Aleks did not know it, but at that very moment, in a different part of the building, Gestapo agents were brutally interrogating Stanisław, the composer of the "Morning Song." They beat Aleks eagerly, joyously, too, and at night he curled up on the cell floor.

Some of the men around Aleks couldn't handle the Gestapo's torture and interrogation and often burst into tearing screams. From other rooms, he could hear the moans of men in different languages. He knew that such savage treatment might also drive him to the edge. To cope, he got an idea. With a scrap of paper and a safety pin, which days earlier he had hooked to his underpants, he pierced holes in the paper to fashion a poem. Each letter took at least twenty-seven pricks. If he focused on the verse he was writing, he found that it distracted him and kept his mind intact. In that moment, Aleks thought of the mystic from whom he'd learned techniques of clairvoyance as a teenager. The last time Aleks saw the man, he said goodbye with a piece of advice: "With thought alone, you can even pierce walls." Now, in this German dungeon, Aleks mulled over that insight. He told himself that with the force of will he could survive.

For his entire stay in Berlin, Aleks pierced out letters with his safety pin, composing a series of poems he called "Engravings with a Safety Pin." Aleks knew the poems held little artistic value. But that wasn't the point. What mattered was that he found a distraction, a way to endure, to deal with the beatings in the jail under the blazing lights. That realization proved essential. From then on, he understood the mental power of composing—poems, lyrics, whatever it might be. That the simple act of writing could divert him from his horrid situation was a powerful lesson.

EARLY ONE MORNING toward the end of May, 1940, the guards marched Aleks out of his cell and put him on a bus on the grounds of the Gestapo jail. His lips and jaw ached from the beatings. His gums had begun to heal, the sockets where each broken tooth had been receded and filled in. With far fewer teeth, however, he could no longer whistle as well as before. Quite possibly, his days whistling Strauss waltzes onstage as the Lithuanian Nightingale were over.

Around him on the bus sat a mixed group of prisoners. There were several other Poles, early captives of the German expansion east. As the vehicle headed north, the capital of the Third Reich receded. Before them, suburbs appeared, followed by towns that dotted the area. The trees had thick clusters of leaves again. The bitterness of that freezing first winter of war had passed.

Aleks sat on the bus for about an hour before it pulled up before a white gatehouse flanked by high walls with razor wire. Nearby, patches of flowers grew. As the bus came to a stop, SS guards circled. Some held dogs on leashes, ferocious German shepherds. Others gripped batons. At the crest of each man's cap there gleamed a silver skull and crossbones. The guards erupted. *"Alles raus!"* ("Everyone out!") Aleks rushed for the door of the bus, and as he and the other men emerged, the guards met them, clubs raised, and beat them toward the gatehouse screaming, *"Schnell, schnell!"* The dogs strained at their leashes, biting the air. Aleks ducked the blows as he and the others ran toward the center of the gatehouse. Welded into the forged wrought iron gate were the words "Arbeit macht frei" (Work sets you free).

Inside, the guards ordered the prisoners to form rows of five. As they were counted, Aleks looked around. Before him was a large semicircular yard covered with black cinder, and on its perimeter, a wide track paved in stone. Beyond that, he could see dozens of long one-story barracks, fanned out like the spokes of a wheel. Everything was clean. Not a scrap of trash lay on the grounds. This facility was unlike the ones Aleks had already seen. In Cieszyn, Breslau, and Berlin, he was detained in jail-like buildings, stone and brick structures with cells and corridors and offices the Germans had taken over. What lay before him was a sprawling camp in the open air on a large plot of land with tall trees standing just beyond the walls. It was as though it had been custom-made for the purpose of imprisoning enemies of the Nazi state. At the camp's edge lay the town of Oranienburg. Aleks could almost hear the chatter of the families who lived outside the walls.

Prisoners at work pushed carts full of dirt or sand. Others carried lengths of wood on their shoulders. Others still, harnessed like oxen to the yoke of a cart, hauled garbage. Every prisoner was gaunt, and some looked so underfed it seemed as though their stomachs and backs would meet. The malnourished shuffled about, perhaps dragging a leg, or bent over, scavenging for cigarette butts flicked by the SS. Aleks immediately noticed there was an otherness about them, a lack of humanness, as though something in the camp had taken an essential part of their spirit. Even before Aleks knew to call these men Muselmänner, the German word for Muslim, perhaps used to evoke a comparison between the prone state of starving prisoners and a Muslim in prayer, something compelled him to begin composing a poem about them. From the very first moments after he arrived at the camp, he began writing verses in his mind, mentally jotting down images, assembling words, memorizing what he created.

All the prisoners had to move on the double, stopping only when confronted by an SS guard. Then each man would slow down, take off his cap, and hold it rigidly against his right thigh until the guard passed. Everyone wore the same clothes—striped shirts and pants made of a stiff-looking material.

The prisoners waited a long time while the guards counted them. Then they marched. Aleks got a closer look at the barracks, squat and dark green. One thing that he didn't expect was to see flower boxes, full of colorful blooms, hung from the gables. Such beauty seemed out of place. Above the flowers, in white Gothic script, painted word by word along the gables, he saw in German, "There is one path to freedom: its milestones are obedience, industry, honesty, order, cleanliness, sobriety, truthfulness, sacrifice, and love of the Fatherland." Aleks could understand it. Unlike many of the men he was with, the Polish intellectuals, the writers and singers and teachers, the professors from universities purged from the streets and flats and cafés of Poland, he spoke fluent German. He'd been speaking it with his grandfather since he was a boy. There was a permanence about the place. Perhaps it was the size of the camp; perhaps it was the guards in uniform. Or maybe it was the fact that so many prisoners seemed to be housed here and that rather than simply sitting around in a cell, they were busy, they were working. Something about the situation seemed terrifyingly fixed.

WHEN ALEKS CROSSED through the gatehouse that day in 1940, he entered the Nazi concentration camp Sachsenhausen, located some 20 miles north of Berlin. Just four years earlier, as athletes from around the world competed in Berlin at the 1936 Olympic Summer Games, weary prisoners felled a pine forest, cleared stumps, and dug sewer trenches for a new concentration camp. German officials, including Heinrich Himmler, believed that constructing a camp near Berlin was essential. Nazi leaders needed a place to detain the ever-growing number of enemies of the state, among them Berlin's communists, social democrats, and trade unionists. The pine forest, at the secluded northeastern edge of Oranienburg, was the perfect place.

The innovative design of Sachsenhausen, in the shape of a near equilateral triangle, with long barracks in concentric semicircles around a central area that was to be the roll call square, enabled a guard—and his machine gun—to surveil nearly the entire complex from a single point—Tower A, which stood at the base of the triangle, atop the white gatehouse. In the very bones of the architecture, the Nazis interwove terror. Sachsenhausen belonged to a new breed of Nazi camps, designed from the ground up, based on what the SS had learned about torture and forced labor in Dachau. The SS planned for Sachsenhausen to be among the biggest camps in the Reich, serving northern and eastern Germany as a place of internment for many of Hitler's enemies. It was all part of a grand plan to detain and punish real or imagined opponents of the Nazi regime. Buchenwald, which was built in 1937, would serve the center of the country. Dachau, which had existed since 1933, would incarcerate people in the German south. With overcrowding and the turmoil of war, however, these plans did not always hold.

Sachsenhausen was meant to be sealed off from the residents of Oranienburg. Once the camp was open, however, the goal of isolation proved impossible. Due to the proximity of the town, residents began to witness the crimes of the SS, especially as more and more transports arrived by train. When new prisoners arrived at the Oranienburg rail station, the SS would march them through town, beating and abusing them along the way.

The real terror, however, began once men passed through the camp gates. By the time Aleks arrived in 1940, Sachsenhausen had already become one of the most important camps of the Nazi system. Given its proximity to Berlin, it was an administrative headquarters for the camp system at large. In a building nearby, senior Nazis officials made decisions about camps all around German-occupied Europe. The camp also housed a training center for young German men who wanted to start a career with the organization that administered the Nazi concentration camps, the SS-Totenkopfverbände (SS Death's Head Units). Recruits arrived at Oranienburg to learn how to become a concentration or extermination camp guard. Over the course of the war, senior commanders regularly met at Sachsenhausen to discuss forced labor, plans of mass murder, or deportation of certain prisoners to the extermination camps. Sachsenhausen quickly became a convenient testing ground. During the early years of the war, camp commanders experimented with the murderous tactics they were developing to commit genocide against Europe's Jews and other groups of people held prisoner in Europe.

ALEKS AND THE other new prisoners were marched to the barracks. These barracks, known as the little camp or quarantine camp, stood apart from

the campgrounds. There the prisoners lined up and waited to be pro-
cessed. When it was Aleks's turn, he gave the inmate behind a desk his
name, date of birth, and profession, which he likely noted as "student." On
the desk lay stacks of dossiers, neatly arranged and organized. The inmate
handed Aleks a slip of paper. Written on it was the number 25,149. He told
Aleks to learn it by heart.

Aleks's clothing and his few belongings—a coat, a jacket, a cap, pants,
several shirts, underwear, shoes, socks, a comb—were taken from him. If a
prisoner wore civilian clothes, he'd lose everything, and if he had a watch,
cash, food, and papers, those items were packed into sacks and removed.
The only thing Aleks could keep were his shoes. Then he and the others
waited for hours—lines of naked bodies, unsure of what the SS might subject them to next. Finally, he was moved to another room, where a man
sat with an electric light and a hair shaver. When Aleks reached him, he
pointed at Aleks's crotch, and before Aleks knew it, the man had shaved
off all the hair on his pubis. Then his armpits and legs. Not long after,
another prisoner, also armed with a shaver, pressed its teeth to Aleks's
forehead and mowed to the base of his skull. Stroke by stroke, his black
hair fell down his bare shoulders. Mounds of hair piled up. The men stood,
heads now like cue balls, stripped and dazed.

Aleks quickly saw that the SS chose prisoners to administer certain parts
of the camp, under what they euphemistically called "self-administration."
Prisoner foremen or clerks, under the surveillance and instruction of the
SS, issued Aleks's inmate number, then led him to the showers. These men
seemed to know the camp system well and were mostly of a certain type,
which is to say they were Germans. Aleks assumed they were arrested as
communists, trade unionists, or criminals and sent to the camp during
the Nazi crackdowns of the 1930s.

As the final step, Aleks and the others were issued a uniform: a shirt,
undershorts, and the striped pajama-like white and blue uniform he'd
seen other prisoners wearing in the yard. The drill fabric was coarse
between Aleks's fingers. Nothing fit exactly right. For some, the pants ran
below their shoes; for others, the sleeves were too short. Stripped, shorn,

and clothed in their new uniforms, Aleks and the others were marched to their barracks. The final step was for Aleks to give the slip of paper with his number on it to another prisoner. In return, the prisoner handed Aleks two strips of fabric, measuring about 2 by 4 inches with his prison number on them. He also got a triangular cloth badge with a red P. The P meant Polish. It was red because he was a political prisoner. The man giving Aleks the badge told him to sew one onto his shirt over his breast, the other onto his pant leg at his thigh.

Aleks's barracks held several hundred men, almost all of whom had come from Poland by a similar route as he. Soon he met the men who would rule and dominate the inmates, who belonged to the same group as those he saw chasing prisoners around the yard, beating them with sticks and cudgels. The Blockältester, or block elder, was a German prisoner who presided over every detail of camp life. He had assistants, also prisoners. Above them was the Blockführer, a man of the SS Death's Head Division. After Aleks and the others entered the barracks, the Blockführer gave a curt speech. "There are no sick prisoners," he said to the stunned inmates. "In the camp, you're either dead or living. The only way out is through the crematorium."

Aleks's barracks was a long rectangular building, split into two wings with central rooms that held about a dozen toilets and urinals—ceramic bowls with no seats—and communal fountains for washing. He and his barracks-mates slept and ate in the wings to the left and right. The rooms were split in two, one part for sleeping, the other with lockers, tables, and a wood-burning stove. A single bed stood near the stove—the block elder's. In fact, he was the only prisoner who had some privacy in the barracks. Everyone else slept on the floor.

At dinner, Alex bent over a bowl of soup. A few potatoes lay in the murky broth, potatoes that provided little by way of caloric replenishment. Around him sat a vast group of Poles newly torn from their lives—priests yanked from parishes, teachers from classrooms, intellectuals from printing houses and cafés, students from lecture halls. Since there was no room for everyone to sit, some men were forced to stand, cupping their bowls in their hands. A sense of shock was palpable. After dinner, Aleks prepared for bed. He lay down on the stinking straw mattress under the single blanket the guards gave him.

Through the barracks windows, Aleks could see the looming watchtowers in the dim light of late spring, the branching tufts of pine trees and the dull sky scraped out behind them. Jammed between a man before him and a man behind him, like spoons in a drawer, he longed for Cieszyn, his home, and for Bożena, the Czech girl. Aleks had always found her powerfully attractive with her large eyes and dark wavy hair. He lay thinking of her. Her memory was respite from what was around him—starving, dirty, sickly men, unable to leave the room until daybreak. Buckets for urine and feces began to fill and stink.

THE BELLS RANG early. During the first few weeks of Aleks's life at Sachsenhausen, the SS and block elder initiated the new prisoners by forcing them to do a routine of exercise distorted by the SS to torture them. The SS and block elder would drill the new prisoners in a succession of knee bends, squat walks, unending push-ups, and running, hopping, or crawling in the barracks. This was called sport. The origins of it lay in military training of new army recruits. But in the hands of the SS, sport served to break prisoners, to weaken and exhaust them. Furthermore, it created the opportunity for the guards and block elder to single out and beat the weaker, older prisoners who could not keep up. Sometimes the guards beat a man nearly to death.

During the endless squats or the chaotic marching up and down the barracks, Aleks felt an overwhelming sense of distress. All around him he saw the frenzy of the camp, the tyranny of his captors. One particularly brutal sport the SS forced on them was called the "Saxon Salute." Prisoners had to squat for several hours with their arms stretched out before them or folded behind their necks. If a prisoner collapsed out of exhaustion, the block elder or a guard of the SS kicked him in the abdomen or in the head. If he fainted during the beating, they would revive him with a bucket of cold water.

To Aleks's surprise, he encountered music almost immediately at Sachsenhausen. As he and the others strode up and down the narrow barracks or squatted with their arms raised, the SS forced them to sing German folk songs. Few of them knew the music, having been raised in Poland away from German culture. If a man didn't know the lyrics or sang the melody incorrectly, a guard or block elder would beat him. For the first time in his life, Aleks realized that music, something in which he had always found joy, could also be sadistic, a tool of evil. "The German songs are nice," he thought to himself, remembering similar folk songs he'd heard as a child. "But they've become poisoned by this tyranny." He hated being forced to sing, to play a role in desecrating something he loved so dearly. To distract himself, and in the hopes that the Nazis could not ruin music for him, Aleks began thinking up lyrics to take his mind off the burning of his muscles and the aching of his joints. He returned to the "Morning Song," which had helped him remain calm at the Cieszyn jail and at the Gestapo jail in Berlin. He wondered if this simple song might again give him strength as it had done before. But he wanted to change the lyrics. It could not be just a lament filled with self-pity and longing for home. He wanted to cry out through the music, to shout at his captors. During a session of sport, Aleks came up with these lyrics:

I will return—even from as far away as Berlin!
to my golden fields. . . .

The more Aleks reflected, the more he believed that a catchy, evocative melody like the one Stanisław had composed for the "Morning Song," coupled with subtly defiant lyrics, might buoy both himself and his fellow prisoners. In the early days of his incarceration, he came to understand that music would be a presence at Sachsenhausen. Instead of letting it be simply another tool of abuse in the arsenal of the SS, Aleks decided that he would compose and sing. He would learn that men turned to culture to survive. Surely, he was not the only prisoner to have this thought. He told himself: "You have to retain everything. You have a good memory for words, for songs, for performance, a memory to show what happened here once the war is over."

Aleks began to write verses to the "Morning Song." When he finished one, he'd file it away in his mind for later reference as he had done in the Berlin jail. Memorization was one of his strongest skills, perhaps even stronger than his performing. The reason for this, as Aleks saw it, traced back to a long bygone summer day in 1926 when he was a boy of eight years old. He and three other children climbed onto the roof of a laundry business in Karwina, a town not far from Cieszyn where a relative lived. It was a harvest day, hot, and workers from nearby fields sat around on their break drinking black coffee and eating potato pancakes, trying to shield themselves from the heat of the sun. As always, Aleks wanted to dazzle the people around him, to put on a show. Among the children he'd been playing with until that moment, most of whom watched him from below on the street, there was one in particular he wanted to impress—a Czech girl he liked named Věruška. On the roof, Aleks found the props he could use for his performance: two wires that fed electricity into the building. Aleks knew that these wires carried a strong current. But something about them tempted him. While the other three children on the roof made jokes to their friends down below, Aleks could only think of the wires. He decided that he'd touch them, gently, just to see. While no one was watching, he brushed a finger against them. Nothing happened. The adults had to be lying, Aleks thought. Now he knew the show he'd deliver. He would pick up the wires and stand triumphant as though their current had no effect on him.

Down below among the children stood Aleks's grandmother, who sensed that the boy was up to no good. She shouted, "Olek, be careful, you are clearly up to something!" Aleks ignored her. Making sure Věruška was watching, he announced, "Ladies and gentlemen! A great and interesting performance is now going to take place! You will see something that will shock you!" The children fell quiet; the workers looked up at him. "Ladies and gentlemen," Aleks continued, "some applause, please! Applause!" A few people below clapped tentatively. And then, very calmly, Aleks put his hand under the wires, not yet touching them. When the adults below saw what he was about to do, they shouted in horror. But he grasped the wires anyway.

When Aleks awoke, he found himself buried up to his neck. The people below had carried him, unconscious, and put him in the ground, believing that the earth might draw the charge out of his little body. He couldn't feel his arms or legs; he could only bob his head from side to side against the loose, sandy soil. All he could remember was the pain that seized his thin being, the incredible whirring in his ears, the certitude that these were the final moments of his life. He thought of all his childhood sins, especially the time, not long before, when he looked up a maid's skirt. He felt an intense longing for his dead mother, Isabella.

That night, back at home under the care of his stepmother, the burn of the electricity returned. He saw the wire; he was standing there on the roof. Buzzing drowned out everything. He was being electrocuted again. He screamed.

IN THE DAYS after the incident, Aleks's physical condition improved, though a wound on the hand that had touched the live wire ached with pain. Of greater concern, however, was a different injury. Since the accident, he had begun to stutter. When he tried to form words, especially those that contained the letters k or g, his mouth grew so tense that only a series of glottal sounds came out. It felt as if he was choking. His whole face contorted as he tried to cough out words. His father, concerned but unable to find a specialist in Cieszyn, took Aleks to another town along the Olza where he had heard a hypnotist and performer was passing through. After watching the man's show, which featured fortune-telling and magic, Aleks and his father visited him backstage. The man was small, inconspicuous. He introduced himself simply as Roob. After listening to Aleks's stutter, Roob told the boy that he knew a treatment that would heal him, make the stutter vanish. But Aleks would have to relearn how he turned thoughts into words, words into sounds. "People think, and then form what they wish to say. But you, you have to write what you wish to say in black letters on a white background in your mind." Whatever Aleks wrote on this blank canvas, Roob said, he could read, and if he followed these instructions, he would overcome the stutter.

In the months after meeting Roob, Aleks practiced the technique. He used it when asking for meat at the butcher, writing out in his mind how much ham or tenderloin or chicken breast his stepmother had asked him to buy. Then he could inform the man behind the counter. At school, when the class recited poetry or passages from Poland's great books, Aleks imagined the words before he uttered them. Little by little, a word starting with the letter k or g ceased to halt him mid-sentence. The frustration and embarrassment began to vanish.

Though overcoming the impediment was significant for Aleks, the encounter with Roob served as an even bigger event in his life. It became an origin story for him. With most of his stutter gone—he still struggled occasionally—Aleks used Roob's technique to develop a remarkable power of memory. When he visualized a word or sentence or paragraph in his mind, he could hold it there. This technique, Aleks believed, enabled him to develop a web of recollections that resembled a memory palace, though instead of using a building where he could place mnemonic images in certain rooms and return to them later, he had begun making a series of long mental notes. Practicing the trick throughout his childhood, Aleks could commit to memory poems or long passages from the books his teachers assigned at school. He saw Roob as the genesis of this ability to memorize, a person who gave him the tools to become exceptional. For Aleks, the encounter with Roob was the foundational moment of his childhood.

During his early days at Sachsenhausen, Aleks tried desperately to find ways to survive, to establish himself as a prisoner of high standing. Memory helped him sharpen his linguistic skills, especially if one of the SS guards or block elders came from a part of Germany where the vocabulary or accent were unfamiliar to him. During sport, when the block elders forced prisoners to memorize German folk songs, Aleks could do so with ease.

Always a man with keen powers of observation, Aleks constantly sought ways to give himself an advantage, to up his odds of survival. As he had realized in the Cieszyn jail, he knew that one of the best ways to do so was to make himself useful to others. Of course, in Cieszyn, among only a few other prisoners, all of whom were Polish like him, making himself essential was not such a tall order. At Sachsenhausen, with prisoners from all over Europe and up against a harsh hierarchy where even among prisoners the Germans dominated, gaining status would be a harder task. Simply pretending to be clairvoyant would not suffice.

The hierarchy of prisoners at Sachsenhausen was highly complex. At the top, as always, were the Germans, especially those whom Hitler had rounded up in the mid-1930s. At the time of Aleks's arrival at Sachsenhausen, German communist prisoners held many of the important functionary positions. Also among the German prisoners were convicts locked up before the war, who sometimes proved eager proxies for SS malevolence. These men mainly made up the block elders and foremen, and they had some freedom of action so long as they obeyed the SS. If an SS guard discovered that a prisoner functionary had circumvented his orders, the functionary would lose his position and face cruel punishment. To ensure order and control, the SS also created a large and sinister network of spies and informants, who, in exchange for their help, received better job posts or camp status. The SS tried, whenever possible, to pit one prisoner group against another and exploit ethnic or religious friction. They knew, for example, how to set political and criminal prisoners against one another to greatest effect.

Below the German prisoners were men that the Nazis considered "Aryan"—the Dutch and Norwegians, for instance, who would begin to arrive at Sachsenhausen later. Europeans from east of Germany came next: Poles, Czechs, and Ukrainians. On the lowest rung were Jews, regardless of nationality, homosexuals, and Russian prisoners of war, who began to arrive a year later. What Aleks saw early on, however, was that these categories were not completely fixed. Other attributes, such as celebrity, language skill, or simply the right personality or relationships, could protect a prisoner, even if he belonged to a lower rung of the Nazi hierarchy. Protection could be as simple as the gift of a crust of bread or an extra portion of soup ladled into the tin bowl of a starving prisoner. But it could also mean a favorable work assignment, one that required less physical exertion or was out of the sight of a particularly sadistic SS guard or block elder.

While Aleks hurriedly invented ways to gain camp status, he also constantly thought about music. The urge to compose lyrics that he had felt when he first arrived at Sachsenhausen and saw the emaciated, sickly prisoners stumbling around the campgrounds had not vanished. In fact, music seemed a place of refuge, somewhere he might find a haven from the sadism and callousness of the camp guards. During the knee bends or push-ups that lasted hours, melodies ran through his mind. He sang to himself the music that he had grown up with, the scout ditties, the patriotic anthems, hymns from church. He also sang the popular songs he had heard at the clubs of Kraków while at university. When he hummed or sang in his mind, he found that the sport the SS or block elders forced them to do was a little less cruel, that he could bear the pain with a little more ease. Though real escape never came, music could, if just for a moment, increase his well-being. Beyond his own mental health, Aleks found that he could also use music to process what was taking place around him, document it, and perhaps, if he could find a means to do it, bring some relief to the other prisoners through performance. He seemed the perfect person for this work—he had a crack memory, a love of music, and a throbbing desire to perform, to be the center of attention, especially if it served the cause of some temporary escape from the torture of the Nazis.

DURING THOSE EARLY weeks of imprisonment, one vivid memory of Aleks's prewar life often came to mind. In early August, 1939, in an act of rebellion against his father and as a result of his attraction to a young stuntwoman called Alice, he had made a quiet exit from Cieszyn, peddling his bicycle after the caravan of a German circus that had passed through town. Aleks had become infatuated with Alice after seeing her perform daring tricks on a bicycle. He had noticed her immediately, and he'd gone back several times to see her perform, riding across trapeze lines or in 360-degree loops in a cage. Perhaps, he thought, if he joined her on the road, he could impress her, and she'd feel the same about him. Yet he harbored another reason to take off on that summer day: his ambitions as a performer, ambitions the circus might indulge.

For much of the 1930s, Aleks had been obsessed with performing—singing or whistling or acting before a crowd and, ideally, onstage. He traced his desire to the earliest days of his boyhood. It all began with a love of music, a love he attributed to his mother Isabella. When she passed, almost nothing of her worldly affairs remained. She left few letters and no diaries, little for her child to remember her by.

As a runaway with the circus, Aleks tried his best to get close to Alice. Sometimes, when she emerged from her trailer, he'd sing, arms open, doing his utmost to get her attention. But she barely acknowledged him and once even splashed him with slop while he stood outside her door singing a folk song. Though his ego was bruised, Aleks persisted, eventually earning some pity, winning her over with the half-lie that she didn't much interest him, that he was unemployed and just wanted a job with the circus. As a result, she introduced him to one of the circus strongmen, who told him that he could haul sand for the arena, a simple, tedious job. But it kept him there, and he could still sing for Alice and watch her acts of daring on her bicycle. The setup was basic: when he wished to sleep, he made a bed of straw and dozed off in the open air near Alice's trailer. It was summer, the skies were clear, and the heat from the day soaked into the earth and kept the ground warm long into the night.

In the circus, Aleks found a place where his personality could flourish. The same spirit of defiance and stubbornness, the decided belief in his own abilities that infuriated his father, led to an audition with the head clown, Max. Aleks put on all of his charm and convinced the clown to make him his onstage assistant, which sent tremors of excitement through him. The first thing Max told him was that he'd have to train his bones, to move and act as a clown does. He learned clown choreographies, especially the footwork, which Max said was essential. Aleks had to stand in the clown's posture—his feet open, at near right angles, a position that made him feel as if he had no balance, as though a light wind would blow him over.

Though Max taught Aleks the fundamentals of clowning, much of Aleks's training would come from observing the other clowns. He watched from the wings of the stage how they moved, how they contorted their faces for comic effect, how they picked up cues from the audience. Aleks excelled as an autodidact. All his life, he'd been watching and copying the cultural figures he admired. During the university term, when he lived and performed in Kraków, he sang music he'd picked up from others—perhaps from the radio, or another cabaret, or a film. He constantly scrutinized the techniques of the singers he loved. He mimicked them, watched how they moved on the stage, tried to imitate the way their gestures could intensify a performance. He observed how a performer should sound and act. And he practiced his singing. From the highest falsetto notes he could reach, to the deepest, richest baritone, Aleks finessed his craft. He could use the same methods to soak in the skills of a clown.

After only several days' time, Max deemed Aleks's skills to be sufficient and let him take to the stage. In full costume, with makeup covering his face, Aleks emerged before the crowd beside his clown boss. Each silly gesture, each bow he made, he was sure to pay attention to the littlest detail. He wanted to do everything perfectly. Onstage, Max beat Aleks with balloon-like cudgels made from pig bladders stitched together and inflated. After several strikes to the head, Aleks would play dead, falling to the sand that covered the center of the arena, lying still like a corpse. Then, with great urgency and surprise, he would shoot up, pretending to have shaky legs, and perform a slapstick couplet to the howling crowds.

Once Aleks proved himself a capable performer, Max even let him sing. Before big audiences, he'd belt out a tune called "Shanghai" in which he pretended to be a Chinese merchant. *I am Chinese, and trade is my art / Oh, oh, oh / I'll put the profit in the drawer right away! / I have braided hair on the front and my eyes are slanted / Shanghai, Shanghai, my beloved country*, Aleks would sing night after night. He found the lyrics banal, but he loved the exhilaration of singing before the crowd, impressing them, holding their attention as he put on a show. It was a feeling greater than any other, and he craved it.

At Sachsenhausen, the memory of singing "Shanghai" inspired Aleks to write musical creations, taking a melody he knew from before the war and overlaying it with new lyrics he composed in the camp. With the melody of "Shanghai," he wrote new verses, often while the SS forced him to do sport. For his first real song creation, he decided to compose lyrics about the Muselmänner, those rawboned prisoners who evoked a haunting otherness he had seen during his first hours at the camp. Aleks began with two lines: *I'm a Godforsaken Polish pagan, / To everyone here I'm less than nothing.* Once he wrote them, he then ran them through his mind to see how they felt. He went on: *They pu- pu- pu- push me around./ Ow-ow-oww!*

As Aleks added line after line, he made sure to write them down in his mind, just as Roob had taught him to do. After all, memory was the only way to preserve anything in the camp. Keeping a journal was out of the question; paper and pencil were forbidden, and anyway, they were impossible to find. If Aleks had managed to find a few blank sheets, it would be too dangerous to risk being caught with them by a guard or block elder. The punishment was brutal—perhaps two dozen licks from a cat-o'-nine-tails while strapped to the trestle, perhaps a beating so severe that one would not recover.

In music and composing lyrics, it seemed to Aleks that he had found something to which he could direct his energy. Perhaps if he was lucky and could survive the camp, and if Hitler's Germany fell, he could leave Sachsenhausen with music and poetry—his own and that of others—and thereby save some of the camp's culture, memorialize this time and its victims as he had begun to do with his song about the Muselmänner. Though he had no means to physically record what he saw, Aleks could bear witness to it with music and memory.

Chapter 4

One night during the first weeks of Aleks's incarceration, he sat hunched over a bowl of soup in the barracks, one of dozens of other prisoners. Laid out on the tables were bread, margarine, cups, mess tins, and spoons. The block elder shouted, "Achtung!" ("Attention!") The men froze. For a moment, the block elder stared. Then he screamed, "Get down!" A flurry of movement erupted, cups flying, hot soup splashing, spilling on the floor as the prisoners fell. "Stand up!" the block elder shouted, "Now back down!" As they rose and fell, panting, sweating, it felt like a battlefield to Aleks. Their food, that precious sustenance they never had enough of, drenched the floor, soaked into their clothes. After the jumping, the block elder made them all sing German folk songs.

Sometimes, the SS would return late at night. "Achtung!" the block elder would again shout, and every slumbering prisoner jumped from the floor to his feet to stand at attention in rows. Then the guards, often reeking of alcohol, forced them into sessions of sport. Aleks and the other prisoners squatted and jumped and ran late into the night, ducking the fists and clubs of their captors. Even on those nights when the guards didn't barge in to interrupt their precious sleep, the rest Aleks got never sufficed. He couldn't recover from the physical strain of the day's abuse. The bowls of thin soup and minuscule ration of bread did little to replenish him.

With every prisoner weaker by the day, it seemed as though any of them could die at any moment. The first to go were the old, the sick, and the weak. The sport overtook them, and if not, an SS guard or block elder might do the killing himself. Along with the deaths from exhaustion and illness, there were murders committed expressly by their captors. A guard or block elder might beat a man to death. But there were more creative, less visible ways of killing. Jerzy Pindera, a Pole whom the SS assigned to a barracks close to Aleks's, witnessed guards shooting a jet of cold water at a man's heart for 10 or 15 minutes. This yielded a clean kill—no blood, not a trace of murder. Sometimes a guard or his henchmen stuck a water hose into a man's anus or down his throat while others watched. That could kill, too.

Aleks could disappear into his mind for hours at a time and find deliverance in his verses. Though he was not a true poet—he had no training, he had not read the Polish or European canon beyond what his schooling required—writing gave him a sense of control, of power. During a session of sport at Sachsenhausen, he could look out at the gloom and begin a poem or a verse meant for a song. Or he could revise a composition he had already created.

Death slinked all around—bodies sometimes appeared in Aleks's barracks, dragged out later to be accounted for at roll call. Death obsessed him. He toiled to avoid it, remaining unseen by the guards or prisoner functionaries as much as possible, yet also staking a claim to being important among prisoners—a near impossible equilibrium to strike. The ambition he'd had as a child and young man had not dimmed. He wanted a life. He refused to be a casualty of the Germans and their insane war. Aleks never believed in Hitler's fantasy of a thousand-year Reich. Survival, though, didn't just happen in a Nazi concentration camp.

Though Aleks now stood on German soil, the little camp of Sachsenhausen at that time was filled with Poles. This suited him. He understood these men—linguistically, culturally—and he could make himself useful as he had done in Cieszyn. What was more, Aleks had several big advantages over the men around him. By comparison, he was young and strong, he had a runner's stamina, and most important, he was fluent in German and Czech, thanks to his childhood in a border town and his Austro-Hungarian grandfather. The SS and their prisoner functionaries gave all instructions in German, and not understanding the camp lingua franca was an easy way to get a beating. Speaking Czech helped him make inroads with prisoners of that group.

But becoming a prisoner of high standing, as Aleks had done on a much smaller scale in Cieszyn, would take more than just a knack for languages. During those early weeks at Sachsenhausen, he realized that relationships—especially with prisoners in functions of power—were essential for gaining stature. These men could determine how much a prisoner ate, what kind of work he did. Aleks understood what made people tick. He tried to give them what they wanted and needed, in exchange for something for himself, possibly just a gift of goodwill at some uncertain point in the future. From a young age, Aleks had carried himself with a self-confidence that bordered on narcissism. Perhaps this character trait developed from a need to look after himself after his mother died and during the many times of emotional distance from his father. At Sachsenhausen, this trait proved precious. Though he never lost his sense of empathy or acted in ways that harmed other prisoners, he set himself up to ensure, to the extent he could, the best odds of survival. He told white lies if they furthered his relationship with other prisoners. He formed friendships and did favors in an effort to become necessary to others, even indispensable.

As Aleks built a network of connections in the little camp, he gathered information from different prisoners about what had taken place in Poland after his arrest. One of the most striking events for him was the mass arrest of professors at the Jagiellonian University in early November of 1939, just months after he had been a student there. By the time he heard about this, many of the professors had been transferred to Dachau. All the while, Aleks wondered about the fate of his father, who was also an educator. Had he been snatched up by the Gestapo? Was he in a Nazi camp? Was he alive?

DURING THESE EARLY weeks, Aleks continued composing his lyrics about the Muselmänner. He wished to convey their torpor, their despondency in the song. Yet what he would do with his creation he wasn't sure.

The more Aleks understood about Sachsenhausen, the more he realized that music was a crucial part of camp life. It affected him most when the guards or block elders used it to abuse prisoners. The SS expected them to sing German folk songs with enthusiasm as they crouched in leg squats or crawled up and down the barracks floor. Like sport itself, this sort of collective singing derived from German military tradition, where officers had long used music to impose discipline and order. In the camp, the SS used singing on command for a more malevolent reason—to intimidate, frighten, or humiliate prisoners—much in the way they used sport to break them. During days of excruciating activity or sometimes in the evening when they finally had some respite, the SS forced them to sing, an arduous task for men already weakened by disease and hunger. There was something perverse about celebrating German culture while being victims of Nazi terror.

The music imposed on prisoners by the guards in the little camp could be dangerous for another reason. At Sachsenhausen, the guards and block elders punished prisoners who violated the contradictory and unattainable rules, even if in the smallest way. Whether caused by a bed made short of military standards or a decree a guard invented on the spot to punish a prisoner, the men in Aleks's barracks lived in constant fear of reprisals for the pettiest infractions. The SS applied the same rigor of enforcement to singing on command. If the guards ordered prisoners to sing and one did not immediately hop to and obey in a way the guards deemed satisfactory—perhaps he sang too softly, too loudly, or did not know the words—they beat him.

It didn't take long for men in Aleks's barracks and those nearby to organize regular artistic evenings. Of course, they had to act with great care, as the SS might consider such gatherings subversive and punish them. They took the risk.

The success of an artistic evening depended on the mood and temperament of the block elder, an influential, usually German, prisoner. Some block elders felt sympathy for the prisoners they oversaw, and their political convictions or sense of humanity drove them to help. Others were by nature callous and cruel, eager to take part in beatings and murder. For Aleks and the Poles, the trick was to find a German willing to help them. With their so-called privilege and the leniency the SS sometimes afforded them, the Germans could help the prisoners decide which barracks and which day and hour were safest.

The most likely allies for the Poles were the German communists and social democrats. They even saw resistance as a duty and did whatever they could to be of help. Over time, Aleks and the other inmates sussed out which block elders they could depend on. Then they organized the evenings, usually during the brief window of time before lights out, when prisoners had some control over what they did. The early gatherings Aleks attended mostly comprised other Poles, as prisoners at that point were often housed by nationality. Before a small group, in a quiet voice if the risk was high, but sometimes more loudly and openly, a prisoner would stand to recite a poem or a passage from a novel.

Often, performers chose famous works from the Polish canon. These works were familiar to most prisoners; in school, they were meant to memorize them and speak them aloud. Perhaps a prisoner would recite a page, even a chapter, of the novel *Quo Vadis* by Henryk Sienkiewicz. Another might perform some of Adam Mickiewicz's verses. Others sang popular prewar songs or the occasional patriotic tune, though these posed risks should a guard or hard-bitten block elder recognize them. Because so many of the Poles who found themselves in Sachsenhausen came from the educated classes—professors, teachers, lawyers, doctors, and military officers—and because of the education they had received in the time of partitioned Poland and the Second Republic, they had often committed to memory vast amounts of literature, especially from the long novels written in the second half of the nineteenth century during the Polish realist period.

Aleks saw that these artistic performances gave his fellow prisoners a sense of being supported, of confidence, of camaraderie. Art had the power, he was convinced, to remind them of their lives before the war. His friend Gabriel Zych, like him a Pole swept up in the mass arrests in the fall of 1939, remembered being touched deeply by these secret performances: "Only choral music could remind us that there were other feelings besides hunger and fear." Most of all, Aleks saw that even in such ghastly circumstances, where the SS hounded and beat them throughout the day, people still found meaning and joy in art. Though composing or performing presented immense risks, Aleks's Polish block-mates believed such acts were worth the threat of SS punishment. They kept them from falling into complete despair and resignation, which seemed as great a threat to their well-being as the blunt edge of a guard's cudgel or the growling dog he could unleash.

Perhaps most important for Aleks, he realized that he, too, could perform in the camp. His passion of striding onstage to sing or whistle or act as a clown had not abated. He now knew that he had something of his own to deliver—the lyrics about the Muselmänner he'd set to the melody of "Shanghai."

What Aleks had begun to do, whether or not he understood it, was to create parodies by overlaying his original lyrics onto existing melodies, those that reminded him of the outside, of the past, those he associated with his hopes and revelations. In parody songs, he found an outlet for his artistic urges, someplace to hide his thoughts when his muscles trembled during sport, when fear made him cringe. During the day, he practiced the song about the Muselmänner as the block elders drove him and the others back and forth in the barracks. When he had a moment to himself, he sang the fifty-odd lines he'd composed for his first camp song, trying to get everything right, every pause, every intonation. At last, he felt ready to perform.

On a warm July evening in 1940, in the dim light of his cell block, Aleks stood before a small group of men. The dazzling brightness of the klieg lights, bolted to the watchtowers, trailed outside, sometimes shining through the window, illuminating the men's ashen faces. Aleks's song was far more mournful than the mere recitation of a passage from one of Poland's great writers. Yet that did not discourage him. More and more, prisoners were performing their own camp creations, which, though they often depicted the macabre conditions, still entertained them. Or at least it seemed so to Aleks. He believed that even the somber performances helped the prisoners process what was taking place around them.

I'm a God-forsaken Polish pagan / To everyone here I'm less than nothing / They pu- pu- pu- push me around. / Ow-ow-oww!" Aleks began the sorrowful melody. The men leaning against the barracks walls or seated on the floor would have strained to catch the lyrics.

Then the refrain, a pained cry: *Oh Muselmann, Muselmann.* He looked at the faces of the men before him. They were mostly Poles, far from their homes, expelled from their lives at the barrels of pistols, subject to the wrath of the Germans. At Sachsenhausen, everyone knew what lay ahead: labor as chattel, snarling dogs, murderous guards, hangings, beatings—with escape possible, according to their captors, only as plumes of crematorium smoke.

Aleks continued: *Beyond barbed wire the sun shines brightly / Beyond barbed wire children play / But on the barbed wire / A sad, charred body droops. / Oo-woo-woo!* To accompany the song, he put on a grim dance whose exaggerated moves he derived from what he thought to be Muslim practices. He jerked his elbows with a dumb, rapturous expression on his face, then quickly shifted to a grimace of despair. With the elbow routine, he tried to imitate the movements the Muselmänner made, their hopeless attempt to warm themselves as they stood all day long in a special detachment for prisoners too weak to work. From sunrise to sunset, through rain or snow, hail or heat, they stood in mute, haunted groups. The SS forbade them to speak or lean upon anything for support. Sometimes, a man collapsed, exhausted, never to rise again.

As his song came to an end, Aleks slowed, quieted his voice to the softness of a lullaby. He knelt and bowed his head, as if it were partially severed. With a wail, he sang the final lines: *Mama, my mama / Let me die in peace.*

Even inside a Sachsenhausen barracks, Aleks was a natural. On the night he debuted his song, which he entitled "Muselmann—Butt Collector," something stirred within him. Something about the macabre routine and the tragic melody he sang both shocked and intrigued the other men in his barracks, and he loved their reaction. After that night, he was surer than ever of the power of performance and the act of collective music making in a Nazi camp.

IN A MORBID sort of way, Aleks drew parallels between his time in the circus and now. "A camp is like a shabby circus of sadists and the condemned," he thought to himself. When he looked down at the striped uniform that covered his thinning body, it reminded him of his clown's costume, though a depraved version of it. All the prisoners around him, dressed in the same stripes, hungry and afraid in an animal sort of way, made him feel as though he was surrounded by a group of demented clowns on whom a ravenous menagerie had been unleashed, dancing like beasts to avoid the whip or club. The other difference: at Sachsenhausen, no sawdust blanketed the floor as it did in the circus and the clubs that struck them were made of wood, not inflated pig bladders. No one had to *play* dead.

When he could, he strolled over to the barracks that held prisoners who had arrived before him and tried to ingratiate himself. All around him, other Poles were doing the same networking. As a group, they began to form a tight bond in the little camp. There emerged a feeling of brotherhood among them, that together they could withstand whatever the Nazis imposed on them. To resist, to survive, was not something a man at Sachsenhausen could do on his own. He needed a cohort of other prisoners around him to call in a favor—friends who might conceal him from a block elder if he fell ill and couldn't work. Perhaps music could increase Aleks's standing among prisoners. Perhaps his status as a singer might lend him some amount of protection.

Once Aleks debuted his song about Sachsenhausen's most emaciated prisoners, he began thinking of a new song parody to compose. When, in midsummer, news of the British evacuation at Dunkirk reached Sachsenhausen, he knew exactly what he would write about. This new song was to be a dark satire, one that took stock of his situation and that of Europe as a whole.

It's the second year, dear God,
And the swastika's still frolicking;
There is no power that can exhaust it,
So we'd all better get down on our knees!

By 1940, the Germans controlled a great swath of Europe. Hitler's troops appeared unstoppable, and with the retreat of the British army at Dunkirk, it seemed that no military force could halt their expansion. To Aleks and the men around him, each defeat of those who resisted Hitler meant a dwindling of any prospects for a brief war and their quick release from Sachsenhausen.

Such a terribly great, ferocious Führer,
Such a robber-goy-with paint brush, yet!
And his head's filled up with dirty dishwater,
While his stupid Volk shriek: "Heil!"

Aleks was growing more courageous about expressing his resentment and anger in his music. In this song, which he titled "Mister C," he openly insulted Hitler, poked fun at him for his failure as a painter, the kind of attack that might get him executed by the SS had anyone discovered the

lyrics. Whereas he set "Muselmann—Butt Collector" to a despairing melody, in "Mister C" he replaced that pure sorrow with a deranged sort of
humor, as if he was sneering at pain and despondency. In the final lines of
the song, though, he added a touch of optimism. He appealed to the last
real hope of Europe at the time: Mister C—British Prime Minister Win-
ston Churchill.

Mister C will snuff out his smoke,
And he'll spit on Adolf's "Sieg!"
He'll pay for Adolf's funeral on the Isle of Rugia—
Maybe as early as '43!

During that summer, Aleks learned his way around the camp. He
observed its rules, the expectations of prisoner conduct. He sought out
those prisoners who seemed to earn respect and deference from the others, and he reflected on what gave them their qualities.

Long before he arrived at Sachsenhausen, issues of class and mobil-
ity had obsessed him. The Poland of his youth had been a place where
vast social programs aimed to provide all with health and unemployment
insurance and affordable housing. Students began enrolling in large numbers in Poland's universities. The new government had made education
more accessible, and illiteracy was cut by a quarter. Class dividing lines
were in flux. Yet Aleks still straddled two worlds, the peasant roots of his
father and the wealthy, if distant, background of his mother. His home
was modest, yet he attended private school with the children of some of
Poland's most notable aristocratic families, though only because his father
taught there. These experiences left him with a keen awareness of class,
and at Sachsenhausen he paid special attention to the pecking order of
the camp. Though a strict hierarchy existed, it did not necessarily mirror
social norms from before the war. A Polish count or a respected university
professor could face the same fate of hard labor and starvation as a mine
worker or stone mason, plucked off the street by the Gestapo for resisting
German rule. What replaced the prewar class system at Sachsenhausen

was the Nazi-imposed hierarchy of prisoners. The SS issued advantages not solely based on blue blood or wealth but on nationality, ethnicity, religion, and sexual orientation. But what Aleks realized early was that as a strong, young Pole, he could, to some extent, rise or fall within the hierarchy if he behaved in the right or wrong ways.

Unlike before the war, when he could no more become an aristocrat than a parrot, at Sachsenhausen it seemed he might be able to exert some control over his rank. Now it mattered who he knew, who liked him, what he could contribute. In many cases, privilege before the war had little bearing. Though there was some room to ascend in the hierarchy, many prisoners never managed to do it. A prisoner needed a certain set of skills, such as fluency in German, a certain amount of luck, and the ability to build a network, to make friends, if glibly, with men of different nationalities, to use his wits to get by. Aleks excelled in these areas, and he quickly built a network of useful inmates.

That prewar social norms no longer held sway pleased Aleks immensely, in part out of a leftist ideal of a more equitable society, an ideal tempered by the emotional wound of once being seen as lowly by some of his peers. Though as a teen and young adult Aleks presented himself outwardly with a confidence nearing hubris, he had carefully concealed his lack of self-esteem. He never quite understood its origins, but he speculated that its source was ill treatment at his private school by the sons of Poland's upper classes. He often recalled moments of being scorned in those days because of his lack of noble blood. It was then that he came to understand the prevailing class stratification of Europe, the feeling of being stuck in the position he was born to. Once, on a visit to the country estate of a family whose son attended school with him, a sense of indignation was codified in him. When he saw the way his school friend lived, in grand rooms with servants, he thought to himself: "The world is divided into lords and nobodies, into the strong and the weak."

Now Aleks looked at the shriveled bodies of the men of the upper classes and intelligentsia around him and felt a strange sense of satisfaction, as though a certain atonement had been made. The tingle of pleasure was not out of a love for watching men suffer, but because the privilege and arrogance they had exercised over him was expiring. "*Sic transit gloria mundi*," he thought. Thus passes worldly glory. In the camp a man could only control his place with his intellect, his cunning, his shrewdness. His fate was not predestined by who his father was or what last name he carried or how much gold lay in the family coffers.

These themes of class, hierarchy, and patriotism, which were so present in Aleks's thoughts during his early months at Sachsenhausen, began to appear in the songs he composed. When he longed for Poland, he wrote lyrics like the opening lines of the song "Krakowiaczek" from 1940. *Oh Kraków, oh Kraków, Lovely city, Everyone's astonished by your beauty!* This song doubled as an homage to Dr. Jan Miodoński, a Kraków resident, who impressed Aleks with the courage and self-sacrifice he showed when he confronted SS guards threatening several older, sickly prisoners. Sometimes, Aleks wrote lyrics addressed to his family back home, as in the song "Don't Cry for Me," which he set to an old Silesian melody he knew from his childhood. *Don't cry about me / That I'm hungry here. / Don't cry about me, / My dear daddy.* He wrote about past loves, such as Helena, a young woman from before the war. *I had a dream today, deceptive, enchanting / You were there with me. / Springtime roses bloomed on the wire—/ I was one of them with you.*

As Aleks composed and performed, he arrived at an essential realization: his culture was completely and incontrovertibly his. The Nazis could control nearly every other aspect in the lives of the men in their dreadful camp fiefdom. But for all the brutal attacks on their humanity, culture still belonged to the prisoners. The SS could not beat the music and poetry and literature out of them. Aleks and any other prisoner could find a way to meet in secret, either in a designated barracks or spontaneously, in the corner of their own block, and recite a poem or a song or a section of a novel, to commemorate a national holiday, to honor the death of a comrade. And they might feel revived, if just for a moment. Aleks believed the others felt the same.

Chapter 5

T he closest thing Aleks had to relaxation was the time on Sunday afternoons when the SS sometimes permitted prisoners to rest, idle, converse with friends. It was likely on one of those Sundays in the early fall of 1940, three or four months into his internment, that a guard announced to Aleks and his barracks that prisoners would now be permitted to mail letters home, on the condition that they were written in clear, readable German and contained nothing the censors might find objectionable. The other stipulation: each inmate had to pay for his own stamp. Aleks yearned to make contact with his family in Cieszyn, especially his father, who seemed at great risk for Nazi imprisonment. Since Aleks's arrest, he had had no word about their fate, nor, surely, would they of his. As far as he knew, the Kulisiewiczs of Cieszyn had no idea that the Germans had deported him hundreds of miles from home and imprisoned him in a concentration camp. But Aleks had no money.

When the Gestapo first shackled him on that long-ago day at the family apartment in Cieszyn, he had no chance to bring anything with him. And the Germans would likely have confiscated any bills or coins he carried.

Yet by means unclear to Aleks, other prisoners seemed to have money. That they could write their families and he could not nearly brought this once proud, self-assured young man, wary of displays of emotion, to tears.

The moment of sentiment soon passed. He decided to approach a group of Czech priests to ask for help. Men of God would surely be generous, take pity on a young man desperately trying to contact his family. They would donate the tiny sum of money he needed.

At the barracks where the Czech priests were housed, Aleks approached the first man he saw. The priest still looked portly from his life before the war. Because Aleks had grown up in Cieszyn, on the Czech border, he spoke the Czech language nearly as fluently as he did Polish—after all, it was the language with which he tried to woo Bożena. Always aware of the effect of a good performance, Aleks recited poems by Jiří Wolker and Jaroslav Seifert, two of Czechoslovakia's greatest literary masters, hoping that the verses would stir the priest. Then Aleks made his case. He beseeched the man for the money, a paltry sum, 6 reichspfennig, to inform his family that he was alive. The priest agreed, but on one condition. He pointed at Aleks's rations—prisoners often kept extra food on them so that no one would steal it—and asked whether he had any margarine. When Aleks replied that he did, the priest said. "I will get that tiny bit of margarine for it, and then all will be settled."

To skip even the smallest amount of food seemed perilous to Aleks, even deadly if the block elder ordered a long session of sport the next morning. Yet sending a letter was too important. Trying his best to contain his anger, Aleks handed over his share of margarine. The priest tossed him the coins.

Only when Aleks left did his anger overflow. To calm himself as he walked away from the barracks, the pennies for which he had traded his margarine in the bottom of his pocket, he began to whistle Monti's "Csárdás," the beautiful, wailing introduction, bowed on the lowest string of a violin—music he'd known and loved since he was a boy. As he strode away, he was reminded of how life in the camp seemed to bring out the worst qualities in people, even Catholic priests, men he had been raised to trust, who should have renounced what they had to help others. While brooding on the unfairness of the camp and what it did to people, another prisoner approached him. Aleks studied the man. He was short and bald, with a broad face and one eye nearly swollen shut—most likely from the blow of a fist or club. Stitched to his striped uniform were two triangles, which together formed a Star of David. Aleks turned away and continued to whistle. The man listened intently, intrigued by the melody Aleks could produce simply by blowing air through pursed lips. Puzzled, Aleks stopped and stared at the stranger. Shyly, the man spoke, almost in a whisper, "Please, keep whistling, sir."

The request came as a shock to Aleks. First of all, the man spoke in Polish. Aleks knew that in some barracks of the little camp, the SS held Jews of Polish nationality. Yet despite their Polish roots or citizenship, many had spent years living and working in Germany—some were even born there. What also perplexed Aleks was the fact that the man addressed him as "sir," with the formal word for "you." This sign of respect from someone who looked to be at least thirty years Aleks's senior struck him as unusual. Though curious, Aleks did not want to talk. He muttered something to the man and kept walking. "Anyway," he thought to himself, justifying his brusqueness, "whoever he is, he likely wants to beg or recruit for some secret camp organizing." Yet the stranger persisted, following Aleks as he walked off.

Eventually, Aleks relented and he and this puzzling prisoner began to converse. The man was known around the camp as Moses Rosenberg, and as they spoke, Aleks began to open up and relate what had just happened with the Czech priest. Moses took Aleks by the arm and led him back to the priests' barracks. From a distance, Aleks pointed out the priest who'd taken his margarine leaning against a wall outside the building, chatting with someone and munching on bread. Aleks wondered if he was eating the margarine with it. Moses strode over to the priest and demanded that he give back the margarine. Speaking sharply, he looked the priest straight in the eye. Other prisoners heard the confrontation and gathered round.

"I have no idea what you're talking about," the priest said, smiling.

Moses pressed, and the priest's smile vanished. He lunged at Moses and struck him on the face, calling him a damn filthy Jew. Other prisoners joined in, kicking Moses and yelling at him.

Moses and Aleks managed to flee, Moses bruised and Aleks even more disgusted by the depths to which human wickedness could sink. But in this new acquaintance, Aleks believed he had found someone honest, someone willing to take a stand even though it would win him nothing. Eventually, they had to part; Jews and non-Jews weren't housed together in the same barracks. As Aleks made his way to his own block, he couldn't stop thinking about this Jewish prisoner who had stood up for him even though they hardly knew each other. Moses seemed a good man to know, a courageous type who, despite his age and low rank at Sachsenhausen, did not fear a bully, would not tolerate abuse.

IT WAS A fellow Pole, a seventeen-year-old cadet called Bolesław Marcinek, who told Aleks about the choir. Bolesław, known to friends as Bolek, came from Cieszyn and left his military academy to take up arms when the Germans invaded Poland. As with Aleks, the SS first detained Bolek in the Cieszyn jail in autumn 1939, where together, awaiting their fate, the two became friends. They reconnected months later at Sachsenhausen where they found themselves assigned to nearby barracks in the little camp. One night after a long day of sport, during the hour or so of time the SS allowed the prisoners before lights out, Bolek mentioned that he knew of a male choir mostly from barracks 37, 38, and 39. Aleks had never been in those barracks, but he knew they housed many of the camp's Jews. Bolek said there were twenty or thirty men in the choir and that it only existed because the block elder in barracks 39, a seasoned German communist, saw value in it and allowed the men to rehearse.

To Aleks, it seemed highly unlikely that a camp choir, especially one composed of Jews, could exist without the knowledge of the SS. Information flowed freely in the camp. Secrets were hard to contain. Being caught could mean brutal punishment. Yet the prospect of a choir in a Nazi concentration camp was too intriguing for Aleks to ignore. The thought lodged in the back of his mind, and he could not let go of it. He had to hear them.

When the next opportunity arose, on a night when Bolek got word that a rehearsal might take place, Bolek and Aleks snuck into barracks 39. The act alone of sneaking into a Jewish barracks posed a risk. In most cases, the SS forbade non-Jewish prisoners to enter the Jewish barracks. But Aleks didn't care. The confidence and swagger he'd possessed before the war emerged, if hesitantly, in times like these.

As soon as the two young Poles entered the barracks, they could tell something unusual was taking place. Perhaps what first tipped them off was the sound of prisoners doing vocal exercises, singing warm-up scales. The two men slipped into the room at one end of the rectangular barracks where the choir had assembled. There, twenty, perhaps twenty-five, prisoners stood. Aleks studied them. They all bore the Star of David on the breast of their uniforms. Some were old, balding, wrinkled around their eyes and across their foreheads. A few of them were young, by their appearance still teenagers, with smooth faces, thick hair, and the ropey muscles of youth. Everyone, though, looked hungry—even more so than the prisoners in Aleks's barracks.

When the group began to sing, Aleks could not believe the sound. It was remarkably refined. Yet none of the singers appeared to be professional. Like the men in his own barracks, they seemed more like traders, clerks, craftsmen, tailors, the sort of people to whom a formal musical education was rarely afforded. Yet more astonishing to Aleks than finding a choir in the Jewish barracks, in the stench of tired, unwashed bodies, among the lice-infested blankets and straw mattresses and hunger, was this: the choir's conductor was Moses, the very man who, just days earlier, had come to Aleks's defense against the Czech priest. It was Moses who drew out the beautiful singing of the group, as if by some magic and the grace of his hands. When Moses noticed Aleks in the back of the barracks, he smiled at him, then continued conducting. Aleks could see a dark bruise around his eye.

Aleks lingered, astounded that despite the ordeal of being Jews in a Nazi concentration camp, these men had found a way to assemble when the sun set, to sing in the barracks—no matter how much of a risk it posed, no matter how high the cost would be if a guard passed outside and heard the music. The image of Moses standing before his choir singing, his hands coaxing out music in such remarkable circumstances, burned itself into Aleks's mind.

He had to see Moses again, although getting to him was complicated. Aleks asked around the camp, desperate for more information. The German communists seemed best informed. From them he learned that many of the prisoners called Moses by his artist's name—Rosebery d'Arguto—and that before the war, he'd been a prominent leftist choral director in Berlin. He also learned that though Moses was Polish by birth, he had spent years, even decades, in Germany. Perhaps days, perhaps weeks later, Aleks managed to meet Moses again. From then on, he called him Rosebery.

On the grounds of the little camp, Aleks got to know Rosebery. During free moments, prisoners often plodded between the barracks, sometimes furtively lest a guard stood near. This was one of the easiest ways to get to know other men and to have some privacy from the crammed barracks. Prisoners meandered in pairs or threesomes between blocks, around garbage bins, wherever they could find a path. They bumped into one other, brushed shoulders as they gave way to passersby. This was often how information circulated, how social interactions took place, where quarrels were had and settled. The Polish prisoner Gabriel Zych described the campgrounds during nonworking hours as a human anthill.

Aleks quickly became fixated on Rosebery. Here was a real musician, a skilled and capable conductor. At the rehearsal, Aleks saw how the men in the choir seemed utterly gripped by Rosebery, following every gesture, every flourish of his hands as he conducted. Rosebery also seemed fearless, bordering on rash—only such a bold man would have the pluck to organize a clandestine Jewish choir in a Nazi concentration camp. And despite his stature and age, Rosebery still addressed Aleks, a young man with few accomplishments to boast of, as sir, in the formal way. Rosebery's demeanor struck him as a mark of the intelligentsia; it signaled the sort of well-bred man with whom Aleks so much desired to be associated.

Over the coming weeks, Aleks met Rosebery as often as he could. This mostly happened on Sundays, assuming the SS did not take away the day off and force prisoners to do sport. With luck, they also found time to meet on weeknights, usually after roll call and dinner. Much depended on the whims of the guards, the moods of the block elders.

From Rosebery, Aleks soaked up knowledge about Jewish music, which he had heard and loved as a boy but had never learned as he did Polish, German, and Czech songs. During the summers of his childhood, Aleks's father often sent him to his grandparents' home in a hamlet near Nowy Wiśnicz. A Jewish community flourished there, and when Aleks visited during the warm months in the mid-1920s, he studied Jewish customs with great interest. He heard village boys speaking Yiddish as they kicked a ball around the fields or scampered down the hamlet's dirt streets. His ears especially perked up at the sound of Jewish music, which often emanated from a nearby synagogue. The wedding and funeral music impressed him the most.

The richness of tones that Aleks absorbed from Jewish music pushed the boundaries of the art for him. He loved the lilt of Jewish music almost as much as the Romani songs he heard in Czechoslovakia or in the Cieszyn town square. Though he tried to mimic Jewish songs, even asking a group of boys in his grandparents' hamlet to teach him, he never succeeded. There was something elusive, something he could never grasp hold of as he could with other music.

Aleks encountered Jewish music again when, in Kraków, while at university, he heard musicians singing in apartment courtyards for a tossed coin. One song in particular stuck in his mind, so much so that he memorized it. *There were six brothers, / they traded geese, / then one of the brothers died, / And there were five.* The chorus went: *Josel will take the violin, / Tefel will take the bass, / from courtyard to courtyard—and one more time.*

Aleks and Rosebery shared stories about their lives before the war. They talked about politics and their country of origin. Rosebery, Aleks learned, came from a small town called Mława, about seventy-five miles northwest of Warsaw. In the winter of 1890, when Rosebery was born, his mother and father, Chawa Zysa and Shimshon Rosenberg, boarded a carriage and rode to the nearby village of Szreńsk, where Chawa Zysa's parents lived, likely so she could bring her child into the world with the familiarity and love of her family. On December 24, Chawa Zysa gave birth to a boy, whom she and Shimshon named Moshe. The clerk working for the Russian occupying administration transliterated the name as Moszek in his Cyrillic records book. Once their newborn grew strong enough, Chawa Zysa and Shimshon took him home to Mława, to their two-story stone house, which stood just off the town square.

Mława was a town of crooked streets and sagging homes made of dark planks of wood. It was a world unto itself. Access to newspapers from the capital was uncertain. Few of the modern pleasures of Warsaw or Kraków had yet arrived there. A town water and plumbing system was decades in the future. Like many others in Mława, the Rosenbergs hired a worker to dig an outhouse in the yard behind their home. To shower, most Mławians had to visit a bathhouse, which offered discounts to children under ten, soldiers, and prostitutes.

Ethnic Poles made up the majority of Mławian residents, and a thriving Jewish community of roughly a third of the population lived among them. Occupying Russians who administered the region—mostly bureaucrats, teachers, and soldiers—also lived in town. Shimshon, Rosebery's father, held a lofty position. Like most of the residents of Mława, he made his living from wheat. He bought up vast fields and stored the harvested grain in a silo until the price per pound reached a profitable level. He then sold it in Poland or to neighboring countries for good margins. Despite rises and falls of grain prices for much of the nineteenth century, Shimshon's business prospered, making him one of the wealthiest residents of Mława. That the Rosenbergs lived in a large stone house at number 5 Niborska Street, just steps from the town square, attested to their prosperity. In Mława, social status radiated out in concentric circles from the town square. The richest resided at the center. The peasant farmers, mostly ethnic Poles, lived on the outer rings, where they sowed wheat on the flat, fertile land that stretched far into the distance.

Moshe, as Rosebery's family and friends called him throughout his boyhood, would have witnessed much action and excitement on Niborska Street. Though few shops stood there, to reach the town square from the north a person had to take this route. Wagons clattered into town from early in the morning on market days, filled with wheat or baskets of potatoes or heaps of vegetables. Geese, ducks, chickens, and turkeys lay in the carts, bound in bunches by their legs or in small wooden cages. Peasants sometimes led a cow or a colt to town. Horses pulled the bigger carriages. But just as often, the farmers themselves dragged smaller, two-wheel carts, their hands and clothes darkened by the rich earth they worked. Others arrived on foot, carrying straw baskets filled with butter, hunks of white cheese, or thick cream in earthen pots. In the summer, they brought plump cherries, strawberries, and tomatoes. The sound of horseshoes striking the cobblestones and the chatter among the rural folk announced the business at hand.

Moshe's hometown was at its busiest when the market came to life. Hundreds of people, including those of his own family, assembled in the town square, with many horses alongside them. Across the square, men and women of all ages and from every ethnic and religious group bought and sold onions and parsnips, cabbages and potatoes, clothing, bread, tools, shoes, caps, kerosene, salt, and home goods. Moshe's father might pass his hand through a basket of barley or rye to gauge its quality. His mother, in search of produce for a family meal, might seize a chicken and blow back its hind feathers to see whether it was plump enough to nourish the family. The overflow from the main square spread to the wet markets for calves and other livestock and stands for freshly butchered meat or poultry. At the market for secondhand goods, housewives jostled one another, bartering loudly for the best price. The noise was tremendous. Sometimes tempers flared and fights broke out.

Moshe grew up at a time when Młdawa and many towns around Poland were suspended between centuries-old traditions and modernity, which unfolded at a dizzying pace in the capital. During his childhood in the first years of the twentieth century, the early yearnings for a new world began to emerge around town. Newspapers from the bigger cities like Warsaw or Łódź began to arrive more regularly, causing a flurry of interest, especially among the town's youth, who craved information about the world beyond Mława. Rumors of new technologies like the phonograph and the telephone began to circulate. Around this time, even discussions about reforming education for Jewish children took place. Up until then, Jewish boys received the most education—girls received some but typically were married young and started families. The boys received their education largely in denominational schools like cheders and yeshivas that focused on religious instruction. Reform movements began to advocate for more practical instruction for boys.

At the same time, a new political movement called socialism began to take hold in the minds of many young Jews, who saw in it the chance to transform society into something more just, more equitable, where opportunities could be accessed by all. Though the basic rhythms of life sustained the old ways, with tradition and religion standing as pillars of any person's life, the pace of change in the Mława of Moshe's youth began to accelerate.

Moshe's father saw the world through the eyes of a devout man. He wore a long beard and played an active role in the synagogue and other Jewish houses of worship around Mława. Shimshon likely belonged to the Hasidic Dynasty of Ger, which originated in a town south of Warsaw called Góra Kalwaria. Though he was deeply religious, he didn't follow all the traditions of Hasidism. He wore a long beard but never grew sidelocks, nor did he don the black, wide-brimmed hat that could be seen on the heads of some men around Mława. Instead, he dressed himself in suits and a common business hat. Shimshon also rejected all forms of mysticism and welcomed modern science and secular thought.

Shimshon's devotion to his faith meant that Moshe and his brother and sisters grew up in a home that followed strict Jewish practice, with Sabbath being the most important day of the week. On Friday, Moshe's mother Chawa Zysa cleaned every surface and corner of the house. Before sunset, when Shabbos began, the family would assemble at their large dining table to watch as Chawa Zysa lit two candles in large silver holders. Then, with her hands, she would draw in the candles three times before covering her eyes to say the blessing. Only when this ritual was complete would she bring the special meal to the table. Shimshon prayed over each dish—the bread, the wine, often a roast chicken, maybe potatoes or homemade noodles. Shabbos at the Rosenbergs was a formal affair. Every member of the family dressed in proper attire. The next day, Saturday, Shimshon conducted no business. Save for going to synagogue, he sat in his study, surrounded by hundreds of religious books, devoting himself to reading. He always encouraged Moshe and Moshe's younger brother, Jacob, to join him.

Shimshon had his heart set on his sons taking a religious path in life, following in his own footsteps. By the time Moshe was seven or eight, when his keen intelligence began to show, Shimshon decided that he ought to be a rabbi. Later, when Jacob got in the habit of singing around the house, Shimshon concluded that with such a gorgeous voice, he should be a cantor.

Though Shimshon tried to attract his sons to the Jewish faith, religion never drew their interest. Moshe felt a near aversion to it. He attended the local cheder, where he studied Hebrew, the Jewish scriptures, and the Talmud, but these schools did nothing to pull him toward the religion of his family and community. Instead, two things obsessed him: music and leftist political ideas. Friends of Moshe's remembered that it was Shimshon's brother, Moshe's uncle, who saw in him an unusual aptitude for music, especially after he heard him sing in a pure soprano voice as a young boy. From then on, Moshe's uncle tried to facilitate music lessons. Moshe was even permitted to audition, from time to time, to sing at local funerals. But Shimshon, a practical man, considered the life of a musician laughably unstable—unless, of course, his son wished to be a cantor. Religious music would be acceptable, but anything secular or popular was out of the question. Ideally, Moshe should dedicate himself to Judaism and become a rabbi. If he refused to do that, he should follow in the steps of his father and become a grain merchant.

Aside from the sporadic training Moshe received through the generosity of his uncle, his foundation in music came from his houses of worship. He heard music at the synagogue, and occasionally, when passing the home of one of the town cantors, he overheard him practicing. Moshe's friend Jacob Grobart recalled that he was most drawn to the music of one cantor, a man known as Rabbi Shalom Lipp. Sometimes, Moshe would sneak away from home to study with Rabbi Lipp. Those rebellious excursions, along with Moshe's secretly securing a violin for himself, tipped Shimshon into anger, and Jacob heard that he bound Moshe to the bedposts. From early on, there was a deep-seated stubbornness in Moshe. He refused to abandon his interest in music.

Socialism was also a point of conflict between Moshe and his father. Later in life, Moshe told friends of his taking to socialism before he reached his teen years, stealing away from home in his school cap to join meetings of young radicals around town. He also likely had some contact with local workers who had begun to organize around the ideas of Europe's revolutionaries. Moshe's friend Jacob remembered the two of them crouched in his attic, reading revolutionary proclamations and pamphlets, strategizing on how best to bring about the revolt. As Moshe became more of a committed socialist, the work his own father did likely began to seem like the sort of dirty capitalism he struggled against. After all, Shimshon was a speculator: he would purchase massive amounts of grain at one price and then sell when the price rose, ensuring himself a profit. The fluctuations of the market drove Shimshon's decisions, not the needs of the people, a great many of whom were impoverished workers and peasants. For Moshe, that sort of manipulation, profit-seeking at the cost of the people's well-being, was difficult to swallow. A sense of rebellion burned within him.

Shimshon saw in his son immense potential and arranged for him to attend a prestigious yeshiva as soon as he came of age. But Moshe always had his own ideas about what he wanted to do. Instead of studying the Talmud and the Torah, he insisted that after his Bar Mitzvah he would enter a mixed public school, learn in a secular environment, and get an education beyond just religion. Reluctantly, Shimshon let him enroll at the public school.

As an adolescent in the time of a partitioned Poland, where the Russian Empire brutally ruled Mława and its environs, paths forward for Moshe were limited. Though some young Jewish adolescents gained entry to major universities to study medicine or law, this was far from a sure path for him, even with his father's wealth. Instead, joining Shimshon as a grain merchant was an option, as was becoming a rabbi or religious scholar. Or he could join the socialist cause, a cause sometimes linked with Zionism. Yet religion and Zionism held no allure for him, and he felt no pull toward medicine or law. And joining the family grain business was exactly the sort of capitalist scheme he was utterly opposed to. What remained, therefore, was socialism and, he hoped, music.

IN 1905, JUST before Moshe turned fifteen, the young socialist got his chance at revolution. For several years, economic conditions had deteriorated in Russian-controlled Poland. Peasants in particular were impacted. Political tensions throughout the Russian Empire, but especially in occupied Poland, began to rise. In industrial cities like Łódź and Warsaw, workers struck en masse, revolting against low wages and poor working conditions. Soon, students, even as young as grade-schoolers, took to the streets, protesting the Russification of the country and the general prohibition of Polish as a language of instruction. As a response to the unrest, Russian police opened fire on workers striking in Łódź. Insurrections and protests exploded across big swaths of the country, even reaching the provincial town of Mława, where a teenaged Moshe had been reading about the revolution, yearning for an opportunity to put his new-formed ideas into practice. So active had he been in local socialist circles, his friends gave him the nickname "Minister of Education" and viewed him as an ambitious, intelligent young man who never missed a political meeting. When the protests reached Mława, hundreds of residents, Christian and Jewish alike, flooded the town square, some on horseback, carrying flags and banners in opposition to Russian imperial power. According to family history, Moshe joined them. With other young Młdawian socialists, he marched the streets of the town holding a large red flag. At one point, wanting to take a more active role in the revolt, he ran to the front of the column of protestors, turned around to face the people, and marched backward, leading them in anti-Russian chants and fierce revolutionary singing. At fourteen years old, not physically striking in any distinctive sense or known beyond his own circles, Moshe was an unlikely leader. Yet the marchers saw something in him, in his personality. He possessed a magnetism, an alluring quality that drew people in.

Moshe caught the eye of the Russian police, who, in the days after the protests, clamped down brutally on anyone seen as oppositional. He knew what it meant to fall into the hands of the Russians. In fact, he had already spent time in custody two years earlier for distributing revolutionary leaflets around town, some of which he copied from the originals by hand. To evade arrest this time, he told friends later, he took refuge for a time in the home of a friend, hiding in a nook between a bed and a wall, narrowly escaping when a group of Russian policemen arrived and searched the house. In the weeks that followed, he likely kept a low profile, waiting until the unrest passed.

What drove Moshe permanently from Młdawa took place two years later, in February 1907. As part of a Młdawian offshoot of the Marxist-Zionist movement, Poale Zion, he conspired with other local leftists to rob a town bank so that their organization could further its political goals. Yet when they arrived on the chosen day of the crime, the Russian police were waiting for them—someone had ratted them out. It was then that Moshe realized he was in serious trouble. He understood the brutality a person could face in Russian custody. In all likelihood, no form of due process would be afforded to him. If caught, he could be detained indefinitely—even executed if the Russians chose to accuse him of political insurrection. With the Russian authorities, the deep pockets of his father would not be able to help him. The only option was to flee—and not just from Młdawa. He would have to leave Russian Poland. With money from his father and the names of people he could contact in several European cities, he left and snuck into Austria, then less repressive than the other two empires that had carved up and ruled his country.

During the time spent in Austria and Italy, Moshe studied music and laryngology, though his exact whereabouts and educational affiliations are unclear. It was during this time that he likely adopted the artist's name Rosebery d'Arguto, which, alongside Martin—his choice for a German transliteration of Moshe—he soon used in most interactions. Though he might have arrived sooner, Rosebery officially registered with the city government of Berlin on February 1, 1909. On the streets of the city, Rosebery found himself wide-eyed, gazing at a massive, noisy, gorgeous capital on the tipping point of modernity. The culture and music and life that he didn't know he craved as a boy in Mława because he didn't know it existed was suddenly all around him. Berlin was unlike anything he'd experienced in his childhood. Berlin, it seemed, might be a place where he could settle.

IN THE AUTUMN of 1940, Aleks and Rosebery shared tales from their lives before Sachsenhausen. Their friendship, which would have been utterly improbable had the Germans not plunged Europe into war, grew deep. The two men were starkly different. Aleks was born in a soon-to-be liberated Poland, one of the majority group, to a relatively prosperous family. He enjoyed the freedoms and opportunities these privileges afforded him. He could enter one of Poland's most prestigious universities without trouble and set off on a path toward a life among Poland's elite. A future as a wealthy, music-loving man with a family and a townhouse in a leafy district of Kraków awaited him, even if work as a lawyer was sure to bore him.

Rosebery, on the other hand, came into the harsh world of the Russian Empire, twenty-eight years before Aleks, when imperial oppression gripped the population and opportunities for Jews were limited, even those from wealthy, respected families like the Rosenbergs. What was more, even if Aleks and Rosebery had been raised in close proximity, in the same period of time and in similar circumstances, there existed a certain mystery, indeed aversion, in the views of both Jews and Poles as to how the other group lived, the cultural and religious practices they followed, and the norms that guided their lives. Though both of these men were born on Polish land within one generation of each other, they inhabited two wholly different worlds.

In Aleks's youth, he interacted with Jews, he heard their music, visited their shops and stands, but he never understood them in a nuanced way. Rosebery's strict religious childhood meant that the Poles of Mława remained foreign, beyond his childhood world, most living on the wheat farms beyond the borderlines of town, only to appear on market days when they hauled their grain to the square or when Shimshon bought up their harvest. From towns like Mława, where change unfolded at a sluggish pace, and even to an extent in the big cities like Warsaw, Lwów, and Kraków, tradition reigned. Jews and Poles interacted, they conducted business, fought alongside one another in wars and insurrections. Yet on a day-to-day basis, the two groups were deeply unfamiliar with each other. The lack of understanding birthed lore and mythology, often of the venomous sort. In any other circumstances, Rosebery and Aleks would never have crossed paths. The soon-to-be lawyer in Kraków and the leftist choral director in Berlin would have attended different parties, eaten at different restaurants, read different newspapers. It was Sachsenhausen that laid the groundwork for their friendship.

Learning about Rosebery's background had an immediate effect on Aleks. In Rosebery he saw a man with complete commitment to a set of ideals that advanced equity and justice no matter a person's background. Over the course of his career, he wove these ideals into his music, aiming to give culture to those who needed it, never for his own glory or eminence. Again and again, Rosebery seemed to defend his values with a near impetuousness, ignoring the risks to himself, putting aside his own needs and safety to help people around him. Aleks recognized this in the choir, in that magnificent group of prisoners who risked much for a chance to sing for brief periods of time when the guards weren't abusing them. He would never forget how, when they first met, Rosebery, with one eye nearly swollen shut, defended him over a measly ration of margarine.

Aleks had long since abandoned the chauvinism and the worldview that had drawn him to the nationalist student group in Kraków. Notwithstanding, the half-life of certain anti-Semitic views continued to hold sway in his mind. Perhaps he still wondered why Jews seemingly held such control over money and business. He might still, if absentmindedly, use an anti-Semitic slur to describe a situation or repeat a trope about Jews or their culture.

Yet in the camp something in Aleks began to shift. His view of the world eroded; the facile, naive teenager's understanding of life could no longer hold. Back in 1936 when he belonged to his right-wing youth group, Jews were the students he observed from afar in the segregated lecture halls of the Jagiellonian University. They manned the registers in shops he sometimes patronized. They were the families dressed differently as he passed them on the street. They were the people about whom adults cracked jokes from time to time. There was a foreignness, an otherness to them.

Aleks felt an immediate intimacy with Rosebery, a closeness to a Jewish person he had never experienced before. In Rosebery, he saw generosity, a deep caring for the people around him, and an unfettered commitment to music. He found a mentor, a confidante, a person who possessed the qualities he'd sought throughout his teen and early adulthood. Rosebery was a trained musician, a man who understood music from a technical standpoint, who had ideas and theories about how to build a choir, how to arrange melodies and harmonies. Yet he never lost his sense of humility.

What perhaps impressed Aleks most of all was Rosebery's courage. The values he believed in from his early days in Mława never waned. At Sachsenhausen, where once-virtuous prisoners frequently turned into schemers or villains, like the Czech priest, ready to do anything to advance their interests, to assure their survival, Rosebery remained true to himself. Even when his captors threatened to snuff out his life when his skills were at their most refined and most precious, he didn't cower or shrink. He responded with defiance by forming a choir in a Jewish barracks of Sachsenhausen.

Chapter 6

⌒

Though Rosebery's revolt against the Russian occupiers and his flight from Mława in 1907 had cut a deep rift between him and his Orthodox father, Shimshon, a devoted if disgruntled parent, pledged his son financial support. He even put Rosebery in touch with several of his business contacts in Berlin to help him get settled.

Over several years, Rosebery found a rhythm to life in his adopted city. He spent countless hours reading at the Königliche Bibliothek, the Royal Library. He trained his singing voice, learning counterpoint and composition under the guidance of Gustav Ernest and James Jakob Rothstein. At night, he frequented a community of leftist intellectuals. He made inroads with the radical workers' movements then gaining great momentum. On some nights, he worked as an extra at the opera, partly for the wages, but also so that he could listen from the wings to the singers onstage, especially Mattia Battistini, Enrico Caruso, Frieda Hempel, and Herman Jadlowker. Rosebery gazed at them, observing how they finessed their craft, analyzing what made them great.

By 1915, with Europe entrenched in war, Rosebery sang as a tenor in the operetta choir of the Theater des Westens. During the day, he participated in coursework at Berlin's Charité Hospital. Under the guidance of erudite professors, he delved into the anatomy and function of the human voice. Now aged twenty-four, the voice his uncle had recognized years earlier when he was a boy in Mława had reached its maturity. Yet as war consumed the continent, the Prussian government began to view aliens as a threat and apprehended Rosebery with many other foreigners and sent them to be interned. The authorities released him not long after, but forced him to work for a time as an industrial laborer in Berlin. Now music became a nighttime affair. Only at the end of a day's work for the Prussian state could he sing, compose, or study music theory.

During the First World War, Rosebery's professional life began to take shape. By 1918, he had already published his ideas about musical reform—especially regarding voice training—in scholarly journals. He applied those ideas with private students as a master coach. Yet when peace returned to Europe, he flourished—especially as it related to his leftist politics. With Germany in turmoil, the men and women with dreams of a revolution began to organize, and Rosebery, seeing another chance to raze the system he despised, joined them. At rallies and events for the collective cause, he sang revolutionary music. In Red newspapers, he wrote broadsides against the ruling class and spoke of the power that workers could wield if they organized.

During these years, Rosebery lived in two worlds. Change on a massive scale was unfolding all around him in Germany. In fact, a new, modern Europe had begun to emerge from the mud and carnage of the Great War. For this young, quixotic man, the ideals he'd fought for and the notions of a more just world seemed finally to be coming into reality. Alongside his radical friends, he worked in any way he could to bring about the downfall of capitalism and advance the cause of the German Communist Party. This radical Rosebery copublished an anarcho-communist newspaper called *Die Weltrevolution* (*The World Revolution*), which boasted an initial circulation of twelve thousand. This Rosebery wrote fiery articles, such as one from 1919 entitled "Revolutionary Spirit, Revolutionary

Action," or another in which he reminded class-conscious proletarians, socialists, communists, and anarcho-communists of the "hell of capital and private property."

As part of a community of like-minded leftists, he worked to destroy the old systems that kept workers living in cramped Berlin tenements, where coal soot laced the air and children sometimes fell asleep with hunger gnawing their bellies. At rallies, he called for unity among workers so they could emancipate the proletariat and bring a higher humanity, a purer humankind into the world. When the authorities, suspecting subversive behavior, raided the offices of *Die Weltrevolution*, Rosebery and his copublisher, Ludwig Bergmann, fled for a time to Leipzig. Either there or through friends back in Berlin, they found a book printer who, despite using a hodgepodge of fonts, including an ornate letter D in the title, *Die Weltrevolution*, and printing two typos in the word "proletariat" in the top headline, published the next planned editions of the paper. After the discovery of Rosa Luxemburg's corpse in a lock of the Landwehr Canal in May 1919, Rosebery published a lengthy obituary for a woman he so admired, entitled "Rosa Luxemburg, Her Suffering and Her Final Journey." In rich, lucid German he eulogized, "Bareheaded and shoeless, we enter the temple of the spirit and soul. Free from any external form—the hallmark of spiritual and mental holiness—we bow deeply, broken and shaken before the tragic fate of one of the rarest martyr heroines of all time: Rosa Luxemburg. . . . Go in peace! Greet the brave ones in the hereafter! Christ of women, savior of the proletariat!"

The other Rosebery resided in a far more genteel world, that of classical music and the bourgeois artistic scene. He developed theories about how to regard the human voice, especially when injured or during puberty's mutation. In this world, Rosebery wore well-cut suits, often with a waistcoat, sometimes over shirts with wing collars. He wrote erudite, elaborate articles about his ideas, such as one in 1918 for the magazine *Signale für die Musikalische Welt* (*Signals for the Musical World*) entitled "Solving the Voice Mutation Question. Safeguarding the Noble Classical Vocal Art." His writing helped to build his reputation as a quasi-medical authority.

It gained him a following and placed him among the leading thinkers of laryngology. A colleague once wrote of Rosebery, "One should not picture him as a pedantic singing teacher with crooked glasses and warts on his face, but as a trembling man, a hotblooded fighter for his ideas, who teaches with an eager dizziness."

To earn a living, Rosebery gave master voice lessons to prominent Berlin singers. Seated at the piano in his flat, he worked with them to help them heal their voice injuries, improve their technique, or simply finesse their command of the craft. He likely felt a certain ease among Berlin's monied classes. He spoke a rich and beautiful German, sometimes drawing on archaic words or sentence constructions. He also possessed a certain anachronistic charm and charisma that drew wealthy students to him.

Yet working so closely with the wealthy made him ill at ease. He never saw a problem with publishing musical pedagogy in highbrow journals— this did not conflict with his political beliefs. But allying himself only with Berlin's elite left him weary, unfulfilled. What he craved most was to work with Berlin's working classes, especially their children, who received little or no musical education. Of course, this stratum of society would never have the means to pay him a living wage. He had little choice but to give private lessons to the wealthy.

What brought an end to Rosebery's bifurcated life was a charge of libel leveled at him in July 1921 by the Berlin police after he accused them in a communist newspaper of employing criminals. The authorities issued an arrest warrant. When they captured him and locked him in a police cell, they reviewed his papers and discovered that he did not have a valid residency permit. With his deep ties to the Berlin radicals and no valid papers (he was still seen as a Russian citizen), the authorities sent him to the Stargard Internment Camp in Pomerania, where they began deportation proceedings. Terrified at the prospect of losing the life he had built in Berlin, Rosebery called upon his friends, who helped him retain Kurt Rosenfeld, a prominent attorney for Berlin's left and the former lawyer of Rosa Luxemburg. Rosenfeld convinced the judge that the authorities had overreached when they attempted to deport

Rosebery. Rosebery had, after all, only written a newspaper article; he had not committed a criminal act. The judge threw out the case, and later, the administration issued Rosebery a new residency permit.

Though he was free again and now a legal resident in Germany, the experience changed him. He emerged more moderate, less radical, but a man who still felt committed to the working class and passionate in the belief that they needed liberation. Yet his ideas about revolution and his involvement in radical causes shifted. No longer did he write fiery political articles or chatter at leftist cafés about the best ways to end capitalism. Instead, he delved almost solely into music. In music, he believed he could achieve a revolution of a different sort. Rather than the eloquent yet elusive worlds of equality he and his intellectual peers had once imagined, Rosebery recognized that in music he might conceive of a means to improve the lot of the working class in a tangible, lasting way, if simply by raising their spirits. As a trained singer, musician, and composer with a leftist pedigree, he was ideally suited for bringing music to the people who could not afford to attend a symphony or the opera, whose priority on any given day centered on filling the pantry and keeping the cold out of the flat.

But just how Rosebery might bring music to the toiling workers of Berlin posed a problem, one that took him nearly two years to solve. Finally, in 1922, an opportunity arose. For a short time, Rosebery conducted the child singers of the Neukölln Men's and Women's Choir, one of many leftist musical groups composed of Berlin's working class and their children. He wasn't always welcomed. Franz Bothe, the conductor of the adult singers, was known by the choir to call him "Jew-brat" during disagreements. But Rosebery quickly gained the love and confidence of the community. When Franz died and the adult choir suddenly needed a new conductor, Rosebery got the post.

By 1922, the labor movement had found a home in the southeastern borough of Neukölln, which had recently been incorporated into the city of Berlin. Given the major factories nearby, such as one owned by Siemens, workers had been arriving in large numbers from the countryside since the turn of the century, wishing to trade the rigors of rural labor for new, more modern lives. During the day, they toiled in machine and electrical factories, helping build the ever-expanding German capital. At night, they slept in tenement flats.

As more and more workers gathered in Neukölln, the borough became one of the strongholds for leftist political action, radical newspapers, and boisterous rallies. Compared to other boroughs, there was a high number of residents who belonged to or sympathized with the Communist and Social Democratic Parties, and some anarchists lived there, too. Heated quarrels sometimes broke out between the communists and social democrats. Despite the arguments, the groups often reached fragile rapprochements that would last a few days or weeks and then erupt into renewed belligerency.

This passion spilled over into the borough's cultural life, a big part of which were the workers' singing groups. When Rosebery took over the Neukölln Men's and Women's Choir, some seven or eight other ensembles performed in the area. The relative poverty of southeast Berlin and the resulting dearth of art meant that workers had to build their own places of culture and leisure. Smoking clubs were formed. On the weekends, groups of young men and women rode bicycles through the leafy parks nearby. Theaters staged plays. And of course, choirs sang revolutionary songs to eager audiences. In Neukölln, residents created a cultural space for themselves, completely divorced from bourgeois Berlin society. They had their own dance halls, bookstores, watering holes, and restaurants.

In his new role as conductor of the Neukölln Men's and Women's Choir, Rosebery saw the opportunity he'd long sought: a chance to bring music of the highest quality to men, women, and children whom society had dismissed as unworthy. With this vision, Rosebery overhauled the choir. As a group, the community decided to scrap its old name and replace it with *Gesangsgemeinschaft Rosebery d'Arguto*, or the Rosebery d'Arguto Singing Community. In the early weeks of his conductorship, he examined the more than two hundred choir members so that he could assess whether they had been assigned to the right section. To the surprise of many, he never asked them to sing. Instead, he examined the back of their mouths using a silver baton with a little sphere at one end, or he pressed his fingers on the singers' upper arms and the flesh from the neck down to the shoulder joint. One by one, the singers stood before their new conductor as he patiently examined them and determined their singing range—soprano, mezzo-soprano, or contralto for women; tenor, baritone, or bass for men. Often, Rosebery changed a singer's range even if they'd sung there for years. A woman might switch to the contralto after singing soprano all her adult life; a man might ascend from bass to tenor. Finally, and according to both range and skill, he would assign them to a section—first soprano, second soprano, and down the range. He typically divided the choir into eight parts.

With Rosebery as conductor, the choir took on a new culture and form. From the very start, the choristers knew that Rosebery was not a typical conductor. He embodied a seriousness and musical erudition that past conductors might have lacked. He appeared dedicated to the quality of the music in a way they had never seen. No longer did the choir exist simply to give workers and their children something to do, to deliver mediocre performances to distract them from the tedium of their lives. Rosebery saw the choir as a group of men and women who, if given the right guidance, could produce music as sophisticated, as powerful as that performed by any of the bourgeois choirs—perhaps even more so. This new approach made Rosebery immediately popular among the choir members. The same charm and wit with which he had enchanted his private students seemed to help him prevent any backlash as he changed the very fabric of the choir. Though small in stature, when he stood before the choir they quieted, directing their eyes to this man who had a special presence.

All Rosebery expected in return for bringing the choir members his expertise and passion was commitment. As he saw it, if they were to build something extraordinary, each man and woman had to invest time and energy, unreservedly. Every member had to attend the lengthy rehearsals, which typically took place twice a week and followed a strict routine. Members were to arrive on time, and though some had to travel from deep in the borough or beyond it, rehearsals were not to be missed for trivial reasons. Rosebery could be stern, but he never coerced any of the members into this expected behavior. From very early on, their faith in him elicited devotion. To many of them, it was clear that together they could achieve something distinctive. And so, weary after a long day's work, they made the journey, usually by tram, sometimes by bicycle or on foot, to the hall where the choir rehearsed, to sing for several hours.

As the head of the choir, Rosebery found a calling where all the important parts of his life coalesced. Each night the choir assembled—a group of men and women, untaught in the ways of music but eager and open-hearted—to stand in tiers before him, devoted to the commands he gave, the flourishes of his conductor's baton. In the choir, Rosebery found a universe unto its own, a place where his formal musical training together with his beliefs in equality, fairness, and access to culture for all could flourish. Never did Rosebery put in place restrictions for entry; a candidate did not have to sing well, nor read a musical score, nor understand music theory. As long as he or she found pleasure in singing and promised to do the work, the choir was open. Sometimes, one or another member would be embarrassed about their singing. Perhaps they could not strike the right note. Perhaps they had a gravelly voice. Rosebery would reply: "If a person can speak and hear, he can also sing."

ONCE ROSEBERY TOOK over the choir, he halted all performances for a year. Over that time, he shuffled members into the correct vocal groups, strengthened their voices, taught them his techniques. Though it was not at all clear to the singers that his ideas would yield anything of value, no one questioned him, because of his personality, his zeal. On occasion, a singer might find his methods eccentric. Yet above all, Rosebery and his quirky, fervent personality fascinated them. They recognized a man who had the education and expertise to make a great deal more money teaching the bourgeoisie, yet spent most of his evenings among the workers and their children, the people who could spare but pennies for an experience of music.

Whereas past conductors had concerned themselves only with the choir as a whole, Rosebery saw the individual man or woman as equally essential. To train singers, especially those with little prior musical skill, he developed a routine: To start each rehearsal, he guided the choir through a series of breathing exercises and humming, which he believed warmed up their voices but also improved their breathing technique and pronunciation. Then he led them in singing exercises, using nonsense phrases. "Hussa, Tusga, Bidifidibussa" was one such phrase the choir sang as Rosebery stood before them, seemingly coaxing the notes out of each singer. If someone struggled, he might encourage them to imagine a bouquet of flowers, the scent of which they were breathing in, relishing. By focusing on the beautiful smell, they would inhale consciously and regulate their flow of breath. For especially eager choristers, he gave free private lessons in his flat.

When Rosebery saw individual improvement, he praised the singer and scrawled notes in a ledger where he tracked in meticulous detail the development of each member. Occasionally, he would scold someone if he saw that they smoked or drank too much, vices that he believed hampered singing. With such attention and care, Rosebery began to transform even the most discordant into choristers who could sing beautifully and powerfully. Herr Professor, as the members called him, stood before the choir at each rehearsal, his baton fluttering in the air, clearly pleased by the music that resonated. Steadily balding save for a wreath of thick light hair wrapping around the base of his skull, Rosebery conducted the choir with explosive energy. The singers could see it in his face, in his lively gestures, and in his own gorgeous voice, which he sometimes added to theirs.

After a year of revamping, the choir could sing a wide repertoire. It included Rosebery's own exercises and compositions, as well as adaptations, such as medieval madrigals, which particularly pleased him. Rosebery was not satisfied with the ordinary, even banal sort of music that other workers' choirs performed in Berlin. In his group, he saw people with musical promise, people just as musically capable as those who could afford private lessons and opera tickets.

Toward the end of 1923, Rosebery decided that his singing community was ready for a preliminary debut. Their first semipublic concert took place on November 25 at the Neue Welt concert hall in Neukölln. To open, the choir performed a duet from Handel's *Judas Maccabaeus* and ended with *Der freie Mann*, by Beethoven. After two other preliminary concerts, the Rosebery d'Arguto Singing Community made its public debut on December 23.

Though these early concerts did not draw significant attention, over the first half of 1924, the choir achieved breakthrough success. Soon they were performing in prominent cultural venues across Berlin, including the Hochschule für Musik, the old Philharmonie, and the Großes Schauspielhaus. The choir also performed at many working-class venues, such as the Saalbau Friedrichshain, Irmers Festsälen, and frequently at the Neue Welt. Reviewers in both the leftist and bourgeois press began to note an astonishing level of artistic quality achieved under Rosebery. Newspapers praised the unique sound the choir created, describing it as sharper, throatier, and coarser than the ideal other German choirs sought, yet rousing and refined in its own surprising way. The press often compared it to choirs in the east, such as those in Ukraine.

Over the next few years, Rosebery's choir received steady praise. In 1926, a review in the *Dresdner Volkszeitung* noted that "The flow, the undulating and surging of the voices is fascinating." One bourgeois critic wrote, "Rosebery d'Arguto has tremendous vision. . . . The critical seer in him even includes politics in the flow of ideas, rejecting any and all clichés of racial hatred as a concern of capitalism." The communist newspaper *Die Rote Fahne* wrote, "We must openly say that we know of no other musical organization in Germany which could even distantly rival the *Gesangsgemeinschaft* in terms of either technical execution or love and joy of singing itself."

What with the praise in the mainstream press and the chatter in leftist circles, new members flocked to the choir, and it grew to over two hundred members with an additional children's choir, one hundred strong. At a range of events, including rallies for the German Communist and

Social Democratic Parties, Rosebery conducted the singers as they roused audiences around Berlin. At his direction, the choir even performed at the Plötzensee Prison. While they sang, one prisoner in the audience began to cry. At the end of the performance, the man fell to his knees before Rosebery, and after expressing his deep gratitude for the performance, begged him to repeat one song that had particularly touched him. Emmy Schmidt, a choir member present that day, remembered how the man's plea brought several choir members to tears. When the choir finished, Rosebery told them that their singing had been enchantingly beautiful as never before.

THOUGH ROSEBERY NEVER quibbled with positive press, most important to him was what the choir meant to the workers of Berlin, both the singers themselves and the people who attended the performances. The audience, often hundreds overflowing a concert hall, would erupt in cheers and applause at the end of a song or the finale of a performance. Not only was the level of music first-rate; just as important, the workers felt drawn to Rosebery because of his personality and passion as a composer and conductor. Rosebery understood how to turn a trite folk song into a choral work that one member described as a "strike right at the heart." During the performances, choir members marveled at his ability as a conductor. His hands seemed to speak, his facial expressions—lively, passionate— aroused eager and wholehearted singing.

From the time he took over the choir, Rosebery built a community of working-class Berliners centered around the practice and appreciation of music. For one member, Ernst Schmidt, rehearsals were "an enhancement of the feeling of being alive." He and many others studied Rosebery as a personality, this small man with intelligent, kindly eyes, who always dressed elegantly, who completely immersed himself in his method, in his music. Claire Weigel, another member, loved him for his idealism, for his belief in the good in people and the conviction that a better future, especially for workers, was upon them. Rosebery's bald head also left a mark on Claire. Ever since meeting him, she adored bald men, though she never saw a dome as pretty as her choirmaster's.

Perhaps most joyous, most triumphant about the choir was the sentiment the workers felt—that they, the simple folk, the proletarians who possessed no artistic education or regard from the upper classes, could achieve something so remarkable. These laborers, especially the politically active ones, had long felt oppressed by the wealthier stratum of German society, who, they believed, stymied their growth, both intellectually and musically. With Rosebery, these men and women experienced something they had never had before—an awakening of the creative source and skill within them.

Rosebery's goal extended beyond building a well-loved workers' choir. Soon the Rosebery d'Arguto Singing Community added a dance group, a singing school, and a support group for unemployed workers. Under the umbrella of the *Kunstgemeinschaft Rosebery d'Arguto*, or the Rosebery d'Arguto Art Community, they performed in ensemble fashion with a dance component, sometimes even accompanied by an instrumental group. Rosebery wished to build a community around music and progressive solidarity, to offer to the working class the chance to make and witness art at a high level, unaccompanied by the snobbery of the upper classes. The choir often performed when there was a reason to celebrate— a birthday, a festival, at Jugendweihe ceremonies, where parents marked the secular coming-of-age of their children. Several couples got married after meeting at rehearsals. In his artistic community, Rosebery and the members always adhered to a flat social structure, eschewing exclusion or haughtiness as the choir gained status. One young choir member remembered being shocked when he was rebuked by an older member for addressing him with the formal German word for "you."

The members of the choir loved Rosebery for his dedication and musical skill. Yet his humility and generosity affected them, too. Once, while at a restaurant with members of the choir, he learned one singer had lost his job. Without a second thought, he pulled the sausage from his sandwich and handed it to the man. Rosebery ate the bread alone. At Christmas, when he received some extra money from the sale of tickets to the choir's final performance of the year, he always asked the entire choir how many unemployed stood among them. Usually five or six singers raised their hands. Rosebery would then divide his bonus among them.

Often, after several hours rehearsing, Rosebery accompanied his singers to a neighborhood pub where workers went to drink beer. On weekends, he embarked on hikes and singing trips in the countryside surrounding Berlin. Sometimes he and the choir traveled to Dresden or the mountains of Saxon Switzerland 30 miles farther southeast for a week or even two. On their outdoor strolls, he instructed his members to seek music in nature. He might point to a brook to make them aware of the sound and rhythm of its murmuring. He led the group in song as they walked through the forest. One member recalled belting out a song that went, *Today we march to the farmer's night quarters. A cup of tea, chocolate, coffee, and a glass of wine. In the east the young day is blooming.*

Rosebery and his singers often traveled to villages around Brandenburg, where they performed for the locals on farms or at inns. If they roamed too far from Berlin to return the same night, they often stretched out, all together, on stacks of hay in a farmer's barn after chatting late into the darkness. On one such trip, choir member Käthe Jurr remembered, she awoke at dawn to hear Rosebery humming and whispering to himself. She heard him say, "Yes, that's it." Later in the day, when she confessed that she'd overheard him composing, he flashed a mischievous smile at her.

THE YEARS AFTER Rosebery took the helm of the choir in 1922 and before Hitler rose to power were the most artistically fruitful and fulfilling of his life. Aside from a setback in 1927, when a faction of radical singers split from the choir to form their own group, the Rosebery d'Arguto Singing Community flourished and garnered praise from audiences and the press alike.

What Rosebery achieved is clearly evident in how the choir members reflected on these years later in life. Though thirty, even forty years might have passed, and they could have idealized or romanticized the time, they spoke with eager and undivided affection for Rosebery and the choir. Under Rosebery's direction, they felt empowered, self-assured. They could stir a crowd, rouse them to their feet in vigorous applause. Through music, the choir assured the audience—workers themselves—that they were an important class of people, not the dregs of society, incapable of taking part in culture and art. The citizens of Neukölln knew that the bourgeois classes had choirs and ensembles composed of professional singers or amateurs with enough training to imitate them. They also understood that because of their social standing, they could not join the many singing societies in the city. But none of that mattered. The Rosebery d'Arguto Singing Community made them realize that their brothers and sisters, mothers and fathers, daughters and sons could sing in a choir and make an audience explode with enthusiasm. The choir could perform so well that even the bourgeois newspaper critics traveled to the southeast of Berlin to sit in the audience and then write positive reviews for the next day's edition. Bringing music to the masses—this was perhaps Rosebery's greatest achievement.

When not rehearsing, Rosebery often composed and arranged music for the choir. He pushed the boundaries of what an ensemble like his could do. He introduced his singers to a concept he called Absolute Symphonic Chants, in which the group, divided into six or eight parts, sang an arrangement with vocables but no recognizable words. The polyphony resembled an orchestra; in effect, each section of the choir represented a part of an ensemble—their voices were the violins and cellos and wind instruments. He wanted the audience to focus solely on melody and harmonies, to find a purity in music unencumbered by a verbal message. Rosebery also saw great value in this for the singers. With these chants, he sought to free them from the burden of communicating a text. He wanted them to let their voices flow without the need to vocalize the consonant-heavy, often lengthy, words of the German language. He wanted them to breathe, to feel the vibrations of their vocal chords. And so the Rosebery d'Arguto Singing Community continued throughout the 1920s and into the new decade—a place of pride and community in Neukölln, a darling of the press. Rosebery, likely more so than ever in his life, felt contented.

Yet that feeling quickly eroded in the early 1930s. In 1933, Hitler became chancellor of Germany. Later that year, the Reich Chamber of Music, part of the newly established Reich Chamber of Culture, began to set its eyes on workers' choirs around the country. These musical groups presented easy yet important targets. They were the people Hitler saw as enemies—communists, social democrats, anarchists. The first thing the Chamber of Culture did was to force all choirs to join choral unions, which the government controlled. Convinced as Rosebery was that Nazi domination of Germany would be short-lived, and focused above all on his choir, he did not publicly object, and soon the Rosebery d'Arguto Singing Community began to acquiesce to the demands of the authorities. The line "Member of the Reich Chamber of Culture through the choral union" even began to appear on the choir's letterhead. Rosebery also adapted the music of the choir to appease the authorities. He changed its repertoire, moving away from workers' songs and focusing on German folk music, which the Nazis viewed favorably.

The year 1933 also marked the start of direct Nazi harassment of Rosebery. On June 20, the authorities arrested him, ostensibly for political activities. Following a written objection from his choir members, the authorities released him six weeks later and allowed him to continue directing the choir. The arrest, at least his fifth over the course of his time in Berlin, surely troubled Rosebery. Yet it did not unsettle him enough to force a change in his life. He did not go into exile, as other prominent cultural figures had begun to do. Nevertheless, the city and country he had long loved was changing.

Throughout 1934, Rosebery continued to lead the choir and take on private students. In August 1935, however, the Reich Chamber of Culture began enforcing their orders and policies with far more stringency. First, they rejected his application to be a member of the Reich Chamber of Music. The official reason as stated in the letter was that he did not possess the "necessary aptitude in the sense of the National Socialist state leadership." A month later, after the enactment of the Nuremberg Laws on September 15, the authorities informed the choir that "the conductor of the Gesangsgemeinschaft Rosebery d'Arguto, Prof. Rosebery d'Arguto (Rosenberg), as a member of the Jewish race," was to be "prohibited" from public participation in an upcoming performance of several Berlin choirs. Though the choir made a pledge of loyalty to Rosebery, it was clear that the situation would only grow worse. In late November, he was definitively denied membership in the Reich Chamber of Music.

For a few weeks, Rosebery continued to work with the choir. But on December 20, the authorities sent him a letter saying that for each time he violated their rules, he would be fined up to 1,000 reichsmarks, a substantial sum. This decree marked the end of Rosebery's professional life in Germany. By then, most workers' choirs had already been dismantled or harnessed under Nazi control. That the Rosebery d'Arguto Singing Community remained under Rosebery's conductorship as late as it did was an exception. Nevertheless, in a matter of just two years of Hitler's rule, the choir that Rosebery had dedicated his life to since 1922 was taken from him. What was more, from then on, the Nazis banned him from doing any sort of musical work, unless he was doing it with Jews.

Adrift in a version of Berlin he recognized less and less, Rosebery sometimes watched from the gallery as the choir rehearsed under its new conductor. Occasionally, he joined members on a weekend trip, a bitter reminder of the pastoral excursions he led in the late 1920s. One night, he attended the choir's performance at a movie theater in Neukölln. Now the choir no longer bore his name. It performed as the Gesangsgemeinschaft 1917 (the Singing Community 1917). The singers knew that their beloved former conductor was in the audience, awaiting their program—a program that he himself had taught them just months before. Many of them felt a deep sense of distress, so much so that when their conductor gestured for them to begin, they made three false starts, and even after that they were too befuddled to get the opening right. Herbert Schroeter recalled the immense sadness of having to look down at Rosebery, seated in the audience. Singing seemed nearly impossible to Herbert with Rosebery no longer standing before his choir.

Throughout 1936 and 1937, Rosebery scraped by, secretly taking on students in his flat in the western Berlin locality of Charlottenburg. Teaching in secret, however, was short-lived. In 1937, someone tipped off the authorities that he was giving lessons to non-Jewish students. One day, the police burst in and caught him in the middle of a lesson. With proof that he had been breaking Nazi laws, the authorities imposed the ruinous 1,000-reichsmark fine on him, a sum that in his own estimation constituted nearly a year of his earnings.

By September 1937, Rosebery's life was in pieces. He tried to negotiate with the authorities over the fine, but they refused to lower it, even though he had no way of earning a living. He was solely dependent on his fast-diminishing savings. Despite his troubles, he refused to lose faith in a better future for himself in Germany, something he explained when, in the third week of the month, his teenage nephew, Justus Rosenberg, the son of his brother Jacob, came to visit him. For several days, Rosebery and Justus took walks around Berlin, discussed music and politics, reposed in Rosebery's flat. Despite his troubles, Rosebery still lived in a spacious and well-furnished residence, which he likely paid for with dividends from stock he had received from his father years before. A grand piano and an upright piano, with candle holders near the stand to shine light on the sheet music, took up much of one room. On the wall above the instruments hung a replica life mask of Beethoven, one of Rosebery's favorite composers. During the visit, Rosebery, despite the turmoil of his life, seemed to Justus to be utterly focused on his choral music, which he talked about at length. The conversations spilled over into the night, when Rosebery took Justus to restaurants in Berlin still friendly to Jews.

On most days, Rosebery wore his fine suits, even though his professional life was, in effect, over. He told Justus that the Nazis were simply an evil wind that would soon pass. After all, how could a society that produced Beethoven and Goethe descend any further?

Perhaps Rosebery's unwavering belief in the German people came from how bound he was to their culture. With the exception of his love for several Polish composers, he had long felt little connection to the country of his birth, which in his years of absence had changed considerably. After nearly three decades in Berlin, Rosebery spoke fluent, nuanced German. He didn't celebrate Polish or Jewish traditions, religious or otherwise. Though he did take some nostalgic joy in traditional Polish music, he was far removed from the life and culture of his homeland, and of his father, who still lived in the two-story stone house in Mława.

In the months after Justus left for Paris at the end of September, 1937, Rosebery realized that his hope had been misplaced. He continued to negotiate with the authorities over the fine, employing creative arguments and calling on the Polish embassy in Berlin for help, but to no avail. It was only then that Rosebery, mourning the complete loss of his world, once again fled a country, leaving Berlin for Warsaw. Before he left his flat, he hired movers to take his grand piano, together with several trunks of his belongings, and transport them to the residence of Wilhelm Becker, the administrator of the choir, and his wife Agnes. When he saw Agnes that day, he told her that he didn't believe he would be gone for long.

Among the last things Rosebery did before leaving Berlin was to put all of his compositions, a collection built over decades, as well as books and musical publications and his own personal writings, into a cabinet in the cellar of the building where he resided. When he returned, he told himself, he would draw upon the ideas and skills from his entire career to write a groundbreaking book on vocal pedagogy and choral music.

FOR THE REMAINDER of 1938 and into 1939, Rosebery worked several jobs, mainly on a freelance basis at a conservatory in Warsaw. He made trips to Mława, an hour and a half by train from the city, to visit his father, sister, and several other family members on Niborska Street. For a short time, he was even involved in a Jewish girls' choir in town.

Midway through 1939, Rosebery learned that the Nazi government had begun to allow Polish-Jews expelled from Germany on short notice— especially during the *Polenaktion* in October 1938—to return on a temporary visa to liquidate their residences, hand over businesses to the state, or settle other affairs permanently. In late August, he traveled to Berlin on a short-term visa. Back in his beloved city, he spent time with old friends and did his best to close up his life in Germany for good. When German forces invaded Poland on September 1, he knew the situation had become extremely dangerous for him.

Rosebery spent his last day in Berlin in Rudow, a quarter of Neukölln, the borough where he had lived so much of his adult life. He passed the afternoon with Catenia von Malottki, a dancer with whom he'd had a romantic relationship in the late 1920s and early 1930s. With Tenja, as he called her, Rosebery saw many of his old friends from the choir. He told them that he planned to report to the police station to obtain an exit visa before leaving. Everyone begged him not to, pleading that he leave immediately for Switzerland or another country not under the control of the Nazis. Despite the warnings of his friends, on September 2 or 3, he walked through the doors of the police station at Zoologischer Garten to request the visa. The authorities detained him as a citizen of an enemy state. On September 13, together with many other Berlin Jews, the police forced him onto a northbound train destined for the Sachsenhausen concentration camp.

Chapter 7

⌒

From the Oranienburg train station, Rosebery and hundreds of other Jews began their forced march to Sachsenhausen. Like Rosebery, many of the other prisoners were Polish by nationality but had spent years, even their entire lives, in Germany. Flanked by Death's Head Units, the SS who guarded Sachsenhausen, they were marched quickly through town. Often, when new prisoners arrived in Oranienburg, the townspeople emerged from their homes or shops to gawk. Leon Szalet, a Jew of Polish origin who arrived around the same time as Rosebery, remembered townspeople sneering at him, bloodthirsty, shouting "Kill the Bromberg murderers!" and "Blood for blood!" Some hurled rocks and lengths of wood. Upon arrival, the SS registered Rosebery as prisoner number 9299.

During Rosebery's first weeks at Sachsenhausen, the SS confined him and hundreds of other Jews in barracks 37, 38, and 39 in the little camp. He and the men had no beds or tables or stools to use. And the SS had far more heinous plans in store for the Jewish prisoners of Sachsenhausen. Harry Naujoks, a German communist prisoner of high status who held the functionary position of camp elder, remembered that a few weeks before the Jews were marched into the camp, the SS ordered the air shafts on barracks 37, 38, and 39 to be boarded up and then sealed with paper and glue. In barracks 38, where Rosebery and Leon were held, the SS or block elders made the prisoners do sport through much of the day in the stinking, airless space. Rosebery suffered from the push-ups, knee bends, and sprints that Aleks did some eight months later. But unlike Aleks, he carried a slight paunch and lacked the strength and resilience of a man fit and in his early twenties. Between sessions, Leon remembered, the block elder sometimes forced everyone to lie on their stomachs with their hands crossed behind their backs. Other times, they attacked them with the legs of wooden stools or forced them to lie on the floor so they could trample them.

The heat became unbearable. When the men did push-ups and squats, it seemed to Leon that their sweat vaporized. The room turned as steamy as a Turkish bath. If a man had to urinate, he did so on the floor. If he had to defecate, he held it in until he absolutely had to relieve himself. Asking to use the toilet was reason enough for the block elders to beat a man.

At night, prisoners feared suffocation. Squeezed in with over a hundred men in each wing of the barracks, they lay on straw mattresses, sweating, agonizing, dying. With no water to drink, they licked up the salty droplets of perspiration clinging to the windows or their bodies. They drank their own urine.

The SS frequently assembled the Jews after hours of sport or labor and forced them to sing, sometimes for hours on end. Exhausted and with little in their bellies, many of them found it nearly unbearable to sing cheerful German folk songs. Yet sing they did. They had no choice.

On one occasion, several SS guards entered the barracks.

"Can you sing?" one guard asked the group. The prisoners responded with an emphatic "Yes."

Since they had not decided what they would sing, each man belted out a song of his own choosing. The SS men listened for several minutes to the discordant, earsplitting mess of music, and then interrupted. Leon Szalet remembered one guard shouting, "This isn't a synagogue." The guards began to beat them severely. When the pummeling ceased, Leon recalled, Rosebery stepped forward, stood at attention, and said, "I am a professor of music; may I lead the prisoners in song?"

"So, a professor. Not a doctor?" one guard responded before striking Rosebery across the head. Rosebery fell to the ground. Blood trickled from his forehead.

"Stand up!" the guards screamed.

Rosebery clambered to his feet.

"Come forward and show us your degenerate art."

Rosebery was pale. The only color in his face was the red of the blood on his forehead. Unsteady on his feet, he wiped the blood with the back of his hand and tried to compose himself.

"We will sing 'Das Roeslein auf der Heiden'" ("Little Rose on the Heath"), Rosebery said, choosing the German folk song, his voice breaking.

The prisoners who knew the song began to sing. Those who didn't pretended to know it, lest the SS punish them. The guards listened for a time, and then shouted stop.

"Professor, step forward," a guard screamed. "You Jewish dung. First you said you were a professor, and now you act as if you were the governess of these scoundrels and sing nursery songs." The guard beat Rosebery until he lay on the barracks floor, motionless.

TOWARD THE END of the month, on Yom Kippur of 1939, the SS beat the men in Rosebery's barracks with more ferocity than usual. They knew the importance of the day and wanted to disrupt it. When the SS had had their fill and left the barracks, Leon took note of what happened. He remembered the pain and the fear he felt that the SS would return, as they had threatened to do. Through a crack in the boarded window, he saw a cloudless sky, set with sparkling stars. The moon shone faintly into the barracks, giving the faces of the men around him a pale, ghostly appearance. Then a voice broke the silence. In a mournful tone, a man began to sing the Kol Nidre, a prayer performed at synagogues on the eve of the Day of

Atonement. Leon raised his aching body to see where the voice was coming from. Up against a barracks wall, an old man whom Leon and others admired for his piety and quiet strength was the source of the music. For Leon, the prayer seemed to lift the other prisoners from their stupor of pain and fatigue. He watched as the eyes of men around him searched the darkness and fixed on the singer. At the end of the chant, the old man softened his voice. It quavered. "When at last he was silent," Leon wrote, "there was exaltation among us, an exaltation which men can experience only when they have fallen as low as we had fallen and then, through the mystic power of a deathless prayer, had awakened once more to the world of the spirit." Around midnight, the SS made good on their threat. A group of them entered the barracks and assaulted the prisoners.

The conditions Rosebery and the other Jews underwent lasted for seventeen days until, at the end of September of 1939, a senior SS guard entered the barracks. He announced that the campaign for Poland had ended with victory and ordered the boards covering the windows to be removed. Though those terrible, breathless weeks had ended, Rosebery had fallen into depression. Prisoners who knew him before the war hardly recognized him. He was wretched, his body shrunken and malnourished. Not yet fifty, he was wasting away.

For the men confined in barracks 38, the first three weeks at Sachsenhausen had made the intentions of the Nazis absolutely clear. The torture they faced was not the product of a single deranged SS guard or prisoner functionary; the horror of it was not arbitrary. It was part of a precise plan of annihilation, and they knew it.

For the Jewish prisoners in the little camp, the abuse signaled what was to come, and for the first time, Rosebery and the other men had to face the fact that they likely would not leave the camp alive. Hans Hüttner, a Jewish prisoner confined to neighboring barracks 39 and a friend of Rosebery's, recalled that most of the men in his block believed that resistance was pointless. The Nazis held complete control. In their free time, few prisoners plotted against the SS. Instead, they chatted wistfully about the foods they loved, their favorite hobbies, their lives before the war.

AS ROSEBERY SANK deeper into despondency after the first weeks in Sachsenhausen, several prisoners decided they had to intervene. To them he was a significant figure, perhaps not as famous or influential as Bertolt Brecht or Hanns Eisler but well known and loved in leftist Berlin circles. In prisoners such as Hans Hüttner and Gerhard Schwarz, who advocated for him in the politically active barracks 39, Rosebery had allies.

Soon, his situation improved. He began to receive extra food. Other prisoners of influence started to protect him, especially the German political prisoners, many of whom were seasoned communists and sympathetic to a leftist choirmaster. Through the help of Hans, Gerhard, and a third man who worked at the camp office and had admired Rosebery's music before the war, Rosebery got transferred from the brickworks and assigned to the indoor squad, a much less demanding job under the supervision of the block elder in barracks 38. Alongside what Leon described as some of the least deserving prisoners—men who got their jobs based on their willingness to do the block elder's dirty work—Rosebery served food at mealtimes. According to Leon, Rosebery remained stubborn and candid, even in a position such as this, where he wielded extraordinary power: control over how much food the others received. The authority never corrupted him. In fact, he often expressed in no uncertain terms the contempt he felt for his fellow workers. Yet, no matter what he said, no matter whom he angered, no prisoner dared to lay a hand on him. He had the backing of the influential political prisoners and the protection it provided. Instead, they treated him as an old crackpot.

The extra food and protection revived Rosebery. He regained some strength, grew more active, and engaged more with the men in his barracks. Hans even remembered him singing from time to time for the other prisoners, who were quickly drawn to this eccentric yet engaging man.

In early 1940, the SS and block leaders' compulsion to torture Jewish prisoners seemed to wane somewhat. For the first time, circumstances had lined up in a way that might allow Rosebery to do something he had long contemplated: form a clandestine Jewish choir. He would have to be extremely discreet. If word got back to the wrong block elder or just about any SS guard, he and those involved could face vicious, even deadly punishment. With great care, he spread the word around the Jewish barracks about his plans. Prisoners whispered the message: A certain Rosebery d'Arguto of barracks 38 seeks prisoners of any age or musical skill to join a secret choir. As he had done in Berlin before the war, he approached the camp choir in the belief that with the right direction and pedagogy, anyone could sing. In little time, some two and a half dozen Jewish men of different backgrounds and ages volunteered. Even a few teenagers, some of Sachsenhausen's most vulnerable prisoners, joined.

Finding volunteers proved the easy part. A more serious challenge now stood before Rosebery: where could the choir rehearse? His own barracks 38 had a criminal prisoner as a block elder. Though the criminal prisoners were not necessarily cruel, the one who ran barracks 38 was. A man like him might rat out the choir to the SS. He posed a significant risk. Barracks 39, just a few steps from 38, struck Rosebery as a possibility. It held the more politically active Jews like Hans Hüttner, and its block elder was a German political inmate, likely a communist arrested in one of Hitler's dragnets of the 1930s. After some discreet enquiries, Rosebery got the permission he needed from the block elder of barracks 39. Soon, the choir assembled, likely in the window of time after the evening roll call and before lights out. Hans attended one of the first rehearsals. Rosebery exchanged a few words with each man, listening to the tone and timbre of his voice, perhaps feeling his neck or shoulders, and then assigned him to one of four sections. One prisoner who volunteered was Max Hüttner, Hans's cousin. Max was a classically trained musician, a violinist who before the war had performed in some of Berlin's major concert halls, such as the Großes Schauspielhaus and Wallner Theater. Rosebery's skill astounded Max, not only his sense of where to place each man without hearing him sing, but also his ability to name any note just by hearing it. Later, in a private moment, Max told Hans that he believed Rosebery had perfect pitch.

Leading a choir in a Nazi camp proved an extremely tall order. Prisoners rarely had time to themselves, and even before bed, in the hour or so when they could sometimes do as they pleased, the block elder or SS men might burst in to inspect the barracks or make the prisoners do sport. A network of SS informants also posed a significant risk. For Rosebery to succeed, discretion and secrecy were essential. Over time, and with the help of several influential prisoners, he devised a system for when and how the choir should gather. When a window of time seemed safe, he and the members would find their way to barracks 39, where they rehearsed in one wing of the building. They always made a carefully chosen prisoner serve as the lookout, lest a guard or a prisoner they didn't trust pass or enter the barracks. Hans sometimes played this role. He would stand in the corner holding a rag, pretending to clean something. Though tasked with keeping the lookout, he could not help but glance over at Rosebery standing before the choir. He noticed that Rosebery appeared to sing with the choir, although Hans could not hear his voice. It turned out that Rosebery sang with what he called a "head voice," a soft falsetto, which the choir members could hear but the audience could not.

During rehearsals or in spare moments, Rosebery worked tirelessly with each member. He grew obsessed with the choir and its music, spending the little free time he had instructing the singers or creating compositions or adaptations. Even though the circumstances were starkly different from his workers' choir in Berlin five years earlier, he still knew how to draw out beautiful songs from singers with no musical education. Despite their constant need to dodge the SS and the threat of death looming all around them, the choir quickly achieved an impressive level of refinement. Hans never joined the choir, but regularly listened in on its rehearsals. He could not believe the music he heard. Rosebery, Hans realized, could sing every part of each composition or adaptation. He knew every bar, every note of the music. He could teach the melody and harmonies to these men who, with few exceptions, had lived as shop owners, traders, workers, distant from music but for the odd film or accordion performance in the neighborhood bar.

Rosebery described the founding of the Jewish choir to Aleks as they got to know each other. He recounted how the choir rehearsed whenever possible during the spring of 1940 before Aleks arrived at Sachsenhausen, how much he loved to work with the singers, especially during those still moments when they could all assemble in relative safety. It was such a rehearsal that formed the foundation of their friendship, the evening when Aleks, recently arrived at the camp, snuck into the barracks on the recommendation of Bolek Marcinek and found himself astounded, watching the man who had taken a blow to the face for him conducting a choir. That night began the most pivotal relationship of Aleks's life.

THE TEMPERATURE CONTINUED to drop in the autumn of 1940. Rosebery worked on the indoor squad, which left him enough strength to rehearse with his choir. Aleks was not as lucky. After nearly four months in the camp, the block elder informed the men in his barracks that they would soon be put to work. Aleks knew this meant joining the thousands who toiled as slave laborers of the Nazi state.

To the distress of Aleks and many of the men in his barracks, the camp administration assigned them to the brickworks. Starting early on in their incarceration, they had heard rumors about this work detail. It was known as the deadliest of all assignments. Men perished by the dozen some days, and the survivors had to haul their corpses back to the camp at night to be counted on the roll call square. Would the brickworks be worse than sport? No one knew whether to rejoice at the end of one evil or to fear the unknown ahead.

On Aleks's first day, a bell sounded before the sun rose. After three-quarters of an hour to wash and dress, he and the other men devoured a meager breakfast—likely a form of coffee made of burnt root vegetables. Then, with dawn just breaking, they formed rows outside their barracks. Once each man was accounted for, the SS marched them through the gates and a little over a mile's distance to the Oder-Havel Canal, beating them with clubs or flogging their backs with whips. Children often chucked stones at them as they marched.

What stood before Aleks when the march ended was the world's largest brickworks. Hundreds of prisoners scurried about, carrying sacks of sand, stumbling, falling, beaten by foremen. From then on, Aleks would be forging bricks to be sent by barge to Berlin. His labor and that of the others would help build Hitler's grand capital, "Germania."

It didn't take long for Aleks to realize that the rumors were true: the brickworks was brutal. On most days, some two thousand prisoners marched to the canal where the SS worked them at a brutal pace, trying to meet a tight production schedule. As temperatures plummeted and the first snows arrived, he and the other men shivered for want of any shelter.

Aleks coped with the torturous work by composing verses in his head. Some he intended to set to music, others he thought were fine as they were, poems that recorded their labor and suffering. Lost in thought about a love interest from before the war, he wrote these verses as he struggled at the canal: *Water flows to Berlin, black and dirty water. / You are far away, so young, so marvelous. / A crow drinks the black water, / Tell me, love, have you cheated, / I will survive—I will survive. / Water, water, cursed black water.*

To survive, Aleks had to find a way to get transferred. Inmates of high standing could switch work with relative ease. After all, prisoner functionaries had much say as to who was assigned to which labor detail or barracks. To some extent they could even control food rations. As a new prisoner, Aleks had yet to build connections that could get him off the brickworks. It would become his priority.

It was around this time that Rosebery decided his choir was ready for its first performance. After coordinating with several German political prisoners, who were best informed about the safest time for the choir and its audience to assemble, Rosebery chose an evening. Within a tight network of Jewish prisoners, the word went around. It was passed from man to man, among trusted comrades, always hushed so that a malevolent block elder or an SS informant would not overhear. A more public gathering would likely put Rosebery and the choir at the most risk, more so than when they just met to rehearse. An organized performance, with a Jewish choir and a Jewish audience crammed into a barracks, might appear to be subversion to the SS, reason enough to snuff out Rosebery's life and those of his singers.

Rosebery took great care, and the SS did not find out about his plans. On the designated night, in the fall of 1940, a small group of prisoners emptied one wing of barracks 39 of its mattresses and furniture. The audience began to arrive, mostly Jews. Several German communists likely came, too, though Rosebery had only entrusted a few of them with knowledge of the choir. Aleks also knew about the performance. He walked the short distance from his block and slipped into barracks 39, where he joined what seemed like an audience of over two hundred men. Because of how secretive Rosebery and everyone involved had been, in all likelihood the men in the many neighboring barracks—the Czechs, the Poles—had no clue a Jewish choir performance was about to begin. Once the audience had settled in, Rosebery gestured to the choir of about twenty-five men.

From the first moments, the pure male voices, the harmonies Rosebery could draw out from this group of untrained, unmusical concentration camp prisoners, astonished the men in the audience. At any moment, a group of passing SS guards could storm in, cudgels raised to beat the men to death. Perhaps that sense of tension made the scene all the more powerful. Perhaps it was Rosebery's charisma that mesmerized the audience. To Hans and Aleks, watching from the back, Rosebery seemed a mythical figure, standing slightly bent over, hands aloft gracefully forming and shaping each man's voice, coaxing their voices into a whole. That Rosebery could organize a choir and a performance was amazing enough. That it could perform at such a high level in a wing of a Jewish barracks in a Nazi concentration camp was nearly beyond belief. Hans sat in awe. Rosebery seemed to take on an ethereal quality. His face glowed. His eyes shone, burning with passion. With his gestures, with the expressions on his face, he controlled the choir as if it were under a spell. Like Hans, Aleks marveled at the scene. He, too, felt that Rosebery had taken on an almost supernatural quality. He thought: he has hypnotized his singers.

When the performance ended, pride swelled among the Jews in attendance, pride and the feeling of incredulity that art so moving could exist in a barracks at Sachsenhausen, in a place where every prisoner incessantly wondered, *will I survive tomorrow?* After hearing Rosebery's choir, Hans and many other men in the audience that night felt a new sense of strength. The music boosted their spirits in a way that little else could do. As Hans saw it, Rosebery wanted to give the singers and the men in the barracks alike a reminder of beauty, if only for a short time. For Gerhard Schwarz, a political prisoner and a man who knew Rosebery's music from before the war, the choir struck him as an act of unbelievable defiance, a means to resist the Nazis who had stolen their freedom and tormented them. It was as though the prisoners could say to their captors, in their minds, and now by their songs, *Though you've robbed us of our freedom and safety, you can never take everything from us. We can still make music.*

At the end of the choir's first performance, everyone returned to their assigned barracks. Aleks strode the short distance to block 15. Rosebery slipped back into block 38. Inside block 39, prisoners returned the mattresses and furniture to their places in the sleeping room. Stillness returned to the little camp. Aleks went to sleep. The music lingered.

WITNESSING THE JEWISH choir's first performance left Aleks even more fixated on Rosebery and the idea of music in the camp. When the choir performed, he soaked up the music with the kind of intensity and eagerness that he'd felt as a boy. He also watched how the other prisoners in the audience reacted, the awe in their expressions. The music buoyed them, filled them with elation. It was definitive proof of what he already believed: that music, even surrounded by the brutality and hatred of a Nazi concentration camp, was a force for life. It could serve as a source of inspiration and pride for the prisoners, from whom nearly every bit of freedom and autonomy had been stolen, where each move they made, each word they spoke, each morsel of food they ingested, fell under the edicts of their torturers.

IN THE WEEKS after the Jewish choir's first performance, Rosebery and
Aleks spent more time together. Rosebery, somewhat recovered in energy
and spirit, poured himself into his work with the choir, spending any free
time he had rehearsing the group or, when this was too dangerous, seeking out individual members or composing or creating adaptations on his
own. Of course, he had no blank sheet music, or even a pencil, so any melodies he came up with had to be committed to memory.

In Rosebery, Aleks found the musical mentor he had long sought. He
also felt a sense of honor, of self-worth, that a man of such stature and
import would become a close confidant. Rosebery carried himself with
grace and humility, never flaunting his title of professor, never seeking the
sympathy of others, never decrying the injustice that led to his imprisonment. As Aleks saw it, Rosebery was a person who stubbornly accepted his
lot in life, no matter how dreadful it might be. Even when it became known
around the camp that he came from wealth, he never acted snobbishly the
way other prisoners who were privileged before the war often did. In fact,
privilege and excess seemed anathema to everything he believed in and all
the work he had dedicated his life to.

When Aleks and Rosebery met, they sometimes spoke about their previous lives, but they mostly talked about music. Music united them. It
was what they each held most dear in these horrible circumstances. They
discussed the composers they loved and what music meant to them. Rosebery spoke of his admiration for illustrious European composers, such
as Edvard Grieg and Felix Mendelssohn and beloved Poles Władysław
Żeleński and Józef Nikorowicz. Sometimes they spoke about popular
music—of the tangos that were so widespread before the war, especially in
Poland. Rosebery once told Aleks that he couldn't stand jazz adaptations
of folk tunes, though he tolerated jazz in its pure, creative form.

Rosebery was the first true composer with whom Aleks formed a close
relationship. Until then, composers and performers, even the minor figures Aleks admired in Kraków's cabarets, seemed distant, impossible to
meet, moving in social circles closed off to him. In all likelihood, Rose-

bery was also the first Jew Aleks got to know closely. Throughout Aleks's life, Jews were always present. As a child, he played soccer with Jewish boys in Nowy Wiśnicz in the summer when he visited his grandparents. Several Jews attended his school and sat near him at university lectures. He caught sight of their weddings, he patronized their shops. He loved the cantor's musical prayers and Jewish funeral music. Yet rarely did he mix with Jews. Instead, he tended to view them with a certain suspicion or doubt. For Aleks, the Jewish community had been segregated from his world, a mystery. Through friendship with Rosebery, that changed. The views he had had before the war faded as Rosebery taught him scores of Jewish songs, hummed him the melodies, and spoke of his life and work. Jewish music had always seemed slightly taboo to Aleks, though he was not exactly sure why. No longer. The music Rosebery shared both inspired and soothed him. He admired its scope and vividness. He could feel the lamentations of the sad songs, the delight of the happy songs. He pondered the mysteries of the allegorical pieces.

Rosebery dazzled Aleks with his erudition. Here was a bona fide musician, a man who not only understood the great masterworks of the past but had also been at the forefront of advancing music before the Germans ended his career. Here was an innovator, a pedagogical reformer, bringing culture to the workers of Berlin through new techniques and ideas. He had published dozens of articles in musical journals across the German-speaking world. And yet the country of his birth had stripped him of his citizenship. The country he adopted and loved, where he had spent most of his adult life, had persecuted him throughout the 1930s, robbed him of his choir, and finally incarcerated him in Sachsenhausen to die.

Aleks sensed that Rosebery never expected to find himself in a camp. Rosebery had long regarded Germany as a land with a superior culture, one that had produced many of his musical heroes. He seemed to wonder how such a country could descend to a state of barbarism, where so many hungered for war, sought territory that didn't belong to them, and were eager to kill to achieve their aims. Yet Rosebery's faith in the German people did not falter. Even the warnings of his brother, Jacob, who fled Danzig with his wife and daughter on a journey to British Palestine, did not convince him of the danger. When he crossed through the gates of Sachsenhausen, beginning what might become the final years of his life, he did not grow bitter, he did not capitulate. He organized a choir.

"I could not look at the people here, knowing that they were to die without ever having sung together," he told Aleks. "It would be a betrayal."

THE COMING WINTER spelled suffering. The uniforms the men wore did little to warm them when the snow began. At night in the barracks, they shivered, huddled together, feeding off of one another's warmth. Though a stove stood near the block elder's bed, rarely was there wood to burn.

With the temperatures dropping below zero, Aleks still toiled at the brickworks. Chunks of ice started to float by on the surface of the canal, and often the plank from the barge to the bank froze over too, leaving it slick. The guards took great pleasure in shaking the plank as prisoners walked across it, hoping that some of them might topple into the canal and drown in the frigid water. During those weeks, Aleks saw many men die in the canal's dark waters. From his first days at the brickworks, he knew this detail would kill him. With the freeze, his survival was even more doubtful.

Yet Aleks's network of connections had begun to elevate him in the prisoner hierarchy; it made a name for him. No longer was he just a number, one of thousands. In a move that surely saved his life, Aleks drew on these connections to get off the brickworks.

It was these same connections, in large part, that also helped Aleks switch barracks and transfer from block 15 in the little camp toward the end of 1940 to block 3, which stood in the first ring of barracks on the main campgrounds. Unlike block 15, which housed Poles who had been swept up in the waves of arrests when the Germans invaded their country, block 3 held people from several different countries, though the strongest presence consisted of Germans of high camp status, the ones who likely helped Aleks get this favorable block assignment. He quickly grew close to many Czech prisoners, too, including the communist Antonín Zápotocký, the cofounder and former secretary general of the Communist Party of Czechoslovakia. Living among such prisoners provided Aleks with slightly better living conditions and access to both information and the prisoner functionaries who held immense authority in the camp.

But it also meant leaving the little camp, which was a seismic change in Aleks's life. Up to that point, he had been surrounded by Poles, at least one of whom he knew before Sachsenhausen. During the initial few months at the camp, the Poles in his and neighboring barracks had built a tight-knit community, where a great spirit of solidarity formed among them. They had supported one another and tried to shield the weak and the old. On the one-year anniversary of the German invasion of Poland, they had gathered to commemorate the loss of their country. Aleks joined a group from Lublin and Cieszyn. The experience marked him strongly. Perhaps it was due to his friend Edward Janiuk's opening address, likely uttered in a hushed voice so as not to draw attention. Perhaps it was because he found himself united with a group of compatriots, many from his hometown on the Olza River. When Edward finished his introductory remarks, the poet Kazimierz Andrzej Jaworski rose and recited several of his verses. Then it was Aleks's turn. To surprise his audience, he chose the form of a tango. It being the anniversary of the German invasion of their homeland, he knew that the men before him would expect something patriotic, perhaps a march or an anthem to rouse their Polish pride. But Aleks's patriotism worked more subtly. His song flowed on a delicate and muted undercurrent of Polish symbols, like the red and white colors of Poland's flag: *When you come back, / at the start of summer, In white and red flowers —/ there will be nothing left of them.*

Aleks sang as tenderly as he could, making sure, however, to add a touch of menace to the song and a promise of retaliation against those who had destroyed his Poland. This was what the men seated before him craved. *Understand / that nothing is over / and no one will stamp out / our red blood.*

Leaving block 15, as Aleks and some other Poles had begun to do, meant an end to this camaraderie and the beginning of a wholly different camp experience. Now on the main campgrounds, Aleks found himself in a huge prison ecosystem with thousands of incarcerated men. He had to recalibrate, to learn quickly how the main camp functioned and to determine his place in it. In a way, it was as if he had been sent to a new camp altogether.

Leaving the little camp had another significant drawback; he was now far away from Rosebery and the Jewish choir. Officially, the SS forbade prisoners from the main camp to travel freely to the little camp, though in practice the rules at Sachsenhausen were contradictory, and prisoners with the right connections could sometimes circumvent them. For a time after Aleks joined the main campgrounds, he and Rosebery likely lost touch. Sometimes he heard news through a German political prisoner about a rehearsal or just an update as to Rosebery's situation, but for a while, the two men would not see each other.

Instead, Aleks occupied himself by settling in as best he could at the new camp barracks. He navigated this new world, coming into contact with German prisoners, some of whom had been at Sachsenhausen for three, even four years. Many of them had been hardened by their time. Others, especially the leftist political prisoners, remained true to their convictions and used their camp relationships to help others as much as they could.

Aleks focused on his poetry as well as music. In his verses, he took inspiration from the great works of Polish masters he had learned during adolescence, creating camp adaptations of famous poems written by Maria Konopnicka, Adam Asnyk, or Adam Mickiewicz. He riffed on popular interwar music. Because they were catchy, his songs and verses quickly circulated in the camp. Some of his phrases even became commonly used expressions. The Polish prisoner Gabriel Zych remembered Aleks's compositions as touching records of real experiences. Zych also remembered Aleks's prodigious memory.

In one of Aleks's first performances in the main camp, he debuted the song "Mister C" at an artistic evening organized by a group of German communists in block 3. So that everyone present could understand his lyrics, a prisoner interpreted their meaning in several languages.

As 1940 drew to a close, he returned to a prewar hit called "Old-Fashioned Song" that he'd performed at a commemoration of the outbreak of the war. Now he borrowed the melody of that song and began composing new, far more optimistic lyrics, while tapping into the longing he and so many others felt for their lost countries, families, and lives.

Breeze rustling through the wires lulls me to sleep:
"Do you remember Poland, poor fellow?"
Daydreams of long ago today are no more—
Only a dull ache remains.

Too many days I've waited in vain,
Still I'll wait a thousand more!
Life is hard, but so are my fists!
Remember! Revenge! Say nothing!

Unforgettable song,
My dearest, my only one,
Beloved song that stifled their "Heil!"

Dear song about things that once were,
About things past—but that will endure!
Dear God, with a song on my lips let me die.

All my Poland will sing out,
With wings reborn again she'll soar!
We all will return again, there,
Where the Vistula awaits in spring.

PART II

Chapter 8

⌒

In Aleks's new block assignment, he found himself among more German political prisoners than ever before. On music nights, he observed with great interest their musical traditions. He listened to the popular or leftist songs the men performed, the same ones they sang before the war. Like the Poles Aleks knew in the little camp, the Germans seemed to view music as an essential tool for keeping morale high. Harry Naujoks, a German prisoner of high standing and an acquaintance of Aleks and Rosebery, even went so far as to say that music could lessen a man's despondency and hopelessness, dangerous states that could hasten death. Harry tried his best to arrange musical gatherings and protect prisoners from the SS. Even a mere hour of distraction from the tedium and abuse of Sachsenhausen, Harry believed, did wonders for a man's mental state. Another prisoner, named Werner Koch, found the same value in music. Werner remembered how singing together, no matter how short a session, gave him a sense of joy. "We could rejoice together, seal comradeship and friendship, make firm our hope for the day of freedom, and gain new strength for the daily struggle for survival that was demanded of us."

Anyone in the barracks could join in, regardless of his skill or background. Most astonishing to Aleks was that the SS seemed to be aware of the music the Germans created. Prisoners spoke of how guards had on several occasions entered a barracks while prisoners sang. Frozen, waiting to see what the SS would do, these prisoners were shocked when the guards did not intervene to punish them. In stark contrast to the risk and secrecy of Rosebery's Jewish choir or the fear that Aleks and other Poles felt when they sang in clandestine performances, the Germans seemed to have some freedom as to how they entertained themselves. In some cases, they created songbooks, containing dozens of scores decorated with colorful drawings. So confident about their ability to gather for music without SS retribution, some Germans at Sachsenhausen even inscribed their prisoner and block numbers on the songbooks. Why the SS permitted the German prisoners to sing was not entirely clear—to Aleks or the Germans. Perhaps music offered some value to the guards without posing any risk. After all, it kept prisoners calm and distracted. It raised their morale, perhaps even their strength, for the following day's labor.

Seeing the Germans convene to sing in larger groups amazed Aleks. Until then, he had experienced music as a secret, spontaneous, anxious affair. Arranging one of the rare performance evenings for a larger audience in the little camp required planning. One had to seek a sympathetic block elder for information and protection, such as the choice of a night that posed the least risk. The other difference he noticed was that fewer Germans appeared to be composing the parody songs he and other Poles were partial to. Instead, they often sang a repertoire of communist music that was dear and personal to them. Aleks had found in parody songs a way to taunt Hitler, his ideas, and his camp lackeys. He had used dark humor to document the suffering and abuse of the camp, to attack the vicious Nazi ideology. When the German political prisoners sang communist music, that act was an affront to Hitler too, just of another sort.

In mid-December, just after being transferred out of the little camp, Aleks teamed up with Jan Dedina, a student from Prague, to form a singing duet. Since it was near Christmas, the two men rehearsed Polish, Czech, and Slovak carols in the washroom of Aleks's barracks. To make it a proper show, Aleks and Jan recruited the actor Jerzy Kaliszewski to recite a monologue or poem and the dancer Bogdan Chomentowski to do a tap routine. Over the course of three days, the quartet walked between blocks to sing holiday tunes for the men inside, trying as best they could to brighten the mood. Aleks and Jan chose which blocks to visit with care. A malevolent block elder might beat them or betray them to the SS, who viewed the Poles with far more contempt than the Germans. With Aleks's cunning and camp relationships, he could usually gauge where he and Jan were safe, though nothing was certain.

The cold stiffened Aleks's fingers and made nights a wretched battle for warmth. Around the same time that he and Jan toured the barracks singing carols, the SS ordered prisoners to erect a large Christmas tree at the roll call square beside the camp gallows. Now, when the guards hanged a man, his corpse dangled next to that symbol of the approaching holidays.

Yet in the final days before Christmas, Aleks got the sense that the camp had quieted somewhat. Even control over food appeared to loosen, and prisoners with standing managed to get their hands on extra rations. The political prisoners, especially the communists, tried their best to share the extra food with those who were hungriest. What explained the quiet? Aleks speculated that much of the SS guard corps had taken holiday leave. Or perhaps they were distracted by the good cheer of Christmas with their families in Oranienburg. Whatever the reason, Aleks and the men around him welcomed the respite. Between Christmas and the new year, he and Jan sang their carols in the barracks while several prisoners performed a puppet nativity scene, using props they had made from whatever scraps of material they could find.

THE NEW YEAR brought a swift end to the relative calm of Christmas. On a frigid morning, the guards made all prisoners stand on the snowy square during roll call while they searched for a missing man. Aleks watched as a group of guards began to scour the camp, led by the noses of their German shepherds. All the while Aleks and the thousands of other men stood perfectly still, freezing.

A dog began to bark: he had a scent. From what Aleks could see, the missing man was hiding in a ventilation turret in one of the buildings. As the guards hauled him down, Aleks caught sight of the pink triangle on his uniform. He was a German homosexual. As he was dragged toward the roll call square, he began to howl, grasping his left wrist. Then he released his grip and blood from a self-inflicted wound gushed from his veins. As he died, Aleks heard him crying out in a horrifying voice, "Thoughts are free!" The guards dumped his body, their accounting of prisoners complete. Blood soaked the snow, and Aleks marched to his work detail.

BY 1941, SEVERAL German, Czech, and Polish choirs existed in the main camp, some with just a few men, others with as many as forty. A group of prisoners even founded a string quartet, which featured three Czech musicians—including the virtuoso violinist Bohumír Červinka—and the German Eberhard Schmidt, a friend of Rosebery's, on the cello. Even though the SS forbade instruments in the barracks at that point, a block elder helped Eberhard secure his cello. Bohumír had his master violin sent to him by a friend, and a group of Czech students obtained a viola. Other prisoners, who had worked as luthiers or carvers or woodworkers before the war, spent free time fashioning instruments.

During the early days of the Czech quartet, the prisoners themselves arranged their music, but after a time they managed to obtain contraband scores by Beethoven, Brahms, Schumann, Dvořák, and other European composers, which they rehearsed in the camp mortuary. Eberhard Schmidt remembered walking nervously to rehearsals through the rings of barracks, holding his cello, his heart pounding, fearing that an SS guard would stop him. When he reached the mortuary, he and the other musicians would spread out their scores on the porcelain dissecting tables where, during the day, the bodies of prisoners lay.

On Sunday afternoons, members of the quartet invited select prisoners to hear them play. Bohdan Rossa, who attended one of the rehearsals, later recalled the sensation of hearing such beautiful music within the walls of Sachsenhausen: "After the first few notes I thought I had a fever. It ran hot and cold down my back. It was like a dream."

The Poles in the main camp had founded several choirs, though like the Jews they had to be more secretive. Some choirs were well organized, such as the one the Polish prisoner Jan Dunst founded, an ensemble in four-part harmony with more than twenty-five members. Aleks's friend Edward Janiuk, of Lublin, had begun to organize a Polish choir as well. For a time, Sachsenhausen even had a harmonica troupe. At night when it seemed safe, these groups paid visits to various barracks. Aleks was not the only camp troubadour. Soloists, trios, small ensembles, and even multimember choirs toured different barracks. Mirek Pilar, a Czech, founded an eight-voice a cappella group called The Sing-Sing Boys. Mirek's group took inspiration from jazz and improvisation and performed popular music, dance songs, and tunes from prewar films. One member of the group remembered, "From evening to evening, when the wind whistled outside in the barbed wire and the spotlights on the watchtowers were lit, we went singing on the different blocks, regardless of fatigue. No sooner had word got around that the Czechs were singing than the block was packed with listeners. People even sat on the ceiling beams and lockers and we were satisfied to be able to give away some of our modest art."

That so many other prisoners found in music the same potential for hope and escape gave Aleks a sense of optimism. Yet this was not the full story. As he marveled at the unexpected presence of the quartets, trios, and other singing groups that toured the barracks, he was again confronted with music of an entirely different sort: as a tool in the Nazis' arsenal of abuse. Aleks had encountered this before, while still in the little camp. He recalled how the block elders would force everyone to sing during the sprints and leg bends and push-ups. Sometimes, the block elders forced them to sing while standing at attention so they could scrutinize each man and punish those who did not know the lyrics or melody. On the main campgrounds, he was to experience the full extent of music as an SS weapon. At certain times of the day, the call would sound: *"Ein lied!"*—"A song!" Barked from the mouth of an SS guard or a prisoner functionary, it signaled that everyone should begin to belt out a choral work. This singing on command often took place when prisoners were marched to and from work assignments beyond the camp walls. Aleks suspected the intent was to convince residents of Oranienburg that the inmates inside were healthy and in good spirits. The call might also sound at night, when Aleks stood among as many as twenty thousand men at attention on the roll call square to be counted. As the SS guards circulated, gripping their clubs, on the hunt for a man out of line, one would call out, "A song!" and the whole group, those twenty thousand voices strong, would join to sing German folk tunes or military marches in a forced cheerfulness that evoked in Aleks and many other prisoners an acute sense of despair. They were ordered to sing the jovial music of the nation whose soldiers tortured them.

During forced singing, each prisoner had to observe the standards of the SS. He was not to sing too loudly or too softly. He had to know the lyrics by heart. If he did not sing in a satisfactory way, a guard or prisoner functionary would beat him with a cudgel. Even worse, if the commander found the music as a whole inadequate, he lengthened the roll calls to last hours, no matter the weather—it could be snowing or pouring or storming with a cold wind ripping through their thin uniforms, but the men still had to sing.

Often, they sang at the most central point of the camp, beneath the machine gun tower fixed to the gatehouse. Not only did it present the SS with another opportunity to pummel the inmates, it also drained the men of any remaining strength they had. Sometimes, a prisoner grew so exhausted singing at the roll call square that he collapsed. Only when the commander was satisfied did anyone return to the barracks. And even there, the prisoners did not always find respite. Sometimes, forced music continued late into the night in their block. Under the scornful eye of an SS guard, the block elder would stand before the prisoners and conduct them in song, perhaps an upbeat folk melody, perhaps a camp song like the one called "Yes, I

Was in Sachsenhausen." These late-night singing sessions, which exhausted everyone, which smothered any remaining energy they might have had at the end of a workday, could last for hours.

IT TOOK TIME for Aleks to reconnect with friends from the little camp. Many of them had been transferred to the main grounds as well, though they were assigned to the dozens of outer-ring barracks where the SS housed prisoners with little influence. Once back in touch with these compatriots, however, Aleks began to perform regularly.

Communication between the main camp and the little camp where the Jewish barracks stood was infrequent, often unreliable. News from Rosebery came in an often-interrupted trickle—a rumor here, perhaps a greeting there. Aleks had yet to muster the courage to go to the little camp himself. He was still learning how Sachsenhausen worked, and any misstep could be deadly. Yet the lack of news about Rosebery tormented him. For all he knew, his friend was dead. He had to find a way to make contact.

The German communists Aleks lived with were the best means of passing messages from the big camp to the little one. In all likelihood, one of his German contacts arranged a communication through political prisoners assigned to the little camp. The response: Rosebery was still alive. The news lifted the burden of worry off Aleks, at least for a time. The next step: to figure out a way to visit Rosebery in person. This was the kind of act that could attract the deadly attention of an SS guard. Aleks believed it was worth the risk. He longed for the friendship he had with Rosebery, the discourse about music and progressive politics that made up the heart of their discussions. When Aleks's chosen day came and he snuck into the little camp, he was elated to find Rosebery at last, weak and thin, but alive. The Jewish choir was intact too, Rosebery told him, though its members suffered under the hands of the SS and their prisoner lackeys.

That Rosebery's choir still existed must have been an immense relief to Aleks. A Jewish choir at Sachsenhausen posed such an immense risk. Each rehearsal was an act of defiance. Rosebery guarded his secret with great care. Only a handful of Poles knew about it from their time at the little camp at the start of the war. Some of the German political prisoners knew about it, too. Yet countless others, even influential Germans like the communist Harry Naujoks, never learned of its existence. Rosebery's choir was not meant for the rest of the camp. The Germans and Poles and Czechs had their own forms of entertainment—and often, better conditions. Rosebery's group was made up of Jews, for Jews, an ensemble that could never tour the other barracks or write songbooks or hold concerts for the broader inmate population.

Since Aleks had last seen the choir in the fall of 1940, its repertoire had expanded. As its conductor, Rosebery had grown into a near mythical figure in the eyes of his singers and the men who watched the choir perform. Hans Hüttner viewed him as a man of great dignity. Even as Rosebery endured immense abuse, he held fast to the principles he'd believed in since he was a teenager in Mława. What mattered most to Rosebery, as Hans saw it, was the music and the good it could do for the other Jews in Sachsenhausen. Hans, like Aleks, believed that when inmates heard the choir, they were moved enough to forget, if just for a few minutes, the savagery of the camp. Of all the Jewish choir's repertoire—the Yiddish songs and German art music they sang—one piece stuck out in Hans's mind: *"Der König in Thule"* (The King in Thule), whose text Goethe had written and Schubert adapted to music. In the song, the king of the mythical realm of Thule mourns the death of his mistress by drinking from a golden goblet she gave him as she was dying. At the end of the king's life, with all his riches in the hands of his heirs, he hurls the goblet into the sea, then dies watching it fill with water and dip beneath the waves. Hans watched as Rosebery worked with the singers. What struck him was the very choice of song. It was a distinctly German piece of music, drawing on one of the country's most distinguished poets. Why would Rosebery want his Jewish choir to rehearse such a song? Hans speculated that for Rosebery there existed two Germanys— one that contained the prose of Goethe, the symphonies of Beethoven, the vision and passion of the left. The other Germany belonged to the fascists and their many followers, the men who had enslaved him in Sachsenhausen. With this song, Hans maintained, Rosebery was staking a claim for the Germany he loved, one that he believed would reemerge when the war had passed.

OVER TIME, ALEKS mastered the risky task of crossing to the little camp to meet Rosebery. Yet they could never see each other as they once had done, when their barracks stood but a few strides apart. Passing into the little camp required tact, connections, and favorable circumstances, which occurred only occasionally. Unable to attend rehearsals of the Jewish choir regularly, Aleks focused on creating his own music. He composed the parody song "Germania!" to assuage despair over Hitler's unstoppable expansion across Europe. For "Germania!," Aleks chose the melody of a Czech soldier's tune. *Shit-caked country!* Aleks's lyrics went, *Better to be like tiny Monaco / Rather than a Europe like that / My dears, consider castration? / SS-ma-ni-a!*

After Aleks performed "Germania!" at several song evenings, other prisoners began to hum the melody around the camp. To avoid punishment, they got in the habit of singing the single word "Germania." Aleks sang it this way too, especially as he marched to and from the shoe factory, where he now worked. When an SS guard overheard him and demanded, with menace in his voice, the title of the song, Aleks replied: "This song is called 'Germania!'" Satisfied, the SS guard expressed his regret that such a pretty song had so few lyrics.

When music did not consume Aleks's thoughts, he often mused about Bożena, the girl he could never get off his mind. He remembered how hard he tried to make her love him and how it stung when she rebuffed him: "I am a Czech girl, and you, only a prašivy Polák." A lousy Pole, that was how she saw him. Once, when melancholy struck, Aleks bemoaned the fact that he might die within the walls of the camp never having experienced love in a real, adult way. "No one will ever kiss me goodnight," he thought. "No one will cry for me." He hoped that if he died in the camp, someone might at least take pity on him and close the tired eyes of his corpse. In Sachsenhausen, a man could not even rely on that.

As fighting between the Wehrmacht and the Red Army intensified in the latter half of 1941, thousands of Soviet prisoners of war arrived at Sachsenhausen, men captured in the fighting on the newly created Eastern Front. They filed into the camp in tatters, scraggly beards on their faces, sick after the vicious fighting and the long journey west as captives in empty freight trains. These new prisoners intrigued the German communists, many of whom saw Moscow as their political polestar and had forged deep ties with the Soviets before the war. Yet as soon as the Germans began to associate with their communist brethren of the east, the newly arrived POWs started to disappear. Mysteriously, groups of Soviets went missing, simply vanished from the camp. In theory, the SS could have transferred them to a subcamp connected to Sachsenhausen a short distance away. But then an explanation came. At a specially designed facility on the campgrounds, the SS took each Russian and stood him against a measuring stick on the wall. What the prisoner did not know was that behind the stick was a slit, and behind that, a member of the SS holding a gun. As the Soviet soldier waited, ostensibly to be measured, the guard behind the wall squeezed the trigger. All the while the SS blasted upbeat marching music over loudspeakers so that the gunshots could not be heard. During a ten-week period, the SS murdered some ten thousand Soviet POWs, the marches playing over and over. To dispose of the corpses, the SS fired up the crematorium and slid each body into the flames. Flakes floated down onto the streets and houses near the camp in an ashen snow.

Word of this mass murder quickly spread, enraging the German communists in particular. With Hitler now invading to the east and the slaughter of the Soviet POWs in Sachsenhausen, there seemed no hope for them.

WEEKS BECAME MONTHS, and the monotony of Aleks's routine changed little as 1941 drew to a close: exhausting work from the early hours of morning, the constant struggle to avoid the wrath of a foreman, a guard, or the freezing weather. At night, he sang at gatherings. He watched others perform. Sometimes prisoners even put on dance routines. Jan Baranski, a Polish prisoner who arrived just after Aleks, remembered how enthusiastically the men clapped to performances of the Krakowiak, a folk-inspired dance from the Kraków region. Sometimes the dancers even performed wearing makeshift costumes created with scraps of material scavenged from around the camp. Aleks relished these forbidden nights. Afterward, cramped between other men in the sleeping room, he composed his lyrics in his mind.

By mid-1942, Rosebery seemed weaker, from time to time absent of mind, perhaps less unflinching. Aleks learned why on one of those days when they met, likely in the summer of 1942. Rosebery looked at Aleks and explained. He was convinced the Germans were doing something terrible to Europe's Jews. Though the SS tried as best they could to keep Sachsenhausen sealed against news from the outside world, information constantly seeped in, some of it true, some untrue. Rumors, glimpses of murder, were shared by new prisoners, who spread them around the camp. A new detainee might have seen Jews being run out of town or loaded onto trains and deduced from this the mass murder the Nazis had begun to implement. Another new detainee might have come with information about the Warsaw Ghetto and the ghastly crimes committed there. Rosebery and several other Jews Aleks knew began to fear that large-scale murder was taking place across German-occupied Europe.

Broader news of the war effort spread around the camp with surprising speed. Prisoners assigned to work in SS bureaus sometimes overheard bits of news, a few words of hearsay passed between guards. Or perhaps they sighted a headline in a German newspaper left on a desk, though they knew that anything from official Nazi channels was perverted by propaganda. The best information about the outside world and the war came from a group of German political prisoners who managed to obtain a radio. At a hushed volume, these men tuned into radio programs from around Europe, such as the BBC in London, which broadcast far more reliable information than what was transmitted across German airwaves. Aleks and Rosebery almost certainly knew about the ongoing German attack on the Soviet Union, the extent of Hitler's domination of Europe, and the entry of the United States into the war.

Of all the hearsay and half-truths about the war and the outside world that spread around Sachsenhausen, one persistent rumor distressed Rosebery in particular: in Nazi camps on occupied Polish land, the Germans were carrying out a mass killing of Jews, sometimes with the use of poisonous gas. No one knew for sure whether this was true—it was not the sort of information that the British radio broadcast. Yet Rosebery told Aleks he believed it. No longer could he view the Nazi state as merely an evil wind the way his brother Jacob had described it years earlier at home in Danzig. Perhaps that was when all the events lined up for Rosebery— the rhetoric before the war about the Jewish question, the mass arrests, the talk of deporting Europe's Jews to Madagascar, the brutal treatment he and the other Jews endured at Sachsenhausen. Extermination was the end the Germans sought. Hitler had begun to make good on his threats.

Rosebery told Aleks that he sensed his own end was near. He didn't say where it would happen or when, only that it was not far off and he suspected he would be gassed. In facing the prospect of death at the hands of the Germans, a people and culture he so dearly loved, Rosebery began to compose. "I'm preparing a composition," he told Aleks. He didn't yet have the title. All he knew was that it would be a cry of anguish for the Jews at Sachsenhausen and across Europe based on the old Yiddish folk song "Tsen Brider" ("Ten Brothers").

Aleks knew "Tsen Brider" well. Rosebery's choir had already sung it in its traditional form. He also remembered it from his days at university in Kraków, when Jewish musicians strolled from courtyard to courtyard, singing for coins. The song recounted the story of ten brothers who traded in geese, wood, cargo, and flax. One by one, as the song progresses, the brothers die. Popular before the war, the song charted the long Yiddish music tradition about disappearing Jews. At the end of one version, when only two brothers remain, the men trade in bones. The final living brother trades in candles, perhaps an allusion to lighting a Yahrzeit candle to remember the dead. The song ends: *I am one brother, / I fell in love with a beautiful girl, / I married a non-Jew, / Now I'm no-one.*

Other than noting that he believed the melody would be familiar to most of the camp's Jews, Rosebery said little to Aleks about why he had chosen "Tsen Brider" as the basis of his final arrangement. Aleks speculated that it was because the song was uncomplicated and relatable. It also seemed to him that the melody was perfect for a lament sung by a men's choir. Rosebery did make a point about the lyrics he was composing. They would be in German. He wanted everyone in the camp, no matter his background, to understand them.

As Rosebery arranged "Tsen Brider," composing new lyrics as Aleks and others did for their parody songs, he sometimes sang completed sections to Aleks. Those moments touched Aleks deeply. Hearing "Tsen Brider's" melody took him back to his boyhood. He remembered tilting his head to listen to the Jewish funeral music that flowed through the windows of Cieszyn's synagogue onto the street. By then, many of the men at Sachsenhausen knew that the Nazis used music to accompany their murders. And everyone suffered the forced singing of lively German marches and folk songs on the way to work details or at the roll call square. Yet for Aleks and Rosebery and others, the Nazis could not spoil music, they could not stamp out its power.

It was then that Aleks sensed Rosebery's wish to preserve some part of himself, perhaps a bit of music as a lasting remnant, a trace of having lived. The adaptation of "Tsen Brider" might be that legacy. At one of their meetings, Rosebery turned to Aleks, squeezed his hand, and said, almost as though he was touched by some sort of religious epiphany, "You are not a Jew. If you survive, you must sing my song of bitterness and revenge, my death song. You have to sing it all around the world, or else I will curse you and you won't be able to die in peace."

Aleks immediately agreed to Rosebery's plea. The request also put another idea in his head: what about the music composed by other prisoners? And the camp poetry, too? Until that point, Aleks had used his memory mainly to preserve the lyrics of his own songs, now nearly two dozen in number. Yet rarely had he thought of memorizing the compositions of others. All around him men were processing, memorializing, reporting on what was taking place at Sachsenhausen. Many had died, and with them, their artistic witnessing vanished forever. Yet ahead of Aleks likely still lay years of war. Prisoners would turn to culture to endure their days of struggle. Perhaps Aleks could preserve some of the music, some of the poetry if he committed it to memory. Rosebery had yet to finish his song. There was still time.

Chapter 9

~⟶~

Aleks first sighted Aron, a tall, young, and once broad-shouldered Polish Jew, when they were both sweeping the campgrounds as part of a janitorial work detail. They got to talking, furtively, always scanning for an SS guard or a foreman, careful to remain out of earshot. Aron whispered between thrusts of his broom that before ending up at Sachsenhausen he had watched an SS guard shoot his wife through the temple in another camp on occupied Polish soil. Once the guard had dealt with Aron's wife, he smashed his toddler son's head against the wall. Aron believed that he was spared only because the guard looked at the thick muscles on his frame and decided it would be a waste not to save him for work.

Aron claimed that later, he begged the man who guarded the building where corpses awaited incineration to let him spend time with the body of his son. Among the piles of corpses, he composed a farewell lullaby for his child. Now, at Sachsenhausen, he wanted Aleks to memorize it. Aleks never knew how much truth there was in Aron's story. Substantiating an account like this while a prisoner in a Nazi camp was impossible.

Yet Aleks honored Aron's experiences; he believed in the greater truth of the tale and was eager to memorize the lullaby.

Aron, it turned out, knew Rosebery; he likely lived in a barracks in the little camp. Perhaps it was Rosebery who told him to entrust his song to Aleks. Perhaps it was another man. Aleks did not know. In the weeks after Aleks decided his mission in Sachsenhausen would be to memorize the music and poetry of the camp, he began to work with speed, and word spread. A prisoner at Sachsenhausen could die at any moment. For the Jewish inmates in particular, the threat loomed heavily, especially if Rosebery's premonition that he and the other Jews would soon be deported east for extermination came true.

It took several days for Aron to dictate his song. He and Aleks could only speak while they swept, and in whispers. The SS were watching. Day by day, lyric by lyric, Aron shared his song, its melody a sustained wail of sorrow:

Crematorium black and silent
Gates of hell, corpses piled high
I drag stiff, slippery corpses
While the sun smiles in the sky
Here he lies, my only little boy
Tiny fists pressed in his mouth
How can I cast you into the flames?
With your shining golden hair

Aron was not long for the world, Aleks believed. His knees looked thicker than his thighs. The skin on his hands was white, almost transparent, like tissue paper. Sometimes he spat blood. Sometimes, feces ran down his legs underneath his uniform. Still, Aron carried on, bending his head toward Aleks, demanding that he remember the lullaby. "This is my only vengeance!" he wheezed. At the refrain, Aron slowed his pace as if coaxing his dead son to sleep: *Lulai, lulai—little one / Lulai, lulai—only son / Lulai, lulai—my own boy / Oy . . . oy . . . oy.* Then, in verse two, Aron's voice began to build in strength:

Oh, you sun, you watched in silence
While you smiled and shined above
Saw them smash my baby's skull
On the cold stone wall
Now little eyes look calmly at the sky
Cold tears, I hear them crying
Oh, my boy, your blood is everywhere
Three years old—your golden hair

When he reached the final stanza, Aron's voice rose, almost to a shout. Aleks hushed him, "Shut up or we'll attract attention! And anyway, what kind of lullaby is this if you shout it?" Aron glared at him. "All I wanted was for my child to wake up."

In the final measures of the song, Aron returned to his grieving refrain. *Lulai, lulai—little one / Lulai, lulai—only son / Lulai lulai—my own boy / Oy . . . oy . . . oy.* His voice softened until, at the very last line, it trailed off.

IN THE LITTLE camp, Rosebery worked on his composition. He had grown weaker, thinner. A festering infection distorted his face. At times, a sort of haze seemed to hang over him. He repeated the same stories to Aleks again and again, recalling his years in Berlin and the zenith of his career, when people all over the city knew of his choir, when newspapers published enthusiastic reviews of its performances.

Other times, Rosebery was lucid. He talked often and with pleasure and nostalgia about Mława, his hometown some seventy-five miles northwest of Warsaw. He was curious about Poland, asking Aleks and others what was happening there. After so many years of disinterest in his homeland and his past, he seemed to have found a certain pleasure in recalling his life and family and roots in Poland.

As though he were saying his final goodbyes, Rosebery asked Aleks to send wishes to several camp friends he could not easily meet; the movement of Jews, as ever, was restricted. He wished to pass messages along to

Jule Furst and Rudolf Grosse. He asked Aleks to greet their mutual close friend, Edward Janiuk, a Pole Rosebery met while carrying bricks at the Klinkerwerk. Their meeting had greatly impacted Edward, who remembered Rosebery's calm, melodious voice and described him as having "an ascetic, always focused face and restless hands . . . as though he was constantly playing something with them."

Edward once asked Rosebery to arrange several songs in four-part harmony for the choir he was leading. Edward was among the very few non-Jews who witnessed a rehearsal of the Jewish choir, which he attended at Rosebery's invitation. The night of his visit, some of the singers stood while others sat on tables because there was little space in the barracks.

After meeting Aron, Aleks made contact with more prisoners who had songs or poems. He met the young Polish highlander, Stanisław Roszkowski, who during his final hours of life, expiring in agony in the medical barracks, composed a refrain: *When the smoke rises, so will I, so will I . . . whistle.* He also met a young Russian, Aleksey Sazonov, known as Alyosha, at the Schuhfabrik, the shoemaking work detail. The Czech communist Jan Vodička made the introduction, immediately piquing Aleks's interest when he said, "Ah, if you only knew how well he sings!" Alyosha blushed. They worked alongside each other, fashioning shoes out of old officers' boots, rolls of cloth, rubber coats, old leather upholstery. Another source of raw material: women's handbags, some made of crocodile or lizard skin, seized from the victims of German terror in occupied Europe. Gabriel Zych, a friend of Aleks's and another prisoner on the shoe factory detail, remembered dismantling bags whose contents were still intact. He would open them to find handkerchiefs that smelled of perfume, notebooks filled with writing, lipstick, powder compacts, and money.

Aleks learned that Alyosha was seventeen and a Red Army volunteer, though this was all he would say about the army. After exchanging a few words, the men fell silent and focused on their work. Aleks believed that if a foreman or guard saw him talking, especially with a Russian, they would both be punished. A few nights later, though, Aleks saw Alyosha at a song evening. This time Alyosha performed, singing his own parody song based on the melody of "The Cossack Rode Past the Dan-ube." *Szarła-tiuga! Szarła-tiuga!* Alyosha sang with energy, repeating the words again and again. To Aleks, these words seemed to bring together Alyosha's wistfulness and happiness, the long-unheard twittering of birds in his homeland, his boy-like hope, and also his rage and contempt for the Germans. In the chorus, Alyosha sang *Ah-ah-ah / ai, my mother Russia.* Later, Aleks asked him, "Why do you hold that *ah-ah-ah* for so long?" Alyosha sighed. "You know, it makes me feel that I am out there again, free, and there's this large choir of young Russian boys singing with me. And I'm the soloist. You heard me a moment ago. I have such strong lungs, and yet I must die."

Aleks memorized the song and another Alyosha dictated to him some weeks later. Alyosha said he named the song "Sonia" and based it on a mel-ody he heard Aleks humming when he came to pick up supplies from the warehouse where he was working.

Dark and silent as far as eye can see,
Wherever you look—howling wires, howling wind! . . .
The phantom-like camp, panting, sleeping deeply,
And the cold stigma of death grasping the back of my neck!

Do you remember how sweetly your eyes begged of me?
Kiss me again, while you still live . . .
And even though the memory of it has grown faint
And I will be carried away by the black, black smoke—
I will come, I will return, as if an apparition
And I will forever howl at my executioners . . .
Sonia . . . Sonia . . .

As with many prisoners, Alyosha reworked and improved his song. He had time to change his composition while on the work detail, during marches, or at night, crammed in the barracks with hundreds of other dying prisoners. A few days after he dictated to Aleks the first version of "Sonia," he appeared while Aleks was unloading a truck near a camp warehouse and tossed him a shoe. When Aleks looked inside, he found a scrap of paper with lyrics for a new song Alyosha wanted him to memorize.

The last night Aleks saw Alyosha, the young Russian sang the first part of his new song. *Smoke, smoke—the vile smoke / Chokes the weeping, chokes a scream.* Aleks recognized the melody: Ukrainian. He asked Alyosha why he, a Russian from Gorky, had set a song to a Ukrainian melody. Alyosha revealed that his mother had come from Belarus, and as a young boy he often heard the music of that country and its neighbor, Ukraine, which he found enchanting, mournful. His mother's mother had been left behind in Belarus when the war began. He was sure that her village had been burned. The melody was to honor these two women.

Aleks and Alyosha did not have the time to reminisce. A foreman lingered not far off, watching for insubordinate prisoners. The last thing Alyosha said was that he wished his song to be called "Hecatomb." The title surprised Aleks, who thought to himself, how can this young Russian peasant with no education know a word used in ancient Greece to describe a great public sacrifice, usually of oxen? Aleks only knew it because his father taught classics and tried to imbue his son with some knowledge of the past. Alyosha repeated the word, syllable by syllable: "He-ca-tomb." He thought about it for a moment, sighed, and told Aleks to add 1941, presumably to memorialize the mass murder of Russian prisoners of war at Sachsenhausen the year before. Alyosha gave Aleks a firm handshake and went back to his work. Before they could see each other again, the SS transferred Alyosha to a barracks for POWs, which Aleks could not reach. Some days later, Alyosha managed to get word to Aleks and Jan Vodička through the inmate doctor Stanisław Kelles-Krauz that he was alive. Stanisław even smuggled the rest of Alyosha's song to Aleks, written on a scrap of paper torn from a bag of cement: *I beg of you, dearest mother, / That I don't die slowly . . . / Smoke, smoke . . . may it choke / You pack of German dogs!*

Aleks saw Alyosha one last time from a distance; it was too risky to get close to the Russian barracks. Alyosha was sitting on the ground. He

looked weak, and his face bore the bruises and wounds of beatings. "Alyosha! It's me, Aleks, the Pole!" he said, trying to keep as quiet as he could.
Alyosha crawled in Aleks's direction. A German foreman struck him with
a stick and then kicked him. Alyosha clenched his skeletal fingers and let
out a scream. That was the last time Aleks saw him.

By then, Aleks had a method and process for creating camp songs. In
most cases, a song began with a scene he'd witnessed or an emotion he'd
felt. Then he wrote the lyrics as a series of verses, like a poem. When the
lyrics felt right, he would choose which tune to use.

Aleks used this approach when he created the song "Notturno 1941."
Jolted from his sleep by an air raid siren one night, he lay in his wooden
bunk, composing as he listened to the Allied airplanes thundering over
the camp in the dark sky. Imagining the bombers shooting through the
clouds toward Berlin, he wrote:

> *I praise you, birds, confident sailors,*
> *I know—you are avoiding the cursed valley.*
> *On the black sky, black angels*
> *Flapping their black wings: kill!*

Aleks believed that the prospect of death sharpened his creativity.
With the siren still wailing, he thought to himself: "Even though the
bombs could kill us, I will still work on this song." He heard the whine
of falling bombs, the explosions rumbling in the distance. He imagined
Berlin, even Oranienburg just beyond the walls of the camp, aflame, terrified townsfolk fleeing. He thought that most people would expect lyrics
composed under such conditions to be jagged, knotted, a reflection of the
dread under which they were composed. Yet he believed those of "Notturno 1941" to be romantic, even tender at the beginning. Only in the second verse did they grow dark and threatening.

> *And even the moon is black from the smoke,*
> *The stars are scared, pale from pity—*

There is no hope, every weak person weeping,
The wind is crying a hangman's serenade.

When the raid ended and the quiet of the nighttime camp returned, Aleks decided to dedicate the song to his mother, who gave him his love of music.

Though Aleks had tried hard to keep his music a secret, after roughly two years of performing and composing, the SS had taken notice. Once, while he was whistling Monti's "Csárdás" for a group of prisoners in a barracks, a mid-level SS guard walked in. Aleks recognized this guard, a Viennese man named Engelbert Schroder. As punishment for the music, Schroder punched Aleks in the mouth, breaking a tooth. Later, Schroder brought Aleks before Sachsenhausen's chief doctor, Heinz Baumkötter. Aleks discovered why he was there. Schroder and Baumkötter would try to silence him by injecting bacteria—Aleks speculated that it was diphtheria—into his neck.

That night, Aleks pleaded with several friends who worked in the medical barracks to steal an antitoxin for him. Josef Čapek, a well-known Czech painter, and Walter Thate, a paramedic, did him the favor. Aleks believed they helped him because they appreciated his music. After the treatment from Josef and Walter, Aleks experienced no symptoms.

Schroder returned a few days later to give Aleks a second dose. Once again, Josef and Walter treated Aleks. When Schroder visited Aleks a third time, he said, with sarcasm in his voice, "Maestro Aleks, would you please sing something, master." Aleks sang for him in Italian, his voice unchanged. Schroder stormed out of the barracks. Some five days later, he returned, this time, with Baumkötter. Aleks sang before the two Nazis. His voice was still unchanged. Baumkötter looked surprised. He whispered something to Schroder, then shrugged and said, "Let that dog continue to sing!"

IT WAS IN the early fall of 1942 when Rosebery told Aleks that he had completed his song. Its title was the "Jüdischer Todessang" (Jewish Deathsong). Aleks heard it in full for the first time at one of their meetings. After Rosebery sang it, he explained measure by measure what each section signified, why he had chosen each lyric, each musical feature.

The song began with bass voices in unison. *Bom, bom, bom, bom.* This, Rosebery explained, represented a warning of death, the omen of the end for him and the other Jews. He told Aleks that he intended the vocables to be sung at a slow, heavy pace, one that expressed the many emotions he and the other Jews felt—the rage, the resignation, the will to survive. He also envisioned each line of vocables to be sung in one breath, and compared the technique to playing a bagpipe. Then, in a falsetto voice, he sang *lee-lai, lee-lai, lee-lai,* lullaby-like sounds that signified the murder of Jewish children, which Rosebery believed to be taking place across Europe. He rarely talked about the fate of his family, which almost certainly was dire. Save for his brother Jacob and that part of the Rosenberg family, and possibly his sister who fled to the Soviet Union, none of Rosebery's family had left Poland.

Aleks never knew whether Rosebery seldom mentioned his family because he wished to keep their plight private or because he simply had no information. Once though, with tears streaming down his cheeks, he told Aleks about some news he had received. Before the war, he had grown fond of a little girl, the daughter of distant relatives or friends he visited in eastern Poland. Now he had discovered that when German soldiers detained the girl's father, she ran to him, embraced him round the knees, and, crying, begged him not to leave. The soldiers trampled her in the mud and deported her father. How Rosebery had learned about the girl's fate, Aleks never found out.

Aleks believed that Rosebery chose to open the "Jewish Deathsong" with vocal music but without lyrics because of his work with his prewar choir. Perhaps as far back as the late 1920s, Rosebery had thought that songs without lyrics brought forth a certain purity in choral music. A melody sung without words produced a fullness of emotion free of anything to obstruct it. Over time, Rosebery's lyric-less arrangements became what he called Absolute Symphonic Chants. When the choir sang them, it seemed to him that each man and woman could let their voice flow, uninhibited. They could put lyrics out of mind, forget about forming and pronouncing words. All they had to do was breathe, feel the resonance of music in their bodies. The audience, in turn, no longer had to strain themselves to decipher lyrics. They could hear the music alone, in pure form.

Yet the "Jewish Deathsong" was not just vocables. After the *lee-lai, lee-lai, lee-lai*, Rosebery added verses, which he had translated into German so that everyone in the camp could understand them. The song began much as Aleks knew it, as he remembered it sung by the passing Jewish musicians in Kraków. However, Rosebery had changed the lyrics.

Ten brothers were we together
All of us merchants of wine
One brother died one day
Now we're only nine
Oy-yoy! . . . Oy . . . yoy!

Then, only when Rosebery reached the chorus, did Aleks discover why he called his composition the "Jewish Deathsong."

Yidl with your fiddle
Moyshe with your bass
Play oh sing a little
We're bound for the gas!
For the gas!
For the gas!

In the final line of the chorus, Rosebery lengthened the word "gas" so that it sounded like a wail.

One brother now alone I remain
With whom shall I whine?
Nine brothers murdered all

Left: Aleks as a young man, in the late 1920s or early 1930s.

(Courtesy of Krzysztof Kulisiewicz.)

Above: An illustrated score of Aleks's song "A Dream of Peace." Created by Aleks while imprisoned in Sachsenhausen on a document that describes rules for inmates.

(Courtesy of Krzysztof Kulisiewicz.)

Left: An illustrated score of Aleks's song "Le Crucifié." Created by Aleks under his artist's name, Alex Alicouli, while imprisoned at Sachsenhausen.

(Courtesy of Krzysztof Kulisiewicz.)

Gruss aus Mława   Neidenburger Straße.

The Rosenberg family home in Mława (white, two-story house on the right). Photo likely taken before the First World War.

Above: Jewish residents of Mława protesting during the 1905 Russian Revolution.
(Courtesy of The Ghetto Fighters' House, Israel/Photos Archive.)

Right: Rosebery d'Arguto, Berlin, 1920.
(Courtesy of the United States Holocaust Memorial Museum.)

Rosebery's article about Rosa Luxemburg in *The World Revolution*, c. June 1919.

(Akademie der Künste, Berlin, Sammlung Rosebery d'Arguto (Rosebery d'Arguto Collection), No. 451.

With kind permission. Hereafter: Courtesy of the AdK, Berlin, Rosebery d'Arguto Collection No. 451.)

An early performance of the Rosebery d'Arguto Singing Community at the Berlin Philharmonie, May 1924.

(Courtesy of the AdK, Berlin, Rosebery d'Arguto Collection No. 451.)

Rosebery conducting a rehearsal with the children of workers, Neukölln, Berlin, 1925.
(Courtesy of the United States Holocaust Memorial Museum.)

Rosebery with one-time romantic pa
Catenia von Malottki.
(Courtesy of Tamar Israeli.)

Rosebery at the piano in his Berlin apartment. The replica mask of Beethoven hangs on the wall.
(Courtesy of Tamar Israeli.)

Left: Rosebery on a visit to Mława from Berlin, 1930. From right to left: Rosebery, his sister Lea, his nephew Josef, his father Shimshon, his nephew Izo, his sister Chana, and his brother-in-law Moshe Citrin (Lea's husband).
(Courtesy of The Ghetto Fighters' House, Israel/Photos Archive.)

ight: Rosebery ing with choir embers, likely veen 1930 and 1935. *(Courtesy of the AdK, Berlin, osebery d'Arguto llection No. 451.)*

Rosebery and members of the choir on an outdoor excursion, June 1935.
(Courtesy of the AdK, Berlin, Rosebery d'Arguto Collection No. 451.)

Rosebery with the choir of the Jewish gymnasium in Mława, 1937.
(Courtesy of the United States Holocaust Memorial Museum.)

The Rosenberg family home sometime after the German invasion.
(Courtesy of Jarosław Janiszewski.)

A gaunt Aleks poses for a photo immediately after the end of the war.
(Courtesy of Krzysztof Kulisiewicz.)

Aleks performing in his later years (date unknown).
(Courtesy of Krzysztof Kulisiewicz.)

Above: Aleks performing in a Nazi camp uniform, likely at the end of the 1960s.
(Courtesy of Krzysztof Kulisiewicz.)

Left: Aleks with his guitar at a performance of camp music (date unknown).
(Courtesy of Krzysztof Kulisiewicz.)

Self-portrait, painted by Aleks in the 1960s.
(Courtesy of Krzysztof Kulisiewicz.)

Aleks's painting of the grandmoth[
he encountered on the death mar[
(Courtesy of Krzysztof Kulisiewicz.)

Aleks, late in life (date unknown).
(Courtesy of Krzysztof Kulisiewicz.)

Remember all nine?
Oy-yoy! . . . Oy . . . yoy!

Yidl with your fiddle
Moyshe with your bass
The last, I'll sing a little
Now I'm bound for the gas!
Yidl with your fiddle
Moyshe with your bass
The last, I'll sing a little

Then came the last lines: *Ten brothers were we together / We never hurt another soul.* Finally, Rosebery sang in his falsetto voice, *lee-lai, lee-lai, lee-lai* once more: a lullaby to bring the lament to an end.

In that menacing autumn, when Rosebery chose an old Yiddish song as the basis of his requiem, he was following a long tradition of adapting folk music. There were already several versions of the original song "Tsen Brider." The one Aleks knew from his university days in Kraków had lyrics slightly different from the one Rosebery had grown up with. Still another version appeared in a film in the 1930s. In all likelihood, most of the Jews in Sachsenhausen knew the melody. Rosebery's choice of "Tsen Brider"—a distinctly Jewish song—must also have held personal meaning for him. Not since his childhood in Mława, under the religious stewardship of his father, had he lived in a world where Jewish culture or religion dictated life. During his rebellion as a teenager and his years living in Berlin, he had rejected Judaism and what came with it. Even in the name he used as an artist, he concealed his Jewish ethnicity. If someone did call him by his first name, they likely used Martin, not Moshe. His friends in Berlin never knew him to visit a synagogue or socialize with the city's many assimilated Jews. His nephew Justus saw no religious books or objects for worship in his uncle's apartment when he visited him before the war. Rosebery likely did not obscure his origins because of embarrassment or to shield himself from anti-Semitism. The faith of his forebears simply did not interest him. His peers remembered him as an atheist, dedicated to socialist ideals through and through, unmoved by the devotional and cultural traditions of his home and his parents and the pious families around whom he grew up.

Yet in creating his final musical work, he did not look to the working-class traditions that had directed his musical life. Like many before him, it seemed that as he aged before the war—and perhaps, like other assimilated or atheist Jews incarcerated by the Germans, this shift in him intensified while facing death in a Nazi camp—he returned to his ethnic origins and chose a distinctly Jewish song to create a distinctly Jewish lament. Perhaps, at what he thought was the end of his life, he wished to forge connections to the culture of his past. Perhaps he was moved, if only faintly, by the faith his parents had followed so closely. Aleks never found out. He could only surmise.

Not long after Rosebery sang Aleks his song, he asked him for a favor. After the war, would he get it published somewhere? Aleks promised that he would. Implicit in Rosebery's request was the acceptance that he, as a Jew, as an aging man in a Nazi camp, would not live to see what lay beyond the war. He did not know whether he would perish there, at Sachsenhausen, or in a camp to the east. He did not know how he would die—whether by hunger, by bullet, by gas. He simply sensed that death approached.

Aleks, on the other hand, had a chance to walk out the camp gatehouse alive. His odds, they both thought, were better. Like most other prisoners, Aleks was thin and weak, but he no longer toiled at the brickworks or on another detail where the probability of death was high. He spoke fluent German and had even told the fortunes of several SS men who occasionally sought his advice on matters of the heart. Aleks only had to ride out the remainder of the war—however long that would take. This was no simple or certain task, to be sure, but possible if he was careful, cunning, and lucky. One essential concern: he couldn't get sick. Even a prisoner of high standing could only do so much to avoid the viruses and bacteria that festered around the camp. If he grew too sick to work, his utility to the SS would vanish.

Hearing the "Jewish Deathsong" affirmed Aleks's dedication to Rosebery. Here was a man who, despite his education and age and erudition, spoke to Aleks as an equal. For over two years, Rosebery had taken the time to expose Aleks, this mere stripling, barely out of his teens, to music. He took him seriously as both a young man and a singer. If Rosebery was right and the Germans soon killed him, Aleks would have to make the most of their remaining time together.

BY SEPTEMBER 1942, life in Sachsenhausen had deteriorated. Food was scarce, disease widespread. The flowers that once adorned the camp were gone. Prisoners were eating them, so the SS ordered their removal. A swelling population of prisoners meant that the barracks had grown desperately crowded. Men were dying in appalling numbers.

Rosebery felt rushed by time. Rumors of death camps in German-occupied Poland were now rampant among the camp's Jews. Though they already suffered terribly, many feared deportation to the unknown destinations of the east. At Sachsenhausen they had a chance of survival; this camp's primary purpose was not extermination. Thus far, so long as they could endure the work, elude illness, and avoid the ire of the SS and camp foremen, it seemed possible to live to see the next day, and the day after that—at least for some amount of time.

With the "Jewish Deathsong" complete, Rosebery began to rehearse it with the choir. As always, they could only assemble at certain times and with the help of a select few German prisoners. With the crowding of the barracks, there were more eyes and ears and risk. The SS had also ordered three-tiered wooden bunks to be installed in each block, which filled the space where the choir usually assembled. But assemble they did. Rosebery's commitment had not wavered. Singing, both for the choir members and the men who were lucky enough to hear them, remained his priority.

The first time Aleks heard the choir perform the "Jewish Deathsong" was during a nighttime rehearsal in early October 1942. That night, Aleks remembered, a gloom hung in the air. A hard rain fell. The wind whipped and whistled through the trees just beyond the camp walls. Aleks looked up at the sky. It seemed blacker and more unforgiving than ever.

Aleks departed block 3, where he lived in the first ring of barracks, and snuck through the darkness of the campgrounds. He walked toward the little camp and the Jewish barracks. He entered the block where the rehearsal was to take place—likely number 39. The men were preparing. They shivered with cold. Their bodies had shrunk so much that their bones pushed up against the skin—visible around the cheeks, hidden beneath drill uniforms but no less present on the ribs and hips. Several of the men were wearing wooden clogs, the rough shoes a man got when the ones he had on when he arrived at Sachsenhausen wore out or were stolen and he couldn't secure a new pair. Aleks marveled at how Rosebery had managed to create a choir under these conditions. Assembling that night involved an enormous risk for everyone. The risk extended to Aleks. After all, it was forbidden for him—a non-Jew—to be present in a Jewish block.

When Rosebery stood before the choir, Aleks noticed how each member stared at him. Despite their physical weakness, they exuded what Aleks noted was a boundless confidence, a rare and profound trust. It reminded him of the Christmases of his childhood, when Grandfather Frost visited schools, and all the children would greet him with a look of awe. As Aleks remembered it, that night there was a blackout. Seated in the back of the barracks, wrapped in a blanket, he held a dim flashlight, one of the only sources of light. His flashlight drew long shadows on the floor, a powerful image, he thought. He made sure to point the beam downward so as not to attract attention from outside. He could hear footsteps, people moving about the grounds. He watched the men of the choir in the dim light as they waited. Rosebery raised his hands, and the singers, standing in their striped uniforms, cast their eyes on their conductor. In the feeble light, with his hands aloft, Rosebery appeared to Aleks like a great bird with wings spread wide. With a flourish of his hands, the choir began. They had likely warmed up with some of Rosebery's exercises, perhaps one of his Absolute Symphonic Chants, perhaps a tongue twister set to a melody. Then, he directed them in his latest composition, the "Jewish

Deathsong." First, the unison of bass—*bom, bom, bom, bom*—and then again—*bom, bom, bom, bom.* The intro, sung in just a few somber notes, was like a funeral procession—each *bom*, Rosebery's omen of death, like the footsteps of the men on the way to their demise. From the back of the barracks, it seemed to Aleks that Rosebery looked at the face of every man in his choir, giving each member his attention. Then came the *lee-lai, lee-lai, lee-lai,* sung in a pained falsetto by the youngest members of the choir, a few prisoners likely in their late teens, whose voices most closely resembled the pure tones of preadolescent males.

A soloist stepped forward. Aleks looked him up and down. He was tall, young. He still possessed the ropey, thick neck of a man newly arrived at Sachsenhausen. Aleks thought to himself: this man wants to live at all costs. In a rich baritone, the man sang the first verse, as the rest of the choir sang a supporting melody. *Ten brothers were we together, / All of us merchants of wine.* At the end of the verse, the man broke off abruptly. Aleks perceived this as representing the broken thread of many lives, including the lives of the Jews at Sachsenhausen. Then, after a short pause, the whole choir lamented *Oy-yoy! . . . Oy . . . yoy!*—followed by the chorus, *Yidl with your fiddle / Moyshe with your bass / Play oh sing a little / We're bound for the gas! / For the gas! / For the gas!* The men held the final syllable of the word "gas" for a long time, the note fading before the soloist began the second verse.

The scene mesmerized Aleks. The men sang with skill and refinement, but also with chilling emotion. There were none of the honeyed tones, the euphony of Rosebery's other arrangements for the Jewish choir. It struck Aleks that the "Jewish Deathsong" was not a song at all, but a sob of despair, an elegy created by one of them for all of them. Rosebery, its author, burned with intensity, singing in his special lead falsetto to guide this group of anguished, suffering men.

Partway through one of the subsequent verses, a group of SS guards burst in. They kicked and beat any man they could reach. Aleks saw a guard grip one of the youngest inmates of the barracks and smash him against a window. He fell in a heap, his head bloodied, shards of glass across the floor. Aleks slipped out a back window and disappeared into the maze of blocks and the darkness. As he ran off, he heard screams. When he got back to his bunk, he spent the night memorizing everything he had just witnessed.

Aleks never saw Rosebery again. On October 8, only a few days later, the SS loaded him onto a train and sent him, weak and consumed, south to the Dachau concentration camp. When Aleks managed to get back in touch with some of the other choir members, he learned what happened. The SS had marched them to the roll call square. Standing in the mud, soaked through by the rain, they continued to sing, *bom, bom, bom, bom*. Then they fell silent, the last of their strength spent. The SS beat them in the mud and forced them to stay there the night. Not everyone survived to see the light of dawn.

ROSEBERY'S DEPORTATION WAS an incalculable loss for Aleks. For more than two years, he had been the mentor and companion Aleks had always sought, the kind of intellectual confidante who, because Aleks was not a student of music, would never have been in contact with him had there not been the war. In fact, the chances of Aleks meeting a man like Rosebery, a former radical leftist, a supremely talented composer and conductor, a Polish Jew who had assimilated into Berlin's proletariat society, were next to zero. The war was what brought them together. Perhaps Dachau would protect Rosebery from the gas chambers for a time. Yet a transfer to Auschwitz would arrive sooner or later, and with it, near certain death.

That very month of October 1942, Heinrich Himmler, the commander of the SS, signed an order requiring that all Jews in camps in Germany be sent to Auschwitz for extermination. On October 22, just shy of two weeks after Rosebery had been put on a train for Dachau, the SS marched 454 of Sachsenhausen's Jews to the roll call square and then to the disinfection facility.

Hans Hüttner, the friend of Rosebery's who often watched the Jewish choir rehearse and whose cousin Max sang in it, remembered lining

up two arms' lengths to the next man. Once they reached the disinfection facility, the SS forced them to undress while they harassed them. In
exchange for any warm clothing the men were wearing, the SS issued each
man a thin, summer uniform made of canvas. Watching what was taking place, Hans began to fear that the SS did not plan to deport them
to another camp but rather to murder them right there on the grounds
of Sachsenhausen—perhaps with the neck-shooting setup used on the
Soviet prisoners a year earlier. Hans was not the only man in the group to
come to this conclusion. To him and several other prisoners, all that lay
ahead was death at the hands of the Nazis—either at Auschwitz or here at
Sachsenhausen with a bullet through the neck.

Later that day, when the SS sent the Jews back to their barracks, Hans
overheard a group of his close friends asking, "Can we go to our death
without resistance after we have experienced so much?" Isolated and
unable to contact the German communists who had long helped Jews
at Sachsenhausen, Hans and his friends came to a decision: rather than
being shot in the back of the neck or being sent to Auschwitz, they would
make the SS shoot them right there, on the roll call square of Sachsenhausen, for everyone to see. That evening, he and a group of some seventeen
other Jewish prisoners, mainly young and dedicated communists, jumped
out a window in their barracks and made their way to the roll call square
where, as it happened, the men of the main camp were being counted at
the end of a day's work. Hans remembered the rain that chilly late October
evening, the brightness of the camp's floodlights, the incredible silence
even though so many people stood there. They began to shout at the SS,
"Shoot now, you cowards!" They did not create an overtly political slogan,
something with communist zeal, because they did not want to endanger
their German colleagues. Several guards approached them. Hans and the
others wrestled them to the ground. More guards soon appeared, guns
drawn, ready to fire.

Then a voice rang out. It was the SS guard in charge of the camp that
night. "Don't shoot!" he yelled. "Don't shoot!" Instead, the guards, who
now far outnumbered Hans and the others, seized them and beat them,

with clubs and fists and boots. Yet Hans did not feel the blows. Instead, for the first time in the camp, he felt a sense of freedom. He relished the small rebellion against the Nazis who had destroyed nearly everything about his world. He would never truly experience that feeling again.

That the camp leader refused to shoot struck Hans as significant. He wondered if a deportation east was actually in the works for him and the other Jews. After all, the machine gun on Tower A could easily have cut them down in a spray of lead. Perhaps the bullets would have sliced through the flesh of other prisoners standing at attention on the roll call square. Surely, though, the SS would have seen it as little more than collateral damage, bodies to be ticked off of their accounting. Hans speculated that killing him and the others would have resulted in the need for a report. Perhaps it would have meant a reprimand of the camp leader, a seemingly capable man, someone who could quell a rebellion without a single shot fired.

Once Hans and the other Jews were subdued, the camp leader delivered a speech. As some had suspected, he said that they would soon be transferred to a facility in the east. He swore, however, on his soldier's honor that they would be sent to a work camp, not an extermination camp. As Hans remembered it, the Jews on the square demanded winter clothing and better rations for all who would be deported. The camp leader ordered that they be given sweatshirts and extra food. Late that same night, the SS marched all 454 of Sachsenhausen's Jews, including the members of Rosebery's choir, out of the camp in the direction of the train station. As they marched, some of the younger men near Hans sang "The Sun Doesn't Set For Us," a well-known song among youth movements.

Some prisoners congratulated Hans and the other young men for their rebellion and the moderately more generous rations it yielded, food that they shared. Hans remembered many hugs and handshakes along the way.

At the tracks, a long line of train cars waited. The SS organized the men alphabetically and forced about fifty at a time into each car. Then the train pulled out of the station, leaving the still, dark town of Oranienburg behind, headed to an unknown destination.

THREE DAYS LATER on October 25, when the train came to a stop and the doors slid open, Hans learned where he was: Auschwitz. During an immediate selection, the SS decided he looked strong and sent him to a sub-camp to work at the IG Farben plant—a chance at life. His cousin Max got a coveted work assignment, too, perhaps because, like Hans, he looked fit. Many of the others, including members of the Jewish choir, were deemed too weak for a labor assignment. Soon after, the SS herded them to the gas chambers.

Rosebery departed Dachau on a train bound for Auschwitz a few days before Hans, on October 19. No one could remember seeing him arrive at the camp or heard what became of him, though Hans tried to get information. Given Rosebery's age and his weakened state, he may have perished on the train ride from Dachau. If he arrived at Auschwitz alive, the SS likely sent him straight to the gas chambers. His father Shimshon, the man who wished for him to be a rabbi, and his brother Jacob, a cantor, met the same fate at Auschwitz. Perhaps Shimshon's death came before his child's, perhaps after. The only certainty was that the SS quickly reduced both father and son to ash, mixed into the soil of the flatlands of Oświęcim.

PART III

Chapter 10

―⁓

Sachsenhausen. Spring 1944

T wo punishing winters had passed in the year and a half since the SS marched Rosebery out of Sachsenhausen and put him on a train south for Dachau.

Aleks grieved for him. Sachsenhausen without Rosebery seemed unbearable. Yet to wallow in the cruelty of the world was to put oneself at risk. If he wanted to stay alive, he had to remain focused. He had a promise to keep.

Since Rosebery's deportation from Sachsenhausen, the fighting had begun to go badly for the Germans. At Stalingrad, the Red Army defeated the Wehrmacht. The North African campaign had reached an end, Mussolini had been deposed, and Allied soldiers were invading Italy. These events buoyed the hopes of many prisoners, including Aleks.

Yet as the war effort deteriorated for the Germans, so did conditions at Sachsenhausen. New prisoners streamed in, including groups of Frenchmen.

Almost immediately after Rosebery vanished, Aleks began to perform the "Jewish Deathsong" in barracks on the main campground. He sang it at any opportunity, before any audience that would receive him in their barracks at the end of a long day. In early 1943, he procured a guitar, which he plucked and strummed as he sang. He wanted to give his audiences a sense of what that last rehearsal of the Jewish choir had been like: the gathering in secret to sing in a Nazi camp, the sound of the barracks door swinging open, the thuds of approaching SS boots, the cries of the men being beaten after he slipped out the window. To end each performance of the "Jewish Deathsong," he shouted, *"Alles raus!,"* imitating what he remembered the SS screaming as they burst into barracks 39.

Aleks composed at a rapid pace. Throughout the day, as he toiled, verses streamed across the blank pages of his mind. At the roll call square at night, during seemingly endless prisoner counts, when men around him collapsed into heaps in the freezing temperatures, he closed his eyes and wrote. He entered a trancelike state, where he did not feel the bite of the cold, where he did not hear the footsteps of the guards stomping around him.

He wanted each composition, each poem, to be a record of an event or a thought or a feeling, a type of literary documentation of a concentration camp. He knew that after the war, survivors across Europe—even himself—would reconstruct the life and times of the camp. But a song or a poem, crafted minutes or hours after a prisoner witnessed a hanging or a flogging, would be a truer testimony than anything remembered or read or related long afterward. These assemblages of words were as close as a prisoner could get to the pages of a diary, a roll of film nestled in a camera, anything real to record the terror at Sachsenhausen. These verses were tangible, immediate, lasting.

In various barracks around the camp, Aleks wailed Alyosha's broadside, "Hecatomb 1941," tapping out the rhythm with his fingers on the wooden bedsteads. He performed Rosebery's "Jewish Deathsong" in the hopes that perhaps it would keep some small part of his friend alive. His prisoner audiences were usually keen for the music, no matter how grim it was.

Aleks regularly performed in some ten different blocks on the main camp-grounds, those where he felt welcomed, where it seemed safest. With each block housing four or five hundred men, Aleks often had a great audience, a more substantial one than ever before in his life.

On a lucky day, Aleks and the others might have two, even three hours of respite from the work details, though as the war progressed, free time grew rare. They could sometimes put on a program, so long as they secured the block elder's permission. When they had consent, they had to be more careful about which songs they performed. Block elders inter-acted with the SS. No matter how careful the prisoners were, this was dangerous. Instead of singing Rosebery's or Alyosha's songs, Aleks sang about the Muselmänner, a less embittered song, though still a rebuke and therefore a potential risk.

Aleks's songs often depicted the carnage of the camp. He wrote one in 1942 about Wilhelm Böhm, a German prisoner who worked at the crema-torium, burning corpses, including those of the Soviet POWs shot in 1941. Whenever Wilhelm caught sight of a passing prisoner, this hunched man with dangling arms would grin and call out to him, "Come, come! I'm sure you'll come to me! Why not straight away?"

After encountering Wilhelm, Aleks composed the song "Black Böhm": *Whether it's by night or day, / I smoke corpses—full of joy! / I make a black, black smoky smoke, / 'Cause I am black, black Böhm!* The melody alone, based on a Ukrainian folk song, was simple, even pleasant. Yet Aleks dis-torted it, imitating Black Böhm's voice and menacing laugh. He would sing, *And some chicks and some hags, / I'd like some kiddies, too. / I wish I had a hundred chimneys, / Exactly like in Birkenau! / Hip hooray! Russkies to hell! / But still there are no Jews here! / Oh, my! Could be in '43 / They'll send some SS-guys to me! / Hah, hah, hah, hah, hah!* Sometimes when Aleks performed this song, men in his audience couldn't cope. They cried or entered what he perceived as a kind of nightmarish shock, triggered by the reminder of this wicked cremator. Other times, Aleks watched as pris-oners shivered while he sang—as if an apparition had floated by behind him. Aleks believed they quivered because they knew that Wilhelm Böhm was a real man, a man who one day might slide their own stiff bodies into the fires of the crematorium.

Yet most of Aleks's songs contained an element of uplift—perhaps a broadside against the SS captors, dark satire, or a lyric that said, implicitly or explicitly: *You're going to go home again; that which you see here is only temporary.* Music had to be hopeful in some small way, especially now, nearly four years into his incarceration at Sachsenhausen. If he died, so, too, perished Rosebery's "Jewish Deathsong," so, too, perished the dozens of songs and poems other prisoners had entrusted to him. Since Rosebery's deportation, many other prisoners had sought Aleks out, asking him to memorize a poem or a few verses for a song—some bit of who they were. Men of all nationalities, ages, and backgrounds had been creating poems and songs. Ostensibly, they wanted their verses or camp song to endure even if they did not. Czechs, Germans, Poles, Frenchmen came to Aleks, sometimes in the barracks after working hours, sometimes out of doors, discreetly appealing to him to include their camp creation in the annals of his mind. "Aleks," they would say, "do you have some room in your archive?" He would close his eyes and respond, "Dictate it to me." Sometimes, a man might come back to him a month later to check if he had memorized his song accurately. Aleks welcomed the challenge because he could always reproduce the songs.

Aleks memorized each line that a prisoner brought him, each comma, each semicolon, each dramatic pause, exactly as the hypnotist Roob had taught him to do in 1926 after the shock of a live wire destroyed his ability to speak. Over time, as Aleks memorized more and more songs, it felt as though an octopus of camp culture undulated within him, ever expanding as the hatred and harm and the most intimate longings of so many prisoners filled his being.

Once a prisoner had dictated his song or poem to Aleks, he was relieved of it. It was now sheltered in Aleks's mind, the only way to preserve something, since the SS forbade a prisoner from having pencil or paper. If the SS caught a man keeping a diary, scrawling notes about the camp, they would punish him—perhaps with a dozen lashes from the cat-o'-nine-tails, perhaps with something even more brutal. Still, some prisoners flouted the risks, managed to find pencil stubs, and jotted things down. Sometimes a prisoner approached Aleks with his camp creations recorded on scraps of paper, on shreds of canvas, or in a tiny notebook he had hidden in the ceiling beams in the barracks or buried in an unfrequented corner of the campgrounds. That prisoners came to Aleks to dictate their camp creations made him feel needed, gave him purpose and human connection and a sense of self-worth. From the start, he noted that these prisoners did not come to him to memorize a secret prison manifest or a detailed list of those whom the SS and prisoner functionaries had murdered. Rarely did a man want Aleks to memorize a catalog of perpetrators or the crimes of a particularly brutal guard. Mostly they wanted him to preserve their creative output, raging salvos against the Germans, maudlin scribblings, poems—some naturalistic, some filled with masochism, some blasphemous, some desperate. Yet prisoners did not just come with grim creations. Just as often, a man approached Aleks to share personal verses bursting with blissful confessions of love, the tears shed over the memory of his child's smile, the yearning for the calm of home.

No matter the subject or literary quality, Aleks believed that each creation held an absolute truth, an urgent testimony, be it appalling or uplifting, created by a human under circumstances as bleak and grim as anyone could have imagined. And he struggled to preserve these testimonies at all costs. Aleks knew that these men had become pawns of the German state, as had he, useful only until the SS had wrung out of them every last bit of their strength. For many of them, a song or poem might be the only thing that remained—the sole evidence of a life lived.

In the course of memorizing camp verses, Aleks met men like Henryk Głowacki, who wrote the song "Longing" for a young Polish woman called Janina who came from his hometown, Rzeszów. Henryk told Aleks that Janina grew up in a rich home and loved poetry. She played the piano and even performed in dance bands before the war. Henryk fell in love with her. Janina sent him letters for a time after the Gestapo arrested him. But soon her letters stopped, and Henryk discovered that she married another man while he was locked up in Sachsenhausen. *I play a song of longing for you today / a song of longing—that's all I have in my heart today*, Henryk's composition went.

Aleks learned Józef Denys's poem, "We Poles," a series of patriotic verses that spoke of the strength and resilience of the Polish people, of red and white flags and soaring eagles. Tomasz Poprawka, another prisoner, came to Aleks and dictated a song that went, *I was in a camp once / We will cut those monsters down, / Hollaria! Hollario! / Until our axes grow dull! / Hollaria! Hollario! / We will raise the gallows high, / We will raise the gallows high.* Another inmate, Adam Kowalski, asked Aleks to memorize a carol he had written: *Barbed wire at the doorstep, / Sinister gazes of the cats— / And in the barracks, behind the cot, / Half-nude specters of people. / Hey, carol, carol!* Aleks memorized Jan Vala's song "Kartoszki!," which became a camp hit among the non-German prisoners. Jan performed the satirical song, in which he longed for different foods, in many languages, for example, during the Czech-Polish soirees organized by Josef Kořínek, of Prague: *In a dream I was gulping down a nice fat chicken on my own / And a pork cutlet, and two thick ham hocks. / Coffee with cream and five sweet little cakes / By God, if I were to think of it, I would have to scream: oh, no! / And so, I plead: who will give me potato skins?*

With all these poems and songs packed in his mind, Aleks's absolute priority was to wait out the war and leave the camp alive. The end of the fighting seemed on the horizon, especially after the German defeat at Stalingrad the year before. For Aleks and many other prisoners, the loss represented an immense psychological turning point, so much so that when it happened, he added a second verse to the song "Germania!," which he originally composed in 1941 when Hitler's expansion seemed unstoppable: *You had half the world, Germania! Now you've got crap in your pants / and crap to patch your pants! Shit-caked country!* Then, still euphoric by the news of Stalingrad, he composed another set of lyrics, applied them to the Polish folk song "Nad Ebru falą," and gave it the title "Adolf's Farewell to the World." One night in May 1944, Aleks debuted the song at a musical recital. His close friend, the Russian Andrej Sarapkin, attended the event.

Aleks first sang several Polish national songs, then, in a surprise to Andrej, he performed the new song, tapping as he often did on the wooden beams of the sleeping bunks. Mocking Hitler, Aleks sang: *Bid farewell to me Moscow, farewell Samara, / My distant Leningrad, farewell! / Oh, soon the party will be over, when, in Crimea, / They'll take the crap out of me for good. / Ja, Ja—ist stimmt das* [it's really true] */ Farewell to you mountains, fair Ural Mountains, / You with your army, I bid farewell. / You are Stalin, man-of-steel Stalin, / I'm just an impotent Adolf.* Aleks left the slow melodiousness of "Nad Ebru falą" intact, but he sang "Adolf's Farewell to the World" with a jeer in his voice. It was as if he was wearing a taunting smile, especially when he sang the line, *I'm just an impotent Adolf.* Though Andrej and many of his comrades were elated by the song, he found it almost impossible to believe that someone would have the courage to perform it in a Nazi camp. Every lyric could have led him to the gallows.

Though the war effort was deteriorating for the Germans, Aleks's survival was far from certain. Until that point, he had repeatedly endured physical strain that nearly killed him. Perhaps worst of all was the time when, not long after Rosebery was deported in 1942, he found himself on a camp punishment detail called the shoe-testing track. Every morning, he and dozens of others assembled near the roll call square. With German-issued shoes on their feet, they set off on the stone and gravel track, marching in circles all day, a 45-pound bag of sand strapped to their backs. Like many of the work details, the shoe-testing track had a war-related purpose: to test the performance and durability of various types of synthetic leather meant for the German army and the broader population. When Aleks found himself on the shoe-testing track, it was still bitterly cold, and after hours of marching, singing upbeat German songs, prisoners of higher status would pour his midday meal—a ladle of soup—into his hat. Often, the SS would shout, "Hats on!" and the hot soup would run down his back. It warmed him as it trickled down, but on really cold days it froze. The guards never permitted the prisoners a bathroom break, and so they relieved themselves as they marched. Urine burned their thighs, feces froze against their legs. Soon, sores appeared on Aleks's calves. Any longer than a few days on this detail meant death. Aleks knew he had to use his influence to get a new assignment.

Before Aleks could arrange a transfer, he met Jiří Maleček, a Czech pharmacy student. When they could, they stuck together as they marched in endless circles. Aleks felt drawn to Jiří. Like Aleks, he had studied a sensible if prosaïc subject before the war. Jiří's true love was Slavic literature, and like Aleks with his music, he had devoted much of his free time reading and composing poetry before the Gestapo arrested him.

For distraction through the endless hours of marching, Aleks and Jiří whispered made-up stories to each other. Aleks often told Jiří to pretend that they were walking on a pilgrimage. With each step around the track, they left Oranienburg behind, then Berlin, then Germany. Taking a southeastern route, they passed through Wrocław, then Brno, where Jiří had studied. Finally, they arrived at Olomouc, Jiří's hometown and a site holy to Catholics. As they marched, they counted off each mile, and Aleks would murmur to Jiří: "We've already made it to Wrocław, don't give up!" In a rare expression of faith, Aleks promised God that if he survived the shoe-testing track, he would make a real pilgrimage from Cieszyn to Olomouc, as a demonstration of gratitude and devotion.

Olomouc was on Aleks's mind for another reason. It was the city to which Bożena and her family had retreated when Polish forces occupied the Zaolzie lands in 1938. Aleks longed for Bożena. Even though they had spent time together in 1938, she had never reciprocated his love for her, and though he had had women after her, she remained on his mind. So much did he think of her that he began to credit her, alongside music, for his survival at Sachsenhausen. He often wondered what had become of her, whether she still lived in Olomouc, whether she was even alive. In his mind, he pictured the little market square where she set up her stand on those simple days six years earlier to sell passersby vegetables. Once, while still pursuing her, he spent a week writing a twenty-eight-page letter in which he avowed his feelings, hoping that an epistolary confession might spark a glimmer of love for him. But some weeks later, he found the letter in his mailbox. She had returned it unopened.

Nevertheless, Bożena often continued to appear in Aleks's dreams. One night, he dreamed that the two of them were walking on an overcast day near Olomouc. In the dream, Aleks had grown old and tired. Deep wrinkles furrowed his face. Bożena had not aged a day. She was young and beautiful, just as he remembered her in 1938. She looked at him with great sadness.

In another dream, Bożena gazed at Aleks sweetly, but when he whispered a few words in her ear, her face transformed, and instead of the young woman he loved, Mother Mary stood before him. Aleks wondered what the dream was supposed to mean. The next morning, he began to compose a melody in his head: *Mother of God was with me / she wanted to stay with me for a long while— / she had tears in her eyes.*

AS THE GERMAN war effort worsened, so did conditions at Sachsenhausen. The inmate population had grown to over thirty thousand, a figure reached in part by transports, the year before, of French prisoners numbering twenty-five hundred. Food, as ever, was in short supply. The chaotic nature of the camp only intensified. Yet for Aleks, certain parts of his life had improved. The shoe-testing track was but a memory for him now. He had used his influence to get on a new work detail. To his sorrow, however, the SS deported Jiří to the quarries of Gross-Rosen after they discovered a manuscript of his poetry beneath a pile of hay. Aleks had lost many friends by then. Some died in Sachsenhausen. Others were transferred to camps nearby and died there. One close comrade, Bolek Marcinek, the young Pole from Cieszyn who introduced Aleks to the Jewish choir, had by then staged a daring and successful escape from Sachsenhausen.

When new prisoners were brought to Sachsenhausen, which happened often, Aleks memorized the music or poetry they brought with them, glimpses of the outside world that would connect him and his fellow old-timers to life beyond the barbed wire. Sometimes, a song or poem composed at another camp took on a new life in Sachsenhausen. This happened when Włodzimierz Wnuk, from the Gusen subcamp of Mauthausen, wrote a poem about the quarry there. Entitled "Living Stones," Włodzimierz's verses recounted the plight of thousands of prisoners who excavated granite and died under the weight of the huge rocks they had to carry. In the poem, Włodzimierz wanted to convey the terror of their work, but also what he came to see as the moral toughening and solidarity the work induced in them. He looked at the great blocks of granite lying on the hills all around him. He saw the beads of sweat or the droplets of blood that fell onto the stones he hoisted. He remarked, "We have become more like chunks of rock," and he wrote: *We are like living stones, / Hard, steadfast boulders. / No flames will burn us, / the sun won't blemish us.*

Włodzimierz often recited the poem when the men gathered in Gusen to share culture with one another, as Aleks and so many others did at Sachsenhausen. A few prisoners even memorized the poem because of its simplicity and power. When one of them was transferred to Sachsenhausen, he recited Włodzimierz's poem for the men in his new barracks. The poem circulated until it reached Aleks, who was impressed by it. He decided to set it to music.

This time, for Włodzimierz's poem, he chose to compose the melody himself. He drew inspiration from a work detail where prisoners had to dig heavy clay. In the rhythm of the song, he tried to portray the shuffling of the exhausted men who, he imagined, experienced such immense fatigue that they could hardly lift their legs to walk.

With the melody complete, Aleks introduced the song, which his friend, the Frenchman Roland Tillard, accompanied on an accordion. Many international prisoners attended the performance, and the song took on a new life in translation in Czech, Serbian, and German. From a popular poem in Gusen, Włodzimierz's verses had become a popular song in Sachsenhausen.

SOMETIME IN THE spring of 1944, Aleks used his connections to get a new work assignment: the unit where the SS trained guard dogs. He heard the work was less deadly, even unhurried, to the extent that such work existed at Sachsenhausen. On his first day at this work detail, however, he realized that he had been mistaken. Instead of feeding dogs or cleaning out their kennels as he had imagined, he saw prisoners forced to play the role of thieves or escapees to give the dogs practice in attacking them and yanking them to the ground. A prisoner functionary handed Aleks a padded outfit meant to protect against the teeth of the German shepherds. Then the SS ordered him to dart away before releasing the young dogs. When a dog reached him and clamped its jaws around his legs, Aleks felt the immense force of its teeth. The padding did little to help.

From then on, starting with the morning light, ending when the sun dropped behind the trees, dogs chased and tormented Aleks. Often, a dog's clench drew blood, inflicting teeth punctures in the flesh of his calf or forearm, inviting infection. Yet again, Aleks realized that he had a work assignment that would kill him if he stayed at it for too long. So, as he had done since the earliest days of his imprisonment, he drew up a scheme. One day, he approached a guard he thought would be sympathetic and said, "I am an outstanding expert in the psyche of dogs and a qualified trainer as well." The guard, skeptical, replied with the shadow of a threat in his voice, "We shall see," as though he had just found a way to weed out a lying prisoner who, once caught, could be punished. Yet the lie got Aleks off the training ground. A short time later, the SS assigned him a black German shepherd called Asta.

Now, instead of being pursued by angry dogs, Aleks watched over Asta. He fed her, he cleaned her. He found her intelligent and kind, a welcome companion. During the day, they did exercises together. He led her around the training facility. He gave her commands, trying as best he could to appear authoritative and experienced. Of course, he knew nothing more about training dogs than what he could remember from having a family pet as a boy, but the ruse worked. Though he felt the threat of the SS, who might have killed him if it emerged that he did not possess the skills he claimed and had wasted their time, the work was far better than being chased and bitten. When Asta gave birth to a litter of puppies, the

SS issued gruel to feed them as they grew. Aleks looked longingly at the incredible treasure of food on the tray as he brought it to the dogs. But he noticed that Asta watched him keenly as he portioned the food for each of her offspring. He was too nervous to take any for himself.

One day, Aleks arrived at Asta's kennel and saw that one of her eyes was swollen. Pus dripped thickly from her duct. Over the next few days, her other eye swelled as well, and it seemed that she had gone blind. Every day, he washed her eyes as best he could, and as he cleaned her, she licked his hands, in what he took as an act of gratitude. One morning, Aleks awoke in his barracks with terrible pain behind his eyes. When he opened them, everything seemed concealed in a haze. Each day, the pain and blurriness worsened, and within a week he lost sight in both his eyes. He begged other prisoners to help him. The SS showed little interest in treating their captives. The burden of medicine usually fell on a few prisoners who happened to be trained doctors. But they had too many patients to treat and little by way of medicine or equipment. In most cases, a man healed on his own or he died. That was the camp calculus.

Aleks began to panic. Blindness was a death sentence. After having suffered so much at Sachsenhausen, the thought that blindness from a dog virus would be the end of him—and with him, all the music he had collected—ignited a terrible seething anger in him. He would fail Rosebery and all the other men who had entrusted him with their songs. "There is no grace here," he thought. "A blind man can't escape this hell."

Aleks lay in the camp sick bay. The room stank of disease and death. Around him men moaned in pain. On his cot, in the delirium of his disease, he began to believe that when someone goes blind, musical sensitivities sharpen. And so, with the crematorium looming nearer and an unbearable fear churning within him, he turned again to music.

During these days in the sick bay, Aleks composed some of his darkest, bleakest songs. First, he composed the melody for a poem called "Crucified 1944." He had written the verses some weeks before, when newly arrived French prisoners recounted a story of German soldiers crucifying a three-year-old boy in a village near Nice. Aleks listened to every detail and turned their story into a poem. Now, in his own darkness, he wanted to put the verses to music, to a suggestive melody, one that would suit the tragic story. During the first few bars, he tried to introduce the mood of the song, to represent a scream of desperation, to condemn the Germans before the entire world. He took inspiration from funeral marches as he composed the melody, which he did in a raving state, his mind filled with premonitions of death. In moments of semiconsciousness, visions of the little boy, nailed to the farmhouse gate, swollen and bloodied, appeared to him. The boy's eyes stared at him blankly; his mouth seemed to whisper, though Aleks could not make out what he was saying. Aleks also heard the boy's mother screaming. He wondered if he had begun to lose his mind. In his state of incoherence, he composed his melody. He hummed it to himself, adding the verses he had finished before he got sick: *A son of man was crucified, / A helpless child was crucified! / His eyes poked out with an inch-long nail, / His head crushed, his tongue torn out. / His mother was looking at it while dying: / Both hands nailed to the door!*

Aleks composed another song while in the medical barracks. For "Hymn from the Depths of Hell," he borrowed the verses of Varsovian journalist and poet Leonard Krasnodębski and added a melody, which he based in part on Frédéric Chopin's funeral march. The lyrics went: *Hear our hymn from the depths of hell! / May it keep our killers from ever sleeping well / Sing! Sing! / From the depths of hell— / May it keep our killers, / May it keep our killers / From ever sleeping well.*

Aleks first performed Leonard's hymn at a secret gathering in the camp medical barracks—even among the sick and dying, prisoners found ways to take part in culture. Two prisoner orderlies led Aleks, still blind, from his cot to a place before the gathered crowd. André Gouillard, who was in the audience that night, recalled seeing Aleks stand before a podium made out of a straw sack. André could see that Aleks's eyelids were stuck together, that pus caked his eyelashes. He was terribly thin. When Aleks began to sing, he raised his hands in fists. His voice seemed filled with madness and hatred; his pleading reminded André of a sick, crying child. André later wrote, "The audience gazed upon the soloist

as if upon a statue of revenge. Several sick prisoners became powerless.
I understood only two words: 'choral' and 'attention.' When the word
'attention' sounded for the second time . . . I lost consciousness." Leonard never heard the melody Aleks composed for his poem. After returning from a brutal work assignment one day, Aleks heard that the SS had
forced him to commit suicide. Leonard hanged himself in a medical barracks room.

AFTER WEEKS OF suffering and blindness, terrified that a prisoner functionary or a guard would come to finish him off, a German doctor began
to treat Aleks's eyes. He never learned why. He wondered if he had become
the subject of medical experimentation. Might the treatment have horrific
effects? Was the doctor simply killing him with drugs rather than the lead
of a bullet or the blunt end of a club? Rumors had long circulated that
SS doctors were conducting terrifying experiments on prisoners, such as
slicing incisions into a man's thigh and introducing infections through
patches of dirty cloth to see how different drugs would treat the disease.
Vaguer rumors spoke of children, perhaps Jews from the east, brought to
Sachsenhausen to be used for experiments.

Aleks's sight began to recover. The swelling receded. The oozing pus
dried up. The seal of his eyelids broke. He never discovered what the doctor had given him. He never learned whether he had been the subject of
medical experiments. But what did it matter? Seeing the world again, even
the terrible world of Sachsenhausen, was a relief perhaps more intense
than anything he'd experienced before.

Sight meant going back to work. It meant being useful again to the SS.
It meant life over summary death. When Aleks returned to the camp, his
eyes fully healed, he saw how many new prisoners had arrived at Sachsenhausen. The camp population seemed to have exploded. Among the
arriving prisoners were large convoys of Jews, exhausted and emaciated.
The SS placed them in satellite camps. Aleks learned that many had come
from Auschwitz, where he thought Rosebery had been deported. He likely

asked around for information about his friend, but none of the new prisoners knew anything about him.

As 1944 progressed, Aleks grew more and more confident that it was only a matter of time before the war would end and he could return to Poland and keep his promise to Rosebery. He navigated the camp with utmost care. Men died around him every day. Like the corpse collectors of the plague years in medieval Europe, prisoners roamed the campgrounds, hauling wooden carts piled with bodies. They fetched them from the medical rooms or the barracks or the roll call square, where prisoners had left fallen comrades earlier in the day. Fear still simmered in Aleks and spiked when he came into contact with an SS guard or an infamous prisoner functionary. That same anxiety showed up in many of his songs and also in the way he performed. He tried to convey the nervousness he and others felt by singing with abruptly changing tempos, going from slow to fast, then back to slow again to create an unnerving impression.

One of the big influxes of prisoners began in late August 1944. In Warsaw, the Polish resistance launched an armed uprising. The Germans responded with immense force, killing tens of thousands of Varsovians and carting off thousands of captives to camps, including Sachsenhausen. Between mid-August and mid-September, some six thousand Polish men arrived at the camp. The SS placed the Polish women at another camp called Ravensbrück, which stood about thirty-five miles north. Following these transports of Poles, a month later, some three thousand Dutchmen arrived from the Herzogenbusch camp in the south of the Netherlands, which the SS shut down as the Allies neared the Dutch frontier. The new inmates told harrowing stories. The Poles spoke of how the Germans had bombed Warsaw into heaps of rubble, with only the skeletons of buildings remaining. Some of the Dutchmen recounted how, before they left Herzogenbusch, the SS had shot over one hundred of their comrades.

For Aleks, the most distressing news was that the Gestapo had arrested his little sister, the nineteen-year-old Łucja, and sent her to Ravensbrück. The charge was conspiracy with the Kraków underground to assassinate a Nazi official.

The news stunned him. That Łucja, his only sibling, would end up at Ravensbrück a short distance north from Sachsenhausen, seemed an especially twisted turn of fate for the Kulisiewicz family. Aleks had never felt close to Łucja. She was born seven years after him. But she was his sister, and he knew how brutally the SS treated the women in Ravensbrück. Not long after he learned about her fate, he composed a song for her. Drawing upon a mixture of childhood legends of dragons and villains and the heroes who resisted them, he composed a ballad. *Beyond the mountains, beyond the forests, / Near Berlin, behind barbed-wire, / Near Berlin, in Ravensbrück / There my Wanda waits*, one stanza read.

BY THE TIME the weather turned cold in the fall, Aleks knew that the tide of the war had changed. Broadcasts from London, which some prisoners caught with secret radios, described the Allied advances. They had invaded France, attacking the Germans both from the north and the south. Then they liberated Paris. In the east, the Red Army was advancing toward Germany. The remaining Wehrmacht battalions were in retreat.

Aleks had done everything he could to survive. He had told lies, pretended to be clairvoyant, and used his charm and wits to build inroads into the powerful prisoner circles that could be of use to him. He had to hold on a bit longer. The war would end soon, perhaps in a matter of months. Finally, it seemed plausible that he might leave Sachsenhausen and Germany and this dreadful time behind and unburden himself of the camp music and poetry he had memorized over the course of the war.

At night, Aleks listened to the bombs plummeting earthward onto Berlin to the south. During an intense raid, the sky flushed with the glow of a burning city. Sometimes, he and the others sang in soft voices before they fell asleep. Aleks loved one song in particular: *Kiss me as I fall asleep, / Put your hands where my eyes are / And all my bright dreams / I will tell you, my love, / Kiss me as I fall asleep.* No one knew who wrote the song. It had traveled into Sachsenhausen from another camp with a transport of new prisoners. Those simple words soothed them.

Chapter 11

⟶

The first buds of spring, 1945, signaled the start of Aleks's fifth year as a captive at Sachsenhausen. The snows had melted. The sun rose earlier. The evening light lasted longer. Aleks examined his body. He guessed his weight was no more than 100 pounds. Now, like the Muselmänner he sighted when he first passed through the gates of the camp in 1940, he did not walk, he shuffled. He moved in exhausted, dragging paces, his feet scraping the ground. What was left of him? Bones covered in skin, ashy skin. But a mind full of music and poetry. By then, he had created nearly fifty of his own camp songs and had memorized the compositions of dozens of other prisoners. And he wasn't done.

When Aleks met Henryk Tadeusz Nejman, the young man seemed close to death. He lay on a cot in the hospital barracks, at the crest of his youth, hardly able to move, needlessly, stupidly dying. On his deathbed, in a near paralyzed state of hunger, Henryk composed poems. This is why Aleks sought him out.

It was too late for Henryk. No amount of food could revive him. That he would die seemed especially cruel to Aleks, for Henryk was known to many as one of the finest poets of Sachsenhausen. Seldom had Aleks encountered poetry of such force and refinement. In a world where Germany never launched a war or built concentration camps or attempted to exterminate or enslave whole groups of people, Henryk's verses would have appeared in literary magazines. Perhaps he would have a book of selected verse in the works. And yet, here he lay on his cot forming poems as he slowly died.

A Varsovian student of Polish philology, Henryk had arrived at Sachsenhausen the year before, in the fall of 1944, as part of the huge group of Poles arrested during the Warsaw Uprising, which he and his fourteen-year-old sister had joined. With tens of thousands of prisoners living within the main Sachsenhausen camp and its numerous subcamps now, conditions had deteriorated gravely. New prisoners—even the young ones—who lacked any status and who did not understand the ways of the camp, deteriorated the fastest.

From his deathbed, Henryk dictated his poems to another prisoner, a Polish university professor he knew from before the war. Aleks also sat beside Henryk to hear him whisper his poetry. Henryk was weak, but the poems struck Aleks as deeply powerful.

Aleks could not say how much time elapsed between his meeting Henryk and the young man's demise. But he knew it was short—perhaps days, perhaps a week or two. A prisoner at the medical ward who saw Henryk die speculated that tuberculosis took him rather than starvation. But there were many ways to die at Sachsenhausen; one could rarely be sure of the specific cause.

Because Aleks met Henryk so close to his death, he never got the chance to memorize his poems. To Aleks's relief, the professor who found such value in Henryk's verses wrote them down on scraps of paper a few days before Henryk's death. Aleks took the scraps and memorized what he read. In one final poem, Henryk described the lethargy and stabbing hunger he felt as he wasted away at Sachsenhausen.

Silence on a Hospital Cot

Daily soars the sheer sun across the heavens,
At night soar the mute stars and lifeless doom.

Against the windowpane a fly buzzes, the lazy grouch;
Thus stretches the emptiness, sprawls the boredom

The hours are dragging on, moments pass each other by,
Only hunger, hunger (my God!) piercing your insides.

Seldom a thought will flash somewhere, a spark will burn in hallowed fire,
Hallowed be the memory, that which is nothing.

Around and around glides the wistfulness. With a deranged stride
Life ever escapes into the distance—silently, furtively, sideways.

Daily come down the rains or soars the sun,
At night in mute silence exists the lifeless doom.

In another of Henryk's poems, he gave voice to the hopelessness of every prisoner's lot.

Shooting

Before me muzzles—behind me walls,
Nowhere to find hope!
A bottomless end.
Gray figures. Reverberation. Shackles.
Somewhere a dog howls a lament . . .

Eyes, staring fixedly, it begins to drizzle—
A flash . . . !

The last thought:
It was not worth it to live. . . .

Aleks especially admired a poem Henryk entitled "Parade," in which he ridiculed the industrial magnates and the chauvinistic militarism that was common in Poland before the war. Aleks found the lines captivating. To him, they contained such beauty in their imagery; they were written with an utter mastery of the Polish language. One stanza read:

Lockstep—
Man and horse,
leap abreast—
surge across the countryside
Like gleaming ears of grain.

NOW HENRYK WAS dead, and Aleks mourned him as he had so many other talents who perished at the hands of the Germans. Death, always present, seemed to lurk ever closer. The SS guards appeared jittery. Chatter intensified around the camp about Red Army positions or the proximity of American soldiers. New prisoners, who had been arriving from camps to the east and west, spoke of Allied tanks treading nearer and nearer Berlin.

Toward the end of March, while most of the prisoners stood at the roll call square, the SS herded about a thousand of the first women into the camp. They looked starved and sick, haggard and hollow-eyed. As they walked into the camp, Aleks began to compose a welcoming poem. From some distant part of the camp, Aleks could hear a rhythmic drumming. He adapted the poem's meter to this beat.

A big day, a happy day,
Today, there are a thousand women on the square!
The prisoners brush their yellow teeth,
The prisoners wash their coarse rags—

Because it is a big day, a happy day,
There are a thousand women on the square!

In the days that followed, Aleks searched for his sister, Łucja. Perhaps she had been transferred to Sachsenhausen from Ravensbrück? Maybe a woman had known her and could give Aleks news?

In the women's barracks, Aleks often performed "Song about Wanda" as a way to pique interest in his search. Though he asked every woman he could, he came up empty-handed. No one had heard of a Łucja Kulisiewicz from Cieszyn.

In the men's barracks, Aleks heard constant talk about the female prisoners. Some of the men had mixed feelings, fearing that the SS would assign women to the easiest camp jobs, like peeling potatoes or mending socks. One man exclaimed, "What do we need the damned women for!" Aleks might have thought that being in such close proximity to women after so many years would excite the men. But few prisoners he knew seemed interested in sex. They would sooner spend their extra hours seeking out food. A foreman who held sway where the women lived even offered the men the chance to watch them bathe in exchange for a few slices of bread. But no one Aleks knew took up the offer. Aleks reflected on how strange the world had become. Just a few years earlier, he and so many of the men around him yearned for a lady. Now, with nothing in their bellies, they craved bread or meat or steamed grain. A bowl of unsalted potatoes was far more appealing than the caress of a woman.

When another transport of women arrived at Sachsenhausen, Aleks composed the song "She Was My Little Miss," which opened with sentimental overtones about the beauty of a woman but quickly turned dark by the last line of the song: *Young lips will soon be kissed—by death.*

As the number of women arriving at Sachsenhausen increased, Aleks found himself assigned to a new work detail: delousing female inmates. The delousing facility was divided into three parts—the inspection room, where he worked, the bathing house, and the clean side. The inspection room could hold as many as two hundred women. They stood shaved bald and naked, in lines that moved toward Aleks and three other prisoner-inspectors who sat on stools. The older ones, their bodies sagging, seemed less shy about their nakedness. The young ones, some just teenagers, tried to conceal themselves with their hands or stand behind the women in front of them. Next to Aleks was a small seat that reminded him of a piano bench. One by one, each woman sat on the bench. First she raised her arms so Aleks could inspect her armpits with a wooden stick dipped in chemicals. Then, upright again, she placed one foot on the bench. Aleks shone an electric light on her genitals, searching hair by hair for insects.

After a few days on the work detail, Aleks learned about where the women had come from. There were many Varsovians, captured during the uprising the year before. Some women came from work camps in Germany. Aleks made note of their darkly tanned necks from toiling in the sun, a stark contrast to their pale breasts and stomachs. In the 2 or 3 seconds between each inspection, Aleks gazed at the scene before him. He thought: these women look like the tortured souls of a Goya painting. The blending smells of blood and urine and delousing chemicals was almost unbearable. He lasted a week in total on the work assignment. Though he managed to arrange a transfer, the experience never left him.

ON SOME DAYS, the SS marched Aleks and other prisoners out of the camp and transported them to central Berlin, some 20 miles southeast, to dig up unexploded bombs dropped by the Allies during raids. As Aleks marched, he sometimes passed heaps of piled bodies, civilians killed by British or American bombs. He felt nothing for the German dead. As he glanced at bodies mangled by shreds of steel, no sympathy welled up in him; they looked like mannequins that he once might have seen in the gallery windows of a department store. Even the corpse of a child did not stir his emotion, though his lack of empathy troubled him. "No wonder," he thought. "One evil act creates another, especially when you've been right in the middle of it for so many years."

Sometimes on these trips beyond the walls of Sachsenhausen, Aleks caught sight of German children playing or holding the hands of their mothers. On the face of it, they struck him as cute, similar to the children he had known in Poland before the war. Yet though they held no responsibility for what had happened to Aleks, to Poland, to such large swaths of Europe, he warned his friends later on, during secret poetry evenings: "If you're moved by the sound of a German child crying, you who are forever compassionate, forever noble . . . Go cry over your own children! Every bit of compassion towards the Germans is our loss. We can't afford compassion."

Aleks's close friendship with many Czech prisoners, including important communists like Antonín Zápotocký, elevated him in a certain way. Yet speaking the Czech language, being among that country's people, only reminded Aleks of the woman he missed so dearly. When he performed the song "She Was My Little Miss" at musical evenings or just on his own to pass the time, he often thought about Bożena, especially when he came to the lyrics *She was my painted little miss, / In love with every flower, with the morning dew.*

All Aleks knew was that Bożena had fled to Olomouc when Poland annexed Czech borderlands in 1938. He never received a letter from her at Sachsenhausen. Of course, she had no way of knowing that he was incarcerated in a Nazi camp. To pass the time, especially at night when he could not sleep, he constructed in his mind a version of Olomouc, a city he'd never visited. He drew up the town and its church and buildings, the great expanses of green that surrounded it. So well did he imagine Olomouc that he began to miss it, long for it, as though it were his home. In those moments, he often returned to a poem called "Pilgrimage to Olomouc," which he had written in 1941 and dedicated to Bożena. Through the poem, he could return to his youth and those untroubled days when he wandered the banks of the Olza River or walked through town with his dog.

Aleks knew the war was drawing to a close. Some prisoners even spoke of an impending evacuation of Sachsenhausen, though no one could be sure. Since the start of 1945, the SS had marched thousands of sick prisoners out the gates of Sachsenhausen. No one knew where they were headed.

At the industry square, some two thousand prisoners had vanished, which could only mean that they had been murdered and their bodies burned.

Aleks heard more about the ongoing mass murders. When told by a trusted source that the SS had killed a group of prisoners, including almost two dozen Luxembourgers who refused to join the Wehrmacht, he composed "Execution," one of his last camp songs. The lyrics were short: *Our deep sleep was interrupted at night. / Young hearts beating in us in fear! / And I will never see my mother / A short, gloomy road ahead of us— / and there, there is a rifle at the end. / Ah, how far is Luxembourg / Ah, how far is Luxembourg.* When Aleks performed the song, his friend, Roland Tillard, accompanied him on the accordion.

Aleks heard of another impending slaughter. From prisoners in the know, he got word that as many as a thousand, perhaps two thousand, Poles suspected of having tuberculosis were slated for execution whether they were actually sick or not. One early morning, despite the risk, Aleks made his way to the medical barracks. There he encountered a young friend, Leszek Komornicki from Warsaw. Leszek seemed to have little time to live. He stretched out his hand and said, "Aleks . . . you always sang and composed so much. Write something now, write something for us." Something for the dying. Aleks felt his throat tighten. He handed Leszek the small pencil and scrap of paper he had smuggled with him and said, "You write." When Leszek finished, Aleks looked at the paper. It read: "To the Consumptive." Aleks memorized Leszek's poem on the spot. It began: *You are going on a long journey / The cars are waiting / The guards are waiting / You are so close / Barely three hundred yards away / Chimneys smoke / Chimneys of the crematorium.*

The poems written by prisoners just hours before their death moved Aleks. He noted with awe how the last request of many men was not a slice of bread, not a glass of vodka, not an injection of anesthetic. They wanted to write something.

During those last weeks of the war, Aleks continued to amass any camp music or poetry he could. By then, he had memorized an astonishing collection of material, all neatly cataloged in his mind. There were elegies, hymns, songs of rebellion and sabotage, religious songs, carols, broadsides, sentimental and romantic songs, hit songs, lullabies, parodies, political satires, poems of all kinds.

Around the camp, tension surged. Prisoners sensed that the SS had sinister plans. Rumors circulated about an impending extermination, one on a scale more massive than what Aleks already knew. He heard about a tall, pensive man nicknamed Little Death, who late at night woke prisoners from a list he carried. When the chosen inmate left the barracks, no one saw him again. He vanished into the darkness, led half-asleep to his death, still warm from the breath of his slumbering companions.

Aleks wondered whether he, too, might soon be executed. On some nights, his thoughts wandered as he lay on his cot, half conscious, agonizing that Little Death would come to summon him. For reasons he didn't understand, strangely prosaic thoughts also passed through his mind— things from long ago, perhaps as far back as his childhood. *Maślanka* (buttermilk) was one such preoccupation, though he couldn't say why. On one sleepless night, he thought to himself, "I will neither see death, nor hear it. It will come as an imperceptible moment like the flash of magnesium. Before it penetrates my consciousness, I'll be dead." Yet he knew he had to hold on, to survive a few more weeks, perhaps a month or two. He had come too far to be murdered now. He had heard the thundering power of Soviet artillery to the east. He had seen the fighter planes chasing one another in the skies overhead.

Though prisoners and guards alike seemed edgy, Aleks also perceived in himself and others a palpable sense of pleasure. This pleasure began to appear in his lyrics. In "Return," Aleks's parody of the song "You and I" from the 1935 film *Rhapsody of the Baltic*, he wrote: *The charm of old, good memories, / The same houses sleep—the orchard greets us tenderly / Little sun, I waited for you for so many days! / The birds twitter quietly, there's a drizzle of dew / And I whisper again, / Whisper the sweetest / Of all the words: / Poland!*

The prisoners could almost taste hope. If they could only persist a little longer, they would be freed and could return home. Aleks did his best to impart that feeling of jubilation in another song, "Big Win!," which he based on the Bolesław Mucman title "Panna Andzia ma wychodne" from 1936.

Aleks debuted "Big Win!" one night in mid-April of 1945 at a musical revue organized by a group of Frenchmen, Germans, Czechs, and Poles. Instead of Roland Tillard, who normally played the accordion while Aleks sang, Aleks invited the Italian Giulio Amadeo Bellungi, of Florence, who played several measures before Aleks began to sing:

> *Ladies and gents,*
>   *we've not long to go with this nice little war,*
> *This tall tale's grown stale already.*
> *Ladies and gents, we've not long to go until*
>   *everything's lovely again*
> *Everything's lovely—Ha!*
> *Goebbels with his quill won't be able to help,*
> *Tears will trickle down everyone's cheeks,*
> *And the good ol' Russian boys*
>   *will soon start singing,*
> *Singing—oh boy!*

The melody of the first verse was cheerful. The jeering lyrics lent the song an ironic twist. To heighten the carefree mood, Aleks used theatrical movements and sound effects. He hid a man in a closet who stomped on air-filled bags to create celebratory pops and bangs that mimicked fireworks or perhaps the skirmishes between the Red Army and Wehrmacht that the prisoners believed would soon begin near the camp. In the refrain, which slowed in tempo and sounded like an anthem that might be sung in a beer hall, he directly targeted the Germans, mocking them and their impending defeat:

> *Today's the day of your Big Win!*
> *So start dancing—on your KNEES!*

Today's the day of your big-shit victory,
Today in Berlin, a big jubilee!
And Adolf came—humbled, trembling:
"Hands up! Put your little hands up!"
We don't know the meaning of "capitulation"—
Defascistization, brother, is what it is!

After all the performers had presented their poem or song, the men in the audience chose Aleks's song as the one they liked best, giving him the prize of an intricately carved cigarette box made by fellow Polish inmate Wiktor Simiński.

ABOUT THREE WEEKS into April in 1945, a month shy of the day that marked Aleks's fifth year of captivity at Sachsenhausen, the SS ordered the prisoners to remain in their barracks. Aleks could not remember a time when the guards had not forced everyone to line up at the roll call square to be counted and sometimes punished at the beginning and end of each workday. He and the men in his barracks knew that something drastic was about to unfold.

In the preceding weeks, the camp population had swelled dramatically as the SS transferred prisoners from nearby subcamps to Sachsenhausen. The SS permitted some of the newcomers to find a place to sleep. Others, they murdered immediately. The main camp now held nearly sixty thousand men and women, many diseased, most starving.

Within the walls of Sachsenhausen, everyone could hear the distant roar of Soviet artillery. The rumbles and vibrations were nearly constant. Knowing that the campgrounds might soon be in the hands of the Red Army, the SS rushed to scrub clean all evidence of their crimes. They burned files and index cards. They dumped barrel after barrel of human ash into the Oder-Havel Canal.

The next morning, on April 21, the evacuation of Sachsenhausen began. The first columns of people, which included Aleks, organized themselves by nationality. Aleks tried to stick with his friends and ended up in a column with Gabriel Zych and a group of other Poles he had known since the early days of their imprisonment. Then they marched out through the camp's main gates, escorted by units of the SS. The lucky few at the head of the line, Aleks among them, received a loaf of bread and a bit of meat. Aleks examined his rations. This will have to last me a long while, he thought. No one could say how long they would march or in which direction. For all Aleks knew, they might be on the road for weeks, an ominous prospect given that his legs felt like rubber.

Many of the prisoners, crazed by hunger, scarfed down their rations. But the old-timers, the ones with low prisoner numbers like Aleks, knew that such a shock of food to a deprived stomach would leave a person writhing on the ground, likely too sick to walk.

Aleks marched among some thirty thousand prisoners, though he could only see the five or six hundred men crowded directly around him. They took a vaguely northwest direction, surveilled by jittery SS guards, fingers on triggers, keen to shoot. It took little time for Aleks to comprehend the gravity of the situation. Prisoners and guards alike were in an untested situation. The rules and codes of the camp, which Aleks had followed or broken with great care for almost five years, no longer applied. Keeping his head down, he watched. If a prisoner stopped to tie his shoelaces, the SS shot him. If one faltered, ever so slightly, the SS shot him. The guards, made more homicidal than usual by the encroaching Allied armies to the east and west, drove Aleks and the other prisoners like cattle. Around seven in the evening after the first day of marching, Aleks's column of several hundred men stopped at Löwenberger Land, a collection of villages about 10 miles from Sachsenhausen. After a night spent crammed in an empty barn, the march continued.

Day after day, Aleks watched as exhausted prisoners collapsed or fell out of their column. Some lost consciousness and tumbled into the ditch to the side of the road. There was always a German bullet to finish them. Aleks's column passed farms or hamlets or villages whose inhabitants largely reacted to them with contempt. He likely saw the town of Neuruppin and then Wittstock. Occasionally, a villager might leave a bowl of water or scrap of food on the prisoners' path, but most seemed indifferent if not outright hostile.

Aleks could only think of how urgently he needed to survive. He alone possessed the camp songs and poems, the memories, emotions, and experiences with which prisoners had entrusted him. If he collapsed in a ditch and the SS finished him, so much of such extraordinary human value would vanish forever. He told himself: "I must persist. I must pass on these songs and poems."

The farther Aleks marched, the more corpses lined the road. Hunger pained him. The loaf of bread and the ration of meat had not lasted long, even though he stretched it out, eating only small morsels each day. To cope with the hunger, he composed poetry. One poem, entitled "Agony," recounted the surroundings as he marched:

I look up at the trees, they are so tall.
The green is getting paler, no more green.
My tongue is a dry rag.
I want to scream, but I can't, my throat is drying up.
The outlines are getting paler.
The trees dance above me.
It's very warm in the bowels, very sweet, ever sweeter.
I do not know whether I have already died or was born just now.

The final lines of the poem:

Now I am very full, very quiet, very happy.
I do not sense anything at all, but in my last moment I feel only one
word: mother.

Most evenings, when the sunlight faded, the SS halted the march until morning. Fanning out on the farmland bordering the road, the prisoners dropped to the ground, exhausted. Aleks slept on hay, when he could find it, or the grass that grew on the forest floor. It was April, the turf was wet and cold beneath him. He gazed at the scene. Stretching out far beyond the farm fields in every direction stood dark forest. Thousands of prisoners blanketed the ground beneath the trees, which seemed utterly merciless to him. The Red Army was advancing, its mortars rumbling, and the stutter of its machine gun fire, the blasts from its tanks. The pounding seemed so near, just a bit deeper into the woods.

Before Aleks slept, if a farmhouse was near, he forced himself to search for edible plants in the family garden—a discarded carrot from the previous harvest, an overlooked parsnip, a rotting potato, anything. Gabriel Zych remembered the hunger being so unbearable that at night he and the other Poles in the column chewed on the chance ears of wheat they scavenged in nearby fields, hoping the hard seeds might assuage their pangs. Some prisoners ground kernels between two stones, then cooked the coarse powder over a fire. The method did not work. The flour often contained more stone than wheat. One night, Aleks found the seeds in part of a sunflower and pocketed them when no one was looking. Over the coming days, he ate them, seed by seed, relishing each morsel of sustenance.

By the eighth or ninth day, Aleks could not tell which, the columns of prisoners, until then organized by nationality, started to blend. Women appeared. They looked as wretched and ragged as the men. Aleks recognized some of his non-Polish friends, like the accordionist Roland Tillard, who had often accompanied him when he performed at Sachsenhausen. Then he sighted a woman he knew from the camp. Her name was Danusia, and she was young, perhaps still a teenager. She had arrived at Sachsenhausen in February or March from the Ravensbrück camp, where the Nazis imprisoned her a year earlier for participating in an underground teaching operation. Aleks heard that while at Ravensbrück, she worked as a paramedic, using her delicate hands to treat the boils and wounds of the women around her. Rumor had it that during a typhus outbreak just before she arrived at Sachsenhausen, she even managed to smuggle out oatmeal, carrots, and leftover bread from the guards' kitchen to the barracks to feed the sick. Because of her kindness, prisoners began to call her their shining star. Yet it wasn't Danusia's kindness that drew Aleks to her. He sought her out because it was said that she could sing beautifully. Now, marching nearby, Aleks was sure that he could hear her humming to herself.

Aleks could see that Danusia was losing her strength. She started limping. She began to stumble. The wooden clogs she was wearing, Aleks thought, must have made walking almost unbearable. Though the women to her left and right grabbed her arms and tried to hoist her along, she eventually staggered out of her column, fell to her knees, grasping for support at a birch sapling that stood on the side of the road. An SS guard sighted her. To Aleks, the German looked young, perhaps even a teenager himself. With the barrel of his rifle, he flicked the hair out of Danusia's eyes, and then, instead of shooting her, turned and walked on. "Did he not want to waste a cartridge?" Aleks wondered. The guard turned back one last time and glanced at Danusia. She blew him a kiss, a thank you for sparing her life. He raised his gun and packed several bullets into her head. Then he shot Aleks's friend Roland, the French accordionist, who had jumped in front of Danusia, trying to shield her. Another guard, coming up from behind, kicked the bodies of Danusia and Roland, rolling them into the ditch at the side of the road. As though to ensure she was really dead, or to mutilate her body, he fired off several more rounds into her chest. "Take a good look at this, you dogs," he shouted. Aleks watched the blood soak through Danusia's uniform.

AFTER DAYS OF marching and nights of sleeping on the forest floor, Aleks could tell that the SS guards were growing frantic.

As the anxiety of the guards increased, so, too, did the carnage. The Germans shot prisoners at will, for minor infractions or for no reason at all. Bodies piled up in the ditches. Aleks did everything he could to keep out of sight, not to trip or faint or do anything that might attract the attention of a guard. Marching in his column, he studied the fields and woods around him to distract himself. He made note of the morning dew clinging to the blades of grass. The glistening drops reminded him of a child's tears. Above him, the late April sun shone. He glanced upward. He wondered how it could look down at the suffering, the death. He thought: "Nasty sun—you've been seeing this all along, and you didn't tumble to earth to burn it all."

The moment of Aleks's liberation, a day later, brought no drama. The Red Army did not appear among the trees from the east to cut down the SS and free the prisoners. The Americans did not emerge from the woods in the west. Before a confrontation could happen, the SS vanished. One guard told Aleks's column, *"Macht, was ihr wollt"* ("Do whatever you want") before he disappeared. One by one, or in small groups, the remaining guards slipped away into the night forests. At nearby farms or in villages, they hurriedly stripped off their uniforms and dressed themselves in civilian clothing or in the work clothes of farmers. They tossed their rifles and pistols.

When the men in Aleks's column awoke that morning to discover the absence of guards, they didn't know what to do. Some cautiously ventured off the road, wondering whether the SS were hiding in the forest, ready to shoot deserters. But no shots rang out, no prisoners dropped from a bullet to the chest.

In the first moments of freedom, many prisoners in Aleks's column stretched out on the ground, spent. Others, in their extreme state of hunger, chewed on strips of the inner bark of trees or searched for seeds or grains on the forest floor. Soon it became apparent that the area was not safe. They could hear gunfire in the forest nearby. Aleks joined a group who decided to walk in the direction from which they had come. Eventually, they reached the spot on the road where the young SS guard had shot Danusia the day before. An old woman lay in the ditch, curled up against Danusia's corpse. Aleks stopped. He studied the woman. He could not tell if she was dead or alive.

Later, a friend told Aleks who the old woman was: Danusia's grandmother. She had spent much of the war as a prisoner at Ravensbrück. Once the guards of her column disappeared, she wandered down the road. When she saw the body of her granddaughter in the ditch, she stopped.

AFTER A DAY of wandering, perhaps two, Aleks most likely encountered the 7th US Armored Division on the outskirts of Schwerin, nearly 110 miles northwest of Sachsenhausen.

Nearly six years after the Germans first imprisoned Aleks in Cieszyn, he was free. He looked around: the liberated prisoners straggled, the American soldiers patrolled. Some former prisoners entered pubs or restaurants and demanded food. Those who ate too fast or too much often grew ill and ended up in army medical facilities, their stomachs unable to cope after years of starvation. Other survivors simply staggered about, dazed. The transition from incarceration to freedom was so abrupt and so disorganized that many of them did not know what to do with themselves. They looked for places to sleep. Some stole food from local shops. Some rested where they found a comfortable spot. Suddenly, Schwerin had become home to thousands of men and women in concentration camp uniforms.

Edmund Szybicki, a Polish prisoner who was liberated near Schwerin, remembered the chaos of those days. The local residents he saw seemed apathetic and passive, not outwardly hostile but unwilling to help the thousands of men and women who suddenly appeared in their midst and needed food and shelter and medical care.

On one of his first evenings in Schwerin, Aleks wearily made his way around a quiet residential neighborhood. He felt overcome by joy. Still hungry, he had managed to find some food. Yet perhaps most strongly, he felt a terrible anger to exact retribution on these people. As he walked, he studied the modest houses he passed. In all likelihood, he could burst into any of the homes and find a young mother or an elderly couple or children—by then, Hitler had dispatched most men strong enough to hold a rifle to the fighting zones. Even though Aleks was weak and emaciated, he thought he could deliver the vengeance that burned within him, all the anger and hatred he had repressed in nearly six years of incarceration. Something drew him to one house in particular. He passed through the gate. Without knocking, he turned the doorknob. Inside, he found a thin woman. She jumped up in fright at his skeletal gauntness and camp uniform. First he thought: She is twenty-five at most, a great beauty with freckles on her face. And then: Now you will get your revenge. But he balked. His desire for revenge vanished. He left. And as his anger lifted, a sense of guilt welled up in him. He felt as though he was losing his hatred for the Germans, these people who imprisoned him, who murdered Rosebery, who murdered so many of his friends. "What are you doing, you damn camp poet?" he asked himself.

ALEKS SAW HIS hometown of Cieszyn again for the first time since his imprisonment from a border bridge on the Czech side of the Olza River. The trek home had been long. After lingering in Schwerin for days, possibly weeks, hoping to regain some strength, he started the 450-mile journey home.

For a strong person, on foot, making good time, the journey would have taken three, maybe four weeks. Aleks was emaciated and brittle. For a time, he rode a bicycle. When he awoke to find it stolen, he flagged down passing buses, he hitched rides on horse-drawn carts—anything to get him out of Germany and into Poland. Now, finally, he gazed upon the river of his childhood, the one that had coursed through his songs and his dreams these past six years.

When Aleks reached the border guard, he told the man his name. He had no identification papers and scarcely any belongings. One exception was the empty cigarette case with the white eagle that Wiktor Simiński had carved, Aleks's prize for winning the musical revue at Sachsenhausen just weeks earlier.

"Some Czech girl has been looking for you, a sister of the Red Cross," the guard said upon learning Aleks's name.

It was Bożena; Aleks was sure. Cieszyn was a small town and word got around fast. She must have returned as the war drew to a close and asked the border guards to look out for him.

"For God's sake, where is she?" Aleks said. The guard pointed to the other side of the river, the Polish side, where a white ambulance was driving off.

For one reason or another, Aleks and Bożena did not meet, not that day, not in the days that followed. He blamed another bad turn of fate. Though he wanted to take the time to search for her, Cieszyn being small and it being possible to find people, he had to travel to Kraków, where his father and stepmother had spent the war.

It was also then that his symptoms began to appear—the cough, the fever, the chills. He likely brushed them off as a consequence of the camp, of the death march, of the trek home. As he made the journey through the chaos that was Poland in June of 1945, the cough worsened, his fever burned.

When Aleks reached central Kraków, he saw that it stood intact, unlike many Polish cities. At first glance, little seemed changed compared with what he remembered from his university days, six years earlier. Yet the city's Jews were gone—a haunting and colossal absence. At the flat on Sebastiana Street, Aleks found his father and stepmother. He embraced them and clutched his sister, Łucja, who was shockingly gaunt from her own incarceration. And then, his sickness overtook him.

The doctors issued their diagnosis: tuberculosis. They warned that in Aleks's emaciated, exhausted state, he might very well die. At the city's antituberculosis clinic, he lay on a cot, his fever burning, droplets of sweat rolling down his forehead. Perhaps the fear of death forced him to speak. Perhaps he felt as though this was his last chance to make good on his promise to Rosebery. Whatever the reason, he began to mutter.

On rounds, the doctors stopped to listen. They could make no sense of what they took for gibberish. Given Aleks's fever and his skeleton of a body, the only plausible explanation they could think of was that he had gone mad. One doctor even interrupted his recitations to make him do multiplication problems to assess his mental acuity. From then on, the doctors paid him no heed other than to monitor his fever and vital signs.

A nurse listened more closely. She heard sense in Aleks's words. They did not strike her as those of a madman. She sat beside him at his cot, concentrating on what he said. Only then did she realize that he was dictating. What spilled out of him were poems, lyrics. She got up and fetched a small typewriter so she could transcribe what he was saying, each word, each line, each verse.

Aleks believed she feared him. He had a ghastly appearance—few teeth, bones poking at his skin, the pallid hue of a man forty years older. He noticed how, every so often, she turned away from him and signed the cross. He thought to himself that she must think him possessed, that only someone haunted by evil could spit out such horrible lines.

Over the next three weeks, the nurse returned again and again to Aleks's bedside to type what he dictated. All of his songs poured out: "Muselmann—Butt Collector," "Mister C," "Germania!," "Black Böhm," and some fifty others. He made sure to dictate one of his most precious camp mementos, Rosebery's "Jewish Deathsong," with each of its lamenting vocables, each verse, each word, each rise and fall of the sorrowful melody. The music and poetry of others also gushed out, such as his dead friend Alyosha Sazonov's "Sonia" or Henryk Głowacki's song "Longing" or Jan Vala's song about potato skins. He uttered poetry by Wiktor Simiński, the whittler, and that of others like Stanisław Błasiski and Konrad Stanoszek. He recited Henryk Tadeusz Nejman's verses, composed while emaciated, dying, lines that Aleks found so moving, so genuine. It all flooded out of him onto the pages of the nurse's typewriter, a great unburdening of camp culture that had sustained him and other prisoners over their time in Nazi captivity. When he had no more songs or poems to recite, he instructed the nurse to copy down names and events and dates—all the anecdotal detail that gave each lyric, melody, or verse its context and meaning.

When Aleks uttered the last line of his mental archive, the nurse told him that she had typed over seven hundred pages of text. Upon hearing her, a great feeling of happiness enveloped him, even though he lay on a cot among hundreds of other men and women, coughing and wheezing with tuberculosis. He thought to himself: this is the happiest moment of my sad life.

With his mind free of the music and poetry and culture of the wretched camp, Aleks relaxed. He began to recover. He did not want this to be the end of his life. He was only twenty-seven years old.

PART IV

Chapter 12

ᵔ

From the earliest days after the war, life for Aleks had been arduous. When he emerged from the tuberculosis clinic, only then could he take stock of what his country had become.

Postwar Poland resembled little of what he remembered from his university days just six years earlier. While he was imprisoned at Sachsenhausen, as many as six million citizens of his country had perished, among them at least three million Jewish Poles. In all, about 18 percent of the population had died, almost one Pole in five. For Germany, the aggressor, the figure was 7.4 percent. For the United States, it was 0.2 percent. For the USSR, which sustained massive casualties, it was 11.2 percent.

Nearly every Polish city, save Kraków, had to be rebuilt. German bombs had leveled Warsaw. Little remained but the skeletons of buildings, heaps of rubble, and dazed Varsovians, hungry and exhausted, seeking shelter wherever they could find it. Poland's basic infrastructure lay in ruins. The retreating Germans had destroyed all they could. Once the advancing Red Army seized a new swath of Polish land, special units stripped telephone exchanges, tram installations, anything of value, and sent the equipment east for use in the Soviet Union. Everything had to be repaved, relaid, rebuilt. The dead had to be buried.

A massive exodus of people had also ensued. The new Polish authorities expelled, sometimes violently, millions of ethnic Germans and Ukrainians. Tens of thousands of Polish Jews who had survived the Nazi genocide were emigrating. Huge numbers of ethnic Poles were also on the move, repatriating from camps or exile abroad, populating the newly acquired western territories that Poland had annexed from Germany, or being brutally forced off land in the east that now belonged to Ukraine. The Soviets, now more in control, began to push through massive reforms, including of Poland's industries and the Catholic Church. In the panic and chaos of the time, disease spread at a frightening pace. For Aleks and his decimated generation, those young men and women who, in their teens and early twenties, had felt such hope about Poland, the war had extinguished the future. It was no longer theirs to seize.

With some of his strength back, Aleks tried, as everyone else did, to move on. In his pocket lay bills worth 100 zlotys issued by authorities to give him a fresh start. He reflected: "I should get new clothes. I should make myself look presentable." That was no easy task. Aleks weighed little more in 1947 than he had in the camp. His cheeks and chin carried so little flesh that his forehead looked enormous. Shirts and jackets hung from his bony frame, as though wrapped around a hanger. Even if he had managed to find clothes that fit him, he discovered that he could afford next to nothing. A simple meal, meat-filled dumplings or beef gulasz ladled over a potato pancake, seemed to cost far more than before the war. During those first months in Kraków, he would hand a restaurant cashier the cash to pay for his meal, and when she did not give him anything in return, he would say, "Ma'am, please give me the change!" "There is no change," she would reply.

At first, Aleks felt a certain euphoria that he had survived. He convalesced with his family, especially his little sister. His father, Franciszek, and stepmother, Franka, like everyone else, were struggling to make ends meet. But Aleks's elation quickly wore off. He had to feed himself. He had to figure out what lay ahead after nearly six years of imprisonment. Work was scarce. It seemed sensible to him to restart his law studies at the Jagiellonian University. More than a full decade after he began in 1936, he found himself once again in the halls of Poland's great university. Much had changed. A large number of faculty members had been arrested and deported to Sachsenhausen. Only some of those professors had returned. There were almost no Jews in his classes.

Aleks did not remain at university for long. He needed money. He felt the urge to move. Within the year, he withdrew from his courses and took work from a local baker. With bags of fresh bread, he roamed Kraków's squares, selling loaves and rolls to passersby, a simple but pleasant job. Later, he convinced the baker to let him maintain the books, even though he had never worked as an accountant. When that work dried up, he moved on to a new job, and another one after that, eventually finding employment at a mineral water factory. He was doing what everyone else was: trying to make ends meet, trying to rebuild life as best he could, trying to put the war behind him.

Aleks met Elżbieta Bochenek-Szpakowska one day when he entered a garden store just north of Kraków's old town square. Among the bouquets and potted plants, he saw Elżbieta dressed in her employee outfit. She had dark, curly hair and fair skin. There was an alluring beauty to her. After flirting in the shop, they agreed to meet later. She was quick to charm him by the means closest to his heart: music. *No matter how bad things are, always keep your head up and always laugh*, she sang.

Elżbieta soon found herself pregnant, and so the couple married, though for Aleks the occasion was a melancholy affair. When the ceremony ended, he fled and spent the night by himself. He did not quite understand why he had balked at the marriage, though more and more he found his thoughts dwelling on the past. Perhaps now, having fulfilled what society expected of him—to find a wife, conceive a child, put forth a guise of normality—the trauma of the past began to pull him back.

He was growing restless. No longer did a prosperous, if boring, future as a lawyer await him. Instead of joining the disarray of the new

Soviet-controlled Poland, he daydreamed about the life he had led before the invasion, about the music and performance and possibilities of the Second Republic. This had been the best time of his life. With the connections he had formed during six years of imprisonment in a Nazi camp and his standing as a camp survivor, he could have found a decent job, even just as a mid-level functionary or a government clerk. Instead, he spent his time documenting the camps. In canteens around Kraków, where he and other survivors could get a hot meal at cut-rate prices, instead of eating, he approached other diners, asking them to share what they remembered about their incarceration—especially about the cultural gatherings. Few of the diners received him warmly. They reproached him, "Just let us eat in peace, Aleks! Why are you bothering us with talk of Muselmänner or about some prisoner or torture technique? We've had enough of the camps." Undeterred, he continued to amass information. What he would do with it, he did not yet know. But it struck him as an important task.

Shortly after the marriage, Elżbieta gave birth to a boy they named Marek. Having a son did not focus Aleks, it did not transform him into a family man. Instead, he continued to drift. Conditions in Poland worsened. The country's first elected government took office a year later in February 1947, under circumstances that countries in the west denounced. Józef Cyrankiewicz, himself a survivor of Auschwitz, took power as prime minister and quickly transformed a pseudo-democratic Poland into a one-party state.

Aleks decided to leave Poland and his young family. His Czech friends from Sachsenhausen had risen to power, particularly Antonín Zápotocký, to whom he had given a rudimentary blood transfusion in a Sachsenhausen barracks and who now sat in the Czech National Assembly. In recompense for Aleks's friendship in the camp, Antonín arranged a job for him in Prague as a foreign correspondent covering cultural events for publications, including the *Polish Press Agency* and *Dziennik Polski*.

Aleks departed Kraków on October 1, 1947. In the days after his arrival in Czechoslovakia, he checked into a luxurious sanitorium, another benefit of his friendship with Antonín. Before he began sending dispatches back to Poland, he spent a time in the countryside, continuing to recover, breathing fresh air, taking walks in the forest, eating well.

IN CZECHOSLOVAKIA, ALEKS came back to life. He had long loved Poland's neighboring country and its people, literature, and music. As far back as his boyhood in the town of Cieszyn, he had spoken Czech and played with children on both sides of the river frontier. He preferred the food, too, regarding Czech restaurants as cleaner and better equipped than those in Poland. His job as a journalist came with privilege, good pay, and benefits. He lived in a spacious apartment, a few neighborhoods southeast of the old town, near a beautiful park. Most satisfying of all, he felt valued among the residents of Prague. He relished the bonds and camaraderie he had forged with so many of them at Sachsenhausen and delighted in the fact that these men now held top positions in the burgeoning communist era. Antonín, for one, became the prime minister of the country in June of 1948, eight months after Aleks's arrival.

There was another reason for Aleks to love Czechoslovakia—it was the home of Bożena. Throughout his nearly six years of imprisonment, he believed that in addition to his music, three things had kept him alive: his devotion to Poland, his hatred of his captors, and his love for Bożena. Throughout the humiliations and hardships of Sachsenhausen, he had held Bożena in mind, her slender face, her large brown eyes, this great beauty who sold potatoes and cauliflower.

Not long after Aleks and Bożena missed each other at the Czechoslovak-Polish border in 1945, he received a postcard from her. From the return address, Aleks could tell that she still lived in Olomouc. On the front of the card, there was an image of two children in a car, with two linked hearts printed over them. On the back, she wrote: "May the magical melody of love soothe your heart, sir." Aleks never replied. Though his love for Bożena had carried him through the war, he now wanted to forget about her. He knew how to find her; the distance between Kraków and Olomouc was only about 150 miles.

Perhaps it was the camp trauma that was reemerging in him, especially with respect to women, from the times when he had to inspect female inmates of Sachsenhausen for lice. The experience of these women and their suffering and their skeletal bodies left something twisted in his mind. He realized he could only desire a half-naked woman or a naked woman in just stockings.

But in Prague, three years after Bożena's postcard arrived, he could not get her out of his thoughts. When a Kraków radio station commissioned him to sing several popular songs on a broadcast not long after he arrived in Prague, he decided to send her a telegram to inform her about his performance, which would also air in Czechoslovakia. Though he never received a reply, he pictured her the entire time he sang, as though she was the only person who was listening. He said into the microphone: "If someone loves a Czech woman so much and cannot confess his love in Czech, let him sing in Polish! She will understand him." And then he sang, *I was dreaming about you today, my little lady, / That we were dancing together in that tavern of ours / That tavern, so beautifully built! / My little lady built it with golden bricks.*

In the months after the performance, Aleks became obsessed with Bożena, so much so that he decided he had to visit her. He posted a letter to the only address he had, the one in Olomouc. This time, she replied. When their agreed upon day came, he traveled from Prague to Olomouc. Almost a decade after their last encounter, he felt nervous and abashed. He could not find the words as to why he had never replied to her postcard or tried to find her after they had missed each other in Cieszyn. The guilt of being married to another woman weighed on him, too. That night, they stayed up late talking. Both had found spouses. Both had started families. Only then did he learn that she had listened to his broadcast on the radio. She told him that she had been in the hospital, about to give birth to her third child, when his telegram arrived. But she had heard the broadcast—she had insisted that the nurse place a radio by her hospital bed.

That night, Aleks and Bożena slept together in the lodging in Olomouc, although they were not intimate. For reasons he could not quite put to words, he did not want to be. The next morning, they walked 5 miles from the center of Olomouc to Svatý Kopeček, the Holy Hill, a destination for Catholic pilgrims from around the country. Aleks knew of its importance, though he'd never visited it before. Six years earlier, while suffering on the shoe-testing track with his friend Jiří Maleček, he had promised God that if he survived, he would make a pilgrimage there. As Aleks and Bożena walked to the top of the hill where a monastery stood, he noticed how beautiful she still was. Even after the decade that had passed since he stood next to her on the Cieszyn market square as she sold vegetables, he felt the same love for her. They walked into the church. It was empty. The thick stone walls made the interior cool. Side by side, they knelt at the altar. Aleks gazed at Bożena. He loved her, but he knew they could never be together. Life was too complicated now. They each had families. They held different nationalities. The simplicity of their prewar lives had long vanished.

When they left the church and walked into the sun-draped, verdant landscape spreading out before them, Aleks took Bożena's hand. She looked at him sadly and said, using her nickname for him, *"Ali, proč jsi tady teprve dnes?"* ("Ali, why are you here only today?")

It was too late.

IN PRAGUE, ALEKS led a seemingly charmed life. At banquets, he drank fine liquors and mingled with the city's elite. He took on lovers. He met dignitaries from across the European continent, which offered him the chance to speak the four languages he knew fluently. At Christmas, he could afford to send fragrant oranges home to Kraków, an exotic luxury reserved only for the winter holidays.

But the camp music—Rosebery's music, Aron's music—weighed on him. Even if he had wanted to rid himself of these melodies and lyrics and break his promise to Rosebery, he could not. The songs were woven into the fabric of his being. A passing thought or memory or feeling might evoke them, and he would descend back into the barracks within the walls of Sachsenhausen. Life and luck were splendid only on the surface.

On a winter morning in early 1948, Aleks made the short trip from his Prague apartment on Budečská Street to A.R. Studio at Wenceslas Square. It was only a 15-minute walk, just seven blocks and a stroll past the National Museum and the park that surrounded it. Aleks had regained some strength. His once gaunt face had filled in. His ribs were no longer pressed up against the skin of his torso.

At the studio, Aleks stood before a microphone. Modern equipment encircled him. When the engineer gestured that they were live, Aleks started to sing. He chose to begin with the "Unforgettable Song," which he had composed in early 1941 during an intense period of longing for his lost country and life. Aleks tried as best he could to re-create the way he performed at Sachsenhausen, calling to mind the furtive performances— a spontaneous gathering in the corner of a barracks, a discreet show for a holiday. He hoped to communicate the anxiety of those nights.

But the main reason Aleks went to the studio that day was to record something else, a far more important piece of music—the "Jewish Death-song." Preserving this particular camp composition felt essential to him. He would keep his promise to Rosebery. As far as Aleks knew, Rosebery and most (if not all) of the Jewish choir members were almost certainly dead. He felt a responsibility to preserve this song. Perhaps no one would hear it. Perhaps the copies of the record would end up under a layer of dust in attics or cellars, on shelves in cramped salons, their labels peeling off, the disks disintegrating. But at least the song would exist.

Aleks stepped up to the microphone. *Bom, bom, bom, bom*, he began, trying his best to imitate Rosebery and sing the vocables in one breath, the way he taught him. *Lee-lai, lee-lai, lee-lai*, he sang, as the sound engineer watched the turntables spin and the music was cut into a disk that would become the master record. Aleks tried his best to convey the tension and urgency of the song, to transmit the atmosphere of that dark and rainy night in barracks 39 in October 1942, during the final moments before the SS burst in and he slipped away through a window. *Ten brothers were we together / All of us merchants of wine / One brother died one day / Now we're only nine / Oy-yoy!... Oy ... yoy!* At the end of the song he chanted, *Ten brothers were we together / We never hurt another soul.*

When Aleks finished and silence returned to the studio, he felt as though he had just recorded Rosebery's last will and testament. As far as he knew, all that remained of Rosebery was this piece of music. Now, at least, some bit of this man would live on, engraved in the grooves of a record, of which two hundred copies were to be made. These records, Aleks thought to himself, would not be for commercial distribution. He hoped they would be held in archives. He wanted historians and musicologists to study them.

After Aleks recorded the "Jewish Deathsong," he did not sing anymore, he no longer performed. He went silent. Instead, he focused on his articles about Polish-Czech brotherhood and common cultural history.

Back home in Kraków, Elżbieta fumed. He visited infrequently, and when he did, they quarreled. Normal life under the Kulisiewicz roof, even an imitation of it, rarely occurred. During this time, Elżbieta gave birth to a second son, whom she named Roman. She resented that she had to raise the two children on her own while Aleks lived the life of a bachelor.

Yet that breezy life had begun to shift. To the dismay of many of his Czech friends, now high-level functionaries, Aleks refused to join the Communist Party. He distrusted the institution, the centralized force it wielded. Perhaps most of all, he looked askance at Russia, a country that had long wanted to subjugate and rule Poland and that bore so much responsibility for the fate of his country during and after the war.

As the 1950s began and the experience of war faded, the cohort of Sachsenhausen survivors that held power in Czechoslovakia and had remained loyal to Aleks began to feel pressure from a new group of party members. In him they saw an extraneous man of foreign origins who refused to show proper allegiance. This rejection of the party began to damage Aleks's prospects. After all, he had the right pedigree and friends to rise in the communist structure. On his father's side, he had humble roots, his grandfather a carpenter. He had a good, if incomplete, education. Most of all, he had survived a Nazi camp, and while incarcerated he had shown bravery and commitment to fighting fascism, as witnessed by the men now in power—especially in Czechoslovakia and the German Democratic Republic.

Aleks, however, never sought a position, not because he wasn't a leftist or didn't believe in certain ideals of communism. In Poland and Czechoslovakia he was pleased to see workers in new apartments, students attending university for free, the lowest classes of people newly reading and writing. But those important steps forward came at the cost of democracy, a system that Poles had only experienced for a few years between the wars. Aleks wanted nothing to do with an authoritarian regime.

By the time Czech officials forced Aleks to leave Prague, even joining the Communist Party would not have helped him. His Sachsenhausen friends were losing power to a younger, more rigid generation of party members. Sometime around 1954, he packed his belongings, left the apartment on Budečská Street, and returned to Kraków. Aleks's connections and privileges were now no more. His relationship with the Czechs had ended.

Reunited with family, Aleks was soon thrust back into the arduous life he had sought to escape when he fled to Prague. Because he did not belong to the party and would not join now, many of the opportunities he had early on in Czechoslovakia were closed to him. He also lacked connections to the new Polish elite. The lively social life he had led for more than half a decade vanished with a harsh suddenness. No doubt he called on Polish friends he had met in Sachsenhausen, but these men did not hold prominent positions in the party. Some worked as bureaucrats or functionaries, but none he knew stood in the inner circles of power, around Prime Minister Cyrankiewicz.

To provide for Elżbieta and the boys, Aleks took odd jobs. He got hold of a camera and began shooting wedding photos. He learned how to colorize old photos. He began to travel by bus from Kraków to the little villages around the region, stopping to ask peasants whether they needed a photographer or wanted to add a splash of color to their wedding photos. He won many customers this way, though the pay never amounted to more than a pittance—the peasants had just as little as he did. When not doing photography, he constantly searched for work. Anything would do. The newspaper jobs that might have been available to him before the war had gone to party loyalists, those with the connections and devotion to the state.

Now Aleks longed for two past lives: prewar Kraków and postwar Prague. He desired the emancipation he had experienced in Czechoslovakia, the freedom to put his wife and sons in the back of his mind and instead focus on re-creating the young adulthood the war had stolen from him, the gaiety and cheer and music and sex that would have fueled his university life had the Germans not invaded. It was now sixteen years since the summer days of 1939 when he roamed the streets of Cieszyn, carefree, happy, with a tune in his head, a spring in his step. The war had extinguished any glimmer of the future. No longer did fortune—as a performer, as a lawyer—seem to await him. Instead, he was the father of two young children, one-half of a failing marriage, a man who couldn't find a job. Soon, the Kulisiewiczs were destitute. The only steady work Aleks could find was as a street sweeper.

ONE DAY, AS Aleks took the bumpy bus ride to a mountain village to shoot photos, his eyes met those of another man seated nearby. Aleks recognized him as Stefan Tabaczyński, a person of some influence in the party. Aleks got to know Stefan while in Prague, where Stefan would visit on business. They had become friends, though they had lost touch ever since Czech officials forced Aleks to return to Poland.

"Where are you going, dear colleague?" Stefan asked, pointing at the camera around Aleks's neck. "To do a photo report," Aleks replied proudly, though in fact he would only shoot a wedding. As they rode up to the mountain village, Aleks gradually shed his veneer of confidence and success and admitted to Stefan the desperation of his life. He explained how he had lost his correspondent's job in Prague and since had fallen so spectacularly low that he now made his living sweeping the streets of Kraków and taking pictures of newlywed couples.

When they reached their destination, the two men parted. But a few days later, Aleks received a letter from Stefan. Stefan wanted him to travel to Warsaw for a meeting. Not long after, Aleks boarded a train headed for the capital. Stefan, Aleks discovered, worked for the Press Documentation Office, a part of the Workers' Publishing Collective "press-book-movement." To Aleks's surprise, Stefan offered him a job. In exchange for a decent wage and travel privileges, all Aleks would have to do was travel the country selling restricted news to regional government offices. Aleks accepted the offer without hesitation.

From then on, Aleks had steady work. Again, he often found himself away from home, though now, instead of writing by day and mixing with Prague's elite by night, he sat on rickety trains, traveling to cities and towns across Poland to sell his booklets of restricted news to local authorities. The work might have been dull, but receiving a steady income improved the lot of his young family.

The income and stability could not save Aleks's marriage. The fighting, the financial struggles, and Aleks's years-long absence in Prague had cut wounds too deep to heal. Aleks's camp trauma roared back. At home, small disagreements between him and Elżbieta rose to tempestuous fits of rage. Aleks would shout that she did not understand him, that she would never comprehend how the experiences of the camp never receded from his mind—the stench of corpses, the sickness, the torture. As he saw it, they were poor, but they had what they needed—a flat, food, warmth. What else could they desire? Only a short time later, Aleks and Elżbieta separated. The children stayed with her.

As a bachelor, largely free of family duties, Aleks once again became absorbed by his research into the music of the Nazi camps. The new job at the Press Documentation Office offered a key perk that enabled his obsession: unfettered travel. Aleks could indulge his compulsion to meet survivors and collect documents for the budding archives in his flat.

During the war, Poles of all backgrounds were imprisoned in nearly every major Nazi camp. Now, in the 1950s, these survivors gathered at camp associations to give one another support, share stories, attempt to track down lost loved ones, eat a cheap meal. Each time Aleks arrived at a new city or town, he sought out the local camp group, hoping to meet with fellow survivors and learn about any camp music and culture they could recall.

In cities all over Poland, he heard harrowing stories. But he also heard about what had kept the survivors alive. Just as Aleks and Rosebery and so many other prisoners at Sachsenhausen had done, incarcerated men and women across the camp network had turned to culture to cope and survive. In Auschwitz, Buchenwald, Theresienstadt—just about any Nazi camp—inmates had gathered to share music and poetry and literature. Some prisoners composed lyrics and laid them onto prewar melodies, just as Aleks did. Others composed original scores—from popular songs to classical or modern music, many of genuine artistic quality. Aleks heard tales of art as well, of illustrated songbooks, of crafted rings or cigarette boxes, carved out of chunks of scrap wood with homemade whittling knives. He noted each anecdote with care.

When Aleks wasn't on the road, he perused Polish newspapers, reading for any mention of the camps or their survivors. Most of all, he sought articles about camp culture. When he found such an article, he clipped it out and added it to the many folders he kept, each with a specific theme. He also kept track of the early postwar concerts that memorialized the men and women who suffered in the camps. Whenever he encountered a survivor's name, he sent an inquiry. Over time, he had a network of contacts with people around the country who had spent the war in Nazi camps. These stories fascinated Aleks. They struck him as an invaluable piece of cultural history, culture perhaps for its purest purpose—to elevate and bear witness during some of the most barbaric moments of modern history. In collecting them, Aleks had found a calling.

ON A NIGHT train, in transit to Warsaw on business for the Press Documentation Office, Aleks struck up a conversation with the woman sitting across from him. Her name was Barbara Seweryn and she was young, with sandy blond hair that fell in loose curls around her face. Throughout the trip on that spring evening in April 1956, Aleks recounted stories of his life. As the locomotive heaved north toward the capital, he spoke of the culture that had long obsessed him, the music, the poetry, the languages. He told her about Prague and the Czech politicians he had befriended at Sachsenhausen, about the parties and the writing, which became the dispatches Poland's national newspapers and magazines published. He described his travels abroad before the war, especially to the Balkans, Vienna, and Brussels. Basia, as Aleks began to call her, was enamored. Here was a man of the world. He understood culture and art; he could quote lengthy verses from the Polish and foreign canons. She herself had only reached adulthood after the war, when travel restrictions took force. She could only dream about a world beyond Poland.

In the eyes of Basia, Aleks was a man with a bright future, someone who might one day hold a leading cultural role in Poland. He had the credentials: He'd studied for a time at the Jagiellonian University. His job gave him the means to buy the well-cut suits he wore. His suffering and ultimate survival at a Nazi camp gave him social capital. His war experience particularly spoke to Basia. Her father, Tadeusz Seweryn, had played an important role in Żegota, the Polish Council to Aid Jews, during the war. On several occasions, she had snuck around Kraków with false papers. She had once even been struck by a Gestapo agent. The war drew them together into a besotted kind of love. He scrawled love notes to her on napkins, she signed off letters with a lipstick kiss.

Yet Aleks's swagger soon wore off, and over the next year, their infatuation turned stale. He traveled the country for days on end, going from city to city selling his packets of news by day and collecting camp music by night. She wrote him pained letters pleading for his attention. Yet not long after the courts finalized Aleks's divorce from Elżbieta, he and Basia married on a fall day in September 1958. She wore a white veil with lace flowing to her shoulders.

Over the next couple of years, with Aleks back on the road, the newlyweds quarreled in letters. They slung insults at each other and seemed to be reaching a breaking point by the spring of 1961 when Basia learned she was pregnant. Ever on the road, Aleks wasn't in Kraków to learn of the news. Instead, Basia wrote to him. She had done a urinalysis, she explained in her messy scrawl, "It is positive, which means I am pregnant, even one month along." Yet what should have been a joyous letter quickly turned somber. "I realize that you will worry about this a lot as you have admitted yourself that you have almost no feelings for me anymore," she added in the next line.

Basia gave birth to a son eight months later in December 1961. They named the child Krzysztof. For a time, Aleks put on a convincing imitation of the good father. He held his bundle of a child, smiling for pictures. Yet something about the infant sent Aleks back to the camp. With Krzysztof in her arms, Basia would say to him, *look, look at your beautiful son*. But to her sorrow, an expression of quiet anguish would form on his face. Something in the baby seemed to trigger in him the terror of Sachsenhausen, yanking him back into the camp with the patrolling SS, the starving prisoners, the growling dogs. To Basia, it seemed as though Aleks couldn't handle having brought another child into a world that could be so cruel.

Instead of being a parent and provider for their future, Aleks was ever more absorbed by the past. One priority of this work was to discover what happened to Rosebery and learn more about his life in Berlin before the war. He came up empty-handed. Finding information about survivors and the dead alike was a complicated task. Even if Aleks had managed to track down the address of Rosebery's last flat in Berlin at Kleiststraße number 6 or the location of his childhood home in Mława at Niborska number 5, any letter would have been returned. The apartment building on Kleiststraße and Rosebery's childhood home lay in ruins. All that was left of the Rosenberg home in Mława were the scorched outer walls. The roof had caved in. The old homes that stood on either side and up and down the street where farmers once brought their harvest to the market square were piles of charred wood and twisted metal.

What Aleks never learned was that Rosebery's father, Shimshon, and the rest of the Rosenberg family in Mława had fled to Warsaw before the invasion, hoping to find shelter and a safe place to wait out the war. Eventually, the Germans forced them into the Warsaw Ghetto. Living at number 35/85, Nalewki Street, Shimshon was desperate for information about his family. He might have known about Rosebery's incarceration at Sachsenhausen, but if he did, there was no course of action he could take. Before the war, his youngest son, Jacob, had emigrated with his family from Poland with the intent of settling in Palestine, but Shimshon had not heard from them directly. The only information he had came from a Jewish organization in Danzig, which informed him that Jacob and his wife and child had been sent to the island of Mauritius because, in the eyes of the British authorities, they did not have a valid reason to remain in Palestine. Among the only family contacts that remained was Justus, Shimshon's grandson and Jacob's son, who had visited Rosebery in Berlin in 1937.

Shimshon did not know where Justus was. The best addresses he had were those of two Americans—one in Dayton, Ohio, the other in Pennsylvania—presumably friends of his grandson who could forward a missive. In a letter dated October 1941 sent to Dayton, Shimshon pleaded with Justus to find information about the family. He told him to ask everywhere, to visit the consulate, to inquire with the Red Cross. "How I long to see a message from my children in their own handwriting," he wrote. "My, why do the children let me remain in sorrow for such a long time and don't let anything be heard from them." Little did Shimshon know that Justus was in Marseille, where he had been working as a courier for Varian Fry and the Emergency Rescue Committee, which helped evacuate anti-Nazi and Jewish refugees. Justus only received the letters when, in 1946, he sailed across the Atlantic and settled in the United States. By the time he opened the envelopes, Shimshon had been dead for three, perhaps four years.

In the pile of rubble that was postwar Berlin, some of Rosebery's friends and former members of the Rosebery d'Arguto Singing Community searched for him, though they likely knew that their attempts were futile. Ernst Lindberg, one of Rosebery's singers and for a short time the conductor of the choir after the Nazi Party removed Rosebery from his post, asked the Berlin authorities in 1945 to search the wreckage of Kleiststraße number 6 in Schöneberg. Ernst knew that Rosebery had left a cabinet full of his musical publications, scores, and personal writing in the cellar. Though they rummaged among the ruins of the building, they found nothing. The structure had collapsed in flames, and all of Rosebery's possessions likely burned in the blaze.

Another of Rosebery's friends from the workers' movement tracked down two conductor's batons, which Rosebery used with his choir in the 1920s and '30s. This friend also found the 8-inch silver rod with the sphere at one end that Rosebery used to inspect his singers' throats. But that was all. The Nazi state had not only murdered Rosebery, it had destroyed his life's work as a composer, all but erasing him from history. What remained of him were a few dozen prewar compositions, those personal effects, the memories of his friends, and the "Jewish Deathsong."

Of the members of the Jewish choir of Sachsenhausen, only one man was known to have survived the war: Max Hüttner, the violinist. Max's cousin, Hans, survived, too. With the war behind them, they tried to begin new lives. Max immigrated to America and settled in Buffalo, New York. Despite all he had suffered as a Jew in German-controlled Europe, Hans spent four months in London, two and a half years in Paris, then returned to Berlin and settled there.

In the years that followed, Aleks sought out former inmates of Dachau, Auschwitz, Bergen-Belsen, and camps across Central Europe. With each encounter, he pressed the men and women to return in their memories to the camp for a moment, just long enough to call to mind an anecdote, a song, a poem. Some obliged him, though not every survivor he met welcomed him with warmth. More than fifteen years had passed since the end of the war, and former prisoners were now engineers, lawyers, teachers, laborers. Some had joined the Communist Party to work as government functionaries or politicians. They had wives and husbands, children to look after, meals to cook, flats to clean. For many of them, the passage of time meant the war had faded, leaving them in a place of welcome respite. Instead of answering his questions, they might shoot him a cross look or reply to his queries with a brusque retort. The trauma they had endured might still be simmering just beneath the surface, though so many of them wore a convincing imitation of normalcy and got on with life.

Aleks could not do that. His inability to forget had nothing to do with a weakness of will. Rather, it was his promise to Rosebery and the belief that someone had to gather the music, poetry, and art of the Nazi camps. At home in his flat, stacks of papers grew—clippings, interviews, notes. His network of connections expanded, too. A man who survived Dachau might tell him to seek out a camp poet he remembered. Another survivor might mention a writer at Mauthausen, or a singer at Gross-Rosen, or a composer at Auschwitz. Some former prisoners even invited Aleks to sing his own camp songs when he passed through their town on business. For the first time in years, Aleks felt an awakened urge to perform, to stand before a crowd of people and sing his camp repertoire.

These early performances were small affairs. A group of fifteen, maybe twenty people would assemble in a recreation room. Aleks might sing half a dozen or ten songs from Sachsenhausen while strumming an old guitar. When word got around that Aleks had performed at several camp associations, he began to receive an occasional invitation to sing. One came from a group of Polish priests the Nazis had imprisoned at Dachau.

Perhaps this could be a way for him to keep his promise to Rosebery and the other men and women who did not survive the camps. Aleks started to seek out opportunities to perform. Yet the reasons why he now sought the limelight had changed. No longer was he attracted to singing at cabarets or nightclubs. His interest in popular music had vanished, both the prewar repertoire he had loved and the modern songs of the generation of young rock musicians like Czesław Niemen and Niebiesko-Czarni now producing records in the communist era. He never went to concerts or music halls. It was the music of the camps that consumed him—his own songs, what he carried out of Sachsenhausen by memory, and those works he was still collecting.

But Aleks soon discovered that Poland's cultural institutions had little interest in him or his work. At first, he seemed to get traction from the camp associations. The men and women who belonged to them appeared to understand the value of what he was doing. Yet when he went to the authorities to ask permission to organize larger concerts of camp music, they often refused. Aleks never found out why, though he had a feeling that his refusal to join the Communist Party years earlier before moving to Prague had not been forgotten or forgiven. That suspicion intensified when a Polish official offered him the freedom to perform widely, to sing on television and radio broadcasts. The proposal heartened Aleks. After all, he believed that the party shared his renewed goal: to decry fascism and memorialize its victims. But he came to realize that the rubber stamp of the state hinged on his joining the party and taking an active role in communist circles. To spread camp music, he would have to join the tightly controlled narrative transmitted to Poland from Moscow. He refused.

By and large, the cultural elites of Poland offered little support as well. As far as Aleks could tell, the academics—historians, musicologists, anthropologists, journalists—disregarded the topic of camp music. If they did pay attention, it was only to criticize it. The broader cultural institutions saw camp music of any sort—Polish, Russian, Jewish, or otherwise—as popular at best and vulgar at worst. They panned or ignored the lyrics and melodies Aleks was unearthing.

Among average people, Aleks also found little traction. In part, this was due to his character. On his best days, he was demanding. On a bad day, he was contentious, brawling, ready to explode if he felt offended. Yet the reasons why people showed little interest in Aleks's work reached beyond his difficult personality. Most people in Poland in the early 1960s, camp survivors or not, were focused on the struggle of daily life. They had enough on their hands to afford meat or flour or toilet paper. The youth desperately wanted ties to the West. The war was the world of their parents. They craved jazz records and the pop songs of the Beatles; they dreamed of a single pair of American jeans. Poland was not West Germany with the financial and cultural support of the United States. It was a country at once recovering from the decimation of the war and being strangled by the grip of the Soviets. Anti-Semitism existed in Poland after the war, yet it wasn't a dislike of Jews that drove people to ignore Aleks. After all, he sang dozens of songs written by Russians and Catholic Poles. He sang about Nazi atrocities in France. He attacked Hitler. More pressing problems existed for Poles: earning a living, getting medicine, staying on the right side of the authorities.

Nevertheless, each rejection intensified Aleks's indignation. He believed unreservedly in the importance of camp culture—the music in particular—and the stories of the people who created it. He knew that without his archival work and the concerts he wished to give, the music that had kept him and so many others alive would be lost to the postwar world. The touch of narcissism he had always possessed began to reemerge. He viewed the Polish cultural authorities as fools who lacked the intelligence to recognize the value of his work. Anger stirred inside him.

Chapter 13

⌒

In February 1963, a letter bearing an East German stamp arrived at
Aleks's apartment in Kraków. It came from a musicologist named
Inge Lammel, who wrote that she worked at the Deutsche Akademie
der Künste (German Academy of Arts). Inge, whose parents were killed at
Auschwitz six years after they sent her and her sister to the United Kingdom as part of the Kindertransport, had been collecting music from the
Nazi camps for several years. Now she and the academy planned to publish a comprehensive academic article on this topic, and she hoped that
Aleks might share the songs he knew. "Dearest Comrade Kulisiewicz,"
she wrote, "we sincerely ask you to support us in our work and hope to
hear from you as soon as possible."

By 1963, Aleks's life had grown more stable. Basia now worked as a veter-
inary surgeon, an arduous vocation yet one that provided some privileges
under the communist regime, such as extra allotments of meat and other
supplies that were not always in stock at grocery stores. Aleks's job at the
Press Documentation Office was another source of income, a stream of
modest but steady paychecks. At home, the couple's son Krzysztof, by then

over a year old, toddled around the apartment. The Kulisiewicz household may not have been prosperous, but the ground beneath their feet felt firm.

Inge Lammel's letter raised Aleks's hopes. Finally, there appeared a glimmer of interest in the camp songs he had composed and collected at Sachsenhausen. Several Poles, most notably the ethnomusicologists Józef Ligęza and Adolf Dygacz, had paid attention to his repertoire over the years. Another Pole, Jan Tacina, helped him to write out each song as a musical score. Yet Aleks had struggled to find broader interest. With East German support, perhaps he could perform the songs he longed to sing; perhaps he could expand his archives.

About two weeks after receiving Inge's letter, Aleks drafted a detailed, nine-page response. He offered his support and made reference to thirteen songs, including "Muselmann—Butt Collector," "Mister C," "Black Böhm," and "Adolf's Farewell to the World." He also mentioned the "Jewish Deathsong," which, he noted, had been composed by a man he once knew well: Rosebery d'Arguto.

During the next two years, Aleks and Inge corresponded at length, discussing individual camp songs and Inge's work on a new archive within the Academy of Arts called the Workers Song Archive. The praise Inge offered Aleks, the reassurance that the work he was doing held value, was exactly what he craved. She eventually asked him to record a selection of camp songs, which he did with pleasure at the headquarters of Polish Radio in Warsaw. There, he recorded ten songs from Sachsenhausen, including "Adolf's Farewell to the World" and "Big Win!" As soon as the record was complete, Aleks sent a copy to Inge in East Berlin. Some weeks later, he received a reply. "We were surprised to hear what a skilled singer you are. The songs are performed in a truly authentic, poignant way." This was the validation Aleks had so long desired. That it came from the cultural organization in the German Democratic Republic made it all the better. Finally, someone of import was paying attention. Even if she was East German and the impetus of her work had far more to do with documenting the effort political prisoners—primarily leftists—had made to defeat fascism than in memorializing Nazi persecution, all that mattered was that she was a respected musicologist at a prestigious institution. With Inge's affirmation, Aleks enveloped himself fully in his music and ever-growing archives, much to the detriment of his home life. His wife and children once again receded to the periphery. The calm he and his family had enjoyed began to wane.

In 1965, Inge sent a copy of Aleks's recordings to the composer and ethnomusicologist Sergio Liberovici, of Bologna, Italy. Equally impressed by Aleks's singing, Liberovici took a chance and invited him to perform at an upcoming international festival, Musiche della Resistenza (Music of the Resistance), which was to be held at the Teatro Comunale di Bologna. On the day of the performance, Aleks took to the stage wearing an authentic Sachsenhausen prisoner's uniform. He had long ago discarded his own camp clothes, but he borrowed an outfit from a fellow Polish survivor who had likely worn it home after the death march. While Aleks sang, he believed he could feel the shock of the audience, even though they probably understood very little of the Polish or German lyrics. It struck him that the men and women seated before him instinctively understood the music. They stared at him, wide-eyed, as though hypnotized. Reflecting later, he thought that the crowd had been most affected by the song "Muselmann—Butt Collector," which he performed with an improvised dance just as he had done at Sachsenhausen at musical gatherings. He hoped to imitate the starving men and their shuffling gait to keep warm. One Italian journalist described Aleks's European debut as "something macabre; a slow dance of death and pain." The success of the performance in Bologna led to an Italian tour. Aleks took to the stage at seventeen other venues around the country. Each time, the audience reacted with the same shock they showed in Bologna. Partway through the tour, he considered having some of the lyrics translated into Italian for a greater effect. But after giving it more thought, he balked at the idea. "I sing only what was translated in the camps. Otherwise, it would be false, a false document from those times."

Not everyone welcomed Aleks and the other anti-fascist singers with whom he toured. At one concert in Turin, with protest singers from all over the world, neofascists planted a bomb under the stage, hoping to prevent some ten thousand people from hearing the music. Before the concert began, someone tipped off the police. They rushed to defuse the device.

Aside from the touring and press coverage, an important outcome of the Musiche della Resistenza festival was a record called *Il Canzoniere Internazionale dei Ribelli* (*The International Songbook of Revolutionary Songs*), which included the "Hymn from the Depths of Hell" and the "Jewish Deathsong." Aleks tried to sing with intensity, from deep baritone to high falsetto, especially on the "leelay" vocables of Rosebery's lament. He never polished the songs, rubbed them clean of a certain ugliness. Authenticity was paramount.

Now, with the newfound attention and audiences around Europe, Aleks felt a renewed urgency to make known the music of the Nazi camps, especially Rosebery's final composition. The promise he had made to his friend over twenty years earlier was still fresh and vital. It was as though Rosebery's spirit would haunt him if he did not keep his word. Earning money never concerned him. He cared little about luxuries. Being a good husband or father was not his calling. Only music from the Nazi camps seemed to matter.

AFTER PERFORMING IN Italy, Aleks received even more invitations to sing his camp repertoire. Initially, the letters came mostly from West Germany. Student groups and progressive organizations had read the news coverage of his concerts and now wanted him to sing at festivals and private events. With each letter he received, Aleks felt drawn more deeply into the music.

In 1967, Aleks received a request to perform that especially excited him. The organizers of the Burg Waldeck music festival, which would take place at a castle ruin in the Hunsrück Mountains in West Germany, wanted him to take the stage alongside folk and popular singers from around the world. The Polish authorities, after interrogating Aleks as to why he wanted to travel beyond Moscow's reach, acquiesced and issued him a passport. In May, he boarded a train in Kraków and headed west.

When Aleks arrived at the Waldeck Castle ruins, he saw thousands of young West Germans who had journeyed from around the country to a place where the paved roads ended and many tall oaks and hornbeams stood, dense with deep green spring leaves. He studied the young spectators. He knew that these were the sons and daughters of the men who had reigned terror across Europe. Most of them looked to be in their twenties, which meant they came into the world during the war. Yet when he gazed at them, he did not feel a rush of hatred. These people, he thought, were not his torturers.

This gathering of the Burg Waldeck Festival marked the fourth time in as many years that thousands of German youths had come to this spot in the middle western part of the country. Four years earlier, the festival was founded here in the Rhineland-Palatinate with little by way of organization or sanitation but with the worthy goal of rebuilding the German democratic tradition of folk song. Now, it had acquired a clear leftist political tone, though it had also become more commercial. The progressive spirit of the festival gave Aleks a sense of calm. It seemed that these young Germans all around him wanted to understand the past, to reckon with it. They, in the west, had enough money and food and comfort to reflect on the past, to recognize that their fathers, just twenty-five years earlier, had presided over terror in Europe. These young men and women wanted nothing to do with war. Like Aleks, they were horrified by the missiles, rockets, and bombs that were lighting up the skies over Vietnam. They did not condone warmongering. They wanted to be sure the world knew they were nothing like their fathers.

In the sunlight of those warm days, clad in jeans and colorful shirts like those seen in Haight-Ashbury, thousands of these young Germans stretched out on the grass to watch dozens of performers sing on a small stage. There were earnest voices, acoustic guitars, and lyrics about peace, love, and resilience. Among the performers were local acts—Romani jazz bands, for instance—and big names from overseas, including Sydney Carter, who played the song "Turn Him Up and Turn Him Down," and Hedy West, a banjo-playing folk revivalist inspired by the Appalachian culture of her upbringing. Inge Lammel gave a talk about folk music. While she was onstage, members of the audience subjected her to intense questioning about cultural suppression in East Germany.

Then it was Aleks's turn. He had aged. His hair was graying. Thin wrinkles ran across his forehead and around his eyes. Instead of the jeans and hip jackets the other performers sported, he was dressed in the modest clothes he always wore—loose slacks, perhaps a woolen sweater over a striped shirt, all in different earth tones. Before he began, he stood before the microphone and said nothing for a time, drawing the audience's attention. Then he uttered a few words about his songs, noting only that they came from the concentration camps and that some of their composers had perished there. He closed his eyes and drew in his breath before plucking the strings of his guitar.

A young German teacher, Georg Bündgens, sat with a group of friends in the crowd. Like so many others, his father had fought as a Wehrmacht soldier on the Eastern Front. Clear in his mind was the holiday photo he, a mere toddler, and his parents posed for while his dad was on leave. Next to the Christmas tree behind them hung a portrait of Hitler. The songs Aleks sang shocked Georg. "My god, what has this man gone through?" he thought. When he looked around, the people near him seemed to have the same thought. No one sipped from their wine. Cigarettes burned down, unsmoked. They watched the thin man onstage singing some of the ghastliest songs they had ever heard. When Aleks finished, the crowd remained silent. Applause was unseemly. Georg looked around him. Only after a long pause did anyone move. Then, people got up to leave. There was a break in the set. They walked quietly, whispering as though they were passing on a secret.

AFTER ALEKS'S PERFORMANCE at the Waldeck Castle, the British Sue Ryder Foundation got wind of his singing and asked him to visit the United Kingdom for a tour. This represented another breakthrough for Aleks. An invitation from the British made him feel like a respected cultural figure, someone whom the press covered, who deserved attention. He arrived in the fall of the same year and began his tour at the Theatre Royal in Windsor. But his debut in the United Kingdom did not begin smoothly. Upon learning backstage that Aleks would perform "Hecatomb 1941," the song his friend Alyosha Sazonov had composed about Sachsenhausen's crematorium, the concert's organizer, a British diplomat formerly assigned to the embassy in Warsaw, forbade him from singing it. The diplomat explained that this song had not been included in the official program. What was more, the Theatre Royal followed certain customs and etiquettes, and this song did not meet them. Aleks replied: "Am I to sing Polish, Yiddish and German songs but not a song about the Russians, who had the greatest losses?" The diplomat refused to change his mind. Aleks said, "Either I sing this song or I don't sing anything at all." The diplomat did not say another word. He walked onstage and addressed the crowd. From the wings, Aleks strained to catch what he said. But he could not hear him, and besides, Aleks spoke little English.

When the introduction was complete, he walked onstage. He tried to sing with great intensity that night, swinging from low melancholy tones to high falsettos, which he hoped sounded diabolical. Often during performances he took on a persona, gesturing with his hands, making hideous faces, which he had practiced in front of a mirror at home like an actor. This, he thought, made his performances more intense, more emotionally authentic. Each time he sang, he felt transported back to the years of Nazi imprisonment, as though he had returned to the song nights in the Sachsenhausen barracks among hundreds of suffering men in their striped uniforms. Some years later, Aleks put that feeling into words: "Every time I sing, I go back to that accursed camp. Once again, I have to live through it, not just re-create it through the sounds, but through all that was macabre, the bitterness, the sarcasm, the despair, the spiteful subtexts contained in one song or another. I'm paying back a debt of memory to millions of my murdered fellow prisoners, whose voices were choked back there, in the camps. They are always with me. When I sing, I feel their presence behind my back. That is why the feeling of stage fright is practically alien to me."

After the show, a journalist asked Aleks about Aron's song, "Lullaby for My Little Son in the Crematorium," the same question Aleks himself had asked Aron on the campgrounds of Sachsenhausen when he first heard it: "What kind of lullaby is this, if you shout in it?" To answer the journalist, Aleks repeated what Aron had said to him: "All I wanted was for my child to wake up."

AFTER PERFORMING HIS camp repertoire in twenty-four towns around England and Scotland, Aleks returned to Kraków, tired but satisfied with the work he had done. Soon after, he received an invitation to perform in Poland for a group of progressive students at the youth club Żak in the northern city of Gdańsk—another satisfying accomplishment. It seemed the European public was finally showing him the admiration he thought he deserved. In Germany and the United Kingdom, he had basked in the attention he received, the taste of fame. Often, an audience would sit stunned after his performances, as though he had affected them in a way no one else had done before. He relished those moments.

But then his luck turned, as he believed it always would after any taste of success. Such was his life, a series of inexorable misfortunes.

The first signs of his failing health crept in slowly; his hearing dulled, his balance faltered. Having recently celebrated his fiftieth birthday, he entered the time of life when many people who had spent their twenties in the Nazi camps would begin to decline.

Aleks saw doctors who examined his ears but said that no hearing aid would help. They examined his back and legs but said no pills would stabilize his gait. More and more often, his head would spin with little warning, and he found himself thrusting out his arms to a table's edge or the back of a chair—anything solid to steady his balance. Sometimes, he felt so wobbly on his feet that passersby shot him a contemptuous look; he looked like an old man staggering around town with vodka rushing through his veins.

Though he cared little about the thoughts of people on the street, the idea of falling during a performance did concern him. He imagined himself standing onstage, a few thousand listeners in front of him. He thought: "I am not allowed to collapse, to do badly, to go out for a while, take a break, drink some water."

Then a doctor informed him he had diabetes. After the shock of the diagnosis wore off, he tried to adjust to his new restricted life. The doctors forbade him from eating more than tiny amounts of bread or butter. Sugar of any kind was now out of the question. He most regretted that he could no longer eat pears, which he loved. He could not ignore the realization that he had begun to fade away. He knew it was the beginning of the end, and yet there remained so much to accomplish.

As Aleks's symptoms intensified, he decided to disregard his doctors and diagnose himself. He bought a large medical book and studied it until he found an ailment he believed fit with his symptoms. He landed on Ménière's disease, a disorder of the inner ear whose symptoms matched his: vertigo and hearing loss. Though he felt confident about his self-diagnosis, others around him viewed it with doubt, especially his wife, who had a medical background. In addition to his balance problems, doctors told Aleks that his liver and stomach were in bad shape, even though he almost never drank alcohol and ate very little. The few teeth the Gestapo didn't knock out in the Cieszyn jail in 1939 troubled him, too. Sometimes he stood before a mirror examining them. He would think: "I can't sing in front of a crowd with these teeth. It's terrible!" The starvation and stress and beatings of the camp were catching up with him. A specialist in Malmö, Sweden, told him that he had a choice: to give up performing his camp repertoire or die young and sick. Aleks refused to let the music go.

More than any of the physical ailments, what troubled Aleks most was the psychological burden he carried. He had seen men whipped on the trestle until the flesh on their backs turned to pulp. He had observed men strapped to wooden carts like oxen, collecting bodies for burning. He had inhaled the stench of rotting flesh and feces and pus in the medical barracks. A Polish doctor diagnosed him with KZ syndrome, a type of depression that survivors of Nazi camps often experienced. That was one diagnosis Aleks trusted. The symptoms added up—the insomnia, the images of dying men flashing into his mind, the resignation to the world, the anxiety. The scenes from the camp appeared in his mind at random times, day and night, pulling him back to a barracks or the brickworks or the roll call square. What little mental health care existed in Poland in the late 1960s could offer him nothing. And anyway, he had grown to despise doctors. More and more, he avoided treatment and medicine. When he observed so many camp survivors around him moving on, he felt indignant, as though living a decent life meant betraying the memory of those who did not survive the camps. When a former prisoner of Auschwitz or Dachau or Sachsenhausen seemed to be leaving those times behind, Aleks saw it as a breach of loyalty. He simply could not grasp how others could move on. Even his friends, many of whom survived a Nazi camp, did not want to attend his concerts or reply to his lengthy questionnaires about camp music. They wanted to buy a flat or a car, holiday on the Baltic Sea, spend time with their children. In letters and at coffee houses, they urged Aleks to move on. "Close your archives, stop singing, forget the past." The more they rebuffed him, the angrier he grew. In a letter to a recalcitrant former prisoner, Aleks wrote, "We suffered so much only to be silent now!!"

At home, life was no better. Basia found herself working a full-time job while also taking care of nearly every household task. Aleks never shopped for potatoes or meat or milk. He cared little about his clothes or whether his sons had a jacket or proper shoes. At best, he fathered from a distance. Instead of looking after Krzysztof, he typed letters to musicologists and camp survivors. He organized his papers with pedantic detail, filing them away in folders, which took up more and more space in the tiny apartment the Kulisiewiczs called home. Basia believed that Aleks loved her and Krzysztof even though he showed little interest in them. Yet she struggled to accept that he contributed so little, that he never wanted to go to the cinema or take a holiday in the summer, perhaps to the Masurian Lake District or up into the mountains not far from Kraków.

In 1971, after about a decade of marriage, Basia asked Aleks whether he thought he would always be so distracted and distant from her and their son. She was at the end of her patience. Though she had not grown bitter toward Aleks—she understood the trauma that war could inflict on someone—she knew that their marriage could not continue. Aleks told her that he expected never to improve. In fact, he predicted that his problems would only intensify. He explained that mentally he still lived in the camp. He couldn't promise her or Krzysztof that he would ever change. He agreed to the divorce. Basia and Krzysztof moved out. Due to Aleks's modest means, he took his few belongings and many files and moved into a room in the apartment where Basia's mother and father lived.

Only months after the divorce, Aleks learned that his father was dying. He boarded a bus and traveled to Cieszyn, where Franciszek lay in the hospital. Franciszek stroked Aleks's hand. Aleks remembered the song he had composed for his father at the camp: *Don't cry about me* / *That I'm hungry here.* / *Don't cry about me,* / *My dear daddy.*

As Aleks watched his father dying, he thought about his own demise. He recalled a line from a Czech poet who said that death is not as terrible as the last moments of life. Thoughts of death frightened him.

Aleks did not stay in Cieszyn long. He could not stand watching his father die. It was wrenching to witness loved ones perish. He had seen it happen so many times at Sachsenhausen. As his father dozed, Aleks stroked his hair. Franciszek seemed serene, unearthly on the hospital bed, and Aleks wondered whether the strange calmness no longer came from this world. Then he kissed Franciszek on each cheek, and his father wrapped his arm around Aleks's head, drew him downward, and kissed him back.

On the bus headed toward Kraków, while a storm gathered in the sky above, Aleks felt guilty about abandoning his father. Though they had not always seen eye to eye, Aleks respected him. He regarded Franciszek as a man of so many talents, who could recite whole sections of the *Odyssey* and *Iliad* by heart. As the bus drove toward Kraków, he tried to compose an elegy in honor of his father. But each melody that came to mind resembled a song he already knew. After several tries, he gave up.

———

THE TWO FAILED marriages, the broken homes, and the death of his father affected Aleks deeply. During much of the coming year, he diverted his sorrow by engrossing himself in his archives. He also began what he hoped would be the capstone of his life's work: a comprehensive book about music in the Nazi camps. Entitled *Polish Concentration Camp Songs of 1939–1945*, it would contain every song Aleks composed or collected—during and after the war—with an analysis of each one. To Aleks's great satisfaction, Polskie Wydawnictwo Muzyczne, a music publisher in Kraków, agreed to publish the book.

When not writing, Aleks continued to travel around Europe to sing. Research and touring helped distract him. But the diversion only worked up to a point. Regret and loneliness always found a way to creep back in. In the years after he and Basia split, he was often alone on holidays. One Christmas, he wandered aimlessly through Kraków's central train station. He found a restaurant that was open despite the holiday. Sitting before a meal of mushroom soup, carp, noodles with poppy seeds, and prune juice, Aleks looked at the others around him and tried to figure out who they were. Some must be unlucky travelers, he thought. A uniformed soldier sat at one table. He seemed drunk. There was a man with one leg. A group of women chattered at another table. Aleks thought they must be prostitutes. When he finished his meal, he slipped the holiday menu into his bag to add to his personal files.

Bitterness grew in his letters and interactions. Sometimes he came off as arrogant, as though he and only he knew about music in the camps and how it should be memorialized. In an audio journal he taped, he grumbled with jealousy after seeing Bolek Marcinek, the man who introduced him to Rosebery's choir in 1940 and who, after escaping Sachsenhausen, immigrated to Canada. "I looked at him and thought that, despite his wealth, he is far from me in terms of skills and ability. Nobody will make a film about Bolek Marcinek." With friends and colleagues, he assumed a tone of hostility and resentment. In one letter to a former prisoner, he wrote: "You are an ordinary, egoistic monster without a heart, devoid of any feelings of inmate solidarity. My name is said with respect around the world. I will repay you for such an affront." He signed off: "Without any respect."

At night, sitting at his small desk encircled by cabinets of neatly arranged files, Aleks often read books about the war or the camps. In the margins he scribbled comments and corrections, sometimes hundreds in a single book. Then he would ask Krzysztof, now a teenager, to send the book back to the publisher with an angry letter explaining in minute detail the mistakes of the author, often insulting him or her in the process. Sometimes he telephoned authors to argue with them directly. Whenever he found errors, he noted them down and added them to a special file in his archives, which he labeled, semi-humorously, "Tilting at Windmills"—attacking an imaginary enemy.

By the mid-1970s, Aleks's archives had grown enormously. They now took up a considerable part of his bedroom. During much of the day, he wrote letters to former camp prisoners across Europe, asking them to share their experience of music and to send him written testimony, scores, maps, drawings—whatever they might have. Aleks hoped to create a repository for the culture of the camps before those who created and experienced it died. Almost every day, he received replies from men and women who had survived Auschwitz, Gross-Rosen, Dachau, Buchenwald, Majdanek—nearly every major camp in the German system. He met people like Krystyna Żywulska, a Polish Jew who survived Auschwitz and Birkenau. In Aleks's opinion she was a fine poet. He was thrilled when she sent him a reproduction of her diary, in which she wrote poems, lyrics, and notes while hiding in an attic in a town near Oświęcim after she escaped the Auschwitz death march in January 1945. In the diary, Krystyna scrawled all sorts of notes, including personal confessions about prewar love affairs. What caught Aleks's eye was a poem entitled "Excursion to the Unknown."

Two hefty bodies,
And one of a child—
Now this is a job
Truly German.

One just has to
Pay close attention,
To how the fat melts,
And the meat cooks,
The shovel's movement
Makes the bones crack,
Bodies sizzle,
Bones stick out:
Children's bones
Innocent bones!

Aleks got his hands on more material from Krystyna, including a long song entitled "Medley from the Effektenkammer," the personal effects room, which had, by Aleks's count, over fifty verses. In one verse, Krystyna wrote about an heiress she met who always chattered about how she would, in a sexual way, live big after returning from the camp.

In the Pągów forest,
something shines in the distance,
The young heiress
Kindles the hearts.
She's making up for the five sad years,
She is now everyone's and she is no one's.

In another poem, Krystyna wrote about a young Jewish girl from France she saw twirling naked outside the personal effects room of the camp. Krystyna tried to figure out why the girl acted so merrily when in all likelihood she would be raped and then murdered. Krystyna wrote a poem in her head as she watched.

Dance, dance, dance, girl,
With a happy expression,
With a cheerful face.

The lords of death are in a good mood today,
They've killed mothers, fathers,
Brothers and sisters,
Pain tears the heart,
Sharp pain,
The gentlemen are watching . . .

Dance, dance, dance, girl,
Dance, girl, dance a waltz,
Legs are flowing, flowing, flowing,
Giving the executioners shivers.

Whenever Krystyna sent Aleks a poem or a letter or a document, he added it to the Żywulska file in his archives. He did the same when Józef Kropiński, a former prisoner of both Auschwitz and Buchenwald, sent him manuscripts and scores to revolutionary and prisoner songs he composed. Aleks believed that Józef stood among the most prolific, heroic, and talented camp creators. Among the songs Józef shared were "The Echo of the Uprising," about the Warsaw Uprising. At Buchenwald, Józef played the violin in the men's prisoner orchestra. By night, in the glow of a candle, he wrote hundreds of compositions in the quiet of a pathology lab where German doctors dissected bodies by day. He often drew on prewar forms like tangos and waltzes. Sometimes, corpses lay in the room as he composed. He even wrote an opera while at Buchenwald. On the death march in 1945, he burned most of his scores. The night was freezing, and the warmth of a fire might have made the difference between life and death. Though he had been on the brink of a professional career as a violinist and conductor when the Germans invaded Poland in 1939, at the time Aleks met him in the 1960s he was working in Wrocław as a clerk in the Agricultural Department of the Provincial National Council. Most days, he summarized figures on the production of state-owned farms.

Aleks regularly received twenty to thirty letters a day related to his archival work. The quantity of mail—particularly from Western Europe—

raised flags among Polish authorities. Aleks began to notice that much of his mail bore a Polish stamp pressed over the original French or West German ones. This could only mean one thing: the secret police were rerouting his mail through Warsaw.

As Aleks saw it, if the authorities were screening his mail, they had likely tapped his phone as well. But he didn't care. He believed he was doing essential work, gathering information from people like Krystyna and Józef and hundreds of others, including Szymon Laks, the conductor of the Auschwitz men's orchestra who survived the camp because of his musical skill. Another was Elżbieta Popowska, a great poet who endured the Majdanek concentration camp.

Through Inge Lammel, of the East German Academy of Arts, Aleks also met friends of Rosebery's from before the war. Whenever he traveled to East Berlin, he gathered with them and recorded interviews about the Rosebery d'Arguto Singing Community. He even reconnected with Hans Hüttner, the man who often served as the lookout while Rosebery's choir rehearsed in Sachsenhausen barracks 39.

When Aleks returned home with new recordings or documents, he added them to his archives, sometimes with the help of his sons. His eldest child, Marek, now in his mid-twenties, remembered how the scene would unfold.

"Take this piece of paper and put it in the Krystyna Żywulska file," Aleks would say.

"But dad, where do I find it?"

"Seventh file from the left, third page in the middle."

When Marek climbed the ladder and opened the folder, he always found the file he was looking for. Aleks was always right.

THOUGH ALEKS'S RENOWN continued to grow during the 1970s, he slipped into a near-constant state of depression. He rarely laughed. If he did see a friend, he dominated the conversation, tying it back to the war and the camps at every chance. His urge to attend a cabaret, to drink with friends, to hear the latest popular music never returned. He hardly drank anything, just a Czech beer once a month or so. He took little pleasure from food. He barely ate, believing that consuming less would help his diabetes. Though placing music at the center of his life kept his sense of dread somewhat at bay, he always felt a constant, simmering depression. It blocked out the light; it kept him locked in Sachsenhausen forever.

Rosebery occupied his thoughts more and more. Whenever he missed Rosebery or received bad news from a friend, his depression intensified. In a letter from this period, Aleks wrote, "It's nice to hear that you some-how made a reasonable life. At least you did—mine is broken. It's hor-rible. I'm just dejected, sad, I have become a recluse, and sometimes I don't feel like living, even if from the outside I burst with propaganda and initiative." His misery faded a little whenever he performed, especially in West Germany, where he had made several good friendships and where he felt appreciated.

However much Aleks tried, Poland's cultural elites never accepted him. In part, he was convinced, his rejection stemmed from his not belonging to the Communist Party. For years, the authorities asked him to join, but each time he refused, skeptical in his bones of the fanaticism of it. He also refused to network, to seek the right friends, to drink vodka with local party leaders. Had he built connections with influential people as he did in Sachsenhausen, perhaps he would have been able to publish essays or memoirs more widely, to gain some prominence in Poland.

But not belonging to the communist institutions was only part of the problem. More damaging to Aleks's effort to memorialize was the fact that the cultural elite of Poland still found his camp music vulgar and crude. They viewed him personally as eccentric at best, a quack a worst. They hated the way he howled, trying to re-create the anxiety and fear of a Nazi camp. They saw camp music broadly as unsophisticated, deformed, lacking the complexity of the music a trained composer might produce. That opinion frustrated Aleks intensely. To his way of seeing it, they missed the point. Camp music did not seek refinement. These songs and verses were never meant to be beautiful in the way of a symphony. This was music created in some of the most barbaric circumstances of the century, often by amateurs. How could anyone expect it not to be coarse?

The rejection from the educated classes combined with his increasing intellectual myopia and hostility left Aleks bitter and defensive. He bristled at criticism. When former prisoners challenged him or did not want to fill out his questionnaire, he erupted in anger. He began to repel people. One German musicologist described him as a peacock, concerned chiefly with drawing attention. But several others, like Inge Lammel, could see past his difficult personality. They understood the importance of his work, that as a former prisoner he was unique in his collecting and documenting of camp culture. They also recognized that his prickly behavior fundamentally came from his utter devotion to his work. This is how the famous German singer-songwriter Dieter Süverkrüp perceived Aleks when the two men met in West Germany. Being well known, Dieter was accustomed to adulation. But when Aleks approached him backstage at a festival in West Germany before they both were to perform, the first thing Aleks blurted out was that he had spent the war in a Nazi concentration camp. Then he pulled a thick album from his bag filled with photos of former prisoners and explained who each of them was. Dieter had heard of Aleks from other Germans on the folk music scene. Some of them disliked Aleks. They found him aggressive and domineering in his views. But that did not deter Dieter, especially after he heard Aleks sing. "He probably just wanted to process the trauma of the war," Dieter thought.

When in Poland, Aleks still worked at the Press Documentation Office, which sent him on the road, but at home he had few people around him. By then, he had moved his archives and a few belongings into a small apartment south of the Vistula River in Kraków. His eldest son, Marek, had emigrated to Chicago. His relationships with Roman and Krzysztof were strained. His complete obsession with the music of the camps consumed him.

On the night of Christmas Eve in 1975, Basia and Krzysztof paid him a visit. He proudly served Basia wine for diabetics and gave Krzysztof some presents. But he was in a foul mood. Life frustrated him. Everyone seemed to be doing their best to stifle him. His anger often poured out when his family tried to connect with him.

"I wish you good health, good fortune in the New Year," Basia said. "I wish that you finally finish that book of yours, and may no more zealous Poles keep blocking it at the publishing house—"

"Oh, and what else, what else?" Aleks put in, cutting her off.

"And I also hope that with the increase in benefits for veterans, you'll get everything they're promising. Both money and pension—"

"Yes, yes?" Aleks interrupted her again, his tone of voice impatient, aggressive.

Basia raised her voice to finish. "I just want you to get the money you need."

When Basia and Krzysztof went home, Aleks was left to the quiet of his apartment. Throughout Kraków, in the stillness of a Christmas night, most everyone sat around their dining tables to begin a festive meal, laughing and drinking and exchanging presents. All Aleks had were his countless documents stored neatly in folders and binders in the cabinets around his apartment. He had the pile of his typescript and stacks of musical scores. He was alone with the camp music and horrifying memories of Nazi terror. And he was lonely.

Chapter 14

~⌐

New York City, 1979

In the moments before Aleks began to strum his guitar, to let out the howling songs composed within the electrified fences of Sachsenhausen, the crowd of young people went silent. They sat shoulder to shoulder on the parquet floor of a Greenwich Village studio apartment. They spilled out the door, standing in the corridor and down the staircase outside, craning their necks for a glimpse of the frail concentration camp survivor. A few steps away on the street below, cars rushed up Sixth Avenue. Washington Square Park lay just a short distance to the southeast. Manhattan's size and noise and smell were nothing like Kraków or Prague or even Berlin, the cities Aleks knew well.

The apartment belonged to Peter Wortsman, the child of Austrian Jews who fled Vienna just before the war to eventually settle in Jackson Heights, Queens, and restart their lives. While on a fellowship in Vienna in 1975, Peter had heard from Austrian camp survivors about Aleks and arranged to meet him in Warsaw. In the hotel room, the two men spoke about music in the Nazi camps, about Rosebery d'Arguto, about the Jewish choir. Aleks had brought his guitar, and Peter had a shoddy tape recorder. Before Aleks sang, he revealed a piece of matzo bread, which they divided. Aleks always kept matzo, a rarity in 1970s Kraków, in his apartment in large part because he believed it helped his digestion. "Now," he sighed, "I have to go back . . . there." Peter remembered him shutting his eyes, a moment of silence, and then his voice flooding the room. It was Aron's song, "Lullaby for My Little Son in the Crematorium." As Aleks sang, Peter glanced at his tape recorder. He saw that the spools weren't turning. Nothing of Aleks's music was being recorded. Nearly in tears, he told Aleks about the malfunction. Aleks drew in his breath and said with no anger or frustration in his voice, "Don't think I sing for you or for myself. No! I sing for Aron." Peter fixed the spools. Aleks began again.

Four years later in 1979, in front of a group of young American artists and poets and writers, Aleks prepared to sing. Since he had never learned English, Peter interpreted from the German. Before the music began, Peter asked the audience to hold their applause—clapping, he explained, would not suit the spirit of the songs they were about to hear. Then he introduced the first song, "Hymn from the Depths of Hell."

Aleks put himself back in the camp. He saw the grounds of Sachsenhausen. He heard the screams and tumult. He watched the emaciated prisoners shuffling about. Perhaps he remembered the feeling of the jutting bones of his own body. Then, with all the macabre images, the bitterness, the black humor, the despair of the camp, and the spirits of his dead friends there with him, he began. *Hear our hymn from the depths of hell! / May it keep our killers from ever sleeping well.* This was the song Aleks had composed in 1944 using the lyrics of the Varsovian journalist and poet Leonard Krasnodębski and adding a melody based in part on Chopin's funeral march. It was the very song Aleks had debuted thirty-five years earlier at a secret gathering in the camp medical rooms, where he lay blind, sick from the virus that filled his eyes with pus, certain that at any moment the SS would order him to the crematorium.

Aleks's debut in the United States, even informal as it was in a Lower

Manhattan apartment, felt to him like an immense accomplishment. For most Poles, America held a near mythic status in the world. People in the east of Europe craved ties with the United States. Many families remained afloat in villages and towns across Poland thanks to boxes of supplies sent from relatives in New York or Chicago. Even a package containing used clothing, purchased for a few dollars at a thrift store anywhere in America, was valuable on the Polish black market. For Aleks, a man of sizable ego, singing here meant reaching a high point of success. It was more gratifying still because a young man—a young Jewish man—had organized it. That Peter had seen value in Aleks's work, had written about him in the magazine *Sing Out!*, and had organized a trip for him to visit New York and record an album with the Folkways label was a triumph for Aleks.

When Aleks finished Leonard's song, the audience was speechless, their eyes fixed on the thin singer with graying hair. No one forgot what Peter had said; there was no burst of spontaneous applause. Clapping would have breached the somber atmosphere. After a silent pause, Aleks plucked out the introduction to the next song, "Lullaby for My Little Son in the Crematorium," the solemn notes that foretell the piercing lyrics to follow. *Here he lies, my only little boy,* Aleks sang, trying as he always did to reproduce every nuance, each cadence of the way Aron had sung it at Sachsenhausen in 1942. *How can I cast you into the flames? / With your shining golden hair.* When the song came to an end, Aleks could see tears running down the cheeks of several people in the audience. Though they didn't understand Polish, they knew of the fate of Aron and his wife and child. Peter had told them in his introduction, mentioning how Aleks learned the song while sweeping the grounds of the camp and how Aron's voice had risen pleadingly at the end of the song, imploring anyone or anything to make his son wake up.

As Peter watched Aleks sing, he had the feeling that he was conjuring forth the disembodied voices of the dead, men like Leonard and Rosebery and Aron, who had perished at the hands of their German captors. The effect of Aleks's singing, the dramatic flourishes he used to re-create life in a Nazi camp, struck Peter as deeply powerful, almost exaggerated, but appropriate for the purpose of conveying to the audience the anxiety and fear of living in Sachsenhausen. Peter's brother Harold was also in the room that evening. To him, Aleks's voice seemed to live in a space between life and death. His was not a conventionally beautiful voice, but it was a powerful one.

In the days after the performance at Peter's apartment, Aleks recorded an album for Folkways Records. Peter produced it and Moses Asch, the legendary founder and head of Folkways, oversaw the process. When it was time to record, Aleks stood in a sound booth in the Midtown Manhattan studio, his guitar in hand. On the other side of a glass window, Peter and an engineer, seated before the controls, signaled for him to begin. Aleks sang the "Jewish Deathsong," the "Hymn from the Depths of Hell," "Heil Sachsenhausen," and a dozen other camp songs in what Peter remembered was a single take. For the cover, he and Peter chose a postwar pen-and-ink drawing of Aron clutching the corpse of his dead boy, the boy for whom he composed his searing lullaby. They named the album *Songs from the Depths of Hell.*

On one of Aleks's final evenings in America, he sat in the dining room of the Wortsman family home in Jackson Heights, Queens, where he had been staying while in New York. It was a Passover Seder, and Peter's whole family had assembled to observe the occasion. On the table lay the Seder plate with its symbolic foods. A copy of the Haggadah was also within reach, probably in German, as this was the common language of the group.

Seder at the Wortsmans, which that night included Peter's siblings, parents, and aunt, was not a formal affair. Over a meal of gefilte fish and matzo ball soup, followed by roast chicken, potatoes, and vegetables, Peter's parents spoke about the Jews' exodus from Egypt, and then wove in their own flight from Vienna. Aleks sat quietly, a yarmulke resting slightly askew on his gray pate, observing a ritual blended with laughter and warmth and candlelight. Peter remembered a look of boyish contentment on Aleks's face as he absorbed the stories and songs and food. At the end of the night, Aleks ate a piece of the afikomen matzo over tea, and then went to bed. That was to be the first and only Passover Seder Aleks ever attended.

TRAVELING ACROSS THE Atlantic Ocean to New York proved to be an immense strain for Aleks, both physically and psychologically. Yet when another request to perform in the United States arose just a few months later, he immediately consented.

In October of 1979, Aleks boarded a flight from Warsaw, and after layovers in New York and Chicago, he arrived in Milwaukee, Wisconsin. This time, his hosts were two men from the Jewish Community Center, Rod Eglash and Howard Karsh. More than a year earlier, Rod had happened upon Peter's article in *Sing Out!* magazine. Gripped by the "singer from hell," as Peter had described him, Rod spent the intervening months trying to arrange for Aleks to visit the Midwest.

Over the course of ten days, Aleks performed in as many venues as Rod and Howard could arrange. He sang on Milwaukee Public Radio, at high schools, including one across state lines in Chicago, and repeatedly at the Jewish Community Center. He even came to Howard's Sunday School class to share his story. Aleks's performances in Milwaukee were small affairs—they were casual, in school gymnasiums or multipurpose rooms. Sometimes, people had gathered for a free meal and heard his singing by chance. Compared with the concerts he gave to thousands, even tens of thousands of people at festivals in West Germany or Italy a decade earlier, these could be seen as minor events of a long career. Yet there was one difference: for the first time, Aleks was singing for audiences made up primarily of Jewish people.

For years, he had yearned to perform for Jewish listeners. Perhaps more than any other group, he felt that Jews needed to hear Rosebery's elegy or Aron's lullaby, songs written about the Holocaust from within the walls of Nazi camps. Until those performances in Milwaukee, Aleks's audiences had largely been German, Italian, British, or French, with few—if any—Jews among them. He had long dreamed of traveling to Israel. But diplomatic tensions between Jerusalem and Warsaw had prevented travel between the two countries, and though Aleks repeatedly tried, he never secured the permission he needed.

In America, Aleks got as close as he could to what he desired. To a nation far more able and willing to memorialize German crimes during the war, he told the story of Rosebery, of Aron, of Alyosha. He sang the music they composed in Sachsenhausen. In Milwaukee with the Jewish community and in New York with Peter and his friends and family, Aleks had come full circle to where he had begun with the music of the camps: a day in the summer of 1940 when a man he knew only as Moses defended him against the Czech priest in the little camp of Sachsenhausen. On that day nearly forty years earlier, he met Rosebery, a man who would change his life more profoundly than any other person.

Before he flew back to Europe, Aleks spent a Sabbath morning at Howard's synagogue, the Congregation Beth Jehudah. Over a meal, he met the congregants. Some spoke Polish well, and most greeted him hospitably. Though the spread of food was enticing, he mostly ate matzo—a food he knew would not upset his stomach. That he ate so much matzo, out of season at that time, seemed to please the congregants. Little did they know it was his favorite snack when he visited his grandparents in Nowy Wiśnicz in the 1920s.

IN MID-NOVEMBER, ALEKS returned to Kraków and his increasingly quiet life. He often strolled to Park Krakowski, a few minutes south on foot from his apartment, and sat on a bench by his favorite duck pond to think. He could still feel the energy and youthful spirit of Peter's circle in Manhattan. The satisfaction of singing for the Jewish community in Milwaukee pulsed through him.

The American performances, small as they might have been, marked a consummation of Aleks's work memorializing the camps. On those chilly fall days, he could still feel the warming buzz of the eager American crowds, see the tears shed in the audience at Peter's apartment, recall the Milwaukee newspapers that printed his photograph. One reporter from the *Milwaukee Journal* who saw him perform wrote, "You cannot watch the man and not believe that he is, indeed, resurrecting the dead with each word. The songs and thoughts about those people might make me weep, but they make Kulisiewicz full of tenderness and not just a little joy. The people are, for a very few minutes, alive again."

A sense of pride welled up in Aleks, the sort of defiant pride that spawns after years of indignation. For a time, the attention put him in a remarkable humor. Peter had noted his youthful smile at Passover dinner in April. Rod and Howard had thought of him as sweet and exceptionally humble. These were words that few people in Europe would ever use to describe Aleksander Kulisiewicz.

The afterglow could only last so long. In times like these spent at the duck pond, Aleks could equally reflect with regret on the chauvinism he had embodied before the war. A flash of such remorse could send him plummeting into the darkness. He would fantasize about a retreat to a dense mountain forest, where he would live in a cottage without radio or television, with just a wolfhound he would name Reks. He would rid himself of every book and document and letter about the concentration camps and finally forget it all. Perhaps, he thought, if he did this he might return to the folk music he knew and loved as a child: "I'm a different man when I'm in the mountains."

But Aleks could not withdraw to the mountains. Work remained to be done. By the close of the 1970s, he had retired from the Press Documentation Office and was collecting a modest pension. That covered his basic costs but little else. A few years earlier, he had moved back into the flat at 10 Henryk Sienkiewicz Street that belonged to the Seweryns, Basia's parents. Likely in an aim to save money, the three lived together until both Seweryns died and Aleks had the place to himself.

By any honest account, Aleks now lived in squalor. The apartment may once have been modern and beautiful, a place where in the 1930s, the Seweryns had held dinner parties for Kraków's intellectual elites. But they had changed little of it in the nearly fifty years that had passed, other than swapping out much of the prewar furniture for communist-style replacements.

By the mid-1970s, the building wore Kraków's soot like a coat of paint. The cream or white or tan of the facade's plaster was darkened yellow-black. Inside, the paint on the walls chipped off in flakes. The floors were stained and filthy. The bathroom had fallen into disrepair. Nothing but the toilet still functioned. The windows, installed in the 1920s, let in the cold winter wind, which, no matter how hot the coal stoves burned, left the apartment in a frigid, dank state whenever the outside temperature fell. One benefit was that it was now owned by a state cooperative and was cheap. His rent and bills combined cost him next to nothing, perhaps the equivalent of a few restaurant dinners each month.

Aleks spent his days at a simple wooden desk, writing letters, filing new documents in his archives, and working on his manuscript, a particularly sore subject, since the music publisher in Kraków who had promised to publish it had put him off for the past several years.

Though the flat was cold and neglected, Aleks preferred life this way. He often said as much to his son Krzysztof. His previous flat before returning to Sienkiewicz Street was far more comfortable—it was a short walk from the wide Vistula River, across the water from the Wawel Castle, and was quiet and centrally heated. When Krzysztof asked why he wanted to go back to the Sienkiewicz apartment, Aleks replied that in order to work well, to remain focused on his camp music, his archives, and his promise to Rosebery, he needed to live in a derelict setting, one with few comforts that stood near the old Nazi landmarks of Kraków. A few paces from the Sienkiewicz flat, Aleks reminded his son, stood Pomorska, the former city headquarters of the Gestapo. Aleks wanted to live among the ghosts. He wanted to pass his final years in darkness.

Even though Basia's parents were dead, Aleks inhabited but one room of the spacious apartment. Aside from a desk with a prewar German typewriter, a single bed, a lamp, and a small coal stove in one corner, his archives filled his living space. Hundreds upon hundreds of files stood on shelves in wardrobes that almost touched the ceiling. By his own count, he had collected some 820 songs from the Nazi camps all over occupied Europe. Over two thousand works of camp poetry were in his neatly organized files. He possessed thousands of microfilm frames, leaflets, notes, statements, maps, reports, and radio and television broadcasts;

a hundred original and reproduced camp drawings and paintings; and almost a hundred recordings of camp music. Over a quarter century of focused work building the archives, his correspondence and attached camp testimony now amounted to some twenty thousand pages. He carefully filed away each letter in a folder in his room. Having lugged his weighty tape recorder around for two decades, he had over 165,000 feet of audio tape, which held the interviews he conducted with camp survivors. The archives also included his interviews with scholars, collected music, his own autobiography, and hundreds of personal files—the letters Basia signed with a lipstick kiss, stamped tickets from the Paris metro, blood test results, a butter wrapper, unsmoked cigarettes. His manuscript had swelled to three thousand pages and contained music and poetry, as well as related research and analysis, from thirty-four Nazi camps and their subcamps.

Practically every day, Aleks posted letters to camp survivors he had tracked down, imploring them to return to their war memories just long enough to send him their recollections of camp culture or perhaps the lyrics of a song or the verses of a poem. The work felt urgent. Some thirty-five years after the end of the war, many of the men and women who had survived the camp were dying, and with them, their music and poetry and art. Aleks sorted and listed every document the postman dropped off, adding new files to his catalog and bibliography. Whenever a song came with an anecdote, he noted the name of the person and each fact before checking everything with the resources at his disposal and striking anything from his archives or manuscript that he could not verify. Doing this work caused him deep mental anguish. At night, he sometimes shot awake in fear. He looked at the hundreds and hundreds of files and folders and could no longer sleep. He felt surrounded.

Yet he would not stop. Performing in as many venues as possible was one pillar of this work. Building a record of it was another, a set of physical mementos that could be held and studied and analyzed, the final remains of the lives of the friends he loved.

Though for the last fifteen years European newspapers had praised

Aleks, calling him the "Bard of the Camps" or the "Singing Conscience of Europe," by 1980, he could hardly perform, and as he withdrew from the world, his renown quickly faded.

His massive archives were another source of anxiety. Aleks feared that after his death, someone, possibly a relative, would dump all the documents into the trash and record over his tapes. Around this time he told a Polish journalist, "The heart of the matter is to save the archives." As he searched for a new publisher for his manuscript, he also inquired of institutions around Poland, urging them to take his collection. He wanted the material to remain in his home country, yet available to scholars from all over the world.

He tried to convince the library of the Jagiellonian University. He approached the Auschwitz Museum and the Institute of Literary Research at the Polish Academy of Sciences. The National Library in Warsaw even sent staff to inspect the archives and assess their importance. But in the end, no institution would commit to taking the collection, not even one of the many new Nazi camp museums that had been founded since the end of the war and had growing archives themselves.

By 1981, Aleks believed he was fast approaching death. On some days, he took stock of his accomplishments—his performances around the world, sometimes for thousands of people, the records of camp music he had made, his manuscript, his book of camp verse called *Poetic Memories*, his archives. The accomplishment that gave him the most pride was surviving the camp at all, of marching out of Sachsenhausen with hundreds of pages of music and poetry stored in his mind, and then unburdening himself to the nurse in Kraków's Antituberculosis Clinic. Thirty-five years later, he still felt that this act of bearing witness was the most fulfilling of his life.

Despite Aleks's postwar struggle, there had been moments of immense happiness since his liberation. When he held one of his records for the first time, a rush of satisfaction came over him. With each recording, he believed he was leaving behind a bit of himself, a bit of Rosebery and Aron and Alyosha and everyone else whose music he so wanted to keep alive. None of the records struck Aleks as perfect. He knew that to some, his

was the voice of an amateur. And most certainly, every so often a string
on his guitar might ring sharp or he might hit a note flat. Yet his goal was
never to be regarded as a master artist. He only wanted to evoke interest
in the camp songs, to memorialize the camps' victims and the suffering
they experienced so that young men and women of the future might know.

He recalled with great pleasure a performance at the Sorbonne, in Paris,
after which a French studio made a recording of his music. He could still see
with vivid detail the streets of Moscow, where he visited a friend from Sachsenhausen, Andrej Sarapkin, and performed on the radio. He had friends
throughout the world, as far east as Japan and as far west as California.

In reflecting on his life, Aleks recalled a prophecy Rosebery had made
in the camp: "Remember, when your days are almost over, they will cover
you in gold." He continued: "As long as you don't betray my song and aren't
greedy for money or fame, I will do everything in my power to make you
shine with my song and other songs all over the world." Had Rosebery
gotten it right? Aleks wondered. For a time in the postwar years, the Germans had treated him well enough, the Italians, too. Their newspapers
had written laudatory articles about him. Studios there had been keener
to record his repertoire. But that had faded as the spirit of the 1960s and
'70s gave way to a new decade. What Aleks longed for was more attention
in Poland. When he had performed in his home country, he thought he
deserved more adulation. In his diary, he complained. "In Italy I received
a loud ovation, and here, in my home region, I got some applause, but the
audience should have risen from their seats."

What Aleks knew for certain was that he had not betrayed Rosebery. At
the cost of his family, his health, his friendships, he had sung the "Jewish
Deathsong" around the world. In fact, alongside Leonard Krasnodębski's
"Hymn from the Depths of Hell," it was the title he had sung the most over
the course of his performing career.

THE NEARLY SIX years Aleks endured as a captive of the Nazis caught up
with him. His three sons, Marek, Roman, and Krzysztof, saw him as a

man with a destroyed psyche. They knew that he struggled to sleep, that day and night visions of violence and anguish flashed through his mind, yanking him from the present back behind the walls of Sachsenhausen.

His sons could not remember a time when he wished to attend the cinema or visit a concert hall or read a trendy novel. At the cost of his relationships, his book about camp music, the archives, and the singing were all that held his attention. Unlike other camp survivors, many of whom turned to drink, he never guzzled vodka or struck his wives or children in rage. His depression simmered, a constant low burn.

His health began to worsen so intensely that he found it hard to leave the apartment. Being confined angered him. He believed that now, in his sixth decade, he was reaching his creative zenith, that the world shimmered with opportunities to spread the music and message he had dedicated his adult life to preserving. He wanted to visit Japan and Brazil, perhaps the United States a third time, a country whose citizens he was convinced wanted to hear more from him and would arrange a concert if he would only make the trip across the Atlantic.

Aleks brooded in Kraków. He wondered why God or the universe would stifle him when all he wished to do was sing for the dead, stand up and accuse those who were culpable, keep the memory of men like Rosebery alive. "God is giving everything to the murderers," he grumbled to himself, thinking about how so many ex-SS and Wehrmacht soldiers in West Germany had prospered. They drove Mercedes-Benz cars, holidayed in Spain. In Kraków, he struggled to get enough toilet paper to wipe himself clean.

Aleks's legs ached constantly. The left one felt cold, as though blood had ceased to circulate so far from the heart. His once straight frame, the runner's body that helped him survive sport at Sachsenhausen, had bent and grown stiff. Mysterious ailments had sent him to a plethora of doctors, most of whom he did not like or trust. Between official and self-diagnoses, he now believed he suffered from diabetes, rheumatism, Ménière's disease, and Buerger's disease. The function of his kidneys and prostate had deteriorated, and the excruciating pain of kidney stones tormented him. A nurse began to visit him to administer injections, but he thought they did little to help. As the months passed, his left foot grew colder, as if it were dead flesh and bone. At night, he covered it with a wool blanket.

Sometimes, Aleks mourned the final heady years of the 1930s, when he felt as though he was coming into himself as a person, with music and literature and friends as the focal points of his life. And then came the German invasion, which ruined that life so completely and permanently. He grieved for the life he likely would have begun under pressure from his father—that of a lawyer distracted by singing, of a man who had the capacity to love his wife and pay his sons the attention they desired. In that fantasy, Aleks would have been a contented man in the year 1981, with grown children, a good wage, a mind free of trauma. Instead, here he sat alone under his blanket in the dilapidation of his flat, feeling the creeping approach of death in the tedium of late Soviet-era Poland, his relations with his family strained and his head filled with the mournful music of the Nazi camps. He hoped a heart attack would kill him. He wanted to leave the world like his friend Józef Ligęza: collapsing among family after a walk with his dog at Christmas time. It was a death that lasted little more than an instant. "A beautiful death," Aleks thought. "I envy him very much."

This was how Aleks envisioned his end: he would be at the library of the Jagiellonian University and his heart would stop. It would be a quick, fashionable way to go, and he prayed to God that this is how he would die. His final desire: to be buried next to his mother at the Salwator Cemetery in Kraków.

Aleks had long given up trying to find Rosebery or any of his family. He was sure that what remained of his old friend was mixed into the soil around Auschwitz, blended with the shards of bones of countless others. What often returned vividly to him was the evening of the Jewish choir's final performance, cut short by the SS. As if it were just weeks earlier, he remembered the sorrowful day when Rosebery left Sachsenhausen for Dachau and the moment, two weeks later, when the SS marched most of the other Jews like Hans and Max Hüttner out of the camp, forced them onto trains, and deported them east. Most of all, Aleks recalled the time when Rosebery looked him in the eye and said, "You are not a Jew. If you survive, you must sing my song of bitterness and revenge, my death song." This simple instruction had determined the rest of Aleks's life.

ALEKS TOOK TO the stage to sing his repertoire of camp music for the last time in July 1981. A few months earlier, an invitation to perform in Nuremberg had arrived at his apartment in Kraków. He agonized over whether to make the trip. He had little energy. His whole body felt frail, as though he might topple over at any moment. Yet he agreed, under the condition that he be accompanied by a nurse.

On the day of the performance, Aleks hobbled up to the microphone wearing a short-sleeve white shirt and a green sweater vest. A nurse from the Red Cross trailed behind him onstage.

While he sang, he looked out at a youthful crowd of West Germans, two generations removed from the war, to his eyes wealthy and materialistic in a way he had never before seen. They struck him as disinterested in his music, almost suspicious of it. These were not the eager students he'd sung for in the 1960s at Burg Waldeck, with their modest means, their search for truth about the crimes of their parents. No, this generation was coddled by a life in one of the richest countries on earth. They listened to electronic music. They used modern technology—even early computing devices. On Aleks's way back to Poland, he scoffed at the unfairness of the world. In Germany, the land of the aggressors, life seemed opulent, lavish. In Poland, the country vanquished, shop shelves were empty, poverty was pervasive, and the government was oppressive.

When Aleks returned to Kraków, he slowed to the pace of an old man. From the window, he stared at the broad acacia tree outside. He watched as ravens pecked at its green leaves. Other birds sat on its branches— mainly pigeons and turtledoves. He studied them until he perceived an avian order. The bigger black birds sat on the solid boughs. The smaller, timid ones seemed to choose the unsteady branches, prepared to dart away. A little brown-white pigeon often alighted on the windowsill. It seemed too old and weak to fight for its spot in the pigeon hierarchy. Perhaps this bird reminded Aleks of himself. By now, he had accepted that his role in the world was over. The public's memory of and interest in the war had dimmed, and Europe, especially Poland, was facing new troubles. In Poland, the collective memory of Nazi crimes never completely disappeared, but it was now only an undercurrent, superseded by a preoccupation with the Solidarity movement and the fight against the communist state and the Soviets in Moscow.

Aleks mostly stayed at home. He tamed the brown-white pigeon, which he named Rumcajs after a character in a Czech children's series, by feeding it from his window. When Rumcajs alighted on the sill and pecked at the glass, Aleks dropped whatever he was doing to feed it. After a while, he left leaves on the ledge. Rumcajs would land on this simple nest and hide his head beneath his feathers to slumber. Aleks no longer had the strength to walk to the park and sit beside the duck pond. "I at least have them," he thought, watching the birds.

He looked forward to a small joy, the near-daily presence of a young graduate student named Marta Urbańczyk, who had chosen to write her master's thesis on his life and work. Over the years, Aleks had been the subject of documentary films, and dozens of newspapers around the world had written articles about him. The well-respected Cracovian journalist Konrad Strzelewicz was even in the process of assembling a book based on an oral history he conducted with Aleks. Yet all these press accounts, which often relied on clichés and superlatives to describe him, seemed cursory. They recounted his story, they mentioned the music of the camps and his desire to spread it around the world. But they never broke the surface to examine the deeper, more complicated questions of music and trauma in a place like a Nazi camp. Even Strzelewicz's oral history struck Aleks as painting the music in the broadest of brushstrokes, skimming over much of the detail that he recorded with such rigor in his manuscript. Aleks believed that through Marta's thesis, he could leave behind an accurate record of the music of the camps, something that future musicologists could study and appreciate. As he saw it, the thick stack of papers that made up his manuscript might be stuffed in a trash bin upon his death, but at least Marta's thesis would be preserved at her university's library.

On most weekdays over the next year, Marta sat at Aleks's bedside, listening to the sick man speak. His physical condition had deteriorated to the point that only rarely could he summon the strength to rise from beneath the covers. Despite his physical suffering, to Marta his mind seemed perfectly sharp. Reclining against pillows in his bed, he would often tell her to retrieve a document from the thousands and thousands of folders in file cabinets around the room. As he did with his son Marek, he would point, "There, on the second shelf, in the fourth package, take the third file you find. Inside, eight documents from the left, you'll find a certain letter from Krystyna Żywulska or testimony from Hans Hüttner or a program from the Gesangsgemeinschaft Rosebery d'Arguto." Each time, she would follow his instructions and there, invariably, would be the document he wanted. His memory struck her as uncanny, astonishing, especially because he seemed so debilitated.

Each day, Aleks dictated to Marta from his bed. He told her about the most important camp songs. He recounted the circumstances in which they were composed. He spoke of the source melody and composer of each song, analyzing the lyrics and explaining the symbolism. Then, when she had noted everything down, he would sing for her. Marta watched as this tiny, feeble man, dressed in pajamas, suffering from a catalog of ailments, would draw in his breath and let out a voice so powerful, so sonorous that it stunned her. When he sang, she watched as the muscles in his body tightened. It was as though he could expand. He could consume the space around him. He seemed to channel someone else, someone only he could see or feel. Anger or fear sometimes flashed across his face. The muscles of his jaw and cheeks grew taut. Watching him often left a look of fright on her face. When he finished, he would ask, "What, have you seen the devil?"

Without the company of Marta or Konrad Strzelewicz or one of his sons, Aleks spent his days alone, musing about the past, about God, about heaven, which he believed awaited him. He fantasized about heaven being a place where he would see old friends, speak many languages, show his father all of the records of camp music he had made. Perhaps, he thought, he might even impress his father, who had never gotten over the fact that his son hadn't become a lawyer and kept the Kulisiewicz family rising up the social ladder.

Sometimes, Aleks looked at the little cross Bożena had given him when they met in the late 1940s at the Holy Hill near Olomouc in Czechoslovakia. The cross lay on his bedside table. He had long lost contact with Bożena. But he often thought of her and the times they spent together before the war at her vegetable stand, how much the memories of her had buoyed him during the most torturous moments of Sachsenhausen. He still dreamed of a life with her, a version of the world where, had luck been with him, the war would never have happened, where they lived in a simple apartment or country cottage in Czechoslovakia.

Once, when Krzysztof visited, Aleks handed him a photograph of Bożena, a portrait from before the war. He asked him to slip it and the cross into his coffin when he died.

OUTSIDE, BEYOND THE secluded world of Aleks's flat, protest began to shake Poland. During the previous thirteen years, the Solidarity movement had grown in numbers and begun to oppose the communist authorities, who quashed the unrest when it flared up. Since the early days of the movement, Aleks had followed it closely. He even asked Krzysztof to bring him a television set so that he could monitor what was happening outside, though most of the broadcasts were skewed by government propaganda.

As Solidarity gained momentum, its charismatic leaders and nearly ten million members struck Aleks as wielding the might needed to overthrow the regime. But any hope for that in the short term vanished when, on the morning of the December 13, 1981, he awoke to the menace of tanks on the streets of Kraków and learned from his sons of the presence of army checkpoints at many main intersections. General Wojciech Jaruzelski had launched a coup and imposed martial law. Aleks's sons passed along information to him as to what was happening, and though the press did not share the full picture, Aleks knew that in all likelihood, the military had begun a dragnet of arrests, taking thousands into custody. The playbook of human oppression, he had come to understand, so often repeated itself. Nevertheless, he believed in his bones that Solidarity would prevail, perhaps not in his lifetime, perhaps not in five years or ten, but someday. The communist system was so deeply broken that it could not be fixed. Though he might never again experience a free Poland, he was dying with the confidence that his children would.

During a visit from Krzysztof, now aged twenty, Aleks told him that he needed to go to the hospital. He felt unbearably weak. Pain rippled through his body. His doctor, worried about Aleks's kidney function yet unsure of the scope of the problem, asked him to check into the hospital to run some tests. It would not be a long hospital stay, Aleks assured Krzysztof—perhaps at most two weeks away from home.

On the day in late February 1982, when Aleks was to report to the hospital, he dressed in the old woolen clothes in muted colors that he had worn for decades. On the sidewalk below the apartment, he hobbled with an arm around Krzysztof's for support, snow crunching under their feet, a low gray sky above, until they could flag a taxi near Plac Inwalidów, Invalid Square.

As the taxi took off through the city's streets, Aleks caught sight of the tanks that had posed both a physical and psychological threat to residents since December. He implored his son not to get involved with the resistance in any way. Krzysztof was now almost the same age as Aleks when the Gestapo arrested him for opposing the Nazis. Aleks couldn't bear the thought of his child ending up in custody. The only tragedy worse than what he had endured would be if his son experienced something similar.

On most days, Krzysztof visited his father at the hospital. Sometimes, a look of great suffering passed over Aleks's face, but rarely did he complain. At first the doctors explained to Krzysztof that they could not be sure what the exact problem was, though they warned him that because of martial law, medicine was in short supply and getting treatment for his father could prove complicated.

When, some days later, the doctors told Krzysztof that his father had pneumonia, he knew the situation was dire. During normal times, Krzysztof would have sent a telegram to Georg Bündgens or Hans-Christian Tittelmeier or any of the other West German friends of his father's, who would have gladly sent any needed medicine. Yet under martial law, communications with the West were cut off. With tanks again patrolling the streets and men armed with guns and the permission from an oppressive state to arrest anyone who dared resist, Aleks died in his sleep.

He died knowing that he had remained faithful to Rosebery, to the music they and so many others had created in the depths of their misery in Sachsenhausen. Yet so much remained undone. His mission had not come to an end. He had not found a publisher for his book. His archives lacked a home. Death, at the young age of 63, in a Europe either not ready to receive what he had to say or tired of hearing it, was another instance of his bad luck.

On a frigid day a week later, a small crowd gathered to watch as Aleks's wooden coffin was lowered into the snow-dusted ground. In accordance with Aleks's wishes, his family put him to rest in the Czorba-Bromowicz grave in Kraków's Salwator Cemetery, beside his mother, the woman who gave him his love of music. Though he had made hundreds of international friends over the course of his performing, only one, a German who organized his final appearance on stage, managed to arrange a visa to attend the service. Before the coffin was sealed, Krzysztof had slipped in the photo of Bożena and the little cross she gave to Aleks in Czechoslovakia in 1948.

The cemetery was a quiet, pleasant spot on a hill with a view of Kraków in the distance. A few hundred yards west stood the opulent townhouse that, a lifetime ago, in a different world, had belonged to Aleks's Austro-Hungarian grandfather, where Aleks had played as a boy. A few months later, when spring came, the tall, wind-worn trees that dotted the cemetery would grow dense with a canopy of new leaves. Inscribed on his tombstone were the words "Bard of the camps."

Acknowledgments

I am deeply grateful to Dr. Barbara Milewski, of Swarthmore College, and Dr. Bret Werb, of the United States Holocaust Memorial Museum, who showed me immense generosity throughout the research and writing of this book. Barbara and Bret were the first scholars to examine the Aleksander Kulisiewicz archive in detail and have, over three decades, become the leading experts on Kulisiewicz and music in the Nazi camps broadly. Without their exceptional and groundbreaking scholarship, this book would not have been possible. Barbara was also kind enough to allow me to print her excellent translations of Kulisiewicz's song lyrics from the Polish and Krystyna Żywulska's poetry also from the Polish.

In 2020, I was lucky enough to meet Peter Konopatsch, of the Academy of Arts, Berlin. Over the last eight years, Peter has made many of the most important contributions to our understanding of the life and work of Rosebery d'Arguto. Thanks to his keen analysis and understanding of the academy's d'Arguto Collection, which he oversees, and his extensive general knowledge of history, he and I have been able to piece together the life of this remarkable man. Over the course of writing this book, Peter was exceptionally generous with his time, input, and expertise.

I owe another debt of gratitude to Barbara, Bret, and Peter for having read my manuscript and offered valuable feedback. I would also like to thank Dr. Günter Morsch, the former director of the Sachsenhausen Memorial Museum, who very kindly helped me fact-check and verify the sections of the book that take place in Sachsenhausen.

I would like to express my gratitude to the descendants of Aleks and Rosebery. Krszytof Kulisiewicz, Aleks's youngest son, spent innumerable hours with me in Poland and Germany, on the phone, and in letters discussing the life of his father. On three separate occasions, he drove me around the greater Kraków area to show me the landmarks of his father's life, from the townhouse where Aleks played as a child to the site of his grave. Krszytof's wife, Małgorzata, his daughter, Karolina, and his daughter's partner, Oskar Potapowicz, were kind and hospitable to me. Marek and Roman Kulisiewicz, Aleks's older sons, provided essential information that helped me build a narrative of their father's life. They also entertained my seemingly endless questions over several years with attention, kindness, and humor. I am also grateful to Małgorzata Łuczaj for arranging interviews with Marek and Roman.

For the first year of my research, I, like many others, believed that none of Rosebery's family survived the Holocaust. Thus, when I came into contact with Sharon Rozov, Rosebery's great-grandniece, I nearly fell off my chair. I was stunned even further when Sharon informed me that Rosebery's nephew, Dr. Justus Rosenberg, was living in New York State, near Bard College. Sharon and Justus were instrumental in filling in the substantial gaps in Rosebery's private life, particularly about his childhood in Mława. Sharon, an excellent researcher in her own right, helped me track down records, understand the dynamics between Rosebery and his family, and comb through archives in Israel. Justus, who died at the age of one hundred in November 2021, and his wife Karin, welcomed me into their home in Rhinebeck just weeks before the pandemic shuttered the world. Over two days, Justus shared his memories of summer vacations in the Rosenberg home in Mława, of his uncle Rosebery (whom he knew as Moshe), and of his grandfather Shimshon. The details and documents he gave me made the sections on Rosebery come to life.

The family of other characters also provided me with important insight. I would like to thank Dr. André Laks for repeatedly meeting with me in Paris over the last two years to discuss the life of his father, the composer, musician, and Holocaust survivor Szymon Laks. I am very happy to have met Isabella and Caroline Marcinek, the wife and daughter of Bolesław (Bolek), the man who introduced Aleksander to the Jewish choir of Sachsenhausen. Isabella, who died in 2021, shared important information about Bolek's life, and Caroline was kind enough to show me fascinating primary source documents. Jonathan Huttner, the descendant of Hans Hüttner, gamely sifted through family documents in search of information. I'm grateful to Tadeusz and Jacek Andrzejewski, who allowed me to print two poems written by their late mother, Krystyna Żywulska.

I owe a great debt to Sarah Nägele, a journalist who helped me report and research in Germany. Sarah was instrumental in tracking down obscure information, interviewing certain sources, helping me parse historical records, and much more. She made many important discoveries that give the book color and depth and helped weed out my errors and repetitions. I am equally indebted to Agata Majos, a journalist who helped me report and research in Poland. Agata's reporting skill, keen eye, and breadth of knowledge were crucial throughout the research process, especially in regard to piecing together the prewar lives of Rosebery and Aleksander. She made many contributions to this book. I would like to thank Joanna Suchomska and Katarzyna Wrona who translated hundreds of documents from Polish and German into English, including some of Kulisiewicz's lyrics and poetry.

Many friends of Aleksander's welcomed my inquiries and shared their recollections. I would like to thank Georg Bündgens, Brigitte Hege, Walter Gunther, Rod Eglash, Howard Karsch, Tom Schroeder, Carsten Linde, Hans-Christian Tittelmeier, and Dieter Süverkrüp. I'm especially grateful to the writer, poet, and dramatist Peter Wortsman, whose memories and information were crucial to reconstructing the events in chapter 14. Peter was also kind enough to let me print his translations of the "Jewish Deathsong" and "Lullaby for My Little Son in the Crematorium" from the German.

I relied on the expertise and work of many scholars and researchers over the course of this book. I would like to thank Marta Urbańczyk for her pivotal master's thesis on Aleks. Dr. Astrid Ley, head of the Sachsenhausen Memorial, was generous with her time and expertise. I'm grateful to Dr. Juliane Brauer for her work on Rosebery d'Arguto and the music at Sachsenhausen. The musicologist Dr. Dorothea Kolland helped me understand the intricacies of interwar Neukölln and Rosebery's role in it. Barbara Zaborowska, director of the Muzeum Ziemi Zawkrzeńskiej – Mława, and Jarosław Janiszewski, citizen historian, welcomed me warmly and shared their deep knowledge of Mława's history. I would also like to recognize the pioneering work of the late German musicologist Dr. Inge Lammel. Dr. Lammel was central in collecting music from the Nazi camps and building what became the Rosebery d'Arguto Collection at the Academy of Arts, Berlin.

Grace Ross found my proposal for a different book in the depths of her email inbox, then eventually sold the pitch for this book to W. W. Norton. I'll always be grateful to her for her guidance, faith, and enthusiasm. My agent, Markus Hoffmann, has been the ideal literary partner. His presence and counsel were essential. It was a privilege to work with John Glusman of W. W. Norton. John's skill and wisdom are evident on every page of this book. Helen Thomaides, also of W. W. Norton, provided much support throughout the process. Thank you to Seyward Darby and *The Atavist Magazine* for publishing an abridged version of this story. I'm also grateful to Kate Wheeling for fact-checking key elements and scenes that appear in the book.

I owe a great deal to Harrison Hill, my comrade in book writing. Not only did Harrison read an early draft of my manuscript and offer excellent suggestions, he also came up with the title, *Sing, Memory*. My close friend, Bianca Heyward, read an early version of the manuscript and gave me excellent suggestions. Jack Knych and Virginie Actis were crucial in helping me refine the idea behind this book and untangle narrative problems over many late evenings in Paris. I'm grateful to Tancrède Chambraud for his friendship and for his advice as I learned how to discuss this story in French.

I've been fortunate enough to encounter superb teachers over my life. I would like to thank Samuel Freedman, whose book writing seminar at the Columbia Journalism School and dedication to excellence changed the course of my career. Dale Maharidge taught me invaluable lessons in long-form writing, dogged reporting, and seeing the art in nonfiction. Nicholas Lemann, Walt Bogdanich, Sheila Coronel, Laura Muha, Charles Ornstein, Jim Mintz, Steve Eder, Sam Sanders, and Derek Kravitz, all from Columbia, gave me a solid journalistic foundation. The attention and encouragement of Dr. Dari Sylvester put me on a good path. John Chalmers showed me the power of books. Sue Lautenslager gave me a love for stories.

I'm lucky to have many great friends around the world. Thank you to Rory Richard Martin, Matthew Terrance Ching, Sean English, Valerie Shaindlin, Michael Powell and the late Hiroshi Tagami, Tyler Payne, Karelli Cabral and Caelan Urquhart, Spencer Ton, Jordan Schreiber, Chris Sullivan, Taylor Hughes, Dylan Walker, Lameece Gasser, Ellis Rua, Jon Allsop, Martin Goillandeau, Natasha Rodriguez, Deanna Paul, Joshua Hunt, Patrick Mulholland, Ted O'Reilly, Andrew Calderon, Marianna and Pierre van Kampen, Bruno Gonzalez, Cecilia Butini, Temima Shulman, Amanda Darrach, Heather Radke, Alison Cheeseman, Benoît Morenne, Rick Noack, Marc Guidoni, and Thomas Saintourens. I'd also like to thank Christopher Caines for his friendship and wise edits of my writing over the years. *Je veux remercier Kisito Bélibi de m'avoir permis de travailler dans son charmant café et Thomas Guillemin pour ses blagues et ses bons cappuccinos.*

I'm grateful to my family. Above all, I am indebted to my parents. My mother, Hoku Chong, has been an unwavering presence throughout my life. Her unconditional support and warmth have fundamentally shaped me. My father, David Eyre, has been equally present and devoted, especially when it comes to my writing. During the pandemic lockdown, he worked countless hours editing the first draft of my manuscript, an immeasurable contribution that improved this book immensely. Thank you to my siblings and their partners for their love and good company over many years: Sintra Eyre and Odd Bech-Hansen, Lisa Eyre and Magnus Sarin, Emma Eyre and Emil Mattsson, Alea and Haʻaheo Keliʻikoa, and Kamakani Chong-Enos. I'm also thankful to Eva Thunstam, Conard Eyre, Alan Chong, Crocker Clark, Megan Clark, Lee Liddell, Moana Liddell, Tad Sewell, Jolanta Hańska, Agnieszka and Tomek Winek, Alicja Szopińska, and Andrzej Wyka. My nieces and nephews are a great source of joy. My love goes to Chandra, Hadje, Cynthia, Elise, Emmeline, Forest, Eugene, Nāʻiwa, Kaleohano, Louis, Julia, and Jaśminka.

This book is dedicated to my partner, Ewelina Szopińska. In the most literal of terms, *Sing, Memory* would not exist without Ewelina's steadfast support, love, and patience in times past and present. This book is also dedicated to the author and historian Dr. Gavan Daws. If I have a claim to make as a writer, it is in large part because of Gavan's attention, wisdom, and instruction over fifteen years of friendship.

Notes

Primary Archives and Libraries

Alexander Kulisiewicz Collection. United States Holocaust Memorial Museum Archives, Washington, DC, US

Sammlung Rosebery d'Arguto. Akademie der Künste, Berlin, Germany

Arbeiterliedarchiv der Akademie der Künste, Berlin, Germany

Leon Szalet Collection. Leo Baeck Institute, New York, US

Ghetto Fighters House Archive, Western Galilee, Israel

Gedenkstätte Sachsenhausen Archiv, Oranienburg, Germany

KZ-Gedenkstätte Dachau Archiv, Dachau, Germany

Gedenkstätte Deutscher Widerstand, Berlin, Germany

Arolsen Archives - International Center on Nazi Persecution, Bad Arolsen, Germany

Museum Neukölln, Berlin, Germany

Stiftung Archiv der Parteien und Massenorganisationen der DDR im Bundesarchiv, Berlin, Germany

Archiv der sozialen Demokratie der FES, Bonn, Germany

Österreichisches Volksliedarchiv, Vienna, Austria

Universitätsbibliothek Wien, Vienna, Austria

Österreichische Nationalbibliothek, Vienna, Austria

Bibliothek Arbeiterkammer Wien, Vienna, Austria

Chapter 1

3 **Poets, writers, philosophers, and painters:** Norman Davies, *God's Playground: A History of Poland, Vol. 2: 1795 to the Present* (New York: Columbia University Press, 2005), 318.

3 **midst of a revival:** Richard M. Watt, *Bitter Glory: Poland and Its Fate 1918–1939* (New York: Barnes & Noble Books, 1998), 290–92.

4 **meadow of Błonia Park:** Aleksander Kulisiewicz, Jak Umierał Mój Głos. Aleksander Kulisiewicz Collection. United States Holocaust Memorial Museum Archives, Washington, DC.

4 **an ardent sense of freedom:** Patrice M. Dabrowski, *Poland: The First Thousand Years* (Dekalb: Northern Illinois University Press, 2014).

4 **national cause no longer constrained them:** Marci Shore, *Caviar and Ashes: A Warsaw Generation's Life and Death in Marxism, 1918–1968* (New Haven, CT: Yale University Press, 2006).

4 **since the third partition in 1795:** Andrzej Paczkowski, *The Spring Will Be Ours: Poland and the Poles from Occupation to Freedom* (University Park, PA: Penn State University Press, 2003), 1.

4 **homosexuality occasionally appeared:** Shore, *Caviar and Ashes* (introduction); also, Adam Zamoyski, *Poland: A History* (London: William Collins, 2015), 350.

4 **economic and social troubles seethed:** R. F. Leslie, ed., *The History of Poland since 1863* (Cambridge, UK: Cambridge University Press, 1987), 171.

4 **poverty still ravaged:** Watt, *Bitter Glory*, 198.

4 **a bravado not seen in generations:** Paczkowski, *The Spring Will Be Ours*, 18.

4 **no grand state ideology:** Norman Davies, *Heart of Europe: The Past in Poland's Present* (Oxford, UK: Oxford University Press, 2001), 110.

4 **the whole world belongs to me:** Konrad Strzelewicz, *Zapis: Opowieść Aleksandra Kulisiewicza* (Kraków: Krajowa Agencja Wydawnicza, 1984).

5 **vodka-drinking carpenter:** A. Kulisiewicz, Jak Umierał Mój Głos. ms.

5 **gaps in the floorboards:** A. Kulisiewicz, Jak Umierał Mój Głos. ms.

5 **failed the end-of-year exam:** According to student records housed in the archives of the Jagiellonian University.

5 **rumors of war were circulating:** Interview: Sarah Nägele/Bogdan Musial.

6 **strumming his guitar for university friends:** A. Kulisiewicz, Jak Umierał Mój Głos. ms.

6 **called his town and region home:** Interview: Agata Majos/Stefan Król.

6 **hugged it preciously to his body:** A. Kulisiewicz, Jak Umierał Mój Głos. ms.

7 **impress those around him:** A. Kulisiewicz, Jak Umierał Mój Głos. ms.

7 **think of himself as much of a singer:** A. Kulisiewicz, Jak Umierał Mój Głos. ms.

7 **learning scales and doing exercises bored him:** A. Kulisiewicz, Jak Umierał Mój Głos. ms.

7 **nothing of it resembled the waltzes or mazurkas:** A. Kulisiewicz, Jak Umierał Mój Głos. ms.

7 **organ tracks impressed him:** A. Kulisiewicz, Jak Umierał Mój Głos. ms.

7 **highlanders sang in beautiful harmony:** A. Kulisiewicz, Jak Umierał Mój Głos. ms.

7 **the most beautiful sound he'd ever heard:** A. Kulisiewicz, Jak Umierał Mój Głos. ms.

7 **the Pieniny Mountains:** A. Kulisiewicz, Jak Umierał Mój Głos. ms.

8 **she wore braids:** A. Kulisiewicz, Jak Umierał Mój Głos. ms.

8 **fetch his little violin:** A. Kulisiewicz, Jak Umierał Mój Głos. ms.

9 **"He's still a tiny boy":** A. Kulisiewicz, Jak Umierał Mój Głos. ms.

9 **for 123 years:** Dabrowski, *Poland: The First Thousand Years*, ebook location 7615.

9 **Poland did not exist on the map:** Paczkowski, *The Spring Will Be Ours*, 1.

10 **emperor-king in Vienna:** Davies, *Heart of Europe*, 95.

10 **sovereignty from its neighbors:** Dabrowski, *Poland: The First Thousand Years*, ebook location 7590. Also see Davies, *Heart of Europe*, 100.

10 **"an economic impossibility":** This lines and the one before it quoted in Davies, *God's Playground*, 291.

10 **six border wars:** Dabrowski, *Poland: The First Thousand Years*, ebook location 7644.

10 **Polish realm once again:** Davies, *Heart of Europe*, 100.

10 **take control of the city in 1919:** Idzi Panic, *Dzieje Śląska Cieszyńskiego od zarania do czasów współczesnych → tom VI* (Cieszyn, Poland: Starostwo Powiatowe w Cieszynie, 2015), 38. Also see Paczkowski, *The Spring Will Be Ours*, 9.

10 **A year later, in July:** Davies, *Heart of Europe*, 101.

10 **the town was split in two:** Interview: Agata Majos/Stefan Król.

10 **Olza River defined as the frontier:** The Conference of Ambassadors announced the border decision on July 28, 1920, marking the frontier on the Olza line (with local deviations, thanks to which, among others, Larisch-Mönnich's goods were included in the Czech Republic). Source: Panic, *Dzieje Śląska Cieszyńskiego od zarania do czasów współczesnych*, 64.

10 **six currencies circulated:** Watt, *Bitter Glory* 79.

10 **Military commands:** Davies, *Heart of Europe*, 105.

10 **of which Cieszyn was one:** Davies, *God's Playground*, 298.

10 **Three legal codes:** Paczkowski, *The Spring Will Be Ours*, 16.

10 **caused headaches and delays:** Davies, *Heart of Europe*, 105.

10 **build national institutions from scratch:** Zamoyski, *Poland: A History*, 482.

10 **administrative buildings, courts, and schools:** Zamoyski, *Poland: A History*, 482.

10 **Russia, Prussia, or Austria:** Davies, *Heart of Europe*, 105.

11 **and instead, picked up the guitar:** Marta Urbańczyk, "Twórczość i działalność pieśniarska Aleksandra Kulisiewicza w obozie koncentracyjnym Sachsenhausen 1940–1945" (MA thesis, Uniwersytet Śląski, 1981).

11 **at sixteen, he dropped a rope:** A. Kulisiewicz, Jak Umierał Mój Głos. ms.

11 **such an independent son:** A. Kulisiewicz, Jak Umierał Mój Głos. ms.

12 **long and quiet:** A. Kulisiewicz, Jak Umierał Mój Głos. ms.

12 **that same year:** A. Kulisiewicz, Jak Umierał Mój Głos. ms.

12 **Belgrade, Sofia, and Bucharest:** A. Kulisiewicz, Jak Umierał Mój Głos. ms.

12 **slowly and tenderly:** A. Kulisiewicz, Jak Umierał Mój Głos. ms.

13 **stretching out before them:** A. Kulisiewicz, Jak Umierał Mój Głos. ms.

13 **after his inauguration:** Zamoyski, *Poland: A History*, 396.

13 **one to twenty million in 1923:** Dabrowski, *Poland: The First Thousand Years*, ebook location 7794.

13 **the Sanacja regime:** Jerzy Lukowski and Hubert Zawadzki, *A Concise History of Poland* (Cambridge, UK: Cambridge University Press, 2007), 240.

13 **allying themselves with Nazism:** Lukowski and Zawadzki, *A Concise History of Poland*, 249.

13 **Disaffection among Ukrainians:** Davies, *Heart of Europe*, 111.

13 **Jews fear harassment and abuse:** Lukowski and Zawadzki, *A Concise History of Poland*, 249.

13 **newly regalvanized and energetic right:** Davies, *Heart of Europe*, 111.

13 **targeted because of their ethnoreligious:** Paczkowski, *The Spring Will Be Ours*, 20.

14 **the good part of a millennium:** Antony Polonsky, "Jewish Life in Poland–Lithuania to 1750," in *The Jews in Poland and Russia: Volume I: 1350 to 1881* (Liverpool: Liverpool University Press, 2009).

14 **sometimes harmonious:** Eva Hoffman, *Shtetl: The Life and Death of a Small Town and the World of Polish Jews* (Boston: Mariner Books, 2007), 29.

14 **before the Germans invaded:** Davies, *Heart of Europe*, 125.

14 **anti-Jewish boycotts or forced emigration:** Lukowski and Zawadzki, *A Concise History of Poland*, 240.

14 **this was relatively rare:** Peter Stachura, *Poland, 1918–1945: An Interpretive and Documentary History of the Second Republic* (Abingdom, UK: Routledge, 2004), 87. Also see Davies, *Heart of Europe*, 125, Paczkowski, *The Spring Will Be Ours*, 21, and Zamoyski, *Poland: A History*, 478.

14 **a pure ethnic state:** Interview: Agata Majos/Iza Mrzygłód of the University of Warsaw.

14 **brutal attacks:** Interview: Agata Majos/Iza Mrzygłód of the University of Warsaw.

14 **chauvinistic version of himself:** Bret Werb and Barbara Milewski, "From 'Madagaskar' to Sachsenhausen: Singing about 'Race' in a Nazi Camp," *POLIN Studies in Polish Jewry* 16 (2003), 278.

14 **including land in his home region:** Urbańczyk, "Twórczość i działalność pieśniarska."

15 **Jews as a problem:** Interview: Eyre/K. Kulisiewicz. This perspective grew increasingly common among the middle and upper classes during the interwar years, groups to which Kulisiewicz had begun to belong. For more information on increasing anti-Semitism among these classes, see Paczkowski, *The Spring Will Be Ours*, 6, 19.

15 **succeeded too easily in business:** Interview: Eyre/K. Kulisiewicz.

15 **nearby country estates:** Interview: Eyre/ K. Kulisiewicz.

15 **bench ghettos:** Watt, *Bitter Glory*, 363.

15 **anti-Semitic remarks in the classroom:** Interview: Eyre/K. Kulisiewicz.

15 **regularly attacked:** Paczkowski, *The Spring Will Be Ours*, 21.

15 **violence turned into a near daily occurrence:** Interview: Agata Majos/Iza Mrzygłód of the University of Warsaw.

15 **Mandatory Palestine or Madagascar:** Paczkowski, *The Spring Will Be Ours*, 21.

15 **in search of a worldview:** Interviews between Eyre and B. Milewski and K. Kulisiewicz.

16 **operate radios and treat wounds:** Panic, *Dzieje Śląska Cieszyńskiego od zarania do czasów współczesnych.*

16 **damaged several local monuments:** Panic, *Dzieje Śląska Cieszyńskiego od zarania do czasów współczesnych.*

16 **organize a defense:** The Museum of the Polish Army mentions August 30 as the day of general mobilization: http://www.muzeumwp.pl/kalendarium/08-30/. August 24 was "silent" or "card" mobilization, which covered 75 percent of the Polish army.

16 **awaiting what was rumored to come:** Panic, *Dzieje Śląska Cieszyńskiego od zarania do czasów współczesnych.*

16 **invasion on that Friday:** Edward Davidson and Dale Manning, *Chronology of World War II* (London: Cassell, 1999), 14–15.

16 **in the form of radio broadcasts:** Interview: Sarah Nägele/Bogdan Musial. We are sure that Polish Radio informed its listeners about the war early on September 1 (for example, in the account of Franciszek Pasz or https://www.polskieradio.pl/205/3798). Also see note about further radio broadcasts in Dabrowski, *Poland: The First Thousand Years*, ebook location, 8016.

16 **no military significance:** Timothy Snyder, *Bloodlands: Europe between Hitler and Stalin* (London: Vintage, 2010), 119.

16 **killing hundreds of civilians:** Snyder, *Bloodlands*, 119.

16 **a Polish military depot:** Dabrowski, *Poland: The First Thousand Years*, ebook location 8016.

16 **fierce fighting ensued:** Roger Moorhouse, *First to Fight* (London: Bodley Head, 2019), 14.

16 **streaking toward Kraków:** Dabrowski, *Poland: The First Thousand Years*, ebook location 8007. Also see Moorhouse, *First to Fight*, 20, for a note on jets going to Katowice. Also see F. Pasz: Pierwszy dzień wojny w Cieszynie. "Znad Olzy," 1998, nr 1; R. Kaczmarek: II wojna . . ., 344. (Testimony of Cieszyn factory worker. Source: red. Idzi Panic).

16 **Local shops opened, workers arrived:** Interview: Agata Majos/Stefan Król.

16 **blasts rumbled in the distance:** Testimony of Cieszyn factory worker. Source: red. Idzi Panic.

17 **soldiers marched over the cobblestones:** Interview: Agata Majos/Stefan Król.

17 **Luftwaffe aircraft strafed them:** Davies, *God's Playground*, 322.

17 **defense lines would hold:** Interview: Eyre/K. Kulisiewicz.

17 **German rule would be temporary:** Interview: Eyre/K. Kulisiewicz.

Chapter 2

18 **Cieszyn's main synagogue ablaze:** Interview: Agata Majos/Stefan Król.

18 **no longer own a business:** Cieszyn was a part of the Reich, so the Nuremberg laws applied.

18 **commandeered without compensation:** Interview: Sarah Nägele/Bogdan Musial.

18 **slaves of the Reich:** R. F. Leslie, ed., *The History of Poland since 1863* (Cambridge, UK: Cambridge University Press, 1987), 214–215.

18 **on Solna Street:** Interviews: Eyre and M. & R. Kulisiewicz as well as with K. Kulisiewicz.

19 **resilience of the Polish army:** Roger Moorhouse, *First to Fight* (London: Bodley Head, 2019), 19–20.

19 **a million and a half:** Timothy Snyder, *Bloodlands: Europe between Hitler and Stalin* (London: Vintage, 2010), 120.

19 **troops now marauding in Cieszyn:** Adam Zamoyski, *Poland: A History*, 5th ed. (London: William Collins, 2015), 314.

19 **more sophisticated hardware:** Moorhouse, *First to Fight*, 19.

19 **dwarfed by the Wehrmacht's:** Moorhouse, *First to Fight*, 19.

19 **fifth largest military on earth:** Moorhouse, *First to Fight*, 46.

19 **anti-tank rifles, machine guns:** Moorhouse, *First to Fight*, 46.

19 **their own attack on Germany:** Norman Davies, *God's Playground: A History of Poland, Volume II: 1795 to the Present* (New York: Columbia University Press, 2005), 324.

19 **an airfield, a train station:** Moorhouse, *First to Fight*, 100.

19 **military officials fled eastward:** Moorhouse, *First to Fight*, 100.

19 **reduce destruction and bloodshed:** Moorhouse, *First to Fight*, 101.

19 **a gunshot halted him:** Moorhouse, *First to Fight*, 101.

19 **bombs rained down:** Moorhouse, *First to Fight*, 81.

19 **residential neighborhoods:** Moorhouse, *First to Fight*, 157.

20 **seventeen air raids:** Snyder, *Bloodlands*, 119.

20 **destruction by air:** Snyder, *Bloodlands*, 119.

20 **dim blue lights:** Moorhouse, *First to Fight*, 81.

20 **second week of September:** Davies, *God's Playground*, 324.

20 **twenty-five thousand shells:** Moorhouse, *First to Fight*, 201.

20 **Shortages of food:** Moorhouse, *First to Fight*, 202.

20 **the Poles fought well:** Patrice M. Dabrowski, *Poland: The First Thousand Years* (Dekalb: Northern Illinois University Press, 2014), ebook location 8021. Also noted in Snyder, *Bloodlands*, 120.

20 **resisted the Germans for several weeks:** Norman Davies, *Heart of Europe, The Past in Poland's Present* (Oxford, UK: Oxford University Press, 2001), 56.

20 **were still fighting:** Davies, *Heart of Europe*, 57.

20 **to unknown destinations:** Leslie, *The History of Poland since 1863*, 215.

20 **Polish intelligentsia:** Jerzy Lukowski and Hubert Zawadzki, *A Concise History of Poland* (Cambridge, UK: Cambridge University Press, 2007), 256.

20 **the local Gestapo-run jail:** Peter Stachura, *Poland, 1918–1945: An Interpretive and Documentary History of the Second Republic* (Abingdon, UK: Routledge, 2004), 131–132.

20 **Polish journalists had written about:** Interview: Sarah Nägele/Bogdan Musial.

20 **shoot them into trenches:** Interview: Sarah Nägele/Bogdan Musial.

21 **destroy Poland as a functioning state:** Leslie, *The History of Poland since 1863*, 215.

21 **a pliable mass:** Snyder, *Bloodlands*, 121.

21 **held the headmaster's job:** Box 17 / RG-55.003*93. Characteristics of Rosebery d'Arguto. Aleksander Kulisiewicz Collection. United States Holocaust Memorial Museum Archives, Washington, DC.

21 **several newspaper articles:** Konrad Strzelewicz, *Zapis: Opowieść Aleksandra Kulisiewicza* (Kraków: Krajowa Agencja Wydawnicza, 1984), 137.

21 **keeping a low profile:** Interview: Agata Majos/Stefan Król.

21 **wrenched Polish government signs:** Interview: Sarah Nägele/Bogdan Musial.

21 **Adolf Hitler Platz:** Interview: Agata Majos/Stefan Król.

22 **had sat on their hands:** Stachura, *Poland, 1918–1945*, 130. Also see: https://avalon.law.yale.edu/wwii/blbk17.asp.

22 **could withstand a German attack:** For information on the media's portrayal of the army, see Czesław Miłosz, *Wyprawa w dwudziestolecie* (Kraków: Wydawnictwo Literackie, 1999).

22 **war would only last a few months:** Interview: Eyre/ K. Kulisiewicz.

22 **Aleks didn't believe:** Interview: Eyre/K. Kulisiewicz. For facts about war updates—
    Interview: Sarah Nägele/Bogdan Musial.

22 **to straighten its line or regroup:** Moorhouse, *First to Fight*, 100.

22 **Adolf-Hitler-Platz:** Snyder, *Bloodlands*, 131.

22 **to serve the German war machine:** Leslie, *The History of Poland since 1863*, 215.
    Also in Zamoyski, *Poland: A History*, 318.

22 **melted away on September 17:** Leslie, *The History of Poland since 1863*, 212.

22 **Red Army troops crossed:** Moorhouse, *First to Fight*, 163.

22 **drove alongside the infantry:** Moorhouse, *First to Fight*, 164.

23 **evacuation orders:** Moorhouse, *First to Fight*, 173.

23 **fled to Romania:** Leslie, *The History of Poland since 1863*, 212.

23 **divided their spoils:** Dabrowski, *Poland: The First Thousand Years*, ebook loca-
    tion 8050.

23 **demarcation line:** Lukowski and Zawadzki, *A Concise History of Poland*, 255.

23 **vanished from the map of Europe:** Leslie, *The History of Poland since 1863*, 212.

23 **directly into the Reich:** Davies, *God's Playground* 327.

23 **lived in Cieszyn:** Cieszyn (Teschen) was incorporated into the German Reich
    (Teschen District). After the end of the war, the border demarcation of 1920 became
    valid again. Source: Online-Lexikon zur Kultur und Geschichte der Deutschen im
    östlichen Europa, https://ome-lexikon.uni-oldenburg.de/orte/teschen-cieszyn.

23 **Hans Frank as its governor-general:** Bogdan Musial, *Deutsche Zivilverwaltung
    und Judenverfolgung im Generalgouvernement: Eine Fallstudie zum Distrikt Lublin
    1939–1944* (Wiesbaden, Germany: Harrassowitz, 1999), 13.

23 **From the Wawel Castle:** Timothy Snyder, *Black Earth: The Holocaust as History
    and Warning* (London: Vintage, 2015), 145.

23 **incorporating them into the USSR:** Davies, *Heart of Europe*, 57.

23 **in the Polish language:** https://www.dhm.de/lemo/kapitel/der-zweite-weltkrieg/
    kriegsverlauf/kolonisierung-und-vertreibung-in-polen.html.

24 **teaching them in Polish:** Leslie, *The History of Poland since 1863*, 215.

24 **meant a great deal to him:** Interview: Eyre/K. Kulisiewicz.

24 **govern all aspects of daily life:** Davies, *God's Playground*, 330.

24 **racial hierarchy:** Davies, *God's Playground*, 330.

24 **"For Germans Only":** Davies, *God's Playground*, 330.

24 **had to be assigned a group:** Davies, *God's Playground*, 330.

24 **died of intestinal tuberculosis:** Strzelewicz, *Zapis*, 40.

25 **disdain for much of Polish society:** Aleksander Kulisiewicz, Jak Umierał Mój
    Głos. ms, RG-55, United States Holocaust Memorial Museum.

25 **a great impact on Aleks:** Strzelewicz, *Zapis*.

25 **the first songs:** Strzelewicz, *Zapis*.

25 **write in the gothic alphabet:** Strzelewicz, *Zapis*.

25 **the top posts in the region:** Strzelewicz, *Zapis*.

25 **Austro-Hungarian blood:** A. Kulisiewicz, Jak Umierał Mój Głos. ms, RG-55.

26 **an inferior race:** Leslie, *The History of Poland since 1863*, 215.

26 **a Faustian bargain:** Interview: Sarah Nägele/Bodgan Musial.

26 **coupons for more and better food:** Davies, *God's Playground*, 330.

26 **enlist him in the Wehrmacht:** Lukowski and Zawadzki, *A Concise History of Poland*, 257. Confirmed with K. Kulisiewicz.

26 **Warsaw capitulated on September 27:** Davies, *God's Playground*, 326.

26 **national press struggled:** Interview: Sarah Nägele/Bogdan Musial.

27 **owning a radio:** Interview: Sarah Nägele/Bogdan Musial.

27 **Nazi-controlled trusts:** Interview: Sarah Nägele/Bogdan Musial.

27 **corrupted version of German:** Snyder, *Bloodlands*, 122.

27 **sidelocks and long beards:** Dabrowski, *Poland: The First Thousand Years*, ebook location 8072. Snyder mentions sidelocks in *Bloodlands*, 123.

27 **raped Jewish women:** Snyder, *Bloodlands*, 122.

27 **hostilities had ceased:** Snyder, *Bloodlands*, 123. This is also noted in Dabrowski, *Poland: The First Thousand Years*, ebook location 8029.

27 **summarily shot:** Zamoyski, *Poland: A History*, 318.

27 ***Głos Stanu Średniego*:** Barbara Milewski, "Remembering the Concentration Camps: Aleksander Kulisiewicz and His Concerts of Prisoners' Songs in the Federal Republic of Germany," in *Dislocated Memories: Jews, Music, and Postwar German Culture*, ed. Tina Frühauf and Lily Hirsch (New York: Oxford University Press, 2014), 141–60.

28 **On October 25:** Date noted in Milewski, "Remembering the Concentration Camps," endnote 5.

28 **"With a fist":** Strzelewicz, *Zapis*.

28 **bombed and then burned:** The city of Biłgoraj was bombed on September 8 and 11, 1939, and the city burned down in the process. (Source: https://sztetl.org .pl/de/stadte/b/1911-bilgoraj/96-lokalgeschichte/67051-lokalgeschichte and https:// de-academic.com/dic.nsf/dewiki/177009.) Dr. Bogdan Musial also confirms that wooden houses are typical for this region of Poland.

28 **a forest of orphaned chimneys:** Aleksander Kulisiewicz, *Sachsenhausen: Pamiętnik Poetycki, 1939–1945* (Lublin, Poland: Wydawnictwo Lubelskie, 1965), 4.

28 **six-year-old Ewunia:** A. Kulisiewicz, *Sachsenhausen: Pamiętnik Poetycki*, 4.

29 **made the blows less painful:** A. Kulisiewicz, *Sachsenhausen: Pamiętnik Poetycki*, 4.

29 **didn't just shoot him:** Strzelewicz, *Zapis*.

29 **woke him up to the reality:** Strzelewicz, *Zapis*.

30 **"Morning Song":** Urbańczyk, "Twórczość i działalność pieśniarska."

30 **gave him strength:** Urbańczyk, "Twórczość i działalność pieśniarska."

30 **metaphysics, parapsychology:** Strzelewicz, *Zapis.*

30 *Efendi!:* Strzelewicz, *Zapis.*

30 **"Mr. Little Bee, please tell":** Strzelewicz, *Zapis.*

32 **guard slid open the peephole:** Strzelewicz, *Zapis.*

32 **"The idiot talked so much":** Strzelewicz, *Zapis.*

33 **half-interested but jolly lawyer:** Interview: Eyre/K. Kulisiewicz.

33 **disintegrated in the course:** Davies, *Heart of Europe,* 129.

33 **leaning against local bars:** Interview: Sarah Nägele/Bogdan Musial.

34 **were now for German use:** Interview: Sarah Nägele/Bogdan Musial.

34 **deep freeze:** Snyder, *Bloodlands,* 133. Also described as "an unforgiving winter" in Nikolaus Wachsmann, *KL: A History of the Nazi Concentration Camps* (New York: Farrar, Straus and Giroux, 2015), 167.

34 **She fled:** Strzelewicz, *Zapis.*

34 **Zaolzie region:** Lukowski and Zawadzki, *A Concise History of Poland,* 252.

34 **deep into the Czech interior:** Strzelewicz, *Zapis.*

35 **empty box cars:** These details, including the rough date of departure, are located in Bolesław Marcinek's unpublished memoir. Marcinek was a friend of Aleks's both at the Cieszyn jail and at Sachsenhausen.

Chapter 3

37 **in Breslau:** The Polish minority in the concentration camp 1939–1945/Exhibition Catalogue confirms the pattern of Germans putting Poles in local prisons and then, over time, taking them to bigger camps.

37 **a large, damp room:** Aleksander Kulisiewicz, *Adresse: Sachsenhausen, Literarische Momentaufnahmen aus dem KZ* (Gerlingen, Germany: Bleicher Verlag, 1997. For interrogation cells, see https://www.topographie.de/historischer-ort/das -hausgefaengnis/.

37 **enormous bulbs:** Interview: Sarah Nägele/Kay-Uwe von Darmaros, of Topography of Terror.

37 **straight through his eyes:** Marta Urbańczyk, "Twórczość i działalność pieśniarska Aleksandra Kulisiewicza w obozie koncentracyjnym Sachsenhausen 1940–1945" (MA thesis, Uniwersytet Śląski, 1981).

37 **They chewed at blankets:** Urbańczyk, "Twórczość i działalność pieśniarska." For the smile reference, see A. Kulisiewicz, *Adresse: Sachsenhausen.*

37 **Others were silent:** A. Kulisiewicz, *Adresse: Sachsenhausen.*

37 **"end station":** A. Kulisiewicz, *Adresse: Sachsenhausen.*

37 cowered in the Gestapo jail: A. Kulisiewicz, *Adresse: Sachsenhausen.*

37 To cope, he pretended: Urbańczyk, "Twórczość i działalność pieśniarska."

38 *You are a great thing*: Urbańczyk, "Twórczość i działalność pieśniarska." Also recounted in *Aleksander Kulisiewicz: Liedermacher im Kampf gegen Faschismus— Kunst im Konzentrationslager—Lieder als Zeugen der Geschichte*, 1976. Sammlung KZ-Lieder Nr. 2, im Archiv der Akademie der Künste, Berlin.

38 brutally interrogating Stanisław: Urbańczyk, "Twórczość i działalność pieśniarska."

38 safety pin: A. Kulisiewicz, *Adresse: Sachsenhausen.*

38 twenty-seven pricks: A. Kulisiewicz, *Adresse: Sachsenhausen.*

38 "With thought alone": Konrad Strzelewicz, *Zapis: Opowieść Aleksandra Kulisiewicza* (Krakow: Krajowa Agencja Wydawnicza, 1984), 128.

39 no longer whistle: Interviews: Eyre/Milewski and Eyre/R. and M. Kulisiewicz.

39 patches of flowers grew: Interview: Sarah Nägele/Günter Morsch.

39 silver skull and crossbones: These were the SS Death's Head Units, trained specifically for work at the concentration and/or extermination camps. It is not possible to say exactly when the bus arrived. Most likely it arrived during the day rather than at night. It did arrive with certainty in May of 1940, according to Dr. Astrid Ley.

39 The guards erupted: Based on various prisoner accounts. See, for example, Jerzy Pindera, *Liebe Mutti: One Man's Struggle to Survive in KZ Sachsenhausen, 1939– 1945*, ed. Lynne Taylor (Lanham, MD: University Press of America, 2004).

39 "Schnell, schnell!": This was the camp "initiation" according to Dr. Astrid Ley. This is also recounted in various prisoner memoirs. See, for example Bolesław Marcinek's unpublished memoir.

39 dogs strained at their leashes: There were many guard dogs (German shepherds, for example) at Sachsenhausen and in other camps. There was even a dog training unit at Sachsenhausen.

39 rows of five: Pindera, *Liebe Mutti*. Also noted in other memoirs, such as in Hans Reichmann, "Deutscher Bürger und verfolgter Jude."

39 semicircular yard: Pindera, *Liebe Mutti*, 45. Also noted in various other survivor memoirs, such as Harry Naujoks, *Mein Leben im KZ Sachsenhausen, 1936–1942* ; Erinnerungen Des Ehemaligen Lagerältesten. Köln, Germany: Röderberg Im Pahl-Rugenstein-Verlag, 124.

39 wide track paved in stone: Interview: Sarah Nägele/Günter Morsch.

39 Not a scrap of trash: Pindera, *Liebe Mutti.*

40 Muselmänner: For information, see https://www.yadvashem.org/odot_pdf/ Microsoft%20Word%20-%206474.pdf.

40 take off his cap: See Pindera, Reichmann, and others.

40 full of colorful blooms: Alec Le Verny, *No Drums No Trumpets: A Remarkable True Story of Courage and Endurance in World War II* (London: Michael Joseph,

1988). See other survivor memoirs, such as those from Odd Nansen, Jerzy Pindera, and Jan Baranski.

40 **"There is one path to freedom":** Present in various prisoner accounts. See Harry Naujoks, Jerzy Pindera, and Alec le Vernoy, among many others.

41 **terrifyingly fixed:** See Dr. Astrid Ley talking to the BBC about indeterminate sentences: https://www.bbc.co.uk/programmes/p06z3pps/p06z3kbj.

41 **four years earlier:** Nikolaus Wachsmann, *KL: A History of the Nazi Concentration Camps* (New York: Farrar, Straus and Giroux, 2015), 72.

41 **a new concentration camp:** Wachsmann, *KL: A History of the Nazi Concentration Camps.* Also present in Hermann Kaienburg, *Der Ort des Terrors: Geschichte der nationalsozialistischen Konzentrationslager.* Band 3: Sachsenhausen, Buchenwald (Berlin: CH Beck, 2006).

41 **enemies of the state:** Kaienburg, *Der Ort des Terrors.*

41 **innovative design of Sachsenhausen:** Kaienburg, *Der Ort des Terrors.*

41 **surveil nearly the entire complex:** Kaienburg, *Der Ort des Terrors.* Also see Günter Morsch and Astrid Ley, *Sachsenhausen Concentration Camp: Events and Developments* (Berlin: Metropol, 2016), 21.

41 **torture and forced labor in Dachau:** Kaienburg, *Der Ort des Terrors.*

42 **in the German south:** Interview: Eyre/Christine Meibeck.

42 **the goal of isolation:** Interview: Sarah Nägele/Günter Morsch.

42 **witness the crimes of the SS:** Interview: Sarah Nägele/Günter Morsch.

42 **march them through town:** Interview: Eyre/Christine Meibeck. Also, interview: Sarah Nägele/Günter Morsch.

42 **most important camps:** Kaienburg, *Der Ort des Terrors.*

42 **senior Nazis officials:** Interview: Eyre/Christine Meibeck.

42 **housed a training center:** Interview: Eyre/Christine Meibeck.

42 **senior commanders regularly met:** Interview: Sarah Nägele/Günter Morsch.

42 **a convenient testing ground:** Interview: Eyre/Christine Meibeck.

42 **camp commanders experimented:** Interview: Eyre/Christine Meibeck.

42 **the little camp:** Wachsmann, *KL: A History of the Nazi Concentration Camps,* 107.

42 **apart from the campgrounds:** Günter Morsch and Susanne zur Nieden, *Jüdische Häftlinge im Konzentrationslager Sachsenhausen 1936–1945* (Berlin: Ed. Hentrich, 2004).

43 **noted as "student":** Interview: Eyre/K. Kulisiewicz.

43 **number 25,149:** According to various original camp documents (registration forms, letters home, among others).

43 **learn it by heart:** Pindera, *Liebe Mutti,* 46.

43 **his few belongings:** According to Kulisiewicz's intake files in the Sachsenhausen archives.

43 **packed into sacks and removed:** See Pindera, *Liebe Mutti*, 46, among other survivor memoirs.

43 **base of his skull:** See Pindera, *Liebe Mutti*, 46, among other survivor memoirs.

43 **"self-administration":** Interview: Sarah Nägele/Günter Morsch.

44 **cloth badge:** Wachsmann, *KL: A History of the Nazi Concentration Camps*, 144.

44 **several hundred men:** Pindera, *Liebe Mutti*, 47.

44 **Blockführer:** Wachsmann, KL: A History of the Nazi Concentration Camps, 149.

44 **"There are no sick prisoners":** This speech was commonly given to new prisoners, according to Dr. Astrid Ley of the Sachsenhausen Memorial. See Pindera, *Liebe Mutti*, 48, for one description of the speech.

44 **ceramic bowls with no seats:** Le Vernoy, *No Drums No Trumpets*, 155.

44 **communal fountains for washing:** For more details, see https://sachsenhausen projekte.wordpress.com/2013/05/28/haftlingsalltag-im-konzentrationslager-sachsen hausen/.

44 **near the stove:** Interview: Eyre/Astrid Ley. Most barracks had a wood-burning stove, though there was rarely any wood to burn. Often, the stove was present just for appearances when Red Cross visits took place.

44 **slept on the floor:** Le Vernoy, *No Drums No Trumpets*, 155.

44 **A few potatoes:** Jan Baranski, *Mon Pays Perdu (1945–1951)* (Paris: Les Iles d'Or, 1956).

44 **forced to stand:** Kaienburg, *Der Ort des Terrors*.

45 **stinking straw mattress:** See Pindera, *Liebe Mutti*, 49, and Baranski, *Mon Pays Perdu*, 43. Also: https://sachsenhausenprojekte.wordpress.com/2013/05/28/haftling salltag-im-konzentrationslager-sachsenhausen/.

45 **for urine and feces:** Kaienburg, *Der Ort des Terrors*.

45 **a succession of knee bends:** Wachsmann, *KL: A History of the Nazi Concentration Camps*, 49.

45 **served to break prisoners:** Wachsmann, *KL: A History of the Nazi Concentration Camps*, 49.

45 **overwhelming sense of distress:** Urbańczyk, "Twórczość i działalność pieśniarska."

45 **the "Saxon Salute":** Kaienburg, *Der Ort des Terrors*.

45 **bucket of cold water:** Kaienburg, *Der Ort des Terrors*.

46 **forced them to sing German folk songs:** Juliane Brauer, "How Can Music Be Torturous? Music in Nazi Concentration and Extermination Camps," *Music & Politics* 10, no. 1 (Winter 2016).

46 **could also be sadistic:** Brauer, "How Can Music Be Torturous?"

46 **"But they've become poisoned":** As quoted in Brauer, "How Can Music Be Torturous?"

46 **returned to the "Morning Song":** Urbańczyk, "Twórczość i działalność pieśniarska."

46 **longing for home:** Urbańczyk, "Twórczość i działalność pieśniarska."

46 **might buoy both himself:** Urbańczyk, "Twórczość i działalność pieśniarska."

46 **turned to culture to survive:** Aleksander Kulisiewicz: Liedermacher im Kampf gegen Faschismus.

46 **"You have to retain everything":** Aleksander Kulisiewicz: Liedermacher im Kampf gegen Faschismus.

47 **It was a harvest day:** Aleksander Kulisiewicz, Jak Umierał Mój Głos. ms, RG-55, United States Holocaust Memorial Museum.

47 **to put on a show:** A. Kulisiewicz, Jak Umierał Mój Głos. ms, RG-55.

47 **"Olek, be careful":** A. Kulisiewicz, Jak Umierał Mój Głos. ms, RG-55.

47 **"Ladies and gentlemen!":** A. Kulisiewicz, Jak Umierał Mój Głos. ms, RG-55.

48 **longing for his dead mother:** A. Kulisiewicz, Jak Umierał Mój Głos. ms, RG-55.

48 **cough out words:** A. Kulisiewicz, Jak Umierał Mój Głos. ms, RG-55.

48 **simply as Roob:** A. Kulisiewicz, Jak Umierał Mój Głos. ms, RG-55.

49 **overcome the stutter:** A. Kulisiewicz, Jak Umierał Mój Głos. ms, RG-55.

49 **Aleks imagined the words:** Interview: Eyre/K. Kulisiewicz.

50 **German communist prisoners:** Kaienburg, Der Ort des Terrors.

50 **block elders and foremen:** Aleksander Kulisiewicz: Liedermacher im Kampf gegen Faschismus.

50 **face cruel punishment:** Kaienburg, Der Ort des Terrors.

50 **better job posts or camp status:** Kaienburg, Der Ort des Terrors, and interview: Sarah Nägele/Günter Morsch.

50 **one prisoner group against another:** Kaienburg, Der Ort des Terrors.

50 **Nazis considered "Aryan":** Interview: Sarah Nägele/Johannes Tuchel.

50 **arrive a year later:** Interview: Eyre/Astrid Ley. For information about Soviet POWs, see interview: Sarah Nägele/Günter Morsch.

52 **noticed her immediately:** Strzelewicz, Zapis, 55.

53 **gestures could intensify a performance:** Aleksander Kulisiewicz: Liedermacher im Kampf gegen Faschismus.

54 **he craved it:** A. Kulisiewicz, Jak Umierał Mój Głos. ms, RG-55.

Chapter 4

55 **sing German folk songs:** Aleksander Kulisiewicz, "Polskie Pieśni Obozowe 1939–1945," Regiony: Kwartalnik Społeczno-Kulturalny 1 (1976): 5–11.

56 **beat a man to death:** Leon Szalet, Experiment "E": A Report from an Extermination Laboratory (Paris: Didier Publishers, 1945).

56 **jet of cold water:** Hermann Kaienburg, Der Ort des Terrors. Geschichte der natio-

nalsozialistischen Konzentrationslager. Band 3: Sachsenhausen, Buchenwald (Berlin: CH Beck, 2006).

56 **a clean kill:** For a prisoner account, see Jerzy Pindera, *Liebe Mutti: One Man's Struggle to Survive in KZ Sachsenhausen, 1939–1945,* ed. Lynne Taylor (Lanham, MD: University Press of America, 2004), 48. For an academic account, see Kaienburg, *Der Ort des Terrors.*

56 **stuck a water hose:** Kaienburg, *Der Ort des Terrors.*

56 **revise a composition:** Marta Urbańczyk, "Twórczość i działalność pieśniarska Aleksandra Kulisiewicza w obozie koncentracyjnym Sachsenhausen 1940–1945" (MA thesis, Uniwersytet Śląski, 1981).

56 **dragged out later:** Harry Naujoks, *Mein Leben im KZ Sachsenhausen, 1936–1942; Erinnerungen Des Ehemaligen Lagerältesten.* Köln, Germany: Röderberg Im Pahl-Rugenstein-Verlag, 86.

56 **a thousand-year Reich:** Interview: Eyre/K. Kulisiewicz.

57 **emotional distance from his father:** Interviews: Eyre/Barbara Milewski.

57 **He formed friendships and did favors:** Interviews: Eyre/Barbara Milewski.

57 **mass arrest of professors:** Jerzy Lukowski and Hubert Zawadzki, *A Concise History of Poland* (Cambridge, UK: Cambridge University Press, 2007), 260.

58 **transferred to Dachau:** Günter Morsch and Agnes Ohm, *Vergessene Vernichtung: Polnische und Tschechische Angehörige der Intelligenz im Konzentrationslager Sachsenhausen zu Beginn des Zweiten Weltkrieges* (Berlin: Metropol, 2013).

58 **convey their torpor:** A. Kulisiewicz, "Polskie Pieśni Obozowe 1939–1945."

58 **expected them to sing:** Guido Fackler, *Des Lagers Stimme—Musik im KZ: Alltag und Häftlingskultur in den Konzentrationslagern 1933 bis 1936* (Bremen, Germany: Temmen, 2000).

58 **used music to impose discipline:** Fackler, *Des Lagers Stimme—Musik im KZ,* 2.

58 **the SS forced them to sing:** Fackler, *Des Lagers Stimme—Musik im KZ,* 2.

58 **the guards deemed satisfactory:** Fackler, *Des Lagers Stimme—Musik im KZ,* 2.

59 **consider such gatherings subversive:** Shirli Gilbert, "Songs Confront the Past: Music in KZ Sachsenhausen, 1936–1945," *Contemporary European History* 13, no. 3 (2004): 293.

59 **a German willing to help:** Gilbert, "Songs Confront the Past," 285.

59 **housed by nationality:** Szalet, *Experiment "E."*

60 **Polish realist period:** Timothy Snyder, *Bloodlands: Europe between Hitler and Stalin* (London: Vintage, 2010), 134. Also see Gabriel Zych, *Oranienburg, Rachunek Pamięci* (Warsaw: Książka i Wiedza, 1962).

60 **their lives before the war:** Guido Fackler, "Music in Concentration Camps 1933–1945," *Music and Politics* 1, no. 1 (Winter 2007): 12. See many other similar accounts in survivor testimony, such as from Boleslaw Marcinek.

60 **"Only choral music":** Zych, *Oranienburg, Rachunek Pamięci.*

60 **falling into complete despair:** Aleksander Kulisiewicz, "Polskie Pieśni Obozowe 1939–1945," *Regiony: Kwartalnik Społeczno-Kulturalny* 1 (1976): 5–11. This perspective is also widely reflected in other survivor memoirs, such as the one written by Harry Naujoks.

60 **create parodies:** *Aleksander Kulisiewicz: Liedermacher im Kampf gegen Faschismus—Kunst im Konzentrationslager—Lieder als Zeugen der Geschichte*, 1976. Sammlung KZ-Lieder Nr. 2, im Archiv der Akademie der Künste, Berlin.

61 **Aleks stood before a small group:** Barbara Milewski and Bret Werb, Liner Notes for the album *Ballads and Broadsides: Songs from Sachsenhausen Concentration Camp 1940–1945.* United States Holocaust Memorial Museum, 2008. This scene would likely have taken place in barracks number 15, though Kulisiewicz does not indicate the specific block.

61 **klieg lights:** Albert Christel, *Apokalypse unserer Tage: Erinnerungen an das KZ Sachsenhausen* (Frankfurt, Germany: Materialis, 1987), 64.

61 **I'm a God-forsaken Polish pagan:** I am very grateful to Dr. Barbara Milewski, who kindly permitted me to print her excellent translations of Kulisiewicz's lyrics from the Polish.

61 **everyone knew what lay ahead:** Urbańczyk, "Twórczość i działalność pieśniarska."

61 **Beyond barbed wire:** Translation by Dr. Barbara Milewski.

62 **never to rise again:** For information on standing detachments at Sachsenhausen, see from Kaienburg, *Der Ort des Terrors.*

62 **Mama, my mama:** Translation by Dr. Barbara Milewski. This scene is recounted in A. Kulisiewicz, "Polskie Pieśni Obozowe 1939–1945."

62 **"like a shabby circus":** A. Kulisiewicz, "Polskie Pieśni Obozowe 1939–1945."

62 **No one had to *play* dead:** A. Kulisiewicz, "Polskie Pieśni Obozowe 1939–1945."

63 **might conceal him:** Kaienburg, *Der Ort des Terrors.*

63 **a dark satire:** A. Kulisiewicz, "Polskie Pieśni Obozowe 1939–1945."

63 **Such a terribly great:** Translation by Dr. Barbara Milewski.

64 **vast social programs:** Adam Zamoyski, *Poland: A History*, 5th ed. (London: William Collins, 2015), 318, 482.

64 **education more accessible:** Norman Davies, *Heart of Europe, The Past in Poland's Present* (Oxford, UK: Oxford University Press, 2001), 105.

65 **control over his rank:** Interview: Sarah Nägele/Günter Morsch.

65 **once being seen as lowly:** Strzelewicz, *Zapis.*

65 **confidence nearing hubris:** Strzelewicz, *Zapis.*

65 **"The world is divided":** Strzelewicz, *Zapis.*

65 **atonement had been made:** Strzelewicz, *Zapis.*

66 **"Don't cry about me":** A. Kulisiewicz, "Polskie Pieśni Obozowe 1939–1945."

Chapter 5

67 **the time on Sunday:** Sundays were free from work, but often prisoners were forced to give concerts, sing on the roll call square, or endure other harassment. This changed as the war progressed. According to camp survivor Harry Naujoks, Sunday mornings were declared working hours starting in April 1942.

67 **rest, idle, converse:** Shirli Gilbert, *Music in the Holocaust: Confronting Life in the Nazi Ghettos and Camps* (New York: Oxford University Press, 2005), xii, 101.

67 **pay for his own stamp:** Interview: Sarah Nägele/Günter Morsch.

68 **Aleks recited poems:** Box 17 / RG-55.003*93. Characteristics of Rosebery d'Arguto. Aleksander Kulisiewicz Collection. United States Holocaust Memorial Museum Archives, Washington, DC.

68 **any margarine:** Margarine was a common food item in Sachsenhausen. See Harry Naujoks's memoirs, among many others.

68 **"I will get that tiny bit":** Box 17 / RG-55.003*93. Characteristics of Rosebery d'Arguto. Aleksander Kulisiewicz Collection.

69 **He was short and bald:** *Aleksander Kulisiewicz: Liedermacher im Kampf gegen Faschismus—Kunst im Konzentrationslager—Lieder als Zeugen der Geschichte*, 1976. Sammlung KZ-Lieder Nr. 2, im Archiv der Akademie der Künste, Berlin.

69 **formed a Star of David:** Günter Morsch and Astrid Ley, *Sachsenhausen Concentration Camp: Events and Developments* (Berlin: Metropol, 2016), 38. Also see Nikolaus Wachsmann, *KL: A History of the Nazi Concentration Camps* (New York: Farrar, Straus and Giroux, 2015), 36.

69 **living and working in Germany:** Interview: Eyre/Christine Meibeck.

69 **"whoever he is":** Box 17 / RG-55.003*93. Characteristics of Rosebery d'Arguto. Aleksander Kulisiewicz Collection.

69 **if he was eating the margarine:** Box 17 / RG-55.003*93. Characteristics of Rosebery d'Arguto. Aleksander Kulisiewicz Collection.

71 **Bolek got word:** Box 17 / RG-55.003*93. Characteristics of Rosebery d'Arguto. Aleksander Kulisiewicz Collection.

71 **sneaking into a Jewish barracks:** Leon Szalet, *Experiment "E": A Report from an Extermination Laboratory* (Paris: Didier Publishers, 1945).

71 **the SS forbade non-Jewish prisoners:** Szalet, *Experiment "E."*

71 **looked hungry:** For reference, the Jewish prisoners had been in Sachsenhausen for a year by that point. Kulisiewicz would have been incarcerated for roughly four months. Furthermore, the Jewish prisoners were given less food: https://sachsenhausenprojekte.wordpress.com/2013/05/28/judische-haftlinge-im-kz-sachsenhausen-und-der-novemberpogrom-1938/.

71 **dark bruise:** Box 17 / RG-55.003*93. Characteristics of Rosebery d'Arguto. Aleksander Kulisiewicz Collection.

72 **plodded between the barracks:** Box 17 / RG- 55.003*93. Characteristics of Rose-
    bery d'Arguto. Aleksander Kulisiewicz Collection.

72 **get to know other men:** Taking walks was one way for prisoners to get to know one
    another. Kulisiewicz talked in his papers about the walks he took with d'Arguto.
    G. Zych mentions walks and their privacy: "The most convenient occasion for such
    a conversation was a walk." Gabriel Zych, *Oranienburg, Rachunek Pamięci* (War-
    saw: Książka i Wiedza, 1962).

72 **brushed shoulders:** Zych, *Oranienburg: Rachunek Pamięci.*

73 **mark of the intelligentsia:** Interview: Eyre/Barbara Milewski. Kulisiewicz discus-
    ses this in "Polskie Pieśni Obozowe 1939–1945."

73 **time to meet on weeknights:** Prisoners had 1 hour of free time after evening roll
    call and dinner before they had to go to bed. See https://sachsenhausenprojekte
    .wordpress.com/2013/05/28/judische-haftlinge-im-kz-sachsenhausen-und-der
    -novemberpogrom-1938/.

73 **perked up at the sound:** Strzelewicz, *Zapis.*

73 **One song in particular:** Strzelewicz, *Zapis.*

74 **small town called Mława:** Peter Konopatsch, *Martin Rosebery d'Arguto: Dirigent
    von Arbeiterchören, Stimmbildner, Gesangsreformer* (Jüdische Miniaturen) (Berlin:
    Hentrich & Hentrich, 2021). The birth records for d'Arguto in the original Russian
    are in the Polish National Archives.

74 **named Moshe:** Interview: Eyre/Justus Rosenberg.

74 **transliterated the name as Moszek:** According to the original birth records.

74 **two-story stone house:** Interview: Eyre/Justus Rosenberg.

74 **water and plumbing system:** Wojciech Tomasz Smoliński, "Studia i materiały do
    dziejów Ziemi Zawkrzeńskiej t. III," in *Życie codzienne Mławy w latach 1918–1939*
    (Mława, Poland: Towarzystwo Przyjaciół Ziemi Mławskiej, 1996), 61–113.

74 **to dig an outhouse:** Interview: Eyre/Justus Rosenberg.

74 **had to visit a bathhouse:** Smoliński, "Studia i materiały do dziejów Ziemi
    Zawkrzeńskiej t. III," in *Życie codzienne Mławy w latach 1918–1939*, 70.

74 **made his living from wheat:** Yosef Rimon Grenat, "Moshe Rosenberg, Composer
    and Communist Activist," in Szreńsk Memory Book [Fragment], *Kehilat Shrensk
    yeha-sevivah: sefer zikaron* (Jerusalem, 1960), 271–273.

75 **where they sowed wheat:** For an excellent explanation of the economy and town
    life of a small Polish town at this time, see Antony Polonsky, *The Jews in Poland and
    Russia, Volume III, 1914 to 2008* (London: Littman Library of Jewish Civilization,
    2019), 142.

75 **as Rosebery's family and friends called him:** Interview: Eyre/Justus Rosenberg.

75 **a person had to take this route:** Grenat, "Moshe Rosenberg, Composer and Com-
    munist Activist," 271–273.

75 **Geese, ducks, chickens, and turkeys:** Jacob Shatzky et al., *Mława* (New York: Velt-Farband-Mlaver-Yidn, 1950).

75 **cherries, strawberries, and tomatoes:** Shatzk et al., *Mława.*

75 **blow back its hind feathers:** Shatzky et al., *Mława.*

75 **The noise was tremendous:** Shatzky et al., *Mława.*

76 **Rumors of new technologies:** Eva Hoffman, *Shtetl: The Life and Death of a Small Town and the World of Polish Jews* (Boston: Mariner Books, 2007), 150.

76 **reforming education:** Hoffman, *Shtetl,* 146.

76 **in denominational schools:** Tobias Grill, *Der Westen im Osten. Deutsches Judentum und jüdische Bildungsreform in Osteuropa 1783–1939* (Göttingen, Germany: Vandenhoeck & Ruprecht, 2013), 31.

76 **more practical instruction:** Grill, *Der Westen im Osten,* 237.

76 **the basic rhythms of life:** Hoffman, *Shtetl,* 152.

76 **a long beard and played an active role:** Interview: Eyre/Justus Rosenberg. Also see Shrensk Memory book.

76 **the Hasidic Dynasty of Ger:** Grenat, "Moshe Rosenberg, Composer and Communist Activist," 271–273. This also appears in correspondence from Shimshon Rosenberg in the personal collection of the Rosenberg family.

76 **but never grew sidelocks:** Interview: Eyre/Justus Rosenberg.

76 **rejected all forms of mysticism:** Oral history interview with Justus Rosenberg (1998). USC Shoah Foundation Institute. VHA Interview Code: 37656.

76 **strict Jewish practice:** For an excellent description of Jewish faith in small towns, see Polonsky, *The Jews in Poland and Russia,* 184.

77 **draw in the candles three times:** Oral history interview with Justus Rosenberg (1998).

77 **Shimshon prayed over each dish:** Interview: Eyre/Justus Rosenberg.

77 **keen intelligence:** Grenat, "Moshe Rosenberg, Composer and Communist Activist," 271–273.

77 **a near aversion:** Interview: Eyre/Justus Rosenberg.

77 **attended the local cheder:** Interview: Eyre/Justus Rosenberg.

77 **unusual aptitude for music:** See, among other sources: Ernst Lindenberg, "Rosebery d'Arguto—Vorkämpfer der Arbeiterchorbewegung," *Musik und Gesellschaft* 4 (1971): S. 231–240. This is also noted in Ernst Schmidt, *Konzeption für eine Arbeit über Rosebery d'Arguto und seine Gesangsgemeinschaft.* Berlin 1964. Sammlung Rosebery d'Arguto Nr. 115 im Archiv der Akademie der Künste, Berlin

77 **sing at local funerals:** Konopatsch, *Martin Rosebery d'Arguto: Dirigent von Arbeiterchören, Stimmbildner, Gesangsreformer.*

78 **Rabbi Shalom Lipp:** Grenat, "Moshe Rosenberg, Composer and Communist Activist," 71–273.

78 **to the bedposts:** Grenat, "Moshe Rosenberg, Composer and Communist Activist."

78 **crouched in his attic:** Grenat, "Moshe Rosenberg, Composer and Communist Activist."

78 **a prestigious yeshiva:** Justus Rosenberg, *The Art of Resistance: My Four Years in the French Underground* (New York: William Morrow, 2020), 34.

78 **a mixed public school:** Rosenberg, *The Art of Resistance*, 34.

79 **paths forward for Moshe were limited:** Oral history interview with Justus Rosenberg (1998).

79 **economic conditions had deteriorated:** Robert E. Blobaum, *Rewolucja: Russian Poland, 1904–1907* (Ithaca, NY: Cornell University Press, 1995), 51–52.

79 **especially in occupied Poland:** Blobaum, *Rewolucja: Russian Poland, 1904–1907*, 51–52.

79 **struck en masse:** Jörg K. Hoensch, *Geschichte Polens* (Stuttgart: UTB, 1998), 223–224.

79 **the Russification of the country:** Blobaum, *Rewolucja: Russian Poland, 1904-1907.* Also see Wiktor Marzec, "Die Revolution 1905 bis 1907 im Königreich Polen - von der Arbeiterrevolte zur nationalen Reaktion," in *Arbeit, Bewegung, Geschichte, Zeitschrift für historische Studien* (Berlin: Metropol, 2016).

79 **nickname "Minister of Education":** Konopatsch, *Martin Rosebery d'Arguto: Dirigent von Arbeiterchören, Stimmbildner, Gesangsreformer.*

80 **ran to the front of the column:** Interview: Eyre/Justus Rosenberg. Also see Lindenberg, "Rosebery d'Arguto—Vorkämpfer der Arbeiterchorbewegung."

80 **originals by hand:** Konopatsch, *Martin Rosebery d'Arguto: Dirigent von Arbeiterchören, Stimmbildner, Gesangsreformer.*

80 **he took refuge for a time:** Lindenberg, "Rosebery d'Arguto—Vorkämpfer der Arbeiterchorbewegung."

81 **less repressive than:** Andrzej Paczkowski. *The Spring Will Be Ours: Poland and the Poles from Occupation to Freedom* (University Park, PA: Penn State University Press, 2003), 3–4.

81 **officially registered:** Konopatsch, *Martin Rosebery d'Arguto: Dirigent von Arbeiterchören, Stimmbildner, Gesangsreformer.*

82 **interacted with Jews:** Strzelewicz, *Zapis.* Also see A. Kulisiewicz, Jak Umierał Mój Głos. ms, RG-55.

82 **visited their shops:** For information on prewar interactions between Jewish and Catholic Poles, see Antony Polonsky, "Jewish Life in Poland–Lithuania to 1750," in *The Jews in Poland and Russia: Volume I: 1350 to 1881* (Liverpool: Liverpool University Press. 2009). For information specific to d'Arguto's childhood, see the Shrensk and Mława Memory Books.

82 **deeply unfamiliar:** Paczkowski, *The Spring Will Be Ours*, 19.

82 **birthed lore and mythology:** Polonsky, *The Jews in Poland and Russia*, 142.

83 **control óver money and business:** Interview: Eyre/K. Kulisiewicz.

83 **His view of the world eroded:** Interview: Eyre/K. Kulisiewicz.

83 **remained true to himself:** There are many accounts of d'Arguto's generosity and courage at the camp. See, among others, Kulisiewicz (Characteristics of Rosebery d'Arguto, USHMM RG-55) and Johann Hüttner, *Gespräch mit Inge Lammel*, Berlin October 10, 1980, Akademie der Künste, Berlin, Sammlung KZ-Lieder 40. Also: Aleksander Kulisiewicz, *Gespräch zwischen Alexander Kulisiewicz und ehemaligen Mitgliedern der Gesangsgemeinschaft Rosebery d'Arguto*, Berlin. Akademie der Künste, Berlin, Sammlung KZ-Lieder 3.

Chapter 6

84 **several of his business contacts:** Interview: Eyre/Justus Rosenberg.

84 **how they finessed their craft:** Ernst Schmidt, *Konzeption für eine Arbeit über Rosebery d'Arguto und seine Gesangsgemeinschaft*. Berlin 1964. Sammlung Rosebery d'Arguto Nr. 115 im Archiv der Akademie der Künste, Berlin.

85 **Theater des Westens:** Interview: Eyre/Peter Konopatsch.

85 **anatomy and function of the human voice:** Schmidt, *Konzeption für eine Arbeit.* Also mentioned in Ernst Lindenberg, "Rosebery d'Arguto—Vorkämpfer der Arbeiterchorbewegung," *Musik und Gesellschaft* 4 (1971): S. 231–240.

85 **aliens as a threat:** Prussia had above all an anti-Polish policy. Poles were considered "enemies of the empire" in Prussia. They were suspected of trying to reestablish the Polish state, which Prussia, Austria, and Russia had divided among themselves at the end of the eighteenth century.

85 **industrial laborer:** Ernst Schmidt, *Aufzeichnungen über ein Gespräch mit Catenia von Malottki (Malotti, verheiratete Käthe Carsten, genannt: Tenja)*. October 1, 1958. Sammlung Rosebery d'Arguto Nr. 251 im Archiv der Akademie der Künste, Berlin.

85 **he sang revolutionary music:** Lindenberg, "Rosebery d'Arguto—Vorkämpfer der Arbeiterchorbewegung."

85 **downfall of capitalism:** Schmidt, *Aufzeichnungen über ein Gespräch mit Catenia von Malottki.*

85 **circulation of twelve thousand:** Peter Konopatsch, *Martin Rosebery d'Arguto: Dirigent von Arbeiterchören, Stimmbildner, Gesangsreformer* (Jüdische Miniaturen) (Berlin: Hentrich & Hentrich, 2021).

86 **"hell of capital and private property":** Rosebery d'Arguto, "Der Kampftag des

Internationalen Proletariats," *Die Weltrevolution* 1 (May 1919). Accessed via Electronic ed: Bonn: FES Library.

86 **destroy the old systems:** Jurr, *Erinnerungen an Rosebery d'Arguto und seine Gesangsgemeinschaft.* RG-55.003*93. Aleksander Kulisiewicz Collection. United States Holocaust Memorial Museum Archives, Washington, DC.

86 **fled for a time:** For further information, see the notes on edition 3 of *Die Weltrevolution* in the Sammlung Rosebery d'Arguto Nr. 399 im Archiv der Akademie der Künste, Berlin.

86 **"Bareheaded and shoeless":** Rosebery d'Arguto, "Das Märtyrerfest der Kommunisten: Rosa Luxemburg," *Die Weltrevolution* (1919). Sammlung Rosebery d'Arguto Nr. 400 im Archiv der Akademie der Künste, Berlin.

86 **well-cut suits:** Interview: Eyre/Justus Rosenberg. Also based in part on the dozens of photographs available.

86 **"Solving the Voice Mutation Question":** Konopatsch, *Martin Rosebery d'Arguto: Dirigent von Arbeiterchören, Stimmbildner, Gesangsreformer.*

87 **"One should not picture him":** Hans Pasche, "Rosebery d'Arguto: A Psychological Study and Some Words about Singing Lessons in School," *Reform-Zeitschrift Für Musik* 7/8 (1923). This article can be found in Box 17 / RG-55.003*93. Characteristics of Rosebery d'Arguto. Aleksander Kulisiewicz Collection.

87 **heal their voice injuries:** Interview: Eyre/Peter Konopatsch.

87 **charge of libel:** Konopatsch, *Martin Rosebery d'Arguto: Dirigent von Arbeiterchören, Stimmbildner, Gesangsreformer.*

88 **new residency permit:** Konopatsch, *Martin Rosebery d'Arguto: Dirigent von Arbeiterchören, Stimmbildner, Gesangsreformer.*

88 **Finally, in 1922:** Konopatsch, *Martin Rosebery d'Arguto: Dirigent von Arbeiterchören, Stimmbildner, Gesangsreformer.*

88 **call him "Jew-brat":** Konopatsch, *Martin Rosebery d'Arguto: Dirigent von Arbeiterchören, Stimmbildner, Gesangsreformer.*

89 **their own dance halls:** Interview: Sarah Nägele/Dorothea Kolland.

90 **examined the back:** Schmidt, *Konzeption für eine Arbeit.*

90 **might switch to the contralto:** Schmidt, *Konzeption für eine Arbeit.*

90 **lengthy rehearsals:** Konopatsch, *Martin Rosebery d'Arguto: Dirigent von Arbeiterchören, Stimmbildner, Gesangsreformer.*

90 **twice a week:** *Erinnerungen von Hans Altenpohl.* Berlin und Friemar September/October 1958. Sammlung Rosebery d'Arguto Nr. 252 im Archiv der Akademie der Künste, Berlin.

91 **for trivial reasons:** *Erinnerungen von Hans Altenpohl.*

91 **did not have to sing well:** Interview: Eyre/Peter Konopatsch.

91   **"If a person can speak":** Schmidt, *Konzeption für eine Arbeit.*

91   **for a year:** Konopatsch, *Martin Rosebery d'Arguto: Dirigent von Arbeiterchören, Stimmbildner, Gesangsreformer.*

91   **find his methods eccentric:** *Gespräch über Rosebery d'Arguto am 8. Januar 1981, moderiert von Inge Lammel.* Sammlung Rosebery d'Arguto Nr. 249 im Archiv der Akademie der Künste, Berlin.

91   **more money teaching the bourgeoisie:** *Gespräch über Rosebery d'Arguto am 8. Januar 1981, moderiert von Inge Lammel.*

92   **regulate their flow of breath:** Schmidt, *Konzeption für eine Arbeit.*

92   **free private lessons:** Schmidt, *Konzeption für eine Arbeit.*

92   **notes in a ledger:** Schmidt, *Konzeption für eine Arbeit.*

92   **smoked or drank too much:** Jurr, *Erinnerungen an Rosebery d'Arguto und seine Gesangsgemeinschaft.*

92   **exercises and compositions:** *Erinnerungen von Hans Altenpohl.*

92   **medieval madrigals:** *Gespräch über Rosebery d'Arguto am 8. Januar 1981, moderiert von Inge Lammel.*

93   **end of 1923:** Konopatsch, *Martin Rosebery d'Arguto: Dirigent von Arbeiterchören, Stimmbildner, Gesangsreformer.*

93   **the Neue Welt concert hall:** *Gespräch über Rosebery d'Arguto am 8. Januar 1981, moderiert von Inge Lammel.*

93   **the Saalbau Friedrichshain, Irmers Festsälen:** Konopatsch, *Martin Rosebery d'Arguto: Dirigent von Arbeiterchören, Stimmbildner, Gesangsreformer.*

93   **"We must openly say":** Newspaper clipping housed in the Sammlung Rosebery d'Arguto im Archiv der Akademie der Künste, Berlin.

93   **one hundred strong:** Konopatsch, *Martin Rosebery d'Arguto: Dirigent von Arbeiterchören, Stimmbildner, Gesangsreformer.*

93   **German Communist and Social Democratic Parties:** Schmidt, *Konzeption für eine Arbeit.*

94   **enchantingly beautiful:** *Erinnerungen von Emmy Schmidt,* 1976. Sammlung Rosebery d'Arguto Nr. 243 im Archiv der Akademie der Künste, Berlin. Sammlung Rosebery d'Arguto im Archiv der Akademie der Künste, Berlin.

94   **would erupt in cheers:** *Erinnerungen von Claire Weigel an die Chorarbeit mit Rosebery d'Arguto,* 1959. Sammlung Rosebery d'Arguto Nr. 240 im Archiv der Akademie der Künste, Berlin.

94   **"strike right at the heart":** *Erinnerungen von Claire Weigel an die Chorarbeit mit Rosebery d'Arguto.*

94   **His hands seemed to speak:** Schmidt, *Konzeption für eine Arbeit.*

94   **"an enhancement":** Schmidt, *Konzeption für eine Arbeit.*

94   **his belief in the good in people:** *Erinnerungen von Claire Weigel an die Chorarbeit mit Rosebery d'Arguto.*

94   **Rosebery's bald head:** *Erinnerungen von Claire Weigel an die Chorarbeit mit Rosebery d'Arguto.*

95   **a dance group:** Interview: Eyre/Peter Konopatsch.

95   **performed in ensemble fashion:** Lindenberg, "Rosebery d'Arguto—Vorkämpfer der Arbeiterchorbewegung."

95   **when there was a reason to celebrate:** Jurr, *Erinnerungen an Rosebery d'Arguto und seine Gesangsgemeinschaft.*

95   **rebuked by an older member:** *Erinnerungen von Hans Altenpohl.*

95   **pulled the sausage:** *Gespräch über Rosebery d'Arguto am 8. Januar 1981, moderiert von Inge Lammel.*

96   **divide his bonus:** *Gespräch über Rosebery d'Arguto am 8. Januar 1981, moderiert von Inge Lammel.*

96   **accompanied his singers:** Lindenberg, "Rosebery d'Arguto—Vorkämpfer der Arbeiterchorbewegung."

96   **traveled to Dresden:** Jurr, *Erinnerungen an Rosebery d'Arguto und seine Gesangsgemeinschaft.*

96   **point to a brook:** *Erinnerungen von Hans Altenpohl.*

96   ***Today we march:*** Jurr, *Erinnerungen an Rosebery d'Arguto und seine Gesangsgemeinschaft.*

96   **on stacks of hay:** *Erinnerungen von Hans Altenpohl.*

96   **to hear Rosebery humming:** Jurr, *Erinnerungen an Rosebery d'Arguto und seine Gesangsgemeinschaft.*

97   **Absolute Symphonic Chants:** Konopatsch, *Martin Rosebery d'Arguto: Dirigent von Arbeiterchören, Stimmbildner, Gesangsreformer.*

98   **force all choirs to join choral unions:** Interview: Eyre/Peter Konopatsch.

98   **the choir's letterhead:** Konopatsch, *Martin Rosebery d'Arguto: Dirigent von Arbeiterchören, Stimmbildner, Gesangsreformer.*

98   **the authorities arrested him:** Juliane Brauer, Rosebery d'Arguto. *Lexicon of Persecuted Musicians from the Nazi Era*, ed. Claudia Maurer Zenck and Peter Petersen (Hamburg: Universität Hamburg, 2010).

98   **far more stringency:** Konopatsch, *Martin Rosebery d'Arguto: Dirigent von Arbeiterchören, Stimmbildner, Gesangsreformer.*

99   **their beloved former conductor:** *Gespräch über Rosebery d'Arguto am 8. Januar 1981, moderiert von Inge Lammel.*

99   **Singing seemed nearly impossible:** *Gespräch über Rosebery d'Arguto am 8. Januar 1981, moderiert von Inge Lammel.*

99 **secretly taking on students:** Lindenberg, "Rosebery d'Arguto—Vorkämpfer der Arbeiterchorbewegung."

100 **1,000-reichsmark fine:** Letter housed in Sammlung Rosebery d'Arguto im Archiv der Akademie der Künste, Berlin.

100 **By September 1937:** Justus Rosenberg, *The Art of Resistance: My Four Years in the French Underground* (New York, William Morrow, 2021), 34.

100 **came to visit him:** Interview: Eyre/Justus Rosenberg.

101 **nostalgic joy in traditional Polish music:** Rosebery d'Arguto, "Zjazd Śpiewaczy w Berlinie," *Chór Miesięcznik Poświęcony Muzyce Chóralnej, Warsaw* 6, no. 1 (January 1939).

101 **to take his grand piano:** *Gespräch über Rosebery d'Arguto am 8. Januar 1981, moderiert von Inge Lammel.*

101 **write a groundbreaking book:** Lindenberg, "Rosebery d'Arguto—Vorkämpfer der Arbeiterchorbewegung."

101 **worked several jobs:** Brauer, Rosebery d'Arguto. *Lexicon of Persecuted Musicians from the Nazi Era.*

101 **a temporary visa:** Interview: Sarah Nägele/Günter Morsch. Jews who returned to Berlin on these visas were able to sell residencies, but they had to pay a Reichsfluchtsteuer (Reich Flight Tax), and the prices for the apartments were extremely low.

102 **pleading that he leave immediately:** Schmidt, *Aufzeichnungen über ein Gespräch mit Catenia von Malottki.*

102 **On September 13:** Konopatsch, *Martin Rosebery d'Arguto: Dirigent von Arbeiterchören, Stimmbildner, Gesangsreformer.*

Chapter 7

103 **Polish by nationality:** Interview: Eyre/Christine Meibeck.

103 **"Kill the Bromberg nurderers":** Leon Szalet, *Experiment "E": A Report from an Extermination Laboratory* (Paris: Didier Publishers, 1945). According to Günter Morsch, this happened sometimes to other prisoners, but it affected the Jews of Polish origin the most when they arrived in September 1939.

103 **rocks and lengths of wood:** Szalet, *Experiment "E."* Also see Nikolaus Wachsmann, *KL: A History of the Nazi Concentration Camps* (New York: Farrar, Straus and Giroux, 2015), 162.

103 **prisoner number 9299:** The relevant records are housed in the Gedenkstätte Sachsenhausen.

103 **no beds or tables or stools:** Harry Naujoks, *Mein Leben im KZ Sachsenhausen*

1936–1942 ; Erinnerungen Des Ehemaligen Lagerältesten. Köln, Germany: Röderberg Im Pahl-Rugenstein-Verlag.

104 **boarded up and then sealed:** Naujoks, *Mein Leben im KZ Sachsenhausen.* Also
see Wachsmann, *KL: A History of the Nazi Concentration Camps.*.

104 **In barracks 38:** Shirli Gilbert, "Songs Confront the Past: Music in KZ Sachsenhausen, 1936–1945," *Contemporary European History* 13, no. 3 (2004): 293.

104 **lie on their stomachs:** Szalet, *Experiment "E."*

104 **the legs of wooden stools:** Naujoks, *Mein Leben im KZ Sachsenhausen.*

104 **steamy as a Turkish bath:** Szalet, *Experiment "E."*

104 **he held it in:** Naujoks, *Mein Leben im KZ Sachsenhausen.*

104 **block elders to beat a man:** Naujoks, *Mein Leben im KZ Sachsenhausen.*

104 **straw mattresses:** Wachsmann, *KL: A History of the Nazi Concentration Camps.*

104 **licked up the salty droplets:** Szalet, *Experiment "E.,"* 163.

104 **drank their own urine:** Wachsmann, *KL: A History of the Nazi Concentration
Camps,* 163.

104 **and forced them to sing:** Shirli Gilbert, *Music in the Holocaust: Confronting Life
in the Nazi Ghettos and Camps* (Oxford, UK: Oxford University Press, 2005), 152.

104 **sing cheerful German folk songs:** Gilbert, *Music in the Holocaust.*

104 **"Can you sing?":** Szalet, *Experiment "E.,"* 39.

104 **an emphatic "Yes":** Original word is "jawohl" in Szalet, *Experiment "E.,"* 39.

104 **the discordant, ear splitting:** This specific word is used in Szalet, *Experiment "E.,"* 39.

104 **"This isn't a synagogue":** Dialogue from Szalet, *Experiment "E.,"* 39.

105 **"I am a professor of music":** Dialogue from Szalet, *Experiment "E.,"* 39.

105 **"We will sing":** Dialogue from Szalet, *Experiment "E.,"* 40.

105 **beat Rosebery:** Szalet, *Experiment "E.,"* 40.

105 **Yom Kippur of 1939:** According to Jewish calendars, it took place on Friday 22/
Saturday 23 in September 1939: https://www.hebcal.com/hebcal/?year=1939&v=1&
month=x&yt=G&nh=on&nx=on&vis=on&c=off.

105 **took note of what happened:** Szalet. *Experiment "E.,"* 70.

105 **The moon shone faintly:** Szalet. *Experiment "E.,"* 70.

106 **searched the darkness and fixed on the singer:** Szalet. *Experiment "E.,"* 70.

106 **"When at last he was silent":** Szalet. *Experiment "E.,"* 70–71.

106 **lasted for seventeen days:** Juliane Brauer, "Musikalische Gewalt und Über-
Lebens-Mittel Musik. Teil 2: Ein Mensch mit großer Würde—Der Berliner Arbe-
iterchor-Dirigent Rosebery d'Arguto im Konzentrationslager Sachsenhausen,"
mr-Mitteilungen, Nr. 64, musica reanimata. Förderverein zur Wiederentdeckung
NS-verfolgter Komponisten und ihrer Werke e. V., Berlin: 2008, 11–24. Most of the
Jewish prisoners arrived at Sachsenhausen on September 13. According to Wach-

smann, *KL: A History of the Nazi Concentration Camps*, 163, the barracks were returned to normal on September 30.

106 **the campaign for Poland:** *Gespräch über Rosebery d'Arguto am 8. Januar 1981, moderiert von Inge Lammel.* Sammlung Rosebery d'Arguto Nr. 249 im Archiv der Akademie der Künste, Berlin. See Johann Hüttner's testimony in particular. For further information, see Wachsmann, *KL: A History of the Nazi Concentration Camps*, 163.

106 **his body shrunken:** *Gerhard Schwarz: Zum Gedenken Rosebery d'Argutos.* Sammlung Rosebery d'Arguto Nr. 253 im Archiv der Akademie der Künste, Berlin.

106 **a precise plan of annihilation:** Brauer, "Musikalische Gewalt und Über-Lebens-Mittel Musik."

106 **abuse signaled what was to come:** Brauer, "Musikalische Gewalt und Über-Lebens-Mittel Musik."

106 **would not leave the camp alive:** Brauer, "Musikalische Gewalt und Über-Lebens-Mittel Musik."

106 **few prisoners plotted against the SS:** Wolfgang Benz, "Selbstbehauptung und Gegenwehr von Verfolgten. Bundeszentrale für politische Bildung." 2005. Accessed online. https://www.bpb.de/themen/nationalsozialismus-zweiter-weltkrieg/dossier -nationalsozialismus/39560/selbstbehauptung-und-gegenwehr-von-verfolgten/.

106 **their favorite hobbies:** *Niederschrift über ein Gespräch mit Johann Hüttner über Rosebery d'Arguto in den Konzentrationslagern Sachsenhausen und Auschwitz, 1961.* Sammlung Rosebery d'Arguto Nr. 114 im Archiv der Akademie der Künste, Berlin.

107 **Rosebery had allies:** *Niederschrift über ein Gespräch mit Johann Hüttner über Rosebery d'Arguto in den Konzentrationslagern Sachsenhausen und Auschwitz.*

107 **receive extra food:** *Niederschrift über ein Gespräch mit Johann Hüttner über Rosebery d'Arguto in den Konzentrationslagern Sachsenhausen und Auschwitz.*

107 **sympathetic to a leftist:** Gilbert, *Music in the Holocaust*, 136.

107 **to the indoor squad:** Szalet, *Experiment "E."*

107 **an old crackpot:** Szalet, *Experiment "E."*

107 **regained some strength:** *Gerhard Schwarz: Zum Gedenken Rosebery d'Argutos.*

107 **eccentric yet engaging man:** *Niederschrift über ein Gespräch mit Johann Hüttner über Rosebery d'Arguto in den Konzentrationslagern Sachsenhausen und Auschwitz.*

107 **In early 1940:** There is some dispute as to the specific date of the choir's founding. Johann Hüttner says in the Hüttner-Schmidt transcript that it took place "over the course of 1940." Kulisiewicz, in Characteristics of Rosebery d'Arguto, says it was founded before June of 1940. Gilbert notes in her book, *Music in the Holocaust*, that it was founded in April.

107 **seemed to wane somewhat:** Brauer, "Musikalische Gewalt und Über-Lebens-Mittel Musik."

107 **long contemplated:** Brauer, "Musikalische Gewalt und Über-Lebens-Mittel Musik."

108 **of any age or musical skill:** Johann Hüttner, Bericht in Interviewform, Berlin 18. April 1974. Akademie der Künste, Berlin, Sammlung KZ-Lieder 38.

108 **two and a half dozen Jewish men:** Hüttner, Bericht in Interviewform.

108 **a few teenagers:** Hüttner, Bericht in Interviewform.

108 **permission he needed:** Brauer, "Musikalische Gewalt und Über-Lebens-Mittel . Musik."

108 **tone and timbre of his voice:** Hüttner, Bericht in Interviewform.

108 **Wallner Theater:** The "Großes Schauspielhaus" was renamed "Friedrichstadtpalast" in 1945. The Wallner Theater existed from 1864, but in 1894 it was renamed the Schiller-Theater Ost. Some people likely still called it the Wallner Theater, however: https://www.theatre-architecture.eu/en/db/?theatreId=2040.

108 **perfect pitch:** *Gespräch über Rosebery d'Arguto am 8. Januar 1981, moderiert von Inge Lammel.*

109 **keeping the lookout:** *Gespräch über Rosebery d'Arguto am 8. Januar 1981, moderiert von Inge Lammel.*

109 **a "head voice":** Hüttner, Bericht in Interviewform.

109 **worked tirelessly with each member:** *Gerhard Schwarz: Zum Gedenken Rosebery d'Argutos.*

109 **singers with no musical education:** Hüttner, Bericht in Interviewform.

109 **believe the music he heard:** Hüttner, Bericht in Interviewform.

109 **teach the melody and harmonies:** Hüttner, Bericht in Interviewform.

110 **the deadliest of all assignments:** Wachsmann, *KL: A History of the Nazi Concentration Camps,* 119.

110 **a bell sounded:** According to Naujoks in *Mein Leben im KZ Sachsenhausen,* it was a bell. Albert Christel tells of intrusive ringing that woke him and his fellow inmates in the morning: Albert Christel, *Apokalypse unserer Tage: Erinnerungen an das KZ Sachsenhausen* (Frankfurt, Germany: Materialis, 1987), 53.

110 **three quarters of an hour:** Szalet, *Experiment "E."*

110 **burnt root vegetables:** Christel, *Apokalypse unserer Tage: Erinnerungen an das KZ Sachsenhausen,* 56.

110 **the brickworks:** Aleksander Kulisiewicz, *Sachsenhausen: Pamiętnik Poetycki* (Lublin, Poland: Wydawnictwo Lubelskie, 1965). Also see Strzelewicz, *Zapis.*

110 **beating them with clubs:** Günter Morsch and Astrid Ley, *Sachsenhausen Concentration Camp: Events and Developments* (Berlin: Metropol, 2016), 38. Also see Wachsmann, *KL: A History of the Nazi Concentration Camps,* 119.

110 **chucked stones:** Bolesław Marcinek, "Escape from Sachsenhausen" (unpublished manuscript).

111 **largest brickworks:** According to: https://www.sachsenhausen-sbg.de/ausstel lungen/kz-aussenlager-klinkerwerk/.

111 **scurried about, carrying sacks of sand:** From Leon Szalet as quoted in Wachsmann, *KL: A History of the Nazi Concentration Camps.*.

111 **build Hitler's grand capital:** Roger Moorhouse, *Berlin at War: Life and Death in Hitler's Capital, 1939–1945* (London: Vintage Books, 2011), 241. For "Germania," see Morsch and Ley, *Sachsenhausen Concentration Camp: Events and Developments*, 38.

111 **tight production schedule:** Wachsmann, *KL: A History of the Nazi Concentration Camps*, 43.

111 **want of any shelter:** Wachsmann, *KL: A History of the Nazi Concentration Camps*, 119.

111 *Water flows to Berlin:* Strzelewicz, *Zapis*.

112 **emptied one wing of barracks 39:** Hans Hüttner's Report, Berlin (GDR). RG-55.003*93. Aleksander Kulisiewicz Collection. United States Holocaust Memorial Museum Archives, Washington, DC.

112 **an audience of over two hundred:** Aleksander Kulisiewicz, "Polskie Pieśni Obozowe 1939–1945," *Regiony: Kwartalnik Społeczno-Kulturalny* 1 (1976): 5–11.

112 **how secretive Rosebery:** Gilbert, "Songs Confront the Past."

112 **astonished the men in the audience:** *Gespräch über Rosebery d'Arguto am 8. Januar 1981, moderiert von Inge* Lammel (in particular, Hans Huttner's testimony).

112 **a mythical figure:** Hüttner, Bericht in Interviewform.

112 **burning with passion:** Hüttner, Bericht in Interviewform.

112 **under a spell:** Hüttner, Bericht in Interviewform.

112 **hypnotized his singers:** *Aleksander Kulisiewicz: Liedermacher im Kampf gegen Faschismus—Kunst im Konzentrationslager.*

112 **pride swelled:** Brauer, Musikalische Gewalt und Über-Lebens-Mittel Musik. Teil 2: "Ein Mensch mit großer Würde."

113 **boosted their spirits:** Hüttner, Bericht in Interviewform.

113 **an act of unbelievable defiance:** *Gerhard Schwarz: Zum Gedenken Rosebery d'Argutos.*

113 *Though you've robbed us:* *Gerhard Schwarz: Zum Gedenken Rosebery d'Argutos.*

114 **poured himself into his work:** *Gespräch über Rosebery d'Arguto am 8. Januar 1981, moderiert von Inge Lammel.* (In particular, Hans Hüttner's testimony.) Also see *Gerhard Schwarz: Zum Gedenken Rosebery d'Argutos.*

114 **a close confidant:** *Aleksander Kulisiewicz: Liedermacher im Kampf gegen Faschismus—Kunst im Konzentrationslager.*

114 **privilege and excess seemed anathema:** Box 17 / RG-55.003*93. Characteristics of
Rosebery d'Arguto. Aleksander Kulisiewicz Collection.

114 **illustrious European composers:** Box 17 / RG-55.003*93. Characteristics of Rosebery d'Arguto. Aleksander Kulisiewicz Collection.

114 **jazz adaptations:** Box 17 / RG-55.003*93. Characteristics of Rosebery d'Arguto.
Aleksander Kulisiewicz Collection.

115 **Jewish boys in Nowy Wiśnicz:** Interview: Eyre & Milewski/M. and R. Kulisiewicz.

115 **seemed slightly taboo:** Box 17 / RG-55.003*93. Characteristics of Rosebery
d'Arguto. Aleksander Kulisiewicz Collection.

115 **inspired and soothed:** Box 17 / RG-55.003*93. Characteristics of Rosebery
d'Arguto. Aleksander Kulisiewicz Collection.

115 **pondered the mysteries:** Box 17 / RG-55.003*93. Characteristics of Rosebery
d'Arguto. Aleksander Kulisiewicz Collection.

115 **stripped him of his citizenship:** D'Arguto was almost certainly affected by the
German Polenaktion and the Polish legislation that followed, which would have
stripped him of his Polish citizenship and rendered him stateless.

115 **faith in the German people:** Interview: Eyre/Justus Rosenberg.

116 **"I could not look at the people":** Box 17 / RG-55.003*93. Characteristics of Rosebery d'Arguto. Aleksander Kulisiewicz Collection.

116 **wood to burn:** Interview: Eyre/Astrid Ley.

116 **shaking the plank:** Interview: Eyre/Astrid Ley. This is also noted by Kulisiewicz
in Strzelewicz, *Zapis*, and Jan Baranski, *Mon Pays Perdu (1945–1951)* (Paris, Les Iles
d'Or, 1956), 62.

116 **saw many men die:** Strzelewicz, *Zapis*.

116 **to block 3:** Juliane Brauer, *Musik im Konzentrationslager Sachsenhausen* (Berlin:
Metropol, 2009).

117 **built a tight-knit community:** Interview: Eyre/Astrid Ley.

117 **On the one-year anniversary:** Urbańczyk, Marta. "Twórczość i działalność pieśniarska Aleksandra Kulisiewicza w obozie koncentracyjnym Sachsenhausen
1940–1945" (MA thesis, Uniwersytet Śląski, 1981).

117 **opening address:** Gilbert. *Music in the Holocaust*, 107.

117 **as tenderly:** Urbańczyk, "Twórczość i działalność pieśniarska."

117 *Understand / that nothing is over*: Urbańczyk, "Twórczość i działalność
pieśniarska."

118 **rules at Sachsenhausen were contradictory:** Interview: Eyre/Christine Meibeck.

118 **the great works of Polish masters:** Gabriel Zych, *Oranienburg, Rachunek Pamięci*
(Warsaw: Książka i Wiedza, 1962).

118 **riffed on popular interwar:** Zych, *Oranienburg, Rachunek Pamięci*.

118 **quickly circulated:** Zych, *Oranienburg, Rachunek Pamięci*.

118 **commonly used expressions:** Zych, *Oranienburg, Rachunek Pamięci.*

118 **he debuted the song "Mister C":** A. Kulisiewicz, "Polskie Pieśni Obozowe 1939–1945."

119 **in several languages:** Zych, *Oranienburg, Rachunek Pamięci.*

119 **far more optimistic lyrics:** Barbara Milewski and Bret Werb, Liner Notes for the album *Ballads and Broadsides: Songs from Sachsenhausen Concentration Camp 1940–1945.* United States Holocaust Memorial Museum, 2008. Translation for lyrics by Dr. Barbara Milewski.

Chapter 8

123 **Harry Naujoks, a German prisoner:** *Aleksander Kulisiewicz: Liedermacher im Kampf gegen Faschismus—Kunst im Konzentrationslager—Lieder als Zeugen der Geschichte,* 1976. Sammlung KZ-Lieder Nr. 2, im Archiv der Akademie der Künste, Berlin.

123 **music could lessen a man's despondency:** As quoted in Shirli Gilbert, "Songs Confront the Past: Music in KZ Sachsenhausen, 1936–1945," *Contemporary European History* 13, no. 3 (2004): 285.

123 **wonders for a man's mental state:** Gilbert, "Songs Confront the Past."

123 **"We could rejoice":** As quoted in Guido Fackler, *Des Lagers Stimme—Musik im KZ: Alltag und Häftlingskultur in den Konzentrationslagern 1933 bis 1936* (Bremen, Germany: Edition Temmen, 2000).

124 **regardless of his skill:** Shirli Gilbert, *Music in the Holocaust: Confronting Life in the Nazi Ghettos and Camps* (Oxford, UK: Oxford University Press, 2005), 285.

124 **did not intervene to punish them:** Gilbert, *Music in the Holocaust,* 290.

124 **seemed to have some freedom:** Gilbert, *Music in the Holocaust,* 290.

124 **created songbooks:** Gilbert, *Music in the Holocaust,* 285. One songbook contained as many as 150 songs.

124 **inscribed their prisoner and block numbers:** Gilbert, *Music in the Holocaust,* 290.

124 **raised their morale:** Gilbert, *Music in the Holocaust,* 119. Other scholars have written about this, including Juliane Brauer in *Musik im Konzentrationslager Sachsenhausen* (Berlin: Metropol, 2009) and Fackler in *Des Lagers Stimme—Musik im KZ.*

124 **Jan Dedina:** For more information on Dedina, see Brauer, *Musik im Konzentrationslager Sachsenhausen.*

125 **Polish, Czech, and Slovak carols:** Aleksander Kulisiewicz, "Polskie Pieśni Obozowe 1939–1945," *Regiony: Kwartalnik Społeczno-Kulturalny* 1 (1976): 5–11.

125 **to do a tap routine:** Gabriel Zych, *Oranienburg, Rachunek Pamięci* (Warsaw: Książka i Wiedza, 1962), 161.

125 **the course of three days:** Zych, *Oranienburg, Rachunek Pamięci.*

125 **walked between barracks:** A. Kulisiewicz, "Polskie Pieśni Obozowe 1939–1945."

125 **his corpse dangled:** Interview: Sarah Nägele/Günter Morsch.

125 **had quieted:** Interview: Sarah Nägele/Günter Morsch. Dr. Morsch also notes that "some of the food rations were improved at Christmas."

125 **control over food appeared to loosen:** Strzelewicz, *Zapis.*

125 **holiday leave:** Strzelewicz, *Zapis.* Kulisiewicz was right in his speculation, according to Günter Morsch.

125 **puppet nativity scene:** A. Kulisiewicz, "Polskie Pieśni Obozowe 1939–1945."

125 **searched for a missing man:** Strzelewicz, *Zapis.*

126 **stood perfectly still:** Interview: Eyre/Astrid Ley.

126 **ventilation turret:** Interview: Sarah Nägele/Astrid Ley.

126 **Blood soaked the snow:** Strzelewicz, *Zapis.*

126 **German, Czech, and Polish choirs:** Brauer, *Musik im Konzentrationslager Sachsenhausen.*

126 **founded a string quartet:** Gilbert, *Music in the Holocaust,* 104.

126 **a block elder helped Eberhard:** Gilbert, *Music in the Holocaust,* 104.

126 **his master violin:** Brauer, *Musik im Konzentrationslager Sachsenhausen.*

126 **spent free time fashioning instruments:** Fackler, *Des Lagers Stimme—Musik im KZ.*

126 **contraband scores by Beethoven:** Gilbert, *Music in the Holocaust,* 104.

126 **camp mortuary:** As quoted in Brauer, *Musik im Konzentrationslager Sachsenhausen.* Original source: Eberhard Schmidt, *Schmidt, Eberhard. Ein Lied, ein Atemzug* (Berlin: Verlag Neue Musik, 1987), 131.

126 **walking nervously to rehearsals:** Schmidt, *Schmidt, Eberhard. Ein Lied, ein Atemzug.*

126 **on the porcelain dissecting tables:** Schmidt, *Schmidt, Eberhard. Ein Lied, ein Atemzug.*

127 **"After the first few notes":** As quoted in Brauer, *Musik im Konzentrationslager Sachsenhausen.*

127 **an ensemble in four-part harmony:** Brauer, *Musik im Konzentrationslager Sachsenhausen.*

127 **friend Edward Janiuk:** Kulisiewicz wrote at length about Janiuk in various documents, such as "Polskie Pieśni Obozowe 1939–1945." Janiuk and his activities are also recounted in testimony from Kazimierz Jaworski in *Serca za drutem* (Lublin, Poland: Lubelska Spółdzielnia wydawnicza, 1959).

127 **organize a Polish choir:** Brauer, *Musik im Konzentrationslager Sachsenhausen.*

127 **harmonica troupe:** Brauer, *Musik im Konzentrationslager Sachsenhausen.*

127 **paid visits to various barracks:** Brauer, *Musik im Konzentrationslager Sachsenhausen.*

127 **choirs toured different barracks:** Brauer, *Musik im Konzentrationslager Sachsenhausen.*

127 **an eight-voice a cappella group:** Gilbert, *Music in the Holocaust,* 105.

127 **performed popular music:** Gilbert, *Music in the Holocaust,* 105.

127 **"From evening to evening":** As quoted in Brauer, *Musik im Konzentrationslager Sachsenhausen.* Original source: Karel Štancl, (1985), "Auch das Lied ist dort Waffe geworden. Erinnerungen an die Kulturtätigkeit im Konzentrationslager Sachsenhausen in den Jahren 1939–1942. Ústí nad Orlicí." ·

128 **belt out a choral work:** Juliane Brauer, "How Can Music Be Torturous? Music in Nazi Concentration and Extermination Camps," *Music & Politics* 10, no. 1 (Winter 2016): 13.

128 **convince residents of Oranienburg:** Brauer, *Musik im Konzentrationslager Sachsenhausen.*

128 **twenty thousand men:** Brauer, *Musik im Konzentrationslager Sachsenhausen.*

128 **sing German folk tunes:** Brauer, *Musik im Konzentrationslager Sachsenhausen.* For the note about cheerful music, Shirli Gilbert writes about this in her book *Music in the Holocaust.*

128 **sing in a satisfactory way:** Guido Fackler, "Music in Concentration Camps 1933–1945," *Music & Politics* 1, no. 1 (Winter 2007): 2.

128 **snowing or pouring or storming:** Brauer, "How Can Music Be Torturous?" 12.

128 **most central point of the camp:** Brauer, "How Can Music Be Torturous?" 12.

128 **drained the men:** Brauer, "How Can Music Be Torturous?" 12.

128 **exhausted singing at the roll call square:** Brauer, "How Can Music Be Torturous?" 12.

128 **conduct them in song:** *Aleksander Kulisiewicz: Liedermacher im Kampf gegen Faschismus—Kunst im Konzentrationslager.*

129 **could last for hours:** *Aleksander Kulisiewicz: Liedermacher im Kampf gegen Faschismus—Kunst im Konzentrationslager.*

130 **never learned of its existence:** In his various writings, Naujoks claimed he never knew about d'Arguto's secret choir. See, for example, *Mein Leben im KZ Sachsenhausen.*

130 **the good it could do:** Johann Hüttner, Bericht in Interviewform. Berlin 18. April 1974. Akademie der Künste, Berlin, Sammlung KZ-Lieder 38.

130 **the savagery of the camp:** Hüttner, Bericht in Interviewform.

130 **Yiddish songs and German art music:** Juliane Brauer, "Musikalische Gewalt und Über-Lebens-Mittel Musik. Teil 2: Ein Mensch mit großer Würde – Der Berliner Arbeiterchor-Dirigent Rosebery d'Arguto im Konzentrationslager Sachsenhausen," *mr-Mitteilungen, Nr. 64, musica reanimata.* Förderverein zur Wiederentdeckung NS-verfolgter Komponisten und ihrer Werke e. V., Berlin: 2008, 18.

130 **worked with the singers:** Brauer, "Musikalische Gewalt und Über-Lebens-Mittel Musik," 18.

131 **for the Germany he loved:** Hüttner, Bericht in Interviewform. For the assertion that this Germany might reemerge after the war, Interview: Eyre/Justus Rosenberg.

131 **Hitler's unstoppable expansion:** A. Kulisiewicz, "Polskie Pieśni Obozowe 1939–1945."

131 *Shit-caked country!*: Translation by Dr. Barbara Milewski.

131 **singing the single word:** Barbara Milewski and Bret Werb, Liner Notes for the album *Ballads and Broadsides: Songs from Sachsenhausen Concentration Camp 1940–1945*. United States Holocaust Memorial Museum, 2008.

131 **had so few lyrics:** A. Kulisiewicz, "Polskie Pieśni Obozowe 1939–1945."

131 **A lousy Pole:** Strzelewicz, *Zapis*.

131 **"No one will ever kiss me":** Strzelewicz, *Zapis*.

132 **close his tired eyes:** Strzelewicz, *Zapis*.

132 **squeezed the trigger:** Günter Morsch and Astrid Ley, *Sachsenhausen Concentration Camp: Events and Developments* (Berlin: Metropol, 2016), 94.

132 **upbeat marching music:** Interview: Eyre/Christine Meibeck.

132 **murdered some ten thousand:** Morsch and Ley, *Sachsenhausen Concentration Camp*, 94.

132 **an ashen snow:** Interview: Eyre/Christine Meibeck.

132 **there seemed no hope:** Interview: Eyre/Astrid Ley.

133 **performances of the Krakowiak:** Jan Baranski, *Mon Pays Perdu (1945–1951)* (Paris: Les Iles d'Or, 1956), 93.

133 **wearing makeshift costumes:** Baranski, *Mon Pays Perdu*, 93.

133 **something terrible to Europe's Jews:** Kulisiewicz wrote repeatedly that d'Arguto said he sensed that his death was near and that something terrible was happening to Europe's Jews. See A. Kulisiewicz, "Polskie Pieśni Obozowe 1939–1945." Also see Strzelewicz, *Zapis* (among others).

133 **large-scale murder:** Brauer, "Musikalische Gewalt und Über-Lebens-Mittel Musik," In particular, see the note from Max Sprecher about transports to Auschwitz and Zyklon B.

133 **obtain a radio:** Interview: Eyre/Astrid Ley.

134 **use of poisonous gas:** See quote from Max Sprecher, a barracks mate of d'Arguto, as quoted in Brauer, "Musikalische Gewalt und Über-Lebens-Mittel Musik." This view was reinforced in an interview by the author with Christine Meibeck, of the Sachsenhausen Memorial. Other survivor memoirs mention the knowledge of extermination in the east, including in Jan Baranski's memoir, *Mon Pays Perdu*, 107. Other facts make the story plausible, including cases of prisoners being transferred

from Auschwitz to Sachsenhausen around this time. Kulisiewicz is adamant in his writings that the Jewish prisoners knew about mass extermination by gas in camps in occupied Poland.

134 **his own end was near:** A. Kulisiewicz, "Polskie Pieśni Obozowe 1939–1945."

134 **he would be gassed:** Ernst Lindenberg, "Rosebery d'Arguto—Vorkämpfer der Arbeiterchorbewegung,"*Musik und Gesellschaft* 4 (1971): 231–240.

134 **a cry of anguish for the Jews:** *Aleksander Kulisiewicz: Liedermacher im Kampf gegen Faschismus—Kunst im Konzentrationslager.*

134 **already sung it:** Brauer, "Musikalische Gewalt und Über-Lebens-Mittel Musik."

134 **courtyard to courtyard:** Strzelewicz, *Zapis.*

134 **ten brothers who traded:** Gilbert, "Songs Confront the Past."

134 **disappearing Jews:** Joshua Jacobson, "Tsen Brider: A Jewish Requiem," *Musical Quarterly* 84, no.3 (Autumn 2000): 452–474.

134 **trade in bones:** Jacobson, "Tsen Brider: A Jewish Requiem," 452–474.

135 **lighting a Yahrzeit candle:** Jacobson, "Tsen Brider: A Jewish Requiem," 452–474.

135 *I am one brother*: Jacobson, "Tsen Brider: A Jewish Requiem," 452–474.

135 **sung by a men's choir:** Aleksander Kulisiewicz, Jak Umierał Mój Głos. ms, RG-55, United States Holocaust Memorial Museum.

135 **to understand them:** A. Kulisiewicz, "Polskie Pieśni Obozowe 1939–1945."

135 **sang completed sections:** A. Kulisiewicz, "Polskie Pieśni Obozowe 1939–1945."

135 **tilting his head to listen:** A. Kulisiewicz, "Polskie Pieśni Obozowe 1939–1945."

135 **squeezed his hand:** Strzelewicz, *Zapis.*

135 **some sort of religious epiphany:** Strzelewicz, *Zapis.*

135 **"You are not a Jew":** Strzelewicz, *Zapis.*

Chapter 9

137 **sweeping the campgrounds:** Konrad Strzelewicz, *Zapis: Opowieść Aleksandra Kulisiewicza* (Krakow: Krajowa Agencja Wydawnicza).

137 **wanted Aleks to memorize it:** Strzelewicz, *Zapis.*

138 **knew Rosebery:** *Aleksander Kulisiewicz: Liedermacher im Kampf gegen Faschismus—Kunst im Konzentrationslager—Lieder als Zeugen der Geschichte,* 1976. Sammlung KZ-Lieder Nr. 2, im Archiv der Akademie der Künste, Berlin.

138 **not long for the world:** Strzelewicz, *Zapis.*

138 **almost transparent:** Strzelewicz, *Zapis.*

139 **"All I wanted":** Strzelewicz, *Zapis.*

139 **festering infection:** *Gespräch über Rosebery d'Arguto am 8. Januar 1981, moderiert von Inge Lammel.* Sammlung Rosebery d'Arguto Nr. 249 im Archiv der Akademie der Künste, Berlin. (See Werner Rosenberg testimony.)

139 **repeated the same stories:** Shirli Gilbert, *Music in the Holocaust: Confronting Life in the Nazi Ghettos and Camps* (Oxford, UK: Oxford University Press, 2005), 141.

139 **the zenith of his career:** *Aleksander Kulisiewicz: Liedermacher im Kampf gegen Faschismus—Kunst im Konzentrationslager.*

139 **nostalgia about Mława:** Aleksander Kulisiewicz, "Polskie Pieśni Obozowe 1939–1945," *Regiony: Kwartalnik Społeczno-Kulturalny* 1 (1976): 5–11.

139 **curious about Poland:** *Aleksander Kulisiewicz: Liedermacher im Kampf gegen Faschismus—Kunst im Konzentrationslager.*

139 **the movement of Jews:** Leon Szalet, *Experiment "E": A Report from an Extermination Laboratory* (Paris: Didier Publishers, 1945).

140 **mutual close friend:** *Aleksander Kulisiewicz: Liedermacher im Kampf gegen Faschismus—Kunst im Konzentrationslager.*

140 **"an ascetic":** A. Kulisiewicz, "Polskie Pieśni Obozowe 1939–1945," section on Rosebery d'Arguto.

140 **arrange several songs:** A. Kulisiewicz, "Polskie Pieśni Obozowe 1939–1945."

140 **singers stood while others sat:** A. Kulisiewicz, "Polskie Pieśni Obozowe 1939–1945."

140 **When the smoke rises:** A. Kulisiewicz, "Polskie Pieśni Obozowe 1939–1945."

140 **a young Russian, Aleksey Sazonov:** A. Kulisiewicz, "Polskie Pieśni Obozowe 1939–1945."

140 **at the Schuhfabrik:** A. Kulisiewicz, "Polskie Pieśni Obozowe 1939–1945."

140 **"Ah, if you only knew":** A. Kulisiewicz, "Polskie Pieśni Obozowe 1939–1945."

140 **old officers' boots:** Gabriel Zych, *Oranienburg, Rachunek Pamięci* (Warsaw: Książka i Wiedza, 1962).

140 **dismantling bags:** Zych, *Oranienburg, Rachunek Pamięci.*

140 **seventeen and a Red Army volunteer:** A. Kulisiewicz, "Polskie Pieśni Obozowe 1939–1945."

140 **they would both be punished:** A. Kulisiewicz, "Polskie Pieśni Obozowe 1939–1945."

141 **Ah-ah-ah:** A. Kulisiewicz, "Polskie Pieśni Obozowe 1939–1945."

141 **"You know, it makes me free":** A. Kulisiewicz, "Polskie Pieśni Obozowe 1939–1945."

141 **named the song "Sonia":** A. Kulisiewicz, "Polskie Pieśni Obozowe 1939–1945."

141 **Dark and silent:** Translation by Katarzyna Wrona.

142 **a scrap of paper with lyrics:** A. Kulisiewicz, "Polskie Pieśni Obozowe 1939–1945."

142 **Smoke, smoke—the vile smoke:** Translation by Katarzyna Wrona.

142 **honor these two women:** A. Kulisiewicz, "Polskie Pieśni Obozowe 1939–1945."

142 **mass murder of Russian prisoners:** A. Kulisiewicz, "Polskie Pieśni Obozowe 1939–1945."

142 **torn from a bag of cement:** A. Kulisiewicz, "Polskie Pieśni Obozowe 1939–1945."

142 **I beg of you:** Translation by Katarzyna Wrona.

143 **"Alyosha! It's me":** A. Kulisiewicz, "Polskie Pieśni Obozowe 1939–1945."

143 **the last time:** A. Kulisiewicz, "Polskie Pieśni Obozowe 1939–1945."

143 **began with a scene:** Marta Urbańczyk, "Twórczość i działalność pieśniarska Aleksandra Kulisiewicza w obozie koncentracyjnym Sachsenhausen 1940–1945" (MA thesis, Uniwersytet Śląski, 1981).

143 **choose which tune to use:** *Aleksander Kulisiewicz: Liedermacher im Kampf gegen Faschismus—Kunst im Konzentrationslager.*

143 **he created the song "Notturno 1941":** Urbańczyk, "Twórczość i działalność pieśniarska." For information on bombing raids in Berlin, see Roger Moorhouse, *Berlin at War: Life and Death in Hitler's Capital, 1939–45* (London: Vintage, 2011), 67, 136.

143 **air raid siren:** *Aleksander Kulisiewicz: Liedermacher im Kampf gegen Faschismus—Kunst im Konzentrationslager* For more on air raids, see https://www.mdr.de/geschichte/zeitgeschichte-gegenwart/politik-gesellschaft/zivilschutz-sirenen-alarm-katastrophenalarm-100.html.

143 **Allied airplanes thundering over the camp:** Urbańczyk, "Twórczość i działalność pieśniarska."

143 **he wrote:** *Aleksander Kulisiewicz: Liedermacher im Kampf gegen Faschismus—Kunst im Konzentrationslager.*

143 **"Even though the bombs":** *Aleksander Kulisiewicz: Liedermacher im Kampf gegen Faschismus—Kunst im Konzentrationslager.*

143 **He imagined Berlin:** Urbańczyk, "Twórczość i działalność pieśniarska."

143 **dark and threatening:** Urbańczyk, "Twórczość i działalność pieśniarska."

143 **dedicate the song to his mother:** A. Kulisiewicz, "Polskie Pieśni Obozowe 1939–1945."

144 **a mid-level SS guard walked in:** Aleksander Kulisiewicz, Jak Umierał Mój Głos. ms, RG-55, United States Holocaust Memorial Museum.

144 **injecting bacteria:** A. Kulisiewicz, Jak Umierał Mój Głos. ms, RG-55.

144 **because they appreciated his music:** A. Kulisiewicz, Jak Umierał Mój Głos. ms, RG-55.

144 **Josef and Walter treated Aleks:** A. Kulisiewicz, Jak Umierał Mój Głos. ms, RG-55.

144 **"Maestro Aleks":** A. Kulisiewicz, Jak Umierał Mój Głos. ms, RG-55.

144 **stormed out of the barracks:** A. Kulisiewicz, Jak Umierał Mój Głos. ms, RG-55.

144 **"Let that dog continue to sing!":** The detail about the shrug comes from Strzelewicz, *Zapis.* The quote comes from A. Kulisiewicz, Jak Umierał Mój Głos. ms, RG-55.

145 **to playing a bagpipe:** *Aleksander Kulisiewicz: Liedermacher im Kampf gegen Faschismus—Kunst im Konzentrationslager.*

145 **murder of Jewish children:** Box 17 / RG-55.003*93. Characteristics of Rosebery

d'Arguto. Aleksander Kulisiewicz Collection. United States Holocaust Memorial Museum Archives, Washington, DC.

145 **trampled her in the mud:** Box 17 / RG-55.003*93. Characteristics of Rosebery d'Arguto. Aleksander Kulisiewicz Collection.

146 *Ten brothers were we:* Translation by Peter Wortsman.

147 **tradition of adapting folk music:** Shirli Gilbert, "Songs Confront the Past: Music in KZ Sachsenhausen, 1936-1945." *Contemporary European History*, 13, 3, (2004): 301.

147 **no religious books or objects for worship:** Interview: Eyre/Justus Rosenberg.

148 **an atheist, dedicated to socialist ideals:** Interview: Eyre/Justus Rosenberg.

148 **a distinctly Jewish lament:** Gilbert, "Songs Confront the Past": 301.

148 **get it published somewhere?:** A. Kulisiewicz, "Polskie Pieśni Obozowe 1939–1945."

148 **affirmed Aleks's dedication:** A. Kulisiewicz, "Polskie Pieśni Obozowe 1939–1945."

149 **ordered their removal:** Interview: Sarah Nägele/Günter Morsch.

149 **three-tiered wooden bunks:** Günter Morsch and Astrid Ley, *Sachsenhausen Concentration Camp: Events and Developments* (Berlin: Metropol, 2016).

150 **blacker and more unforgiving:** A. Kulisiewicz, Jak Umierał Mój Głos. ms, RG-55.

150 **shivered with cold:** A. Kulisiewicz, Jak Umierał Mój Głos. ms, RG-55.

150 **wearing wooden clogs:** Interview: Eyre/Astrid Ley.

150 **managed to create a choir:** A. Kulisiewicz, Jak Umierał Mój Głos. ms, RG-55.

150 **forbidden for him:** Interview: Sarah Nägele/Günter Morsch.

150 **Christmases of his childhood:** A. Kulisiewicz, Jak Umierał Mój Głos. ms, RG-55.

150 **held a dim flashlight:** *Aleksander Kulisiewicz: Liedermacher im Kampf gegen Faschismus—Kunst im Konzentrationslager.*

150 **a powerful image:** A. Kulisiewicz, Jak Umierał Mój Głos. ms, RG-55.

150 **He could hear footsteps:** *Aleksander Kulisiewicz: Liedermacher im Kampf gegen Faschismus—Kunst im Konzentrationslager.*

151 **preadolescent males:** Interview: Sarah Nägele/Astrid Ley.

151 **ropey, thick neck:** A. Kulisiewicz, Jak Umierał Mój Głos. ms, RG-55.

151 **wants to live:** A. Kulisiewicz, Jak Umierał Mój Głos. ms, RG-55.

151 **broken thread of many lives:** A. Kulisiewicz, "Polskie Pieśni Obozowe 1939–1945."

151 **final syllable of the word "gas":** A. Kulisiewicz, "Polskie Pieśni Obozowe 1939–1945."

151 **a sob of despair, an elegy:** Strzelewicz, *Zapis.*

151 **burned with intensity:** Transcript Johann, Hans "Jonny" Hüttner. Audio recording in RG-55.003*93. United States Holocaust Memorial Museum Archives, Washington, DC.

151 **grip one of the youngest inmates:** A. Kulisiewicz, Jak Umierał Mój Głos. ms,
RG-55.

151 **fell in a heap:** A. Kulisiewicz, Jak Umierał Mój Głos. ms, RG-55.

152 **slipped out a back window:** A. Kulisiewicz, "Polskie Pieśni Obozowe 1939–1945."

152 **spent the night memorizing:** A. Kulisiewicz, "Polskie Pieśni Obozowe 1939–1945."

152 **never saw Rosebery again:** A. Kulisiewicz, "Polskie Pieśni Obozowe 1939–1945."

152 **to the Dachau concentration camp:** According to his transfer documents at the
Dachau Memorial and as published in Peter Konopatsch, *Martin Rosebery d'Arguto:
Dirigent von Arbeiterchören, Stimmbildner, Gesangsreformer* (Jüdische Miniatu-
ren) (Berlin: Hentrich & Hentrich, 2021).

152 **continued to sing:** Date noted in endnote 8, Barbara Milewski, "Remembering
the Concentration Camps: Aleksander Kulisiewicz and His Concerts of Prisoners'
Songs in the Federal Republic of Germany," in *Dislocated Memories: Jews, Music,
and Postwar German Culture*, ed. Tina Frühauf and Lily Hirsch (New York: Oxford
University Press, 2014), 141–60.

152 **the light of dawn:** Strzelewicz, *Zapis*.

152 **be sent to Auschwitz for extermination:** Günter Morsch and Susanne zur Nieden, *Jüdische Häftlinge im Konzentrationslager Sachsenhausen 1936–1945* (Berlin:
Ed. Hentrich, 2004).

152 **the SS marched 454:** Morsch and zur Nieden. *Jüdische Häftlinge im Konzentrationslager Sachsenhausen 1936–1945.*

152 **to the roll call square:** Hüttner, Bericht in Interviewform.

153 **"Can we go to our death":** Hüttner, Bericht in Interviewform.

153 **"Shoot now, you cowards!":** Hüttner, Bericht in Interviewform.

153 **guns drawn, ready to fire:** Morsch and zur Nieden. *Jüdische Häftlinge im Konzentrationslager Sachsenhausen 1936–1945.*

154 **experience that feeling again:** Hüttner, Bericht in Interviewform.

154 **could quell a rebellion:** Hüttner, Bericht in Interviewform.

154 **Late that same night, the SS marched:** Morsch and zur Nieden. *Jüdische Häftlinge
im Konzentrationslager Sachsenhausen 1936–1945.*

154 **younger men near Hans:** Hüttner, Bericht in Interviewform.

155 **on October 25:** Morsch and zur Nieden. *Jüdische Häftlinge im Konzentrationslager
Sachsenhausen 1936–1945.*

155 **Hans learned where he was:** Hüttner, Bericht in Interviewform.

155 **a chance at life:** Morsch and zur Nieden. *Jüdische Häftlinge im Konzentrationslager Sachsenhausen 1936–1945.*

155 **on October 19:** Konopatsch, *Martin Rosebery d'Arguto: Dirigent von Arbeiterchören, Stimmbildner, Gesangsreformer.*

155 **same fate at Auschwitz:** Interview: Eyre/Sharon Rozov.

Chapter 10

159 **groups of Frenchmen:** Günter Morsch and Astrid Ley, *Sachsenhausen Concentration Camp: Events and Developments* (Berlin: Metropol, 2016).

160 **Aleks began to perform the "Jewish Deathsong":** Aleksander Kulisiewicz, "Polskie Pieśni Obozowe 1939–1945," *Regiony: Kwartalnik Społeczno-Kulturalny* 1 (1976): 5–11.

160 **procured a guitar:** A. Kulisiewicz, "Polskie Pieśni Obozowe 1939–1945."

160 **he shouted, "Alles raus!":** A. Kulisiewicz, "Polskie Pieśni Obozowe 1939–1945."

160 **closed his eyes and wrote:** Konrad Strzelewicz, *Zapis: Opowieść Aleksandra Kulisiewicza* (Krakow: Krajowa Agencja Wydawnicza, 1984).

160 **a trancelike state:** Konrad Strzelewicz, *Zapis: Opowieść Aleksandra Kulisiewicza* (Kraków: Krajowa Agencja Wydawnicza, 1984).

160 **wailed Alyosha's broadside:** Marta Urbańczyk, "Twórczość i działalność pieśniarska Aleksandra Kulisiewicza w obozie koncentracyjnym Sachsenhausen 1940–1945" (MA thesis, Uniwersytet Śląski, 1981).

161 **performed in some ten different:** *Aleksander Kulisiewicz: Liedermacher im Kampf gegen Faschismus—Kunst im Konzentrationslager—Lieder als Zeugen der Geschichte,* 1976. Sammlung KZ-Lieder Nr. 2, im Archiv der Akademie der Künste, Berlin.

161 **free time grew rare:** *Aleksander Kulisiewicz: Liedermacher im Kampf gegen Faschismus—Kunst im Konzentrationslager.*

161 **"Come, come!":** A. Kulisiewicz, "Polskie Pieśni Obozowe 1939–1945."

161 *Whether it's by day or night*: Translated by Dr. Barbara Milewski.

161 **nightmarish shock:** *Aleksander Kulisiewicz: Liedermacher im Kampf gegen Faschismus—Kunst im Konzentrationslager.*

161 **Wilhelm Böhm was a real man:** *Aleksander Kulisiewicz: Liedermacher im Kampf gegen Faschismus—Kunst im Konzentrationslager.* Research by Dr. Barbara Milewski and Dr. Bret Werb confirmed that Böhm was a prisoner and crematorium foreman at Sachsenhausen.

162 **implicitly or explicitly:** *Aleksander Kulisiewicz: Liedermacher im Kampf gegen Faschismus—Kunst im Konzentrationslager.*

162 **"Dictate it to me":** Aleksander Kulisiewicz, *Sachsenhausen: Pamiętnik Poetycki, 1939–1945* (Lublin, Poland: Wydawnictwo Lubelskie, 1965).

162 **memorized his song accurately:** A. Kulisiewicz, *Sachsenhausen: Pamiętnik Poetycki.*

162 **as the hypnotist Roob had taught him:** A. Kulisiewicz, *Sachsenhausen: Pamiętnik Poetycki.*

162 **an octopus of camp culture:** A. Kulisiewicz, *Sachsenhausen: Pamiętnik Poetycki.*

163 **to find pencil stubs:** See works by Odd Nansen, Emil Büge, and others.

163 **scraps of paper, on shreds of canvas:** Urbańczyk, "Twórczość i działalność pieśniarska."

163 **made him feel needed:** Urbańczyk, "Twórczość i działalność pieśniarska."

163 **personal verses:** Urbańczyk, "Twórczość i działalność pieśniarska."

163 **held an absolute truth:** Urbańczyk, "Twórczość i działalność pieśniarska."

163 **preserve these testimonies at all costs:** Urbańczyk, "Twórczość i działalność pieśniarska."

163 **pawns of the German state:** Urbańczyk, "Twórczość i działalność pieśniarska."

163 **she married another man:** A. Kulisiewicz, "Polskie Pieśni Obozowe 1939–1945."

164 **Józef Denys's poem, "We Poles":** A. Kulisiewicz, "Polskie Pieśni Obozowe 1939–1945."

164 *I was in a camp once:* Translation by Katarzyna Wrona.

164 **to memorize a carol:** A. Kulisiewicz, "Polskie Pieśni Obozowe 1939–1945."

164 **a camp hit:** A. Kulisiewicz, "Polskie Pieśni Obozowe 1939–1945."

164 *In a dream:* Translation by Katarzyna Wrona.

164 *You had half the world:* Translation by Dr. Barbara Milewski.

164 **Andrej Sarapkin, attended:** Barbara Milewski and Bret Werb, Liner Notes for the album *Ballads and Broadsides: Songs from Sachsenhausen Concentration Camp 1940–1945.* United States Holocaust Memorial Museum, 2008.

165 **a 45-pound bag:** Alec Le Vernoy, *No Drums No Trumpets: A Remarkable True Story of Courage and Endurance in World War II* (London: Michael Joseph, 1988).

165 **it froze:** Strzelewicz, *Zapis.*

166 **he met Jiří Maleček:** Aleksander Kulisiewicz, *Adresse: Sachsenhausen: Literarische Momentaufnahmen Aus Dem KZ* (Gerlingen, Germany: Bleicher Verlag, 1997).

166 **"We've already made it":** Strzelewicz, *Zapis.*

166 **Aleks promised God:** Strzelewicz, *Zapis.*

166 **he began to credit her:** Strzelewicz, *Zapis.*

166 **writing a twenty-eight-page letter:** Strzelewicz, *Zapis.*

166 **returned it unopened:** Strzelewicz, *Zapis.*

167 **furrowed his face:** Strzelewicz, *Zapis.*

167 **In another dream:** Aleksander Kulisiewicz, Jak Umierał Mój Głos. ms, RG-55, United States Holocaust Memorial Museum.

167 *Mother of God was with me:* Translation by Joanna Suchomska.

167 **over thirty thousand:** Morsch and Ley, *Sachsenhausen Concentration Camp: Events and Developments*, 114 [for French prisoners]. See Manuela R. Hrdlicka, *Alltag im KZ. Das Lager Sachsenhausen bei Berlin* (Wiesbaden, Germany: VS Verlag für Sozialwissenschaften, 1991), S.46 [for the overall figure].

167 **SS deported Jiří:** A. Kulisiewicz, *Adresse: Sachsenhausen.*

167 **staged a daring and successful escape:** Bolesław Marcinek, "Escape from Sachsenhausen" (unpublished manuscript).

167 **the music or poetry they brought with them:** *Aleksander Kulisiewicz: Liedermacher im Kampf gegen Faschismus—Kunst im Konzentrationslager.*

168 **excavated granite:** See: https://www.mauthausen-memorial.org/de/Wissen/Das -Konzentrationslager-Mauthausen-1938-1945/Zwangsarbeit-in-den-Steinbruechen.

168 **"We have become more":** A. Kulisiewicz, "Polskie Pieśni Obozowe 1939–1945."

168 **shuffling of the exhausted men:** A. Kulisiewicz, "Polskie Pieśni Obozowe 1939–1945."

168 **the SS trained guard dogs:** Interview: Sarah Nägele/Günter Morsch.

169 **practice in attacking them:** A. Kulisiewicz, Jak Umierał Mój Głos. ms, RG-55.

169 **he drew up a scheme:** A. Kulisiewicz, Jak Umierał Mój Głos. ms, RG-55.

169 **"I am an outstanding expert":** A. Kulisiewicz, Jak Umierał Mój Głos. ms, RG-55.

170 **take any for himself:** A. Kulisiewicz, Jak Umierał Mój Głos. ms, RG-55.

170 **concealed in a haze:** A. Kulisiewicz, Jak Umierał Mój Głos. ms, RG-55.

170 **the camp calculus:** Harry Naujoks, *Mein Leben im KZ Sachsenhausen, 1936–1942*; Erinnerungen Des Ehemaligen Lagerältesten. Köln, Germany: Röderberg Im Pahl-Rugenstein-Verlag, 105.

170 **a terrible seething anger:** A. Kulisiewicz, Jak Umierał Mój Głos. ms, RG-55.

170 **"There is no grace here":** A. Kulisiewicz, Jak Umierał Mój Głos. ms, RG-55.

170 **musical sensitivities sharpen:** Urbańczyk, "Twórczość i działalność pieśniarska."

170 **poem called "Crucified 1944":** Urbańczyk, "Twórczość i działalność pieśniarska."

171 **put the verses to music:** Urbańczyk, "Twórczość i działalność pieśniarska."

171 **the mood of the song:** Urbańczyk, "Twórczość i działalność pieśniarska."

171 **inspiration from funeral marches:** Urbańczyk, "Twórczość i działalność pieśniarska."

171 **nailed to the farmhouse gate:** A. Kulisiewicz, "Polskie Pieśni Obozowe 1939–1945."

171 **begun to lose his mind:** Urbańczyk, "Twórczość i działalność pieśniarska."

171 **Frédéric Chopin's funeral march:** A. Kulisiewicz, "Polskie Pieśni Obozowe 1939–1945."

171 **first performed Leonard's hymn:** Urbańczyk, "Twórczość i działalność pieśniarska."

171 **the gathered crowd:** A concert like this would have been very possible given the SS's unwillingness to enter the sick bay for fear of disease, according to Dr. Astrid Ley.

171 **"The audience gazed upon":** Shirli Gilbert, "Songs Confront the Past: Music in KZ Sachsenhausen, 1936–1945," *Contemporary European History* 13, no. 3 (2004): 294. Original source (with full quote): Gouillard, cited in Carsten Linde, ed., *KZ-Lieder: Eine Auswahl aus dem Repertoire des Polnischen Sängers Alex Kulisiewicz* (Sievershütten: Wendepunkt, 1972), 9.

172 **hanged himself:** A. Kulisiewicz, "Polskie Pieśni Obozowe 1939–1945."

172 **terrifying experiments on prisoners:** Hermann Kaienburg, *Der Ort des Terrors. Geschichte der nationalsozialistischen Konzentrationslager.* Band 3: Sachsenhausen, Buchenwald (Berlin: CH Beck, 2006).

172 **children, perhaps Jews from the east:** Astrid Ley and Günter Morsch, *Medical Care and Crime— The Infirmary at Sachsenhausen Concentration Camp 1936–1945* (Berlin: Metropol, 2007).

172 **seemed to have exploded:** Kaienburg, *Der Ort des Terrors.*

172 **large convoys of Jews:** Günter Morsch and Susanne zur Nieden. *Jüdische Häftlinge im Konzentrationslager Sachsenhausen 1936–1945* (Berlin: Ed. Hentrich, 2004).

172 **many had come from Auschwitz:** Morsch and Ley, *Sachsenhausen Concentration Camp: Events and Developments,* 115.

173 **wooden carts piled with bodies:** Interview: Sarah Nägele/Günter Morsch.

173 **spiked when he came into contact:** Urbańczyk, "Twórczość i działalność pieśniarska."

173 **nervousness he and others felt:** Urbańczyk, "Twórczość i działalność pieśniarska."

173 **late August 1944:** Morsch and Ley, *Sachsenhausen Concentration Camp: Events and Developments,* 124.

173 **carting off thousands of captives to camps:** Morsch and Ley, *Sachsenhausen Concentration Camp: Events and Developments,* 124.

173 **another camp called Ravensbrück:** Morsch and Ley, *Sachsenhausen Concentration Camp: Events and Developments,* 124.

173 **three thousand Dutchmen arrived:** Morsch and Ley, *Sachsenhausen Concentration Camp: Events and Developments,* 124.

173 **over one hundred of their comrades:** Morsch and Ley, *Sachsenhausen Concentration Camp: Events and Developments,* 124.

173 **charge was conspiracy:** A. Kulisiewicz, "Polskie Pieśni Obozowe 1939–1945."

174 **childhood legends:** Milewski and Werb, Liner Notes for the album, *Ballads and Broadsides.*

174 **glow of a burning city:** Urbańczyk, "Twórczość i działalność pieśniarska."

174 **sang in soft voices:** Strzelewicz, *Zapis.*

174 **with a transport of new prisoners:** Strzelewicz, *Zapis.*

174 **soothed them:** Strzelewicz, *Zapis.*

Chapter 11

175 **no more than one 100 pounds:** Konrad Strzelewicz, *Zapis: Opowieść Aleksandra Kulisiewicza* (Krakow: Krajowa Agencja Wydawnicza, 1984).

175 **dragging paces:** Strzelewicz, *Zapis.*

175 **ashy skin:** Marta Urbańczyk, "Twórczość i działalność pieśniarska Aleksandra Kulisiewicza w obozie koncentracyjnym Sachsenhausen 1940–1945" (MA thesis, Uniwersytet Śląski, 1981).

175 **nearly fifty:** Barbara Milewskiand Bret Werb, Liner Notes for the album *Ballads and Broadsides: Songs from Sachsenhausen Concentration Camp 1940–1945.* United States Holocaust Memorial Museum, 2008.

176 **Varsovian student of Polish philology:** Aleksander Kulisiewicz, *Sachsenhausen: Pamiętnik Poetycki* (Lublin, Poland: Wydawnictwo Lubelskie, 1965).

176 **New prisoners:** Günter Morsch and Astrid Ley, *Sachsenhausen Concentration Camp: Events and Developments* (Berlin: Metropol, 2016), 133.

176 **poems struck Aleks as deeply powerful:** Kulisiewicz, *Sachsenhausen: Pamiętnik Poetycki.*

177 **"Silence on a Hospital Cot":** Translation by Katarzyna Wrona.

178 **such beauty in their imagery:** Kulisiewicz, *Sachsenhausen: Pamiętnik Poetycki.*

178 **the first women into the camp:** Interview: Sarah Nägele/Günter Morsch.

178 **to compose a welcoming poem:** Strzelewicz, *Zapis.*

179 **to pique interest in his search:** A. Kulisiewicz, "Polskie Pieśni Obozowe 1939–1945."

179 **assign women to the easiest camp jobs:** Strzelewicz, *Zapis.*

179 **"What do we need":** Strzelewicz, *Zapis.*

179 **watch them bathe:** Strzelewicz, *Zapis.*

179 **the caress of a woman:** A. Kulisiewicz, "Polskie Pieśni Obozowe 1939–1945."

179 *Young lips*: Urbańczyk, "Twórczość i działalność pieśniarska."

180 **dig up unexploded bombs:** See Morsch and Ley, *Sachsenhausen Concentration Camp: Events and Developments,* 120, for an image of such a work detail.

180 **nothing for the German dead:** Strzelewicz, *Zapis.*

180 **looked like mannequins:** Strzelewicz, *Zapis.*

180 **"No wonder":** Strzelewicz, *Zapis.*

181 **they struck him as cute:** Strzelewicz, *Zapis.*

181 **"If you're moved":** Strzelewicz, *Zapis.*

181 **woman he missed:** Urbańczyk, "Twórczość i działalność pieśniarska."

181 *She was my painted litle miss*: Translation by Katarzyna Wrona. Source: Urbańczyk, "Twórczość i działalność pieśniarska."

181 **he began to miss it:** Urbańczyk, "Twórczość i działalność pieśniarska."

181 **a poem called "Pilgrimage to Olomouc":** Urbańczyk, "Twórczość i działalność pieśniarska."

181 **return to his youth:** Urbańczyk, "Twórczość i działalność pieśniarska."

181 **war was drawing to a close:** *Aleksander Kulisiewicz: Liedermacher im Kampf gegen Faschismus—Kunst im Konzentrationslager—Lieder als Zeugen der Geschichte,* 1976. Sammlung KZ-Lieder Nr. 2, im Archiv der Akademie der Künste, Berlin.

181 **where they were headed:** Morsch and Ley, *Sachsenhausen Concentration Camp: Events and Developments*, 126.

182 **two thousand prisoners had vanished:** Morsch and Ley, *Sachsenhausen Concentration Camp: Events and Developments*, 126.

182 **Roland Tillard, accompanied him:** A. Kulisiewicz, "Polskie Pieśni Obozowe 1939–1945."

182 **slated for execution:** Aleksander Kulisiewicz, *Adresse: Sachsenhausen: Literarische Momentaufnahmen Aus Dem KZ* (Gerlingen, Germany: Bleicher Verlag, 1997).

182 **"Aleks . . . you always sang":** A. Kulisiewicz, *Adresse: Sachsenhausen.*

182 **felt his throat tighten:** A. Kulisiewicz, *Adresse: Sachsenhausen.*

182 **"You write":** A. Kulisiewicz, *Adresse: Sachsenhausen.*

182 *You are going:* Translation by Katarzyna Wrona.

182 **They wanted to write something:** A. Kulisiewicz, *Adresse: Sachsenhausen.*

182 **elegies, hymns, songs of rebellion:** Urbańczyk, "Twórczość i działalność pieśniarska."

183 **Rumors circulated about an impending extermination:** Jerzy Pindera, *Liebe Mutti: One Man's Struggle to Survive in KZ Sachsenhausen, 1939–1945*, ed. Lynne Taylor (Lanham, MD: University Press of America, 2004), 121.

183 **vanished into the darkness:** A. Kulisiewicz, *Adresse: Sachsenhausen.*

183 **might soon be executed:** A. Kulisiewicz, *Adresse: Sachsenhausen.*

183 **buttermilk:** A. Kulisiewicz, *Adresse: Sachsenhausen.*

183 **"I will neither see death":** A. Kulisiewicz, *Adresse: Sachsenhausen.*

183 **a palpable sense of pleasure:** A. Kulisiewicz, "Polskie Pieśni Obozowe 1939–1945."

183 **parody of the song "You and I":** A. Kulisiewicz, *Adresse: Sachsenhausen.*

184 *Ladies and gents:* Translation by Dr. Barbara Milewski.

184 **stomped on air-filled bags:** A. Kulisiewicz, "Polskie Pieśni Obozowe 1939–1945."

184 **would soon begin near the camp:** A. Kulisiewicz, "Polskie Pieśni Obozowe 1939–1945."

185 **intricately carved cigarette box:** A. Kulisiewicz, "Polskie Pieśni Obozowe 1939–1945."

185 **About three weeks into April:** Pindera, *Liebe Mutti*, 121. Pindera maintains the date was April 20.

185 **murdered immediately:** Morsch and Ley, *Sachsenhausen Concentration Camp: Events and Developments*, 134.

185 **nearly sixty thousand men and women:** See https://www.sachsenhausen-sbg.de/en/history/1936-1945-sachsenhausen-concentration-camp/. The figure is fifty-eight thousand people in the main camp.

185 **distant roar of Soviet artillery:** Gabriel Zych, *Oranienburg, Rachunek Pamięci* (Warsaw: Książka i Wiedza, 1962).

185 **were nearly constant:** Pindera, *Liebe Mutti*, 123. Also mentioned by Kulisiewicz in *Adresse: Sachsenhausen*.

185 **scrub clean all evidence:** Interview: Sarah Nägele/Günter Morsch. The SS burned documents in the prisoners' kitchen in the weeks before the end of the war.

185 **barrel after barrel of human ash:** Hermann Kaienburg, *Der Ort des Terrors. Geschichte der nationalsozialistischen Konzentrationslager.* Band 3: Sachsenhausen, Buchenwald (Berlin: CH Beck, 2006).

186 **a column with Gabriel Zych:** Zych, *Oranienburg, Rachunek Pamięci.*

186 **a loaf of bread and a bit of meat:** Kaienburg, *Der Ort des Terrors.*

186 **last me a long while:** *Aleksander Kulisiewicz: Liedermacher im Kampf gegen Faschismus—Kunst im Konzentrationslager.*

186 **legs felt like rubber:** A. Kulisiewicz, *Adresse: Sachsenhausen.*

186 **thirty thousand prisoners:** Kaienburg, *Der Ort des Terrors.* For the note about what Kulisiewicz can see, refer to Zych, *Oranienburg, Rachunek Pamięci.*

186 **the SS shot him:** *Aleksander Kulisiewicz: Liedermacher im Kampf gegen Faschismus—Kunst im Konzentrationslager.*

186 **drove Aleks and the other prisoners:** *Aleksander Kulisiewicz: Liedermacher im Kampf gegen Faschismus—Kunst im Konzentrationslager.*

186 **stopped at Löwenberger Land:** Zych, *Oranienburg, Rachunek Pamięci.* Also see Morsch and Ley, *Sachsenhausen Concentration Camp: Events and Developments.*

186 **crammed in an empty barn:** Zych, *Oranienburg, Rachunek Pamięci.*

186 **bullet to finish them:** Kaienburg, *Der Ort des Terrors.*

186 **Neuruppin and then Wittstock:** Zych, *Oranienburg, Rachunek Pamięci.* Also see Morsch and Ley, *Sachsenhausen Concentration Camp: Events and Developments.*

187 **indifferent if not outright hostile:** Kaienburg, *Der Ort des Terrors.*

187 **possessed the camp songs and poems:** *Aleksander Kulisiewicz: Liedermacher im Kampf gegen Faschismus—Kunst im Konzentrationslager.*

187 **"I must persist":** *Aleksander Kulisiewicz: Liedermacher im Kampf gegen Faschismus—Kunst im Konzentrationslager.*

187 *I look up at the trees:* *Aleksander Kulisiewicz: Liedermacher im Kampf gegen Faschismus—Kunst im Konzentrationslager.*

188 **wet and cold beneath him:** Aleksander Kulisiewicz, Jak Umierał Mój Głos. ms, RG-55, United States Holocaust Memorial Museum.

188 **dying prisoners blanketed the ground:** A. Kulisiewicz, Jak Umierał Mój Głos. ms, RG-55.

188 **scavenged in nearby fields:** Zych, *Oranienburg, Rachunek Pamięci.*

188 **more stone than wheat:** Zych, *Oranienburg, Rachunek Pamięci.*

188 **seeds in part of a sunflower:** A. Kulisiewicz, Jak Umierał Mój Głos. ms, RG-55.

188 **relishing each morsel:** A. Kulisiewicz, Jak Umierał Mój Głos. ms, RG-55.

188 **Women appeared:** Strzelewicz, *Zapis*. Also see https://www.below-sbg.de/en/ history/april-1945-death-march-and-forest-camp/. "Near the town of Crivitz the bulk of the Sachsenhausen inmates met women from Ravensbrück concentration camp."

188 **underground teaching operation:** A. Kulisiewicz, *Adresse: Sachsenhausen*.

188 **shining star:** A. Kulisiewicz, *Adresse: Sachsenhausen*.

189 **sing beautifully:** Strzelewicz, *Zapis*.

189 **hear her humming:** Strzelewicz, *Zapis*.

189 **She started limping:** A. Kulisiewicz, *Adresse: Sachsenhausen*.

189 **made walking almost unbearable:** A. Kulisiewicz, *Adresse: Sachsenhausen*.

189 **staggered out of her column:** Strzelewicz, *Zapis*.

189 **young, perhaps even a teenager:** Strzelewicz, *Zapis*.

189 **"Did he not want to waste":** Strzelewicz, *Zapis*.

189 **shot Aleks's friend Roland:** Strzelewicz, *Zapis*.

189 **kicked the bodies of Danusia and Roland:** Strzelewicz, *Zapis*.

189 **fired off several more rounds:** Strzelewicz, *Zapis*.

189 **"Take a good look":** Strzelewicz, *Zapis*.

189 **blood soak through:** Strzelewicz, *Zapis*.

189 **Germans shot prisoners at will:** Daniel Blatman, *The Death Marches: The Final Phase of Nazi Genocide* (Cambridge, MA: The Belknap Press of Harvard University Press, 2011), 169.

190 **reminded him of a child's tears:** A. Kulisiewicz, Jak Umierał Mój Głos. ms, RG-55.

190 **"Nasty sun":** A. Kulisiewicz, Jak Umierał Mój Głos. ms, RG-55.

190 **brought no drama:** Kaienburg, *Der Ort des Terrors*.

190 **"Do whatever you want":** A. Kulisiewicz, *Adresse: Sachsenhausen*.

190 **ventured off the road:** Edmund Szybicki, *To Hope or Die: From Warsaw Uprising to Sachsenhausen Concentration Camp and After. Memoirs of a Survivor* (London: Athena Press, 2007), 84.

190 **chewed on strips of the inner bark:** A. Kulisiewicz, *Adresse: Sachsenhausen*.

190 **shot Danusia the day before:** Strzelewicz, *Zapis*.

190 **dead or alive:** Strzelewicz, *Zapis*.

190 **body of her granddaughter:** Strzelewicz, *Zapis*.

191 **7th US Armored Division:** Kaienburg, *Der Ort des Terrors*.

191 **ate too fast or too much:** Szybicki, *To Hope or Die*, 84.

191 **staggered about, dazed:** Szybicki, *To Hope or Die*, 85.

191 **seemed apathetic and passive:** Szybicki, *To Hope or Die*, 85.

191 **find some food:** A. Kulisiewicz, *Adresse: Sachsenhausen*.

192 **get your revenge:** Strzelewicz, *Zapis*.

192 **saw his hometown:** Strzelewicz, *Zapis*.

192   **hitched rides on horse-drawn carts:** *Aleksander Kulisiewicz: Liedermacher im Kampf gegen Faschismus—Kunst im Konzentrationslager.*

192   **the empty cigarette case:** Milewski and Werb, Liner Notes for the album *Ballads and Broadsides: Songs from Sachsenhausen Concentration Camp 1940–1945.*

193   **bad turn of fate:** Strzelewicz, *Zapis.*

193   **travel to Kraków:** See English translation of Kulisiewicz's "Artistic biography" in the private collection of K. Kulisiewicz.

193   **he might very well die:** Interview: Eyre/K. Kulisiewicz.

193   **multiplication problems:** Strzelewicz, *Zapis.*

194   **signed the cross:** Strzelewicz, *Zapis.*

194   **haunted by evil:** Strzelewicz, *Zapis.*

194   **next three weeks:** See English translation of Kulisiewicz's "Artistic biography" in the private collection of K. Kulisiewicz.

194   **and some fifty others:** See English translation of Kulisiewicz's "Artistic biography" in the private collection of K. Kulisiewicz. Also see Urbańczyk, "Twórczość i działalność pieśniarska."

194   **He uttered poetry:** Box 31 / RG-55.003*93. United States Holocaust Memorial Museum Archives, Washington, DC.

194   **all the anecdotal detail:** *Aleksander Kulisiewicz: Liedermacher im Kampf gegen Faschismus—Kunst im Konzentrationslager.*

194   **happiest moment of my sad life:** *Aleksander Kulisiewicz: Liedermacher im Kampf gegen Faschismus—Kunst im Konzentrationslager.*

Chapter 12

197   **six million citizens:** These figures vary somewhat, depending on the source. Adam Zamoyski, in *Poland: A History*, says the figure is "nearly six million." Norman Davies, in *Heart of Europe*, says the figure is "over six million." According to the United States Holocaust Memorial Museum, between 4.8 and 4.9 million citizens of Poland were killed.

197   **three million Jewish Poles:** Polish Victims. United Holocaust Memorial Museum's Holocaust Encyclopedia. https://encyclopedia.ushmm.org/content/en/article/polish-victims. Also see Patrice M. Dabrowski, *Poland: The First Thousand Years* (Dekalb: Northern Illinois University Press, 2014), ebook location 8284.

197   **18 percent:** Adam Zamoyski, *Poland: A History*, 5th ed. (London: William Collins, 2015), 338. Also see Norman Davies, *Heart of Europe: The Past in Poland's Present* (Oxford, UK: Oxford University Press, 2001), 55.

197   **11.2 percent:** Davies, *Heart of Europe.*

197   **had to be rebuilt:** Dieter Bingen and Simon Lengemann, *Deutsche Besatzungspo-*

litik in Polen 1939–1945. Eine Leerstelle deutscher Erinnerung? (Bonn: Bundeszentrale für politische Bildung, 2019), 86.

197 **sent the equipment east:** Zamoyski, *Poland: A History*, 348.

198 **were emigrating:** Dabrowski, *Poland: The First Thousand Years*, ebook location 8391.

198 **forced off land in the east:** Dabrowski, *Poland: The First Thousand Years*, ebook location 8338.

198 **massive reforms:** Zamoyski, *Poland: A History*, 347–348.

198 **disease spread:** Zamoyski, *Poland: A History*, 338.

198 **"I should get new clothes":** Aleksander Kulisiewicz, Jak Umierał Mój Głos. ms, RG-55, United States Holocaust Memorial Museum.

198 **"Ma'am, please give me":** A. Kulisiewicz, Jak Umierał Mój Głos. ms, RG-55.

198 **a certain euphoria:** Interview: Eyre/K. Kulisiewicz.

198 **locked in Sachsenhausen forever?:** Barbara Milewski and Bret Werb, Liner Notes for the album *Ballads and Broadsides: Songs from Sachsenhausen Concentration Camp 1940–1945*. United States Holocaust Memorial Museum, 2008.

199 **selling loaves and rolls:** A. Kulisiewicz, Jak Umierał Mój Głos. ms, RG-55. The note about enjoying it comes from *Aleksander Kulisiewicz: Liedermacher im Kampf gegen Faschismus—Kunst im Konzentrationslager—Lieder als Zeugen der Geschichte*, 1976. Sammlung KZ-Lieder Nr. 2, im Archiv der Akademie der Künste, Berlin.

199 **maintain the books:** *Aleksander Kulisiewicz: Liedermacher im Kampf gegen Faschismus—Kunst im Konzentrationslager—Lieder als Zeugen der Geschichte.*

199 **Elżbieta Bochenek-Szpakowska:** Interview: Eyre & Milewski/M. and R. Kulisiewicz.

199 *No matter how bad:* A. Kulisiewicz, Jak Umierał Mój Głos. ms, RG-55.

199 **so the couple married:** A. Kulisiewicz, Jak Umierał Mój Głos. ms, RG-55.

199 **he fled:** A. Kulisiewicz, Jak Umierał Mój Głos. ms, RG-55.

200 **life he had led:** Interview: Eyre/K. Kulisiewicz.

200 **best time of his life:** Interview: Eyre/K. Kulisiewicz.

200 **"Just let us eat":** Marta Urbańczyk, "Twórczość i działalność pieśniarska Aleksandra Kulisiewicza w obozie koncentracyjnym Sachsenhausen 1940–1945" (MA thesis, Uniwersytet Śląski, 1981).

200 **first elected government:** Davies, *Heart of Europe*, 5.

200 **into a one-party state:** Davies, *Heart of Europe*, 5.

200 **blood transfusion:** Blood transfusions, though rudimentary, were common at Sachsenhausen. They were often administered by prisoner doctors, and there are documented cases of these procedures saving injured prisoners. In most cases, stronger prisoners (especially the better-treated Norwegians) would be called on

to donate blood to prisoners in need. For more information, see Astrid Ley and Günter Morsch, *Medical Care and Crime: The Infirmary at Sachsenhausen Concentration Camp 1936–1945* (Berlin: Metropol 2007).

200 **October 1, 1947:** Urbańczyk,"Twórczość i działalność pieśniarska."

200 **benefit of his friendship with Antonín:** Interview: Eyre/K. Kulisiewicz.

201 **came back to life:** Interview: Eyre & Milewski/M. and R. Kulisiewicz.

201 **preferred the food:** Interview: Eyre/K. Kulisiewicz.

201 **southeast of the old town:** Interview: Eyre & Milewski/M. and R. Kulisiewicz.

201 **three things:** Konrad Strzelewicz, *Zapis: Opowieść Aleksandra Kulisiewicza* (Krakow: Krajowa Agencja Wydawnicza, 1984).

202 **inspect female inmates:** A. Kulisiewicz, Jak Umierał Mój Głos. ms, RG-55.

202 **something twisted in his mind:** A. Kulisiewicz, Jak Umierał Mój Głos. ms, RG-55.

202 **desire a half-naked woman:** A. Kulisiewicz, Jak Umierał Mój Głos. ms, RG-55.

202 **pictured her the entire time:** A. Kulisiewicz, Jak Umierał Mój Głos. ms, RG-55.

202 *I was dreaming*: Translation by Joanna Suchomska.

202 **she had heard the broadcast:** Strzelewicz, *Zapis*.

203 **he did not want to be:** Strzelewicz, *Zapis*.

203 **"Ali, why are you here":** Strzelewicz, *Zapis*.

203 **It was too late:** Strzelewicz, *Zapis*.

203 **took on lovers:** A. Kulisiewicz, Jak Umierał Mój Głos. ms, RG-55.

203 **four languages:** Interview: Eyre & Milewski/M. and R. Kulisiewicz.

203 **fragrant oranges:** Interview: Eyre & Milewski/M. and R. Kulisiewicz.

204 **in early 1948:** A. Kulisiewicz, Jak Umierał Mój Głos. ms, RG-55.

204 **Budečská Street:** Box 61 / RG-55.003*93. Correspondence with Poles, 1946–1966. Aleksander Kulisiewicz Collection. United States Holocaust Memorial Museum Archives, Washington, DC [Postcard].

204 **A.R. Studio at Wenceslas Square:** A. Kulisiewicz, Jak Umierał Mój Głos. ms, RG-55.

204 **begin with the "Unforgettable Song":** A. Kulisiewicz, Jak Umierał Mój Głos. ms, RG-55.

205 **Rosebery's last will and testament:** A. Kulisiewicz, Jak Umierał Mój Głos. ms, RG-55.

205 **two hundred copies:** Urbańczyk, "Twórczość i działalność pieśniarska."

205 **musicologists to study them:** Urbańczyk, "Twórczość i działalność pieśniarska."

205 **did not sing anymore:** A. Kulisiewicz, Jak Umierał Mój Głos. ms, RG-55.

205 **rarely occurred:** Interview: Eyre & Milewski/M. and R. Kulisiewicz.

206 **more than a pittance:** Interview: Eyre & Milewski/M. and R. Kulisiewicz.

207 **street sweeper:** Interview: Eyre/K. Kulisiewicz.

207 **eyes met those of another man:** Strzelewicz, *Zapis*.

207 **"Where are you going":** Strzelewicz, *Zapis*.

208 **selling restricted news:** Barbara Milewski, "Remembering the Concentration Camps: Aleksander Kulisiewicz and His Concerts of Prisoners' Songs in the Federal Republic of Germany," in *Dislocated Memories: Jews, Music, and Postwar German Culture*, ed. Tina Frühauf and Lily Hirsch (New York: Oxford University Press, 2014), 144.

208 **without hesitation:** Interview: Eyre/K. Kulisiewicz.

208 **she did not understand him:** Interview: Eyre & Milewski/M. and R. Kulisiewicz.

208 **could they desire?:** Interview: Eyre & Milewski/M. and R. Kulisiewicz.

209 **network of contacts:** Milewski, "Remembering the Concentration Camps," 145.

209 **Barbara Seweryn:** Interview: Eyre/K. Kulisiewicz.

210 **spring evening in April 1956:** In correspondence in the private collection of K. Kulisiewicz.

210 **only dream:** Interview: Eyre/K. Kulisiewicz.

210 **snuck around Kraków:** Interview: Eyre/K. Kulisiewicz.

211 *look at your beautiful son*: Interview: Eyre/Barbara Milewski.

211 **trigger in him the terror:** Interview: Eyre/Barbara Milewski.

212 **Warsaw ghetto:** Interview: Eyre/Sharon Rozov.

212 **"How I long to see":** From a letter in the estate of Justus Rosenberg.

213 **Buffalo, New York:** I managed to track down several friends of his. He died in the 1990s.

214 **half a dozen or ten songs:** Interview: Eyre/K. Kulisiewicz.

214 **Polish priests the Nazis had imprisoned:** Interview: Eyre/K. Kulisiewicz.

214 **singing at cabarets:** Interview: Eyre/K. Kulisiewicz.

214 **never went to concerts:** Interview: Eyre/K. Kulisiewicz.

215 **they often refused:** Interview: Eyre/K. Kulisiewicz.

215 **refusal to join the Communist Party:** Interview: Eyre/K. Kulisiewicz.

215 **freedom to perform widely:** Interview: Eyre/K. Kulisiewicz.

Chapter 13

217 **German Academy of Arts:** Known as the Akademie der Künste der DDR starting in 1973.

217 **"Dearest Comrade":** Correspondence in Box 65 & 66 / RG-55.003*93. Correspondence with Inge Lammel, 1963–1981 [East Germany]. Aleksander Kulisiewicz Collection. United States Holocaust Memorial Museum Archives, Washington, DC.

217 **extra allotments of meat:** Interview: Eyre/K. Kulisiewicz.

218 **With East German support:** Interview: Eyre/K. Kulisiewicz.

218 **thirteen songs:** Correspondence in Box 65 & 66 / RG-55.003*93. Correspondence

with Inge Lammel, 1963–1981 [East Germany]. Aleksander Kulisiewicz Collection. United States Holocaust Memorial Museum Archives, Washington, DC.

218 **"We were surprised":** Marta Urbańczyk, "Twórczość i działalność pieśniarska Aleksandra Kulisiewicza w obozie koncentracyjnym Sachsenhausen 1940–1945" (MA thesis, Uniwersytet Śląski, 1981).

219 **prisoner's uniform:** Barbara Milewski, "Remembering the Concentration Camps: Aleksander Kulisiewicz and His Concerts of Prisoners' Songs in the Federal Republic of Germany," in *Dislocated Memories: Jews, Music, and Postwar German Culture*, ed. Tina Frühauf and Lily Hirsch (New York: Oxford University Press, 2014), 146.

219 **as though hypnotized:** Konrad Strzelewicz, *Zapis: Opowieść Aleksandra Kulisiewicza* (Krakow: Krajowa Agencja Wydawnicza, 1984).

219 **imitate the starving men:** Urbańczyk, "Twórczość i działalność pieśniarska."

219 **"something macabre":** Urbańczyk, "Twórczość i działalność pieśniarska."

219 **seventeen other venues:** Milewski, "Remembering the Concentration Camps," 158 (endnote 15).

219 **translated into Italian:** Strzelewicz, *Zapis*.

219 **"I sing only":** Strzelewicz, *Zapis*.

220 **planted a bomb:** Milewski, "Remembering the Concentration Camps" 158 (endnote 15).

220 **especially excited him:** Interview: Eyre/K. Kulisiewicz.

221 **marked the fourth:** Milewski, "Remembering the Concentration Camps," 148.

221 **thousands of German youth:** Milewski, "Remembering the Concentration Camps," 148.

221 **more commercial:** Milewski, "Remembering the Concentration Camps," 148.

221 **horrified by the missiles:** Interview: Eyre/K. Kulisiewicz.

222 **intense questioning:** Milewski, "Remembering the Concentration Camps," 148.

222 **modest clothes:** Interview: Eyre/K. Kulisiewicz.

222 **"My God, what has":** Interview: Sarah Nägele/Georg Bündgens.

222 **burned down, unsmoked:** Interview: Eyre/Georg Bündgens.

222 **whispering:** Interview: Eyre/Georg Bündgens.

222 **a respected cultural figure:** *Aleksander Kulisiewicz: Liedermacher im Kampf gegen Faschismus—Kunst im Konzentrationslager –Lieder als Zeugen der Geschichte*, 1976. Sammlung KZ-Lieder Nr. 2, im Archiv der Akademie der Künste, Berlin.

223 **forbade him:** *Aleksander Kulisiewicz: Liedermacher im Kampf gegen Faschismus—Kunst im Konzentrationslager—Lieder als Zeugen der Geschichte*.

223 **"Am I to sing":** *Aleksander Kulisiewicz: Liedermacher im Kampf gegen Faschismus—Kunst im Konzentrationslager—Lieder als Zeugen der Geschichte*.

223 "Either I sing this song": *Aleksander Kulisiewicz: Liedermacher im Kampf gegen Faschismus—Kunst im Konzentrationslager—Lieder als Zeugen der Geschichte.*

223 front of a mirror: Interview: Eyre/K. Kulisiewicz.

223 "Every time I sing": Urbańczyk, "Twórczość i działalność pieśniarska."

224 "What kind of lullaby": Strzelewicz, *Zapis.*

224 twenty-four towns: Milewski, "Remembering the Concentration Camps," 150.

224 youth club Żak: Milewski, "Remembering the Concentration Camps," 151.

224 basked in the attention: Interview: Eyre/K. Kulisiewicz.

224 failing health: Strzelewicz, *Zapis.*

224 no hearing aid would help: Strzelewicz, *Zapis.*

224 stabilize his gait: Strzelewicz, *Zapis.*

224 head would spin: Strzelewicz, *Zapis.*

224 a contemptuous look: Interview: Eyre & Milewski/M. & R. Kulisiewicz.

224 He imagined himself: Strzelewicz, *Zapis.*

225 "I am not allowed": Strzelewicz, *Zapis.*

225 he had diabetes: Aleksander Kulisiewicz, Jak Umierał Mój Głos. ms, RG-55, United States Holocaust Memorial Museum.

225 no longer eat pears: A. Kulisiewicz, Jak Umierał Mój Głos. ms, RG-55.

225 he had begun to fade away: A. Kulisiewicz, Jak Umierał Mój Głos. ms, RG-55.

225 so much to accomplish: Interview: Eyre/K. Kulisiewicz.

225 large medical book: Interview: Eyre/K. Kulisiewicz.

225 liver and stomach: Interview: Eyre/K. Kulisiewicz.

225 "I can't sing": A. Kulisiewicz, Jak Umierał Mój Głos. ms, RG-55.

225 refused to let the music go: *Aleksander Kulisiewicz: Liedermacher im Kampf gegen Faschismus—Kunst im Konzentrationslager—Lieder als Zeugen der Geschichte.*

225 symptoms added up: Interview: Eyre/K. Kulisiewicz.

226 despise doctors: Interview: Eyre/K. Kulisiewicz.

226 avoided treatment: Interview: Eyre/K. Kulisiewicz.

226 "Close your archives": Interview: Eyre/K. Kulisiewicz.

226 "We suffered so much": Box 15 B-G: 4 / RG-55.003*93. Sachsenhausen. Aleksander Kulisiewicz Collection. United States Holocaust Memorial Museum Archives, Washington, DC.

226 He cared little: Interview: Eyre/K. Kulisiewicz.

226 never wanted to go to the cinema: Interview: Eyre/K. Kulisiewicz.

227 marriage could not continue: Interview: Eyre/K. Kulisiewicz.

227 stroked Aleks's hand: A. Kulisiewicz, Jak Umierał Mój Głos. ms, RG-55.

227 recalled a line from a Czech poet: A. Kulisiewicz, Jak Umierał Mój Głos. ms, RG-55.

227 **so many times at Sachsenhausen:** A. Kulisiewicz, Jak Umierał Mój Głos. ms, RG-55.

227 **serene, unearthly:** A. Kulisiewicz, Jak Umierał Mój Głos. ms, RG-55.

227 **he kissed Franciszek:** A. Kulisiewicz, Jak Umierał Mój Głos. ms, RG-55.

227 **felt guilty:** A. Kulisiewicz, Jak Umierał Mój Głos. ms, RG-55.

227 **by heart:** A. Kulisiewicz, Jak Umierał Mój Głos. ms, RG-55.

227 **he gave up:** A. Kulisiewicz, Jak Umierał Mój Głos. ms, RG-55.

228 **wandered aimlessly:** Strzelewicz, *Zapis*.

228 **found a restaurant:** Strzelewicz, *Zapis*.

228 **must be prostitutes:** Strzelewicz, *Zapis*.

228 **add to his personal files:** Strzelewicz, *Zapis*.

228 **"I looked at him":** A. Kulisiewicz, Jak Umierał Mój Głos. ms, RG-55.

228 **"You are an ordinary":** Box 15 B-G: 7 / RG-55.003*93. Sachsenhausen. Aleksander Kulisiewicz Collection.

229 **mistakes of the author:** Interview: Eyre/K. Kulisiewicz.

229 **telephoned authors:** Interview: Eyre/K. Kulisiewicz.

229 **"Tilting at Windmills":** Strzelewicz, *Zapis*.

229 **"Excursion to the Unknown":** Translation by Dr. Barbara Milewski.

230 **over fifty verses:** Strzelewicz, *Zapis*.

230 *Dance, dance, dance:* Translation by Joanna Suchomska.

231 **manuscripts and scores:** Strzelewicz, *Zapis*.

231 **prolific, heroic, and talented:** Strzelewicz, *Zapis*.

231 **"The Echo of the Uprising":** Strzelewicz, *Zapis*.

231 **wrote an opera:** Interview: Eyre/Barbara Milewski.

231 **summarized figures:** Strzelewicz, *Zapis*.

232 **raised flags:** Interview: Eyre/K. Kulisiewicz.

232 **mail bore a Polish stamp:** Interview: Eyre/K. Kulisiewicz.

232 **tapped his phone:** Interview: Eyre/K. Kulisiewicz.

232 **Elżbieta Popowska:** Strzelewicz, *Zapis*.

232 **Aleks was always right:** Interview: Eyre & Milewski/M. and R. Kulisiewicz.

232 **rarely laughed:** Multiple interview subjects made note of this, including K. Kulisiewicz, G. Bündgens, and Brigitte Hege.

233 **beer once a month:** Interview: Eyre/K. Kulisiewicz.

233 **He barely ate:** Interview: Eyre/K. Kulisiewicz.

233 **his depression intensified:** Interview: Eyre/K. Kulisiewicz.

233 **"It's nice to hear":** Box 61. Correspondence with Poles 1946–1966 / RG-55.003*93. Sachsenhausen. Aleksander Kulisiewicz Collection.

233 **the fanaticism of it:** Interview: Eyre/K. Kulisiewicz.

233 **connections with influential people:** Interview: Eyre/K. Kulisiewicz.

234 **a peacock:** Interview: Sarah Nägele/Dorothea Kolland.

234 **a thick album:** Interview: Sarah Nägele/ Dieter Süverkrüp.

234 **"He probably just wanted":** Interview: Sarah Nägele/ Dieter Süverkrüp.

235 **"I wish you good health":** A. Kulisiewicz, Jak Umierał Mój Głos. ms, RG-55.

Chapter 14

236 **spilled out the door:** Interview: Eyre/Peter Wortsman. Kulisiewicz also discusses this in Konrad Strzelewicz, *Zapis: Opowieść Aleksandra Kulisiewicza* (Krakow: Krajowa Agencja Wydawnicza, 1984).

236 **a fellowship in Vienna:** Interview: Eyre/Peter Wortsman.

237 **"I have to go back":** Peter Wortsman, "Orpheus Raising Hell, Impressions of the Late Aleksander Kulisiewicz," in Barbara Milewski and Bret Werb, Liner Notes for the album *Ballads and Broadsides: Songs from Sachsenhausen Concentration Camp 1940–1945.* United States Holocaust Memorial Museum, 2008.

237 **Aron's song:** Wortsman, "Orpheus Raising Hell."

237 **"Don't think I sing":** Wortsman, "Orpheus Raising Hell."

237 **first song:** Strzelewicz, *Zapis.*

237 **all the macabre images:** Marta Urbańczyk, "Twórczość i działalność pieśniarska Aleksandra Kulisiewicza w obozie koncentracyjnym Sachsenhausen 1940–1945" (MA thesis, Uniwersytet Śląski, 1981).

237 **Aleks had debuted thirty-five years earlier:** Urbańczyk, "Twórczość i działalność pieśniarska."

238 **magazine *Sing Out!*:** Peter Wortsman, "A Singer from Hell," *Sing Out! The Folk Song Magazine* 26, no. 3 (1977).

238 **the audience was speechless:** See Wortsman, "Orpheus Raising Hell."

238 **no burst of spontaneous applause:** Interview: Eyre/Harold Wortsman.

238 **tears running down the cheeks:** Strzelewicz, *Zapis.*

238 **men like Leonard:** For Leonard's death, see Gabriel Zych, *Oranienburg, Rachunek Pamięci* (Warsaw: Książka i Wiedza, 1962).

238 **almost exaggerated, but appropriate:** Interview: Eyre/Peter Wortsman.

239 **not a conventionally beautiful voice:** Interview: Eyre/Harold Wortsman.

239 **a single take:** Interview: Eyre/Peter Wortsman.

239 **final evenings in America:** Interview: Eyre/Peter Wortsman.

239 **the Haggadah:** Interview: Eyre/Harold Wortsman.

239 **their own flight:** Eyre/Harold Wortsman.

239 **warmth and candlelight:** Eyre/Harold Wortsman.

239 **boyish contentment:** See Wortsman, "Orpheus Raising Hell."

239 **first and only Passover Seder:** Wortsman, "Orpheus Raising Hell," and confirmed with K. Kulisiewicz.

240 **dreamed of traveling to Israel:** Interview: Eyre/K. Kulisiewicz.

241 **his favorite snack:** Strzelewicz, *Zapis.*

241 **duck pond:** Interviews: Eyre/K. Kulisiewicz.

241 **"You cannot watch the man":** Alice Anne Conner, "On Ethnic Milwaukee," *Milwaukee Journal Sentinel*, October 28, 1979.

242 **regret on the chauvinism:** Interviews: Eyre/K. Kulisiewicz.

242 **"I'm a different man":** Aleksander Kulisiewicz, Jak Umierał Mój Głos. ms, RG-55, United States Holocaust Memorial Museum.

242 **basic costs but little else:** Interview: Eyre/K. Kulisiewicz.

242 **held dinner parties:** Interview: Eyre/K. Kulisiewicz.

243 **stained and filthy:** Interview: Eyre/K. Kulisiewicz.

243 **equivalent of a few restaurant dinners:** Interview: Eyre/K. Kulisiewicz.

243 **quiet and centrally heated:** Interview: Eyre/K. Kulisiewicz.

243 **stood Pomorska:** Interview: Eyre/K. Kulisiewicz.

243 **live among the ghosts:** Interview: Eyre/K. Kulisiewicz.

243 **some 820 songs:** Strzelewicz, *Zapis.*

243 **microfilm frames:** Strzelewicz, *Zapis.*

244 **over 165,000 feet:** Strzelewicz, *Zapis.*

244 **Basia signed with a lipstick kiss:** All in the personal files of K. Kulisiewicz.

244 **thirty-four Nazi camps:** Dr. Bret Werb, Director of the Music Collection at the United States Holocaust Memorial Museum, speaking to the BBC in "Songs from the Depths of Hell," January 27, 2019. https://www.bbc.co.uk/programmes/po6z4m44?fbclid=IwAR3eqcyz23J_rb9wmbAKj8yjUrozWRT5PoFsZ6R5Qbcvvlk QoagMSdj2SwY.

244 **that he could not verify:** Interview: Eyre/Barbara Milewski.

244 **He felt surrounded:** Strzelewicz, *Zapis.*

245 **calling him the:** Barbara Milewski, "Remembering the Concentration Camps: Aleksander Kulisiewicz and His Concerts of Prisoners' Songs in the Federal Republic of Germany," in *Dislocated Memories: Jews, Music, and Postwar German Culture*, ed. Tina Frühauf and Lily Hirsch (New York: Oxford University Press, 2014), 145.

245 **"The heart of the matter":** Strzelewicz, *Zapis.*

245 **remain in his home country:** Strzelewicz, *Zapis.*

245 **library of the Jagiellonian University:** Strzelewicz, *Zapis.*

245 **Auschwitz Museum and the Institute:** Urbańczyk, "Twórczość i działalność pieśniarska."

245 **National Library in Warsaw:** Urbańczyk, "Twórczość i działalność pieśniarska."

245 **fast approaching death:** Strzelewicz, *Zapis.*

245 **his accomplishments:** Interview: Eyre/K. Kulisiewicz.

245 **most fulfilling:** *Aleksander Kulisiewicz: Liedermacher im Kampf gegen Faschismus—*

Kunst im Konzentrationslager—Lieder als Zeugen der Geschichte, 1976. Sammlung KZ-Lieder Nr. 2, im Archiv der Akademie der Künste, Berlin.

245 **a rush of satisfaction:** A. Kulisiewicz, Jak Umierał Mój Głos. ms, RG-55.

245 **struck Aleks as perfect:** A. Kulisiewicz, Jak Umierał Mój Głos. ms, RG-55.

246 **evoke interest in the camp songs:** A. Kulisiewicz, Jak Umierał Mój Głos. ms, RG-55.

246 **the streets of Moscow:** A. Kulisiewicz, Jak Umierał Mój Głos. ms, RG-55.

246 **"Remember, when your days":** A. Kulisiewicz, Jak Umierał Mój Głos. ms, RG-55.

246 **What Aleks longed for:** A. Kulisiewicz, Jak Umierał Mój Głos. ms, RG-55.

246 **"In Italy I received":** A. Kulisiewicz, Jak Umierał Mój Głos. ms, RG-55.

246 **sung the most:** Andrea Baaske, "Lieder aus der Hölle. Die musikalische Rezeption des Aleksander Kulisiewicz in der bundesdeutschen Folkbewegung" (MA thesis, Universität Freiburg, 1996).

247 **struggled to sleep:** Interview: Eyre/K. Kulisiewicz.

247 **visit Japan and Brazil:** A. Kulisiewicz, Jak Umierał Mój Głos. ms, RG-55.

247 **why God or the universe would stifle him:** A. Kulisiewicz, Jak Umierał Mój Głos. ms, RG-55.

247 **enough toilet paper:** A. Kulisiewicz, Jak Umierał Mój Głos. ms, RG-55.

247 **ceased to circulate:** A. Kulisiewicz, Jak Umierał Mój Głos. ms, RG-55.

247 **like or trust:** Interview: Eyre/K. Kulisiewicz.

247 **diabetes, rheumatism, Ménière's disease:** A. Kulisiewicz, Jak Umierał Mój Głos. ms, RG-55.

247 **administer injections:** A. Kulisiewicz, Jak Umierał Mój Głos. ms, RG-55.

248 **wool blanket:** A. Kulisiewicz, Jak Umierał Mój Głos. ms, RG-55.

248 **the life he likely would have begun:** Interview: Eyre/K. Kulisiewicz.

248 **little more than an instant:** A. Kulisiewicz, Jak Umierał Mój Głos. ms, RG-55.

248 **how he would die:** A. Kulisiewicz, Jak Umierał Mój Głos. ms, RG-55.

248 **buried next to his mother:** A. Kulisiewicz, Jak Umierał Mój Głos. ms, RG-55.

249 **last time in July 1981:** Interview: Eyre/K. Kulisiewicz.

249 **whether to make the trip:** Interview: Eyre/K. Kulisiewicz.

249 **green sweater vest:** Based on an image in the private collection of K. Kulisiewicz.

249 **nurse from the Red Cross:** Interview: Eyre and Milewski/M. and R. Kulisiewicz.

249 **wealthy and materialistic:** Interview: Eyre/K. Kulisiewicz.

249 **acacia tree:** Strzelewicz, *Zapis*.

249 **timid ones:** Strzelewicz, *Zapis*.

250 **to feed it:** Strzelewicz, *Zapis*.

250 **Rumcajs would land on this simple nest:** Strzelewicz, *Zapis*.

250 **"I at least have them":** Strzelewicz, *Zapis*.

250 **seemed cursory:** Interview: Sarah Nägele/Marta Urbańczyk.

251 **summon the strength to rise:** Interview: Barbara Milewski/Marta Urbańczyk.

251 **"There, on the second shelf":** Interview: Barbara Milewski/Marta Urbańczyk.

251 **"What, have you":** Interview: Barbara Milewski/Marta Urbańczyk.

251 **heaven being a place:** A. Kulisiewicz, Jak Umierał Mój Głos. ms, RG-55.

252 **hadn't become a lawyer:** A. Kulisiewicz, Jak Umierał Mój Głos. ms, RG-55.

252 **cross lay on his bedside table:** Strzelewicz, *Zapis*.

252 **simple apartment or country cottage:** Interview: Eyre/K. Kulisiewicz.

252 **slip it and the cross into his coffin:** Interview: Eyre/K. Kulisiewicz.

252 **previous thirteen years:** Norman Davies, *Heart of Europe: The Past in Poland's Present* (Oxford, UK: Oxford University Press, 2001), 12.

252 **ten million members:** Davies, *Heart of Europe*, 16.

252 **overthrow the regime:** Interview: Eyre/K. Kulisiewicz.

252 **menace of tanks on the streets:** Davies, *Heart of Europe*, 20.

252 **imposed martial law:** Davies, *Heart of Europe*, 20.

253 **dragnet of arrests:** Davies, *Heart of Europe*, 20.

253 **unbearably weak:** Interview: Eyre/K. Kulisiewicz.

253 **check into the hospital:** Interview: Eyre/K. Kulisiewicz.

253 **at most two weeks away:** Interview: Eyre/K. Kulisiewicz.

253 **taxi near Plac Inwalidów:** Interview: Eyre/K. Kulisiewicz.

253 **caught sight of the tanks:** Interview: Eyre/K. Kulisiewicz.

253 **not to get involved:** Interview: Eyre/K. Kulisiewicz.

253 **only tragedy worse:** Interview: Eyre/K. Kulisiewicz.

253 **rarely did he complain:** Interview: Eyre/K. Kulisiewicz.

Selected Bibliography

Alter, Jacov, and David Sztokfisz, eds. *Mława*, Vol. 1. Israel: Yots'e Mlavah be-Yiśra'el uvitefutsot, 1984.

Baranski, Jan. *Mon Pays Perdu (1939–1951)*. Paris: Les Iles D'Or, 1956.

Blatman, Daniel. *The Death Marches: The Final Phase of Nazi Genocide*. Cambridge, MA: The Belknap Press of Harvard University Press, 2011.

Blobaum, Robert E. *Rewolucja: Russian Poland, 1904–1907*. Ithaca, NY: Cornell University Press, 1995.

Brauer, Juliane. *Musik im Konzentrationslager Sachsenhausen*. Berlin: Metropol, 2009.

Brykczynski, Paul. *Primed for Violence: Murder, Antisemitism, and Democratic Politics in Interwar Poland*. Madison: University of Wisconsin Press, 2018.

Cała, Alina, Zofia Głowicka, Barbara Łętocha, and Aleksander Messer. *Żydowskie druki ulotne w II Rzeczypospolitej w zbiorach*. Warsaw: Biblioteki Narodowej, 2015.

Cesarani, David. *Final Solution: The Fate of the Jews 1933–49*. London: Pan Books, 2017.

Churchill, Peter. *The Spirit in the Cage*. London: Corgi Books, 1956.

Crome, Len. *Unbroken: Resistance and Survival in the Concentration Camps*. London: Lawrence and Wishart, 1988.

Dabrowski, Patrice M. *Poland: The First Thousand Years*. Dekalb: Northern Illinois University Press, 2014.

Davies, Norman. *Europe at War: No Simple Victory 1939–1945*. London: Pan Books, 2006.

Davies, Norman. *God's Playground: A History of Poland, Vol. 2: 1795 to the Present*. New York: Columbia University Press, 2005.

Davies, Norman. *Heart of Europe: The Past in Poland's Present.* Oxford, UK: Oxford University Press, 2001.

Die Polnische Minderheit im KZ 1939–1945: Mitglieder Polnischer Verbände im Deutschen Reich in den Konzentrationslagern Sachsenhausen und Sachsenhausen und Ravensbrück. Ausstellungskatalog (Berlin: Metropol), 20130

Fackler, Guido. *Des Lagers Stimme—Musik im KZ: Alltag und Häftlingskultur in den Konzentrationslagern 1933 bis 1936.* Bremen, Germany: Edition Temmen, 2000.

Friedländer, Saul. *The Years of Extermination: Nazi Germany and the Jews, 1939–1945.* New York: HarperCollins, 2007.

Galas, Michał, and Antony Polonsky, eds. *Polin: Studies in Polish Jewry Volume 23: Jews in Krakow.* Liverpool, UK: Littman, 2011.

Grochowski, Andrzej. *Materiały źródłowe do historii Żydów Mławy i powiatu mławskiego w XVIII-XX wieku.* Mława, Poland: Towarzystwo Przyjaciół Ziemi Mławskiej, Mława, 2016.

Gwiazdomorski, Jan. *Wspomnienia z Pobytu profesorów Uniwersytetu Jagiellońskiego w Niemieckim Obozie Koncentracyjnym w Sachsenhausen.* Kraków: Nakładem Księgarni S. Kamiński, 1945.

Hoffman, Eva. *Shtetl: The Life and Death of a Small Town and the World of Polish Jews.* Boston: Mariner Books, 2007.

Jaskot, Paul B. *The Architecture of Oppression: The SS, Forced Labor and the Nazi Monumental Building Economy.* Abingdon, UK: Routledge, 2000.

Juszkiewicz, Ryszard. *Los Żydów mławskich w okresie II-ej wojny światowej.* Mława, Poland: Towarzystwo Przyjaciół Ziemi Mławskiej, 1994.

Kalisch, Shoshana. *Yes, We Sang! Songs of the Ghettos and Concentration Camps.* New York: Harper & Row, 1985.

Kändler, Klaus, et al. *Berliner Begegnungen: Ausländische Künstler in Berlin 1918 bis 1933: Aufsätze, Bilder, Dokumente.* Berlin: Dietz, 1987.

Klein, Katja. *Kazett-Lyrik: Untersuchungen zu Gedichten und Liedern aus dem Konzentrationslager Sachsenhausen.* Würzburg, Germany: Königshausen & Neumann, 1995.

Kolland, Dorothea. "Zehn Brüder waren wir gewesen" in *Spuren Jüdischen Lebens in Neukölln.* Berlin: Hentrich & Hentrich, 2012.

Konopatsch, Peter. *Martin Rosebery d'Arguto: Dirigent von Arbeiterchören, Stimmbildner, Gesangsreformer* (Jüdische Miniaturen). Berlin: Hentrich & Hentrich, 2021.

Kubicek, Peter. *Memories of Evil: Recalling a World War II Childhood.* Self-Published, 2012.

Kulisiewicz, Aleksander. *Adresse: Sachsenhausen, Literarische Momentaufnahmen aus dem KZ.* Gerlingen, Germany: Bleicher, 1997.

Kulisiewicz, Aleksander. *Sachsenhausen: Pamiętnik Poetycki, 1939–1945.* Lublin, Poland: Wydawnictwo Lubelskie, 1965.

Laks, Szymon. *Music of Another World.* Evanston, IL: Northwestern University Press, 1989.

Leslie, R. F., ed. *The History of Poland since 1863*. Cambridge, UK: Cambridge University Press, 1980.

Le Vernoy, Alec. *No Drums No Trumpets: A Remarkable True Story of Courage and Endurance in World War II*. London: Michael Joseph, 1988.

Łozińscy, Maja, and Jan Łozińscy. *W przedwojennej Polsce*. Warsaw: Wydawnictwo Naukowe PWN, 2012.

Lukowski, Jerzy, and Hubert Zawadzki. *A Concise History of Poland*. Cambridge, UK: Cambridge University Press, 2007.

Margules, Józef. *Oswobodzenie Sachsenhausen*. Warsaw: Wojskowy Instytut Historyczny, 1995.

Miłosz, Czesław. *Wyprawa z dwudziestolecie*. Kraków: Wydawnictwo Literackie, 1999.

Roger Moorhouse, Berlin at War: Life and Death in Hitler's Capital, 1939–1945 (London: Vintage Books, 2011).

Moorhouse, Roger. *First to Fight*. London: Bodley Head, 2019.

Morcinek, Gustaw. *Listy spod morwy: Sachsenhausen-Dachau*. Katowice: Wydawnictwo "Literatura Polska," 1946.

Morsch, Günter, ed. *The Concentration Camp SS 1936–1945: Excesses and Direct Perpetrators in Sachsenhausen Concentration Camp*. Berlin: Metropol, 2016.

Morsch, Günter. *Sachsenhausen, the Concentration Camp by the "Reich" Capital: Formation and Development*. Berlin: Metropol, 2016.

Morsch, Günter, and Astrid Ley. *Sachsenhausen Concentration Camp: Events and Developments*. Berlin: Metropol, 2016.

Morsch, Günter, and Susanne zur Nieden. *Jüdische Häftlinge im Konzentrationslager Sachsenhausen: 1936 bis 1945*. Berlin: Ed. Hentrich, 2004.

Musial, Bogdan. *Deutsche Zivilverwaltung und Judenverfolgung im Generalgouvernement. Eine Fallstudie zum Distrikt Lublin 1939–1944*. Wiesbaden, Germany: Harrassowitz, 1999.

Nansen, Odd. *From Day to Day: One Man's Diary of Survival in Nazi Concentration Camps*. Edited by Timothy J Boyce. Nashville, TN: Vanderbilt University Press, 2016.

Naujoks, Harry. *Mein Leben im KZ Sachsenhausen 1936–1942; Erinnerungen des Ehemaligen Lagerältesten*. Köln, Germany: Röderberg im Pahl-Rugenstein-Verlag, 1987.

Paczkowski, Andrzej. *The Spring Will Be Ours: Poland and the Poles from Occupation to Freedom*. University Park, PA: Penn State University Press, 2003.

Panic, Idzi, ed. *Dzieje Śląska Cieszyńskiego od zarania do czasów współczesnych (tom VI)*. Cieszyn, Poland: Starostwo Powiatowe w Cieszynie, 2015.

Pigoń, Stanisław. *Wspominki z obozu w Sachsenhausen 1939–1940*. Warsaw: Państwowy Instytut Wydawniczy, 1966.

Pindera, Jerzy. *Liebe Mutti: One Man's Struggle to Survive in KZ Sachsenhausen, 1939–1945*. Edited by Lynne Taylor. Lanham, MD: University Press of America, 2004.

Polonsky, Antony. "Jewish Life in Poland–Lithuania to 1750." In *The Jews in Poland and Russia: Volume I: 1350 to 1881.* Liverpool: Liverpool University Press. 2009.

Polonsky, Antony. *The Jews in Poland and Russia, Volume III, 1914 to 2008.* London: Littman Library of Jewish Civilization, 2019.

Prytulak, Ivan. *Father, Did We Know You?* Self-published, 2018.

Radde, Gerd, et al. *Schul Reform: Kontinuitäten und Brüche, das Versuchsfeld Berlin-Neukölln 1912 bis 1945.* Opladen, Germany: Leske + Budrich, 1993.

Rak, Feliks. *Krematoria i Róże: Wspomnienia Więźnia Obozów w Sachsenhausen i Dachau.* Warsaw: Ludowa Spółdzielnia Wydawnicza, 1971.

Rosenberg, Justus. *Art of Resistance: My Four Years in the French Underground.* New York: William Morrow, 2020.

Shatzky, Jacob, et al. *Mława,* New York: Velt-Farband-Mlaver-Yidn, 1950.

Shore, Marci. *Caviar and Ashes: A Warsaw Generation's Life and Death in Marxism, 1918–1968.* New Haven, CT: Yale University Press, 2006.

Smoliński, Wojciech. "Studia i materiały do dziejów Ziemi Zawkrzeńskiej t. III," in *Życie codzienne Mławy w latach 1918–1939.* Mława, Poland: Towarzystwo Przyjaciół Ziemi Mławskiej, 1996.

Snyder, Timothy. *Black Earth: The Holocaust as History and Warning.* London: Vintage, 2015.

Snyder, Timothy. *Bloodlands: Europe between Hitler and Stalin.* London: Vintage, 2010.

Stachura, Peter. *Poland, 1918–1945: An Interpretive and Documentary History of the Second Republic.* Abingdon, UK: Routledge, 2004.

Stopka, Krzysztof, et al. *The History of the Jagiellonian University.* Kraków: Jagiellonian University Press, 2000.

Strzelewicz, Konrad. *Zapis: Opowieść Aleksandra Kulisiewicza.* Kraków: Krajawa Agencja Wydawnicza, 1984.

Sulimierski, Filip, and Władysław Walewski: *Słownik geograficzny Królestwa Polskiego i innych krajów słowiańskich.* Tom VI and XII– Mława and Szreńsk. Warsaw, 1885.

Szalet, Leon. *Experiment "E": A Report from an Extermination Laboratory.* Paris: Didier Publishers, 1945.

Szczepański, Janusz. *Społeczność Żydowska Mazowsza w XIX-XX wieku.* Pułtusk, Poland: Wyższa Szkoła Humanistyczna im. Aleksandra Gieysztora, 2005.

Szybicki, Edmund. *To Hope or Die: From Warsaw Uprising to Sachsenhausen Concentration Camp and After. Memoirs of a Survivor.* London: Athena Press, 2007.

Ury, Scott. *Barricades and Banners: The Revolution of 1905 and the Transformation of Warsaw Jewry.* Palo Alto, CA: Stanford University Press, 2012.

Wachsmann, Nikolaus. *KL: A History of the Nazi Concentration Camps.* New York: Farrar, Straus and Giroux, 2015.

Watt, Richard M. *Bitter Glory: Poland and Its Fate 1918–1939*. New York: Barnes & Noble Books, 1998.

Weitz, Eric D. *Creating German Communism, 1890–1990: From Popular Protests to Socialist State*. Princeton, NJ: Princeton University Press, 1997.

Zaborowski, Jan, and Stanisław Poznański. *Sonderaktion Krakau*. Warsaw: Związek Bojowników o Wolność i Demokrację, 1964.

Zamojska, Dorota, and Mariusz Kulczykowski. *Żydzi—studenci Uniwersytetu Jagiellońskiego w Drugiej Rzeczypospolitej (1918–1939) [recenzja]*. Kraków: Polska Akademia Umiejętności, 2004.

Zamoyski, Adam. *Poland: A History*, 5th ed. London: William Collins, 2015.

Zamoyski, Adam. *The Polish Way: A Thousand Year History of Poles & Their Culture*. London: John Murray, 1987.

Zych, Gabriel. *Oranienburg, Rachunek Pamięci*. Warsaw: Książka i Wiedza, 1962.

Zygner, Leszek, ed. *Księga Żydów Mławskich [Mława Pinkas]*. Mława, Poland: Stacja Naukowa im. prof. Stanisława Herbsta w Mławie, 2016.

Index